ZIONISM

ZIONISM

The Birth and Transformation of an Ideal

Milton Viorst

Thomas Dunne Books
St. Martin's Press
New York

THOMAS DUNNE BOOKS.
An imprint of St. Martin's Press.

www.thomasdunnebooks.com
www.stmartins.com

Design by Meryl Sussman Levavi

The Library of Congress Cataloging-in-Publication Data

Names: Viorst, Milton, author.
Title: Zionism : the birth and transformation of an ideal / Milton Viorst.
Description: New York : Thomas Dunne Books/ St. Martin's Press, [2016] |
   ì2016
Identifiers: LCCN 2015049507| ISBN 9781250078001 (hardback) |
   ISBN 9781466890329 (e-book)
Subjects: LCSH: Zionists—Biography. | Zionism. | BISAC: HISTORY /
   Middle East / Israel.
Classification: LCC DS151.A2 V56 2016 | DDC 320.54095694—dc23

LC record available at http://lccn.loc.gov/2015049507

First Edition: July 2016

10 9 8 7 6 5 4 3 2 1

To Rabbi Leonard Beerman
and the other peacemakers,
the greatest of the Zionists

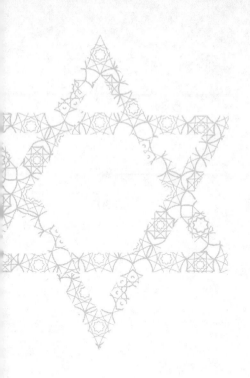

Contents

Preface

I made my first visit to Israel a few months after the Six-Day War. I recall feeling very upset that virtually no one I met during the visit talked of Israel's victory as an opening to a more stable Middle East, in which the Jews could live comfortably in peace. Instead, most exulted over the magnitude of the victory and Israel's obvious military dominance in the region. The few Israelis who expressed concern about the collective intoxication produced by the victory seemed like spoilsports. This book has been gestating in my mind ever since.

I cannot claim that I was immune to the exultation. Until that visit, I had worked as a journalist in Washington, writing chiefly on American politics. Having come of age during the Holocaust, I had long taken pride in Zionism's success in providing a homeland for beleaguered Jews, especially Holocaust survivors. The outcome of the 1967 war imbued in me, as it did in most Jews, a sense of relief. It also established a renewed bond with my Jewish roots. The perils to the Jewish state clearly remained, but I was not then aware how much the Jews themselves would add to them.

As both a journalist and a Jew, I felt at home in Israel, and, over the decades, I returned on extended working visits at least a few times a year. I found Israelis full of ideas—and more than willing to share them with me. I made Israeli friends. I also read Jewish history and explored Jewish thought. Sometimes I crossed into the West Bank and the Gaza Strip for talks with the local Arabs, who introduced me to their own perspective. It was clear in these years that the practices of Israel's military occupation were harsh and growing harsher. I came to know more than a few Israelis who were troubled by the opportunities the state was squandering to advance peace.

In time, I broadened my perspective of the Middle East by making working trips to the Arab world. There was never a shortage of tumultuous events for a journalist to cover in the region: Arafat and the PLO's guerrilla warfare, a civil war in Lebanon, the murder of Anwar Sadat and later of Yitzhak Rabin, Iraq's bloody conflict with revolutionary Iran, rising Islamic radicalism, Saddam Hussein's seizure of Kuwait and two American-led invasions to overturn his tyranny. Even as I worked among the Arabs, however, I looked over my shoulder at what was happening—or not happening—among my fellow Jews in Israel.

As the years rolled by, I produced countless articles on assignment from newspapers and magazines, most combining interpretation with reporting. I also wrote op-eds and other opinion pieces in the *Washington Post* and the *Washington Star,* as well as in *The New York Times.* The French called my kind of work *journalisme engagé,* which meant that my writing, without sacrificing accuracy, reflected a strong personal viewpoint. The core of this viewpoint—more controversial than I had once imagined it would be—was that the interests of Israel, the Arabs, and the United States would all be served by putting an end to the obstacles to Middle East peace.

Having once trained for a university career, I subsequently rejected it in favor of the excitement of journalism. But I increasingly found myself gravitating toward longer works. My first book on the Middle East, published in 1987, was *Sands of Sorrow,* which examined the political divisions among Israelis, principally over the peace issue. I subsequently wrote several books on the Arabs and on Islam. In 2002, I did a follow-up book on Israel called *What Shall I Do with This People?: Jews and the Fractious Politics of Judaism,* focusing on the recurring schisms that occurred in Jewish history and how they mirrored Israel today.

The book I had not written—nor has anyone else, I daresay—was an exploration of the question that first upset me after the Six-Day War. How did Zionism, over the course of a century, evolve from the idealism of providing refuge for beleaguered Jews to a rationalization for the army's occupation of powerless Palestinians? In recent years, though Israel grew stronger and more prosperous as a nation, Zionism became increasingly defined by military power. Meanwhile, Israel, Zionism's offspring, lost much of the sympathy it had once enjoyed from the international community by oppressing the Palestinians under its control.

I began *Zionism* at a time when serious talk of Middle East peace had all but vanished from international discourse. Since then, the American government under President Obama has initiated two major negotiating efforts—and failed dismally in both. Does Zionism's recent silence on the issue suggest that the Jewish DNA contains an immunity to peace? This book follows a steady transformation through the lives and thought of the men who were most influential in shaping Zionism's course. Scholars may disagree on the figures I have chosen and how I depict them. But it is beyond dispute that the history of Zionism is inseparable from ongoing conflict not just between Jews and their adversaries but between Jews and Jews.

The commitment to providing a homeland for a people once scattered across a hostile world represents the Zionist ideal. But Jews have been unable to overcome the obstacles to reuniting after nearly two millennia of living apart. Herzl, Zionism's founder, warned of the difficulty of achieving reconciliation among Jews. The Zionism we know today is not a unified idea but a composite of bitter rivalries between stubborn men and their visions of Jewish statehood. Zionism has created a successful country but it has not made the Jews more secure. The absence of peace, in my judgment, keeps the Zionist achievement in jeopardy.

ZIONISM

Prologue

Theodor Herzl is justly credited with being the founder of Zionism, the movement that in time led to the establishment of the Jewish state in Palestine. But Jewish nationalism, Zionism's foundation, appeared well before him. So did the first tentative Zionist organizations. By the time Herzl threw his prodigious energies into the cause, the seeds sown by dedicated men and women throughout Europe had already begun to bloom.

That is not to say that Zionism would have triumphed without Herzl. Herzl possessed a personal magic, which he brought to the historical stage at a fortuitous moment. The century that preceded him had produced a transformation of Europe and, no less important, of Europe's Jews. The result was that in 1896, when Herzl published *Der Judenstaat,* Zionism's seminal tract, Jews throughout Europe and beyond were prepared to embrace his message.

Herzl's program was a direct challenge to the rabbinic class that had governed the Jews since they were driven out of Palestine early in the first millennium A.D. The rabbis established a law code called *halacha,* which they shaped over subsequent centuries, drawing on rabbinic debates recorded in the Talmud. They also imbued the codes with divine authority, making them easier to enforce. Befitting a people in exile, *halacha* consisted preponderantly of guidance for softening the edges of a painful earthly existence. It is not far-fetched to assert that, even today, Exile is the foundation of rabbinic Judaism.

After the Crusades took thousands of Jewish lives early in the second millennium, the rabbis expanded their authority over religious practices to embrace community defense. The Crusaders' fanaticism had by then passed into the mores of Europe's Christian society. Jews were routinely driven from their homes, murdered by their neighbors, and often forced to convert. Princes confined them to ghettos and limited their means of earning a living. In Catholic Spain, Jews were burned at the stake; in the Slavic east, masses of Jews were butchered by Cossacks.

Without the physical means of defense, the rabbis had to acknowledge the reality of the Jews' impotence. Their response might today be called passive resistance. A Jewish poet in the eleventh century testified to the willingness of the Jews to accept their fate, lamenting, "The young, the fair prepare for death, with 'Hear O Israel' on their lips." By the early Middle Ages, Jewish passivity was recognized not just as a tenet of the Jewish faith but as a characteristic of Jewish culture.

The rabbis' reasoning in adopting passivity as a strategy—often referred to as the Oaths—was that it would evoke compassion on the part of their Christian neighbors. The rabbis maintained that the Jews would be best served by their foreswearing of all rights to challenge the princes as well as the princes' subjects, in whose lands they lived. Absorbed into *halacha*, the strategy of passivity also contained a vow on the part of the Jews—for reasons that were not clear—never to organize to return to their ancient home in Palestine. This vow, too, became a fundamental tenet of rabbinic Judaism.

Developed over centuries, rabbinic doctrine held that only God, having sent the Jews into exile as punishment for their sins, could sanction their return. God would dispatch the Messiah to lead them home, the doctrine held, when He was ready to offer them Redemption. Meanwhile, their duty was to wait patiently. A medieval rabbi, alluding to this divine plan, has God declare, "I made you an oath, my careful ones, lest you rebel. Await the End of Days, and do not tremble."

It is probably true that the doctrine of passivity helped to mitigate—even to legitimize—the suffering of Exile. Passivity, it can be argued, succeeded in saving lives, and without it, Europe's Jews might not have survived at all. What is not evident is that the admonition to wait patiently for the

Messiah had played a positive role in the process. By the mid-1700s, Jews were expressing serious reservations about the Messianic constraints that the rabbis had commanded. By Herzl's time, many Jews had reached a readiness to reject their rabbis' Messianic dogma and take their destiny into their own hands.

ψ

The transformation to activism among the Jews took place within the context of the movement called the Enlightenment, which swept through Europe in the eighteenth century. The Enlightenment was heir to the Renaissance, which, earlier in the millennium, had sown seeds of secularism. On its heels, the Reformation then broke the intellectual dominance of the Catholic Church. Voyages of discovery, meanwhile, quickened the popular imagination. Feudalism fell before the economic surge of capitalism. Population soared and new nation-states scrambled to master unfamiliar political rhythms. Throughout Europe, it can be said the Enlightenment ushered in the modern era.

Europe's rabbis, however, were determined to stop modernity. An early sign was their response to a young Jew named Baruch Spinoza, who had fled the Inquisition in Portugal to settle in Holland. As an early Enlightenment thinker, Spinoza promoted rationalism, a tolerance of diversity, and the suppression of religious authority. His ideas, as the rabbis perceived them, were a greater threat than anti-Semitism to the well-being of the Jewish community. The rabbis judged Spinoza a heretic and imposed on him the rare penalty of excommunication.

Among the innovations derived from Spinoza and his fellow Enlightenment thinkers was the Emancipation of the Jews from the legal inferiority that Europe had long imposed on them. Emancipation offered Jews the prospect of membership as equals in a society that held them at arm's length. It offered them the right to live and work where they chose—and to participate in politics. While many Jews exulted, the rabbis were alarmed. What they saw was not an invitation to live a freer, nobler Jewish life but the dismantling of the traditional structure—based upon their own authority—of the Jewish community.

By the second half of the eighteenth century, Emancipation was being implemented against the will of the rabbis across Europe—a law enacted here, a royal decree there. The process was not a straight line. A ruler, seeing a financial advantage in emancipating his Jews, would lift some prohibition, but often his action generated popular protests, leading him to rescind the measure.

Meanwhile, spreading capitalism provided a new impetus to popular anti-Semitism. Jews proved good at making money. Their schools had fostered literacy, which gave them a leg up within Europe's predominantly rural culture. Their success, however, promoted resentment among their neighbors. To the burdens that the Christian Bible imposed on the Jews was added the stereotype of the merchant and the money changer. Herzl, in his personal gravitation toward Zionism, attributed the resurgence of anti-Semitism in his era to the Jews' pervasive mercantile image.

Emancipation's breakthrough in Europe came on the heels of the French Revolution in 1789. France's Declaration of the Rights of Man abolished the legal inequality of Jews. Victorious French armies, filled with liberalizing ardor, initiated the practice of emancipating the Jews wherever they went. Napoleon, as France's emperor, carried Emancipation to the far edges of the Continent.

To many Jews, Napoleon's message was the realization of the Messianic dream, but the rabbis saw no reason to rejoice. Prague's chief rabbi reminded Jews "not to become insolent and behave with haughtiness . . . We are only guests." With France's armies poised at Moscow's gates, Rabbi Shneur Zalman, the voice of Hasidic Jewry, declared, "If Bonaparte wins, the nation of Israel will enjoy much wealth and prestige. But . . . the hearts of the people will grow distant from their Father in heaven. Whereas if our Master (Czar) Alexander wins, there will be much poverty and suffering, but the people's hearts will draw close to their Father in heaven."

In fact, despite its promise, Emancipation did not impart equality to the Jews, even in France. The Enlightenment's anticlerical ideas brought some acceptance of Judaism, the religion, but little of Jews as individuals. Even Jews who converted to Christianity, remained social pariahs. After his baptism, Heinrich Heine, the great German poet, lamented, "I am now hated by Christian and Jew alike. . . . Conversion has brought me nothing but misfortune."

Still, the Enlightenment continued to excite Jews with the hope of a better life. Jews called it by the Hebrew term *Haskala*. Its followers, known as *Maskilim*, made up a new category of Jews, who abandoned traditional religious practice and aspired to assimilate into the larger culture while still identifying as Jews.

In Budapest, Theodor Herzl's parents belonged in this category. They grew rich under capitalism and moved to a sumptuous home outside the ghetto. The education they gave their children was only modestly Jewish. They gave up Yiddish and proclaimed their loyalty to the Hapsburg emperor. They were stylish in dress. They participated in politics and in the local culture. They understood that Christians had not renounced anti-Semitism, in referring euphemistically to it as the "Jewish Question," but they insisted that in time real equality with their neighbors was inevitable.

As promising as Emancipation seemed to many in West Europe, it brought little hope to the Jews of czarist Russia. Until the eighteenth century, when Russia joined Austria and Prussia in dividing up hapless Poland, very few Jews actually lived within Russia's borders. Then, overnight, Russia became the home of Europe's largest Jewish minority. By the end of the nineteenth century, despite a steady migration to the West, some five million Jews lived under the czar's autocracy.

Determined to limit the Jews' impact, the czar ruled that Jews be confined to the Pale of Settlement, a territory consisting of recently annexed Polish territory plus a few adjacent Russian provinces. Even in the Pale, residence was barred in the large cities and in many prosperous villages. A few rich merchants, university graduates, and army veterans could claim waivers to this exclusion, but most Jews were prohibited even from traveling outside the Pale within Russia.

Some Jews prospered, despite the limitations, but the majority, permitted to work only as small merchants or craftsmen, lived in poverty. The Pale was administered by the czar's police; secret agents intruded into all aspects of the Jews' daily existence. Corruption was rampant. Jewish children were conscripted for as much as twenty-five years as recruits into the czar's army.

Russia did not conceal that its anti-Semitism was official policy. At its root was the czar's deep Christian devotion, imbued with an unmitigated hostility to Jews. Once, when a minion sent Czar Alexander II a memo suggesting he soften state anti-Semitism, he scribbled in reply, "But we must not forget it was the Jews who crucified our Lord and spilled his priceless blood." The czars sincerely believed that Jewish deicide required Russia either to punish or convert the Jews.

Yet even czarist despotism could not erect an impenetrable barrier to the Enlightenment. Both Christians and Jews knew what was happening in the West, and many Russian *Maskilim* were convinced that in time their own Emancipation would arrive. The czars sought to disabuse them of this notion. In midcentury, Czar Nicholas I, identifying the Jews' liberty with Napoleon and the French Revolution, dismissed Emancipation, declaring that, "As long as I live, such a thing will not take place in Russia."

When Czar Alexander II took the dramatic step of freeing Russia's serfs in 1861, he abolished military conscription of Jewish children, but otherwise the constraints on Jews remained intact. Aware that the ex-serfs in the Pale were the Jews' natural antagonists, his regime routinely fanned the fires of hostility. In 1871, former serfs—now legally free peasants—conducted a four-day pogrom against the Jews of Odessa, initiating a new and more violent era in Russian policy.

When Alexander II was assassinated in 1881, the regime turned instinctively for retaliation to the pogrom, though the assassins were Christian revolutionaries. The peasantry, now backed by a rising urban proletariat, responded enthusiastically to the regime's invitation to attack Jews. Most painfully, the Russian intelligentsia, whom the *Maskilim* regarded as supporters of Emancipation, cheered on the bloodshed.

The wave of pogroms throughout the Pale lasted nearly three years, during which some two hundred Jewish towns and villages were overrun. To be sure, the mayhem—forty killed, thousands of homes razed, businesses pillaged, women raped—hardly compared to later ravages at the hands of Hitler and Stalin. But the brutality confirmed that any hope by Jews for a better life in the czar's Russia was a delusion.

For the rabbinate, the pogroms validated the old doctrine that Jews must not threaten their hosts, not even in self-defense. Many Jews instead joined the migratory wave, first to Europe, then to the Americas. Meanwhile, Jews living under Emancipation in West Europe felt no comparable sense of danger. Rather, they scoffed at Orthodoxy's forebodings of disaster, reaffirming their belief in the promises that the Enlightenment had made to them.

By the mid-nineteenth century, several generations of the Jews who grew up in Western Europe had acquired a vested interest in Emancipation. They were oblivious to rabbinic claims of authority and loath to accept any inferior social rank. If Orthodox Jews remained committed to waiting patiently for the Messiah, the Jews who regarded themselves as emancipated were resolute about playing an active role in the state. The signal they sent was that they were ready to shape their own fate.

Such Jews failed to notice that after Napoleon, the Enlightenment had lost much of its appeal to Europe's masses. Romanticism, exalting a simpler past, superseded rationalism at the core of popular thought. Nationalism took on a dose of mysticism and nativism, then of racism. In uprisings in 1830 and in 1848, Jews fought to save the liberal values of the Enlightenment; but these insurgencies proved to be the Enlightenment's last gasp.

By midcentury, many emancipated Jews had lost confidence about their place in European society. It was no coincidence that Jewish thinkers turned to writing articles and books that examined their growing discomfort. Some were influenced by Christian romanticism, others by the secular nationalism rising around them, and some by a combination of both. They wrote of Jews returning to the biblical practice of tilling the soil. They argued for a rebirth of long-suppressed Jewish nationalism. In retrospect, these thinkers were deemed the harbingers of Herzl's Zionism.

Yehuda Alkalai and Zvi Kalischer, born near the end of the eighteenth century, were rabbis who departed from traditional Orthodoxy to urge Jews to embark on a collective effort to return to Palestine. Neither sought out followers among seculars; their vision, rather, was to transport *halacha* to the Holy Land. Having witnessed popular revolts against Turkey in Serbia and Russia in Poland, they urged Jews to absorb the lesson of the non-Jewish nationalists and reach out in a new and specifically Jewish direction.

Alkalai entreated rich Jews to lease Palestine from the Turks, foreshadowing Herzl's diplomatic strategy. "Collective return was foretold by all the prophets . . . ," he argued. "It is well known that a heavenly awakening is dependent on an earthly awakening. . . . The sultan will not object, for he knows that the Jews are loyal subjects." Herzl's grandfather happened to live in the same small Serbian town as Alkalai.

Throwing himself into Jewish nationalism, Kalischer persuaded wealthy Jews to found an agricultural school in Palestine, arguing that Jewish farming would hasten the Messiah's arrival. "Jewish farming," he wrote, "will be a spur to Messianic redemption. . . . Let us take to heart the examples of the Italians, Poles, and Hungarians, who laid down their lives and possessions in the struggle for national independence, while we, the children of Israel, who have the most glorious and holiest of lands as our inheritance, are spiritless and silent. Should we not be ashamed?"

Moshe Hess, born in 1812, had won fame as an advocate of socialism, then shifted his emphasis to Jewish nationalism, publishing *Rome and Jerusalem,* which called for Jews to found a secular socialist state of their own in Palestine. The Rome of his title was neither Imperial nor Papal. It was Giuseppe Mazzini's Rome, the fulfillment of Italy's unification dream. "With the resurrection of Italy," Hess wrote, "begins the resurrection of Judea."

Hess denounced assimilation, the aspiration of most Enlightenment Jews. "The time has come," he wrote, "for you to reclaim your ancient fatherland from Turkey, either by way of compensation *or by other means* [my italics]"—it is not clear if he was suggesting conquest—"where . . . you will be completely healed from all your ills." In the fatherland, he wrote, Jews will meet together on the common ground of Jewish patriotism.

Neither Alkalai nor Kalischer nor Hess, known to Zionism as "Precursors" of Herzl, ever acquired a popular following. But all three had an impact on Zionist ideology. Hess's vision was in time channeled into secular, socialist Zionism, while the ideas of Alkalai and Kalischer flowed into what became a rival wing of Religious Zionism. But, together, the Precursors contributed to the ferment of the times. Oddly, Herzl always insisted, even as he prepared himself to lead a return to Palestine, that he had no knowledge of the works of any of the Precursors.

Though hard to imagine, Herzl was never part of a Jewish intellectual circle, where he might have stumbled into the ideas that led to Zionism. He came late to the idea and formed his vision largely on his own. Nonetheless, it can be said that even if Herzl did not know their works, the Precursors planted in the body of Jewish thought ideas that flowered years later in his seminal work, *Der Judenstaat.*

The Russian pogroms of the 1880s brought to a fever pitch the debate among Jews of Eastern Europe over the future of their community. They met informally in homes and meeting halls to argue over the course they should adopt. Most of the talk was of flight to the West, to which rich Western Jews were willing to donate funds and which the czar, happy to be rid of his Jews, applauded. At the same time, many Jews identified with competing revolutionary doctrines, which widened the breach with the czar's regime. Running behind was a third course: migration to Palestine under the umbrella of Jewish nationalism. The idea particularly excited young

people without money or strong family ties who saw it as offering fulfillment to their lives.

Among the groups that contemplated migration to Palestine was BILU,
whose name was a Hebrew acronym of a biblical verse that exalted hopes
for Jewish freedom. The *biluim* thought about tilling Palestine's soil while
building a framework to shape an independent Jewish society. BILU sowed
the seeds of the movement that would, a few years later, become Zionism.

In 1882, when the first *biluim* arrived, some twenty-five thousand pious Jews already lived in Palestine. They and their forebears had clustered
since the Middle Ages in Jewish "holy cities," chiefly Jerusalem. Called by
the Hebrew term *yishuv,* their community depended totally on charity
from Jews around the world. The *biluim* were appalled by the culture of
mendicancy that they found among Palestine's pious community.

Conflict between the old *yishuv* and the new *yishuv* flared at once.
The men of the old wore skullcaps, heavy beards, and long black coats; the
men of the new *yishuv* dressed in shorts, worked bare chested, and
wore jaunty caps to protect them from the sun. The old *yishuv* considered
charity their due and regarded the newcomers as intruders, diverting
their rightful income into harebrained farming schemes; the new aspired
beyond all else to economic self-sufficiency. To the old, any prospect of
comity with the new immigrants lay in their conversion to piety. The new
yishuv, in contrast, aimed to bring the old into the modern, secular world.

In fact, unable to master the hardships of cultivating Palestine's unyielding soil, the BILU pioneers soon became dependent themselves on
donations from abroad. It pleased the pious Jews that many of them returned to Russia or moved on to America. By normal measure, the BILU
experiment failed.

But the *biluim* had generated a powerful set of ideals, establishing a
heritage that defied the Jewish stereotype in the Christian world. In the
place of merchants and intellectuals, they created an image of tough,
physical Jews, who endured the heat of the sun, and rejoiced in driving
a pick into the earth. They passed on to subsequent generations of migrants a rough-hewn Spartan model, which evolved into a mystique that
would find its way into Jewish nationalist norms.

The *biluim* scarcely took note of their settling on land for which they
had no legal title. They were not hostile to Arabs; some even emulated
the Arabs in food and dress. Rather, their ideals contained no room for
contemplating Arab possession. They deeply believed Palestine was *their*

land. It was not necessarily *holy,* the claim of the pious Jews, but it was intrinsically *Jewish.* BILU left to Herzl the conceptualization of a Jewish statehood, but it never questioned the Jews' right to Palestine.

While *biluim* were struggling to tame the soil, Leo Pinsker, a Jewish doctor from Odessa, published a small book called *Auto-Emancipation.* Its powerful nationalism inspired the founding in Vienna of the journal that coined the term "Zionism," drawn from a historical symbol of the homeland to which Jews in Exile yearned to return.

Pinsker oddly foreshadowed Herzl, forty years his junior, in a wide range of ways. The two were born into successful *Haskala* families, and were educated in secular schools. Both studied law, though Pinsker later became a doctor and was decorated by the czar for his army service in the Crimean War. Both were raised with the conviction that Jews would in due course achieve equality in European society, only to find their convictions shattered by anti-Semitic violence. Their life experiences led both to the conclusion that assimilation was a delusion. As Herzl did later, Pinsker based his book on the premise that Jews would survive as a people only by having a country of their own.

Pinsker argued that Russia's Jews were so beaten down by tyranny that "no Moses" was likely to emerge from their ranks. A Jewish national movement, he said, would have to be led by a free and prosperous Jew from the West. Herzl, after deciding to claim Zionism's leadership for himself, echoed his unawareness of the work of the Precursors by jotting into his diary, "In Odessa there lived a man named Pinsker.... His writings are said to be worthwhile. Shall read them as soon as I have time."

Pinsker maintained that the Enlightenment, having bestowed on Jews a speck of both emancipation and liberalization, left untouched its own "Judeophobia," which he described as a "hereditary psychic aberration" that it had never cured. Emancipation, he wrote, was "a splendid alms ... to poor, humble beggars," which sought to persuade Jews to give up their own nationality, but then swindled them out of the equality they had been promised. Emancipation, he concluded, cannot remove "the stigma attached (by Europe) to this people."

Pinsker contended that only by their own superhuman efforts would Jews be able to free themselves. "We must first of all," he wrote, *"desire to help ourselves ...* [my italics]" even if it was unlikely to bring a happy result. "What have we to lose? At the worst, we shall continue to be in the future what we have been in the past . . . : *eternally despised Jews.*"

Like Herzl, Pinsker was too removed from Jewish culture to grasp the centrality of Palestine in the Jewish mind. "Our goal must be not the 'Holy Land' . . . ," he wrote, "but a secure and unquestioned refuge for those who must leave their homes . . . a piece of land . . . from which no foreign master can expel us." The land that came to his mind was "a small territory in North America or a sovereign Pashalik in Asiatic Turkey."

Again, like Herzl, Pinsker admitted that publishing a book was barely a first step in reaching his goal. In *Auto-Emancipation,* he acknowledged that BILU's young pioneers, having failed to master the soil, were left with the choice of "roaming around without shelter" or returning home in defeat. His book stimulated the founding of dozens more BILU societies throughout Europe, but the number of Jewish migrants to Palestine remained small.

After Pinsker published *Auto-Emancipation,* BILU loosely linked its local societies under the name Hibbat Zion ("Love of Zion"). In search of a leader, it turned instinctively to Pinsker himself. Pinsker, however, was aware that he lacked the skills to bring order to inherently undisciplined organizations, much less the capacity for charismatic leadership that Herzl later demonstrated. Introverted and a self-effacing bachelor, Pinsker, barely sixty, was already in poor health. Nonetheless, in the fall of 1883, he agreed to become the head of Hibbat Zion. He soon recognized that he was not the right man for the job.

In 1884, Pinsker convoked a congress of Hibbat Zion in Kattowitz, a small town in Prussia, beyond the reach of the czar's secret police. Thirty delegates attended. In calling for "rejuvenating our people through agriculture," he followed the script. But to avoid provoking either the Turks, who were then tightening their controls over Jews in Palestine, or the Western philanthropists, from whom he hoped to extract financial support, he was silent about the issue of Jewish statehood. Instead of calling for Jewish independence, he asked only for donations to BILU's hard-pressed, struggling settlements.

Coming to the rescue of Hibbat Zion was Baron Edmond de Rothschild, scion of Europe's famous family of financiers. An observant Jew, Rothschild was outraged by the Russian pogroms but doubted that the most effective answer to them was mass migration to Palestine. While scoffing at Jewish aspirations to statehood, he responded to Pinsker's plea for funds to save the faltering Hibbat Zion enterprise. After his initial contributions, he never stopped contributing, which earned him the honorary title of "father of Jewish colonization."

Rothschild, however, had a personal agenda beyond Hibbat Zion's. He expected his beneficiaries to observe the Sabbath. He also envisaged establishing companies that would create wealth and employment. He built a glass factory and a salt refinery. He founded schools and drained swamps. But, being something of an autocrat, he warned, "In all things, follow the instructions of my representatives. He who fails to do so will cease to enjoy my aid." When BILU settlers protested that his plan for a winery violated their ideals, he dismissed their objections and barged ahead.

Pinsker winced at Rothschild's crude style but understood that defying him placed the entire Hibbat Zion undertaking at risk. Many of the *biluim* regarded the loss of their freedom as an excessive price to pay for Rothschild's charity. Unsure in which direction to turn, Pinsker finally decided to enforce Rothschild's discipline. It cost him much of the pioneers' loyalty.

After eight contentious years at Hibbat Zion, Pinsker died in Odessa, having failed to close the breach with Rothschild. He had also failed to heal the rift between secularism and religion in the settlements, which was wider than ever, and he barely managed to keep at bay the rabbis who tried to take over the Hibbat Zion movement. Despite Rothschild's generosity, Pinsker had also been unable to overcome the financial burdens that limited migration.

At the time of Pinsker's death in 1881, Theodor Herzl, barely in his thirties, had begun thinking seriously about both the plight of Europe's Jews and the role he himself might play in relieving it. When he reached a decision on that role, he found Pinsker's apostles, the veterans of the Hibbat Zion movement, his sturdiest and most faithful collaborators. Though Herzl never met him, Pinsker had set the stage for the Zionist era.

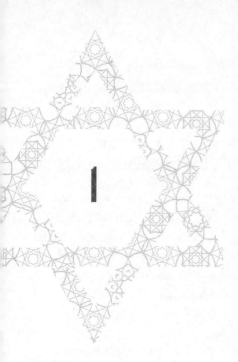

1

Theodor Herzl
1860–1904

PATHFINDER

On August 29, 1897, in the city of Basel in Switzerland, Theodor Herzl announced to the delegates at the first World Zionist Congress that "we are here to lay the cornerstone of the edifice that is to house the Jewish nation." Tall, with majestic bearing, framed by a prophet's black beard, Herzl conveyed a mystical presence on the dais. The cheering delegates responded "Long Live the King." Herzl did not call for Jewish statehood at Basel, but in his diary a few days later, he predicted that "perhaps in five years, and certainly in fifty," the Jewish state will exist.

Herzl's words have long been recalled for their prescience—and for the confidence they expressed in himself and in the Zionist organization that he founded in Basel. But, if they appeared to suggest smooth sailing to statehood, they were misleading. Despite his indefatigable personal efforts, success painfully eluded Herzl in his lifetime. The gestation of the state was a long and tumultuous process. Even today, two-thirds of a century after the establishment of Israel, debate rages over whether the Jews possess the wisdom to safeguard Herzl's heritage.

Herzl, in *The Jewish State*, had only recently introduced Zionism as a movement into the lexicon of international politics. It is true that Jewish thinkers before him had alluded to Zionism, and that the vision of returning home had been kept alive in prayer for nearly two thousand years of Exile. "Next year in Jerusalem" was a promise repeated every day, though Jews did very little to realize it. "Zionism" at first referred to the *sentiment* of Jewish nationalism. Herzl, in devising a strategy and founding in Basel an organization to create a state, gave the word a specific, grander meaning.

Herzl was thirty-seven and at the peak of his powers when, on his own initiative, he convened the Zionist Congress. As an outsider, it took audacity to invite Jews to assemble for what was still his personal project. Even more daring was the vision itself. Rabbinic tradition held that only God, through the Messiah, His agent, had the power to bring His people home. In that sense, Herzl's summons at Basel was a challenge to Judaism, but it was also an echo of the rising drumbeat of the secular nationalism spreading across Europe.

At the start of his journey, Herzl himself did not understand its revolutionary nature. A man of letters, raised as an assimilated Jew, he had been only barely interested in politics, much less Jewish politics. He was recognized as, at best, a minor literary talent yearning for public recognition. He had revealed no intrinsic disposition to lead. Nor did he anguish over Europe's rising anti-Semitism. Herzl loved Vienna, his home city, not for its vibrant Jewish life but for its sophisticated German culture. Before embracing Zionism, Herzl, like many other Enlightenment Jews, had at times even considered conversion to Christianity.

Theodor Herzl was born in 1860 in Budapest, then a provincial capital of the Hapsburg Empire. Alluding to Zionism's conflict with religion, he later described the house in which he was raised as "next to the synagogue where lately the rabbi denounced me from the pulpit in very sharp terms." His parents, Enlightenment Jews, were among the first to accept Emancipation's invitation to relocate their home outside the ghetto. His father, Jakob, was a wealthy merchant and banker; his mother, Jeanette, was the family's literary intellectual. They did not deny their Jewishness, but rarely attended synagogue, and took for granted their ultimate acceptance as Jews into the larger German world.

Theodor's parents enrolled him in a prominent Jewish day school, and, on his thirteenth birthday, invited friends to his bar mitzvah, which in their social circle was called a "confirmation." In secondary school, Theodor was attracted to engineering, but he received poor marks in his technical studies. Private tutors supplemented his schoolwork and also instructed him in good manners and foreign languages.

As an adolescent, Herzl already showed a taste for literature, writing essays, poems, and stories in both German and Hungarian, often with nationalist or antireligious themes. None were on Jewish topics. At fifteen, he transferred to an esteemed Protestant academy, where he showed as much indifference to Christianity as to Judaism. At eighteen, his sister Pauline, a year older than he, died of typhoid fever, a tragedy that left him the unique object of family love and attention. With only final exams remaining until his graduation from the academy, the Herzls decided to move to Vienna, so Theodor could enroll in the fall semester in the imperial university, a center of Germanic learning.

Anti-Semitism was sharply on the rise when the Herzls arrived in Vienna. The Papacy's recent loss of its historic rule over Rome to Italy's democratic *Risorgimento* had inspired it to counterattack against secular liberalism, with which Jews were identified. The impact was particularly strong in Vienna, a Catholic city to which Jews had in recent years migrated in large numbers. Successful in commerce, finance, and the professions, the Jews had provoked laments among disaffected Viennese over the city's "Judaization." Though Emperor Franz Joseph was protective of Jews, political parties found anti-Semitism useful in appealing for the votes of both the working classes and the affluent non-Jewish bourgeoisie.

If young Herzl noticed anti-Semitism around him, it had little impact. Obviously, he did not give it much thought. He lived with his parents in a comfortable apartment in a fine quarter. He happily explored the city's cafés and theaters and, when he returned to Budapest to sit for his final exams, he found his native city unbearably backward. At the university, he enrolled in the law school, but it was a practical move, since his real love was literature. He certainly did not perceive that the ethnic tolerance for which Vienna was known had diminished to a thin veneer.

At the university, about a fourth of the students were Jews, but it was not to them that Herzl turned in search of friends. On the contrary, he sought out the company of German nationalists, who thought of themselves as the student elite. Being Jewish and Hungarian, he was twice an outsider, required to demonstrate his credentials with an extra measure of intensity. The university and its student body, like Vienna itself, were at a tipping point. Though German nationalism still possessed traces of the Enlightenment's liberal ideals, it was moving steadily toward a hostility to everything Jewish.

Herzl signed on to the practices of the young nationalists, who mimicked Prussia's aristocracy. He joined Albia, a dueling fraternity, took lessons in fencing, and fought at least one ceremonial duel. He dressed elegantly and carried an ebony-handled walking stick. He embraced the swords, beer mugs, and caps that accompanied the university's fraternity life.

Biographers have questioned whether Herzl's student antics concealed a secret bond he felt to his Jewishness. Albia required a *nom de combat,* and Herzl chose Tancred, a figure from a novel by England's Benjamin Disraeli, the celebrated writer-politician who was a Jewish convert to Christianity. Tancred, in the novel, promoted a vague Zionism. Herzl never spoke of any hidden allegiance but, much later, having been left with a sour memory of his student years, he mocked his attachment to the "stupid farces" of Christian university life.

Clearly insecure, Herzl was also very moody. Albia had brought him no real friends. Nor did he have romances. A notebook he kept—more intimate than his later diaries—reveals a discomfort with women, even a prudishness, which would reappear in his early published writing. Bored with his law studies, he spent much of his time reading novels in cafes. A friend described him as permanently enshrouded in melancholy, and among Herzl's diary notes was the observation: "I can only be happy when I am absolutely miserable."

Oddly, a book that made a major impact on him was Eugen Dühring's *The Jewish Question as a Problem of Race, Morals and Civilization.*[1] It was one of the works then fashionable among intellectuals across Europe. Inspired by Darwin's genetic research, these works claimed a scientific basis for anti-Semitism. Dühring went beyond the standard religious and social origins of the anti-Jewish phobia to assert the Jews' *racial* depravity. In Vienna, the book was a bestseller.

Dühring, from his seat at the University of Berlin, argued that the assimilation of Jews was poisoning German culture. Being inbred, the faults of the Jews had no prospect of fading away. He called Emancipation a terrible mistake and urged that Jews be re-confined to the ghettos. The backing of intellectuals of both right and left—and most notably the outspoken nationalism of the much admired composer Richard Wagner—added to the power of his argument.

Herzl, now twenty-two, was shaken by Dühring's analysis, though comments he inscribed in his notes suggest he was more confused than angry. Parts of the book, he wrote, were "so informative that every Jew ought to read them." The feeling conveyed by his words was that Dühring asserted some uncomfortable truths. Herzl surely was not alone among Jews of his time who asked themselves whether the scorn directed at them was justified.

Even years later, Herzl described the book as being "as full of hate as it is brilliant. The effect of Dühring's book upon me was as if I had suddenly been hit over the head. I suppose this has been the experience of many a Western Jew who had already completely forgotten his national identity: the anti-Semites reawakened it in him." As he grew older, he often cited Dühring as the real source of his immersion in the "Jewish Question."

After reading Dühring, Herzl drifted away from his companions at Albia, who had grown increasingly hostile to him. In 1883, Albia organized a mourning ceremony for the recently deceased Wagner, sponsored by the Union of German Students. Herzl did not attend, but the press reported that the ceremony degenerated into anti-Semitic rioting. Herzl responded with a letter of resignation from the fraternity, which he signed "Tancred." Albia's board accepted the resignation on the condition that Herzl return his fraternity paraphernalia, including his beloved cap, sword, and drinking mug, which he did.

Even then, Herzl was not ready to abandon his Teutonic infatuations. He snubbed Kadima, a student society recently founded by Jewish students from Eastern Europe to combat anti-Semitism at the university. He also overlooked the appearance of Leo Pinsker's *Auto-Emancipation* and the young organization called Hibbat Zion. Instead, he spent his final years at the university testing his prospects as a playwright. One of the plays, titled *The Disillusioned*, dwelled on his personal anguish, while again skirting the Jewish Question. None of these plays was produced or published.

Depressed about his future as graduation approached, Herzl embarked, at his parents expense, on a tour of Europe. Over the years, family-sponsored tourism became a form of relief to tame his personal demons. Herzl spent much of his life, in fact, on trains speeding to distant places across Europe. These early journeys, from which he mailed back observations for publication, promoted his literary career. In time, the journeys served the cause of Zionism. But they also provided comfort to his troubled psyche.

Herzl finished his university studies in 1884, passed the exam for admission to the Vienna bar, and accepted a position as a lawyer in the Austrian court system. Among his postings was picturesque Salzburg, an experience he called "one of the happiest of my life." But he understood the strict limits faced by Jews in the legal profession and, unlike other Jewish lawyers, he was not prepared to convert. More significantly, he disliked practicing law, so after a year in the courts, he resigned to seek fame and fortune as a writer.

The years that followed were the most rewarding of Herzl's literary career. He wrote plays, stories, and, most notably, *feuilletons,* lighthearted sketches, an art form popular in the press of the day. Many were based on travels he undertook to persuade theater managers to produce his plays. He specialized in comedies, and a few that were produced received positive notices. They brought him a reputation as a sharp-eyed and witty social observer, as well as a sound craftsman, comfortable with a range of topics. But even the most sympathetic critics did not treat Herzl as a serious artist.

Though a recognizable celebrity in Vienna's intellectual circles before he was thirty, Herzl suffered from an internal problem in being a Jew. In one of his letters to his parents about a reception he attended in Berlin, he sneered at "thirty or forty ugly little Jews and Jewesses, not a very refreshing sight." From Rome, he once submitted a journal article describing the ancient ghetto, without once mentioning the Jews who lived there. Another time he admitted his irritation at having an anti-Semitic slur directed at him in a Mainz beer hall. Still, he did not once publicly acknowledge that he was Jewish.

Throughout these post-university years, Herzl continued to live with his parents. He grew the beard that complemented his dark, melancholy eyes and deep voice—and which came to serve as the flag of his identity. He seems to have had a few flings with women, one of whom may briefly have been a mistress. He was a familiar presence in theaters and literary salons, and he issued challenges to duels in response to slights, though nothing much came of them. He privately published two books of his works and, when they failed to produce an audience, he told a friend he was ready to give up his ambition of becoming a major writer.

In 1886, when he may have calculated that he ought to have a wife, Herzl met Julie Naschauer, an eighteen-year-old beauty from a socially prominent Jewish family. A tumultuous courtship ensued, during which the two did not see each other for months at a time. But three years later they married, and children soon arrived, one being a son, Hans, whom he did not have circumcised. Julie, however, was no substitute for his mother. The marriage, in which the partners conveyed little mutual ardor, or much else in common, was marred by recurring separations.

After the marriage, Herzl's reputation as a playwright diminished sharply, and to regain a sense of well-being he again went traveling. The *Neue Freie Presse*, Vienna's most distinguished paper, agreed to publish his *feuilletons* from France. The paper, like many in the Emancipation era, was Jewish-owned and liberal, and had a wide readership, mainly among Jews, throughout German-speaking Europe. So favorably did Herzl's articles impress his editors that in October 1891, they sent him a surprise offer of employment as their Paris correspondent. Herzl accepted it at once, changing the course of his life.

For a year he lived alone in a Paris hotel, seeing Julie and his family only on occasional visits to Vienna. Later he rented a spacious apartment and asked Julie to join him, neglecting to tell her he had also invited his parents to share it. The arrangement aggravated the marital discord, a condition Herzl seemed willing to ignore.

Herzl's preoccupation was mastering the duties of a foreign correspondent, working conscientiously on matters that never before concerned him. He wrote on parliamentary elections and party politics, budgets and the stock exchange. He produced strong articles on the social conditions in fin-de-siècle France, where the rich lived in glittering excess while the working class suffered in poverty. "Paris got hold of me and shook me through and through," he wrote in a letter to a friend. He also acquired an awareness of the impact that anti-Semitism had within France's bubbling cauldron of political instability and social disorder.[2]

It is often said that the anti-Semitism which Herzl found in France made him a Zionist, but that is an oversimplification. France, if anything, forced on him a new sensitivity to anti-Semitism at home. In Vienna, Herzl had once noted in his diary, "the Jewish Question naturally lurked for me around every turn and corner. I sighed over it and made fun of it; I felt unhappy, but still it never really took hold." It was his overall experience in France that primed him for a transformation.

In France, Herzl noted, Jews were blamed for all sorts of offenses. One of his newspaper articles covered street crowds shouting "Down with the Jews" during a scandal they had nothing to do with. He submitted a report of an elaborate military funeral, with full military honors, of a young Jewish officer who was killed in a duel with a notorious anti-Semite. The funeral showed, he wrote, that France's anti-Semites, in acknowledging the humanity of Jews, had more decency, "one could almost say courtesy," than Austria's.

At first, he even spoke well of the intellectuals among France's anti-Semites, who reminded him of Dühring, the racist scholar. He admired their wit and style, he said, and even urged his readers to confront their research for what it revealed about Jewish flaws. Ultimately, however, Paris led him beyond such evenhanded judgment, to a conclusion that Jewish patience would not undo the damage of anti-Semitism. In private letters, he now wrote of Western Europe as "enemy territory."

The Jewish Question had captured Herzl at last. In a series of uncharacteristic delusional musings in his diary in June of 1895, he wrote of fighting duels in Vienna against famous anti-Semites and, if indicted, of defending his honor in show trials. He imagined standing for election to Austria's parliament to serve as champion of the Jews. Most flamboyantly, he envisaged signing a peace treaty with the Pope, solemnized in Vienna's St. Stephen's Cathedral, in which Austria's Jews would agree to convert to Catholicism in return for the Vatican's pledge to bring anti-Semitism to an end.

Yet, even as he dreamed of playing a role in their rescue, Herzl expressed doubts about whether the Jews had the capacity to unite into a viable community. "If the Jews ever 'returned home' one day," he wrote in his diary, "they would discover on the next that they do not belong together. For centuries they have been rooted in diverse nationalisms; they differ from each other, group by group. The only thing they have in common is the pressure holding them together." Having recently learned about Hibbat Zion, he contemplated making an inspection tour to take the measure of its Palestinian colonies.

On one occasion, Herzl's musings on Palestine made a clear and harsh reference to the Arabs. "We shall try to spirit the penniless population across the border, securing employment for it in the transit countries, while denying it employment in our own country. . . . The removal of the poor," he wrote, "must be carried out discreetly and circumspectly."

Anti-Zionists have since pointed to these lines as evidence that even before *The Jewish State* appeared, Herzl intended to expel the Arabs. His defenders reply these were diary jottings drawn from delusional reveries. The idea of expulsion, like the idea of his fighting duels in Vienna, never appeared as formal proposals. To be sure, Arab expulsion—later called "population transfer"—in time entered into Zionist thinking, but there is no evidence it did so at Herzl's behest. In fact, it probably did not need Herzl's help.

These reveries came at what was for Herzl a psychological low point. During a holiday with a male friend at an Austrian spa, Herzl seemed especially gloomy about his future. The holiday began badly when a passerby shouted "dirty Jew" at him. In talks with his companion, he complained that Emancipation had created modern anti-Semitism by offering rights to Jews that Europe never intended to grant. Jews, as a result, behaved as "men who have served long prison sentences unjustly," while being judged for their "anti-social qualities."

This was Herzl's theme in a play he wrote later that year called *The New Ghetto,* his first literary excursion into the Jewish Question. In it, he showed an unfamiliar concern for the Jews' burdens, but he nonetheless came down harder on Jews than on Christian bigots. Modeling its hero on himself, he depicted a high-minded lawyer, son of generous parents and husband of a spoiled wife. His villain was a Jewish speculator for whose shady deals "the victims blame (all) Jews." Herzl's ambivalence at being a Jew clearly reemerged in the last act, which argued that Jews, in being wedded to the sins that perpetuate anti-Semitism, contribute to bringing its ills upon themselves.

On finishing the play, Herzl wrote to a friend, "I don't want to be a sentimental, pathetic poet. . . . I want to unburden my heart. . . . There is a whole springtide still within me, and some day it may break into bloom." Though these words possess a romantic, even self-pitying, ring, they hint at a recognition that he must give up his mystical self-image, in which he makes a deal with the Pope and fights duels to rescue Jews, in favor of a more practical course.

In 1894, soon after writing *The New Ghetto,* Herzl was assigned to cover the trial of Alfred Dreyfus, a French army captain charged with treason as a spy. Like Herzl, Dreyfus belonged to a family of bourgeois, secular Jews who had prospered since Emancipation. Born within months of each other, both he and Dreyfus took their respective patriotisms for granted. Herzl grieved that anti-Semitism had cast a shadow over their feelings. As popular suspicions grew that the charges against Dreyfus were bogus, Herzl identified increasingly with the beleaguered French captain.

"A Jew who, as an officer on the general staff, has before him an honorable career," he wrote in his newspaper, "cannot commit such a crime." Herzl soon expressed his belief openly that Dreyfus had been framed.

As the trial dragged on, rabid mobs screamed anti-Semitic slogans daily on Paris streets. With France torn asunder, Dreyfus was found guilty and imprisoned. But four years later, the discovery of falsified documents within the general staff proved his innocence, and he was pardoned. In time, Dreyfus was fully exonerated and his military rank restored.

The case, however, revealed to Herzl that anti-Semitism—as Leo Pinsker once wrote—was an incurable European plague. The recognition seemed to relieve him of his ambivalence at being Jewish. The trial, he wrote, "embodies the desire of the vast majority of the French to condemn a Jew, and to condemn all Jews in this one Jew." Dreyfus's ultimate exoneration may have saved France's integrity, he wrote, but the French Declaration of the Rights of Man had lost its meaning.

Herzl now embarked on devising a plan to carry out his mission to rescue the Jews. His plays were going nowhere; *The New Ghetto* had not even been staged. His editors in Vienna considered his Jewish concerns a distraction from his duties. He was thinking of making a study of the Jews in the Hapsburg Empire when a friend pointed out that *Uncle Tom's Cabin* had made a huge impact in pre–Civil War America, and he shifted his aim to a novel. Finally Herzl admitted to himself that he had to go beyond his pen to save his people.

Yet, Herzl was unsure of how much of himself he was willing to give to the cause. A visit to Vienna, where he witnessed crowds cheering for a slate of anti-Semites campaigning for local offices, apparently made up his mind. "Out of the realm of the unconscious came the urge to go beyond words," he wrote. Since reading Dühring, "it took at least thirteen years to conceive this simple idea" of direct action. "Only now do I realize how often I went past it."

♆

Herzl was thirty-five years old in 1895, the year in which he started his Zionist diaries, which became a window into his mind. In them, he conceded that his new calling might be impractical and that he could become a laughingstock. "Could I be only a figure in my own novel?" he asks. Only in retrospect is it clear he possessed inner resources that he was just beginning to perceive. "Today I am an isolated and lonely man," he wrote, "tomorrow the intellectual leader of hundreds of thousands—in any case, the discoverer and proclaimer of a mighty idea."

But such a claim was no substitute for credentials. Not only was Herzl's Judaism shallow but he was without popular support. He was, at best, a moderately successful journalist, known to few in the Jewish world. He was also an obvious neurotic, often depressed and given to fantasies. Whether or not he knew it, he was, moreover already suffering from the heart ailment that, within less than a decade, would end his life.

The burden Herzl decided to take upon himself required daring, even foolhardiness. He had to convey an illusion of great authority, much greater than he actually possessed. But he had no idea of how to apply this daring. Then suddenly, an idea came to him, he wrote in his diary. He would initiate his campaign by sending a strong letter to Baron de Hirsch.

Baron Maurice de Hirsch, member of a great Jewish banking family, was a pan-European aristocrat and one of the continent's richest men. He was a generous philanthropist, with a special concern for Russia's Jews. He once offered the czar a fortune to establish Jewish schools in the Pale, which the czar rejected. He also believed in returning the Jews to farming. Unsympathetic to the Hibbat Zion colonization already under way in Palestine, he purchased tracts in Argentina, where he founded farms on which some three thousand Jews were settled. But his settlements, like Hibbat Zion's, were not self-supporting and were in financial decline when Herzl's letter arrived at his Paris home.[3]

Herzl began his letter abruptly: "When may I have the honor to call on you?" He asked Hirsch to arrange an "uninterrupted hour or two" to discuss the Jewish Question. He revealed no agenda, but he called on Hirsch to treat the letter confidentially. Hirsch's reply came from London, where he said he would remain for two months, asking politely that Herzl state in writing what he proposed to say in person.

In reply, Herzl conveyed an even haughtier tone than in the initial letter. "What you have undertaken till now has been as magnanimous as it has been misapplied, as costly as it has been pointless. You have hitherto been only a philanthropist; I want to show you the way to become something more. . . . Although I am unknown to you, all I desire is your fullest attention. I certainly do not expect to convince you right away, for you will have to rethink a number of your present attitudes. . . . I ask you to lay this envelope aside and not to reopen it until you have a completely rested and unoccupied mind."

Herzl's words obviously piqued Hirsch's curiosity. Two days later, Herzl received a letter in which Hirsch said he had changed his plans and would receive him in his Paris home the next Sunday, June 2. In his diary, Herzl says he promptly began making notes for the meeting.

In contrast to the arrogance of his letters, in his diary Herzl does not conceal his anxiety. He notes that he bought a new pair of gloves, which he broke in so that they did not look fresh from the shop. "One must not show rich people too much deference," he wrote. The tactic of covering a weak position with a strong front was one he never abandoned.

On the appointed Sunday, having dressed with "discreet care," he arrived by carriage at Hirsch's home, which he described as a palace where "everything was of genuine beauty," a compliment he then belittled by crediting "someone hired to be in charge of good taste." Hirsch walked out of a meeting then under way to greet him. Suspicious, Herzl wonders if the scene had been set "that way on purpose . . . , for I was not minded at all to become dependent on him." Then he added defiantly, "Either I would bend him to my will or I would leave with my mission unaccomplished."

Herzl admits being aggressive in their encounter, while Hirsch was amiable and attentive. He attacked Hirsch's Argentine colonization, declaring that "the whole thing should not have been started the way you did it." Even more offensively, he continued, "You are breeding *schnorrers*," a scornful Yiddish term for beggars. Hirsch declined to be provoked.

When Hirsch asked what he had come for, Herzl said nothing of his vision of a Jewish state. "The (Jewish) race," he answered, "must first be improved, right on the spot. . . . It must be made strong for war, eager to work and virtuous. . . . You could offer huge prizes in the chief anti-Semitic countries for striking deeds, deeds of great moral beauty, for courage, self-sacrifice, ethical conduct, great achievements in art and science, for physicians during epidemics, for military men, for discoverers of remedies and inventors of products contributing to the public welfare, no matter what—

in short, for something great. . . . People will learn that there are good Jews, too, and many of them. . . . But more important, in this way the moral level will be raised."

What Herzl asked, in other words, was that Hirsch embrace his own nagging belief that the Jews were largely responsible for their own problems. That was not Hirsch's judgment. While willing to support Jewish emigration, Hirsch was not about to give money for a vague project of moral uplift. Forced on the defensive, Herzl hastened to agree that he, too, endorsed emigration, adding audaciously that he would himself ask the German kaiser to "Let our people go." But his vagaries had cost him control of the meeting, which Hirsch ended abruptly, promising to contact Herzl when next he was in Paris.

Herzl knew he had wasted his opportunity. On returning to his lodgings, he began at once to draft a follow-up letter, though its tone was hardly more conciliatory. "Due to your impatience," he wrote accusingly, "you heard only the beginning. Where and how my idea begins to blossom you did not hear." He returned to Hirsch's colonial enterprise, calling it "reactionary," but he insisted that his criticism was aimed only at Hirsch's lack of idealism and passion.

"You are the big Jew of money," the letter explained. "I am the Jew of the spirit." He said it was important for the Jews to adopt a flag. "You would have asked mockingly: a flag, what is that? A stick with a rag on it? No, sir. A flag is more than that. With a flag one can lead men wherever one wants, even into the Promised Land. For a flag men live and die." Then, defiantly, he added, "My plan does not depend on you alone."

Despite its impudence, Herzl's letter was also a step in his search for a course of action. Over the ensuing weeks, he scribbled in his diary page after page of ideas, most of them having to do with raising money to cover the costs of transporting emigrants and building an infrastructure in Palestine. But others touched on Herzl's grand dreams: a Paris built in the "Jewish style," towns surrounded by green fields, electric grids, canals, plantations, a stock exchange, and even dueling laws (swords yes, pistols no). Several of his entries talked of an army. One proposed his father as the state's first senator.

Herzl was aware of the foibles that his scribbling revealed. He conceded a need to "guard against overestimation of myself, arrogance and folly." But he also denounced Hirsch's indifference. In fact, he and Hirsch never met again. Hirsch died a few months later, leaving a bequest to be tapped for the Jews' future. By then, however, Herzl had shifted his focus to the Rothschilds, a family whose wealth was even larger.

Repeating his disdain for rich Jews, Herzl entered into his diary an argument that he was confident the Rothschilds would embrace. Though anti-Semitism is flooding Europe, he wrote, "the Rothschilds have no idea how endangered their property already is. They live in a phony circle of courtiers, servants, employees, paupers and aristocratic spongers." Herzl alludes to financing Jewish emigration by dissolving Europe's great Jewish fortunes before the anti-Semites seize them. "I need the Rothschilds," he wrote. "But what if they refuse? Well, then they will simply take the consequences."

Herzl's chief target within the Rothschild family was Baron Edmond, who was still providing the funds to sustain the Hibbat Zion settlements in Palestine. Edmond, who by now knew Herzl by reputation, declined to grant him an audience. Edmond scoffed at the warning that the family fortunes were in jeopardy. On the contrary, he believed Herzl's Jewish nationalism gave anti-Semites a pretext to demand that Europe's Jews be barred from positions of influence altogether. Edmond also worried that talk of statehood would alarm the Turks and threaten his own struggling network of colonies.

Herzl's diary reveals that he held Rothschild's projects in Palestine in the same contempt as Hirsch's in Argentina. He objected to Hibbat Zion's strategy of bit-by-bit migration to Palestine to endow its settlements with a fragile legality without alarming the Turks. He called it "infiltration," in contrast to his own conviction that a charter would settle the problem of legality in a single startling coup. The Hibbat Zion strategy, he argued, was not just ineffective, it was also dishonorable.

Meanwhile, anxious to avoid the blunders of his approach to Hirsch, Herzl prepared careful notes to present to Rothschild in anticipation of a meeting. He titled them "Address to the Rothschilds," and though they echoed his earlier tone, they flushed out the random ideas he had entered in his diary about the government, the economy, and the army of the forthcoming state. Though Rothschild persisted in his refusal to see him, Herzl's note-taking had its own reward, serving as the transition to *The Jewish State,* the book that stands at the crossroads of Jewish history.

Then, in mid-1895, Herzl was named literary editor of the *Neue Freie Presse* and moved back to Vienna after nearly four years in Paris. It is not clear if he asked for the transfer, or if his editors gambled that the old, reliable Herzl would reemerge once he was home. But by now, Herzl was not about to change his course. Zionism, he wrote in his diary, "possessed me beyond the limits of consciousness. It accompanies me wherever I go. It hovers behind my ordinary talk, looks over my shoulder at my comically trivial journalistic work, disturbs me and intoxicates me."

Herzl's editors, as a gesture of goodwill, permitted him to do much of his writing of *The Jewish State* on office time but, being assimilationists, they refused to let him use the paper's pages to promote his cause. The policy frustrated Herzl, all the more so because the readers of the *Neue Freie Presse* were his natural audience of German-speaking, well-to-do, emancipated Jews. More than once he considered quitting his job, but the credentials of a major newspaper served to open doors for him. No less important, since his father's fortune was in decline, he needed his salary to support his dual responsibilities to his family and to his life's obsession.

Herzl's wife disapproved of his Zionist activities even more firmly than the newspaper. Not only did they leave him little time for her and the children, but their home was invaded routinely by Jews from across Europe, who took over the sitting room to engage in loud conversations about Zionism. At Christmastime, one visitor expressed scorn for the decorated tree in the drawing room; Herzl, while perceiving no inconsistency with his Judaism, decided it would be helpful to Zionism to give the tree up. The episode symbolized the separate roads that husband and wife were taking, with Zionism steadily widening the breach between them.

The Jewish State was ready for publication in early 1896, but Herzl had trouble finding a publisher. His editors gave him no help; in fact, they pressured him to give the project up. Finally, an excerpt that ran in the esteemed *Jewish Chronicle* in London swayed a small Viennese house to publish the book. Before it appeared, a friend gave Herzl a copy of Pinsker's *Auto-Emancipation*, published fifteen years earlier. "It is a good thing I didn't know it," he told his diary, "or perhaps I would have abandoned my own undertaking."

At eighty-eight pages, Herzl's work was more a pamphlet than a book. The German title, *Der Judenstaat,* which translates as "The Jews' State," is a more accurate rendition of its purpose, which is to solve the problem of the Jews. The English title, *The Jewish State,* suggests an emphasis on a Jewish *culture* within the state, which was a matter of little interest to Herzl.

The distinction between the two titles has not been widely recognized but, in the years after publication, a rivalry between the conceptions emerged. Herzl himself came to stand for *political* Zionism, while a competing faction advocated a *cultural* Zionism. Herzl's subtitle, *An Attempt at a Modern Solution of the Jewish Question,* more correctly sums up the book's intent.

Statehood was, in this age of European nationalism, the solution that came naturally to Herzl. Though Pinsker and others had written of it before, Herzl treated it as if it were his personal idea. Statehood fit comfortably into Dühring's premise that Jews were foreigners in whatever country they lived. Herzl shared with Dühring the judgment that assimilation would never work. Herzl, it seems, came to accept Dühring's contention that the Jewish Question was racial. The difference between the two was that Dühring saw Jews as the manifestation of evil. Herzl pledged their rescue from Europe's evil by gathering them in a place that they ruled themselves.

Unlike Karl Marx's famous Communist tract, Herzl's work was not a manifesto aimed at inspiring a following. His thinking contained no call to political revolution. Nor did he encourage the Jews who dreamed of restoring David's kingdom; the glories of the biblical age had no meaning for him. Herzl promised to respect Judaism but, as a child of the Enlightenment, he was secular and rational. His concern was the anti-Semitism of which Jews were victims. Its solution was the establishment of a state—outside Europe's boundaries.

If readers of *The Jewish State* looked forward to the entertainment of a *feuilleton,* Herzl disappointed them. That was no accident; he stated repeatedly in his diary that he was now finished with light entertainment. His book, though utopian in spirit, was a manual of plans for Jewish migration and organization. Save for passing phrases, it is remarkably dry, even tedious. In contemporary terms, it would be called political science, but for the Jewish public the details elicited less attention than the overall vision. Herzl rarely strayed from the theme that a carefully designed and well-constructed state could provide a safe refuge for the Jewish people.

It should be no surprise that Herzl did not feel compelled to place the Jewish state in Palestine. He recognized Palestine as "our ever-memorable historic home," certain to "attract our people," but he declined to be constrained by biblical geography. He had no interest in satisfying a religious nostalgia, as the Precursors had done. Herzl's pragmatism told him, as it had told Pinsker, that a refuge could be anywhere, and there were more promising places than Palestine. The first choice he expressed in *The Jewish State,* despite Hirsch's difficulties there, was Argentina.

Though no authoritarian, Herzl wrote little in his book about Jewish electoral democracy. His experiences in Paris and Vienna led him to conclude that elected regimes were "political nonsense which can only be decided upon by a mob." But neither did he express confidence in the principle of self-government. His advocacy was pragmatic. "Let the sovereignty be granted us over a portion of the globe large enough to satisfy the rightful requirements of a nation," he wrote. "The rest we shall manage for ourselves."

Herzl proposed governing the Jewish state through a "Society of Jews," a body of sages with largely unspecified powers. The state's economic base would not be farming but industrialization, a departure from the era's romantic conventions. He promised an "up-to-date" army that would stay in its barracks and a social system that guaranteed a seven-hour day for all workers.

In his book, Herzl abandoned the worries about the Jewish disunity that he expressed in his diary only a short time before. In the English version, he maintained that the Jews were "one people"; in German he used the word *volk,* which implied a strong spiritual bond as well. No matter where they come from, "the distinctive nationality of the Jews will not be destroyed . . . ," he wrote. "It survived two thousand years of appalling suffering. Whole branches of Jewry may wither and fall away, but the tree lives on."

Herzl took the notion of Jewish distinctiveness a step further in designing a Jewish flag. It was to consist of seven stars against a white background, much different from the flag that serves the present-day Jewish state. The stars were to stand for the seven-hour day, Herzl said, the symbol of the state's humanity. The white field was to represent "our pure new life."

Yet, even in praising the Jews, Herzl could not fully shed his embarrassment about them. The Jewish languages disturbed him. In the new state, he wrote, Jews would speak a European tongue, presumably German. Poking fun, he said of Hebrew, "who amongst us could ask for a railway ticket in that language?" And he went further in dismissing Yiddish as "a miserable stunted jargon . . . a tongue of prisoners."

Little about Herzl's state, as described in his book, was linked to the traditions, much less the practices of Judaism. His social blueprint could have applied to almost any nationality. The book was itself a measure of how his sense of Jewish identity had grown, but there is little religion in the substance. Rejecting piety, Herzl called himself a freethinker, committed to having every Jew "seek salvation in his own way." But his ambivalence about Judaism left a vacuum in Zionist doctrine, which religious Jews have never stopped struggling to fill.

Herzl understood that the Jewish state, unable to stand alone, would have to look for help to Europe's Christian powers, though these very powers were the source of the Jews' problems. This recognition explains his emphasis on safeguarding Palestine's Christian sanctuaries. He went further, eliciting memories of Christianity's historic conflict with Islam to portray a Jewish Palestine as "a rampart of Europe against Asia, an outpost of civilization as opposed to barbarism." His tilt foreshadowed not only his own political practice but a long-term Zionist strategy.

The impact of *The Jewish State* arose not from Herzl's creative formulas, but from its daring. It was as if the Jews, having reached a consensus that Emancipation was a failure, were waiting for Herzl, who assured them that they would lead a richer life within a framework of national independence. He was not modest about the message. "I am sowing seeds in the earth . . . ," he wrote. "It is beautiful, ingenious and worthy of a poet. . . . Until now the plan was missing: now the plan has been found."

Though not a manifesto, the book was nonetheless embraced as a summons to action. Herzl himself did not walk away, claiming his work was finished. It was as if he had issued a summons to himself. Repeatedly he stated that if asked, he would pass on the leadership of the Zionist mission to a more eminent Jew—presumably a Rothschild—but he conducted himself quite differently. Herzl won over much of the Jewish public with his book by setting off personally to transform his vision of Jewish statehood into a political cause.

The popular reaction to *The Jewish State* was not immediately encouraging. Herzl complained to his diary that the local press, including his own newspaper, made no mention of its publication and that friends even asked if he was serious in writing it. The book ignited some dinner-table talk among Vienna's Jews but generated no fervor. Stefan Zweig, the celebrated novelist, recalls in his memoir "the general astonishment and annoyance within bourgeois Jewish circles of Vienna. What has happened, they said angrily, to this otherwise, intelligent, witty and cultivated writer? . . . Why should we go to Palestine? Our language is German, not Hebrew, and beautiful Austria is our homeland. Are we not well off under the good Emperor Franz Joseph?"

Vienna's chief rabbi, Moritz Güdemann, a leader in Herzl's own bourgeois circle, had compared Herzl to Moses when he read an early draft of the book. But, after criticisms from his congregants, he denounced it. As a spokesman for assimilated Jews, he criticized Herzl for abandoning the fight against anti-Semitism at home to urge Jews "to grow vegetables in Palestine." In irritation, Herzl decried Güdemann for being "used by wire-pullers who some day will get their just deserts."

But Güdemann also made the astute point that a state based on Jewish nationalism—built, he said, on "cannon and bayonets"—was likely over time to acquire a strong resemblance to the warlike, intolerant states produced by the Christian nationalisms. Herzl could not imagine this happening. He gave no thought to parallels between Jewish and European nationalism. Güdemann, it is true, drew his warning from the bourgeoisie's view that assimilation was the Jews' best hope, a view discredited by the atrocities of the twentieth century. Still, Güdemann was prescient in warning that excessive Jewish nationalism could produce serious dangers of its own.[4]

Disappointed as Herzl was by the book's reception in the circles that were familiar to him, he was slow to notice the quite different reaction it was stirring among Jews he did not know at all. Eastern Europe paid far more attention to *The Jewish State* than did the West. Enthusiasm, first generated by word of mouth, grew as translations appeared in Russian, then in Yiddish and Hebrew, the languages Herzl disdained. Herzl hardly knew what to make of the reports.

In Vienna, Kadima, the Eastern European student group he had snubbed when he was at the university, liked Herzl's book and invited him to speak on it. Founded to fight anti-Semitism, Kadima had been reshaped, like Herzl himself, by Jewish nationalism and had grown in the East into a chain of societies with loose links to Hibbat Zion. Kadima helped spread Herzl's ideas throughout Russia. Some Kadima members even talked of initiating a campaign to *liberate* Palestine, leading Herzl to note as he prepared his talk, "I didn't want to arouse any beery enthusiasm . . . or unhealthy fanaticism."

Ill at ease with fanaticism, Herzl deeply believed that the Jewish state had to be founded within a legal framework. Zionists since Rabbi Alkalai had imagined a deal with the Turks in which Jewish financiers paid off the empire's many creditors in return for a charter. The charter's nature was never precise, but its purpose was to give Jews a right to return legally to their ancestral land, a notion that fascinated Herzl.

Herzl envisaged enlisting a European power that would happily be rid of its Jews as an intermediary with the Turks. His first candidate was naturally the kaiser's Germany. In April 1896, he actually obtained a written introduction from the Grand Duke of Baden, a German nobleman who had become a strong supporter of Zionism. The kaiser declined to receive Herzl, however, thwarting Herzl's first foray into what would soon seem like an endless cavalcade of unsuccessful diplomatic voyages.

But, far from being deterred by the kaiser's rebuff, Herzl was excited by the chase. Convinced that the sultan, Jewish financiers, and the Christian states would soon grasp the logic of his vision, he took for granted its ultimate success. If no major power sponsored his mission, he decided, he would go directly to the sultan himself. He was not acquainted with the sultan and his government, of course, and had no promises whatever from Jewish financiers. It did not occur to him, as a neophyte in diplomacy, that the waters in which he swam might be over his head. He simply paddled ahead.

Herzl's records leave no hint that he grasped the Ottoman's wariness of Europeans, particularly of French and British imperial designs. As caliph, the head of Islam, the sultan had a duty to safeguard Muslim holy places, especially Jerusalem. But, over the centuries, weakness had forced successive sultans to grant concessions, called "capitulations," to diverse European states, most notably to France, which won the right to establish Catholic missions and to protect French subjects throughout the realm. Understandably, the sultan was not happy with Jewish overtures that ignited memories of his weakness.

The British, in the nineteenth century, began competing with France for influence in Ottoman territories. Lord Palmerston, Britain's foreign secretary, announced that his government would place all Jews in the Ottoman realm under its protection. He also observed to his ambassador in Constantinople, "There exists among (Europe's) Jews a strong notion that the time is approaching when their nation is to return to Palestine," which he surely took as an opportunity for Britain to exploit.

Little came of Palmerston's effort, but a few years later Britain forced the sultan to cede to it control of Cyprus. In 1882, Britain captured the region's biggest prize when it occupied Ottoman Egypt, which included the newly inaugurated Suez Canal. Herzl's vision for Palestine was proclaimed in *The Jewish State*, with which the Ottomans were surely familiar. It sent the sultan a message that the threat to Ottoman Palestine was just beginning.

By the early twentieth century, the Jewish threat was underway. Jewish pioneers, most of them from Poland, were asserting a claim to Palestine that bewildered the local Ottoman authorities. These authorities had long tolerated the bearded pietists who recited their prayers at the Wailing Wall and made no political trouble. Now the Turks faced young, energetic seculars who were far more difficult to handle.

With France ruling the Ottoman provinces in northwest Africa, and with Britain expanding in the east, the sultan's empire had been reduced to a fraction of what it once was. In a desperate move, the sultan turned to wooing Germany as an ally, which transformed the mosaic of power in the region. This was the situation Herzl faced as he made his plans to visit Constantinople, unaware that the sultan had made up his mind to yield no more authority, and certainly had no intention of granting the Jews a Palestine charter.

On June 15, 1896, Herzl boarded the Orient Express headed for the Ottoman capital. At a layover in Sofia, the capital of Bulgaria, a huge crowd, notified in advance, was waiting to greet him at the station. Bulgaria, long an Ottoman vassal state, had in recent years come under Russian domination, intensifying the feelings of insecurity of the Jews living there. Herzl was overcome by the enthusiastic welcome of the Jews on the platform, who looked unlike any he had seen before.

The multitude, Herzl recounted in his diary, was composed of "men, women and children, Sephardim, Ashkenazim, mere boys and old men with white beards . . ." The Grand Rabbi hailed him as the Heart of Israel, king of the Jews. "I stood there completely dumbfounded," he wrote. For Herzl, who knew only the bourgeois Jews of the great cities of the West, it was an introduction to the people who had, in fact, become his real constituency, the imperiled Jews of the czarist East.

On arriving in Constantinople, Herzl had no idea how to proceed. He relied on a mysterious Polish nobleman who had been recommended to him as a broker in the sultan's court. The Pole arranged to have him received by high-level palace courtiers, who warned him that Turkey's toleration of a few thousand pious Jews in Palestine was far different from Herzl's plan to organize a large-scale Zionist migration. In return for substantial bribes, however, the courtiers promised to bring his case directly to the sultan.

Though denied an audience, Herzl received via the Polish nobleman, a message from the sultan. It stated that the Jews should curb their expectations. In his diary, Herzl quotes the sultan's prescient words: "The Turkish empire belongs not to me but to the Turkish people. I cannot give away any part of it. Let the Jews save their billions. When my empire is partitioned, they may get Palestine for nothing. . . . Our corpse will be divided."

It was a melancholy utterance, to which Herzl added in his diary: "I was touched and shaken by the sultan's truly lofty words . . . though they dashed all my hopes. There is a tragic beauty in this fatalism." Though Herzl returned to Constantinople again and again, the message never changed. In retrospect, the sultan prophesized exactly what transpired at the end of World War I, when the Ottoman Empire collapsed and its eastern segments shattered into fragments.

Herzl left Constantinople after two weeks with nothing to show but an empty purse and a handsome military decoration, a token of the sultan's esteem. On the trip back to Vienna, he stopped once more at Sofia, where he addressed hundreds of Jews in the main synagogue. He remained in Vienna for only a few days, visiting with his family and conducting some routine Zionist business, then departed for London, where he was scheduled to meet with Jewish financiers. His failure in Constantinople had not discouraged him. In his diary, he insisted, disingenuously to be sure, that the sultan's words left ample room for a Palestine deal.

He kept up the deception in London, where he told his moneyed listeners that the Turks had left him with a feeling of "near certainty" that the Jews would soon regain Palestine. He assured them that if Baron de Rothschild agreed to embrace his project, he would happily surrender the leadership of the Zionist movement. He also theorized in his diary that, whatever the skepticism of his audience, these rich Jews would certainly make their fortunes available once Rothschild was aboard.

Herzl's chief reward during his London visit came not from the financiers but from a talk he delivered in the heavily Jewish quarter of East London. The audience was drawn largely from the tens of thousands of Russian refugees who had found asylum in England after the pogroms of the 1880s. Herzl was as elated by their cheers as he had been on the railway platform in Sofia. In his diary, he gave it a more grandiose meaning: "I saw and heard my legend being born."

But Rothschild's shadow darkened his path. Members of Hibbat Zion, still reliant on Rothschild's largesse, complained that publication of *The Jewish State* had triggered increased intrusions by the Turkish police on the lives of their pioneers in Palestine. Soon afterward, Herzl received an invitation to the long-awaited meeting with Rothschild, but it was not what he had hoped for. The invitation notified him that its purpose was solely to protest that Herzl's meddling had placed Rothschild's own Palestinian venture in jeopardy.

In his notes on the meeting, Herzl expressed offense at Rothschild's cold, businesslike manner, a contrast with the warm reception in Baron de Hirsch's salon. "He looks like an aging youth," Herzl wrote of Rothschild. "His movements are quick and yet shy, and he has a light brown beard on the verge of turning grey, a long nose and an offensively large mouth. He wore a red necktie and a white waistcoat which flapped about his thin body." When he talked, he "began to spout."

Rothschild scolded Herzl for his overtures to the Turks. Neither the sultan's minions nor London's Jewish financiers could be trusted, Rothschild said, even if Herzl succeeded in negotiating a deal. Opening the gates of migration to Palestine, Rothschild claimed, would bring in "150,000 *schnorrers* who would have to be fed." Twice Rothschild accused Herzl of having eyes bigger than his stomach. As for Jewish statehood, he made no effort to soften his earlier denunciations of Zionism's objective.

After two hours of verbal sparring, in which nothing was resolved, Herzl picked up his umbrella and made his way to the door. "You were the keystone of the entire combination," he declared in parting. "If you refuse, everything I have fashioned so far will fall to pieces. I shall then be obliged to do it in a different way. I shall start a mass agitation." Herzl was referring to the course—admittedly more difficult and uncertain—that he would need to fall back on. He decided, after his frustrating encounter with Rothschild, to turn for support to the hordes of Jews, who he now believed were waiting for him.

But Herzl, at a crossroads, was also forced to reevaluate. Since meeting with Hirsch a year before, he had become reasonably well known as a player in the diplomatic arena. He was accepted in the sultan's court and in the drawing rooms of the Western elite. But what did it mean? The Zionist movement remained Herzl's alone. In the West his popular following was negligible, and in the East fragile. His bargaining with the Turks, based on a hypothesis of access to big money, was a bluff. With neither funds nor an organization, he risked being dismissed as a charlatan. Unless he rebuilt on a sturdier foundation, the Zionist movement was bound to fail.

Ψ

In the months after his meeting with Rothschild, Herzl made no headway. In vain he argued with his editors to support his cause; he even conducted discussions, all futile, about moving to another paper or founding a paper of his own. His informants in Constantinople transmitted only useless gossip. Though Zionist societies were sprouting up across Europe, they did not strengthen his hand. In Vienna, meanwhile, anti-Semitism was growing violent, leaving Jews increasingly alarmed.

Herzl admitted to his diary in early 1897 that he was demoralized. "The general torpor of the movement is getting into my bones," he wrote. A less driven man might at this point have given up the enterprise, but not Herzl. By spring his sense of purpose had reemerged.

Herzl had long been engaged by the idea of convoking a congress, drawing a lesson from Pinsker's tiny Hibbat Zion conference at Kattowitz in 1884. He had no intention, however, of emulating its furtive character, adopted out of fear of the Russian secret police. The congress that took shape in his mind would advertize Zionism to the world and serve as an instrument to mobilize Jews everywhere. It would create an administrative framework to reinforce his own personal efforts, mainly in widening his access to funds. No doubt he also saw a congress as the way to strike back at the personal insults of Rothschild and the Jewish financial aristocracy.

Herzl's diary entries reveal the evolution of his plan. By March 1897, he had reached a decision to call the congress in Munich in August. Though he was uncertain who would attend, he found encouragement from Kadima students and Hibbat Zion veterans working for him across Eastern Europe. He himself supervised the unfolding arrangements, demonstrating his talent for organization, propaganda, and drama. As the planning developed, it became clear that this would be Herzl's personal congress.

Naturally, he ran into obstacles. Some putative Zionists whom he had counted on turned out to prefer Rothschild's formula of philanthropy to the goal of Jewish statehood. A segment of Hibbat Zion refused to help him for fear of antagonizing Rothschild. Given the *Neue Freie Presse*'s refusal to back him, he felt he needed an organ to spread his message. He founded his own paper, which he called *Die Welt,* and sustained it with his personal funds, but they were rapidly shrinking.

Then the German Rabbinic Association vetoed Munich as the site of the Congress. Its Orthodox wing repeated the position that collective Jewish migration violated the messianic edict; its Reform wing argued that the assimilated Jews had a prior duty to serve their European fatherland. Herzl answered sharply, "The latest vogue in Judaism," he wrote "are the protest-rabbis. These people sit in a safe boat using their oars to beat the heads of drowning men who try to hang on to the sides." The "drowning men" were an obvious reference to Eastern European Jews, toward whom the movement was already gravitating. In response to the rabbis, Herzl shifted the congress from Munich to Basel.[5]

In supervising arrangements, Herzl emphasized the objective of imparting dignity to the Zionist movement. On arriving in Basel to look over the site, he was embarrassed to find that local organizers had set up headquarters in a vacant tailor shop. He ordered a banner to cover the tailor's sign. He then moved the sessions from a seedy *bierstube* to an austere concert hall of the Municipal Casino. To add to the solemnity, he ruled that delegates to the congress must wear formal attire.

But even on the eve of the congress, Herzl was unsure how many would attend. Kadima and Hibbat Zion volunteers had extracted promises, but unless a substantial number actually appeared, the Zionist movement could collapse. Herzl trembled even as he waited for the delegates to gather. At last, the trains rolled in to the Basel station. Many delegates did not register, fearing spies and visits by the police on their return home. So the exact attendance was never established, but it was roughly 250, considered by Herzl a satisfactory number. More important was the exhilaration they exhibited as they assembled for the opening session.

Most of the delegates were Eastern Europeans, and even among the Westerners many were Eastern transplants. "It seemed," one observer quipped, "that Dr. Herzl had come to their congress and not they to his."

Notably absent were not only the West's recently emancipated bourgeoisie but the great financiers, the Orthodox rabbinate, and even the intellectual luminaries whom Herzl had hoped to attract. It was the Eastern Jews to whom Herzl had been introduced in Sofia and East London who had gathered in Basel to cheer him on most enthusiastically.

"There rose before our eyes a Russian Jewry the strength of which we had not even suspected . . . ," Herzl wrote in his diary. "What a humiliation for us, who had taken our superiority for granted! . . . They possess the inner unity that has disappeared from among the Westerners. . . . They are not tortured by the idea of assimilation. . . . They are ghetto Jews, the only ghetto Jews of our time! Looking on them, we understood where our forefathers got the strength to endure. . . . They are steeped in Jewish national sentiment."

In reality, few were "ghetto" Jews. The majority in Basel were Eastern *Maskilim,* Jews who had prospered under opportunities presented by Russia's small but surging capitalism. They were also students, professors, writers, doctors, lawyers, and artists. A few were women. Christians sat as observers in the galleries, shoulder-to-shoulder with czarist and Ottoman spies. There were also reporters from Europe's major newspapers though, conspicuously, not Herzl's own. But most of the delegates would not have been there at all had it not been for Pinsker's Hibbat Zion, which had sown the seeds of Jewish nationalism well before Herzl came along.

Rabbi Samuel Mohilever, a direct heir to the rabbinic Precursors, was a major force in obtaining Hibbat Zion's endorsement. Having given much of his life to infusing Judaism into Pinsker's Zionism, he turned in his final years to infusing it into Herzl's. Mohilever maintained that the Basel congress was itself messianic. Herzl, though pleased, had no intention of allowing religion to interfere with the congress's political objective and ruled that the delegates could pray, or not, as they themselves chose.

Still, Herzl had come to understand Zionism as more complex than he once believed. The Dreyfus affair in Paris, as well as his exposure to anti-Semitism on Vienna's streets, lay behind his own Zionist aspirations. But Zionism's real dynamism stemmed from the persecution experienced by the Jews of Eastern Europe, whose concerns were the driving force behind the Basel agenda.

Herzl recognized that he could not ignore the dedication of the Easterners to their religious traditions, though its depth remained a mystery to him. On the Sabbath eve, he mounted the *bima* at the Basel synagogue to read, with difficulty, from the Torah. By now, he had learned from the Eastern Europeans that though a Jewish state could not be defined by Orthodoxy, it had to be more than a religiously neutral, uncommitted, Enlightenment-oriented refuge for the Jewish oppressed.

Even before reaching Basel, Herzl expressed in his diary his anxieties about the presence of discord among the delegates. He noted a need to "dance on eggs" to avoid a rift with Orthodoxy. But he also compiled a list of potential troublemakers that included Edward de Rothschild, Jewish financiers, and even Hibbat Zion. Also on his list were the *Neue Freie Presse,* Russia, the sultan, modernists, Austrian patriotism, and Christian denominations in Palestine. What he had not foreseen was the demand of many Eastern *Maskilim* that Zionism, though free of Orthodox Judaism, be imbued with a substantial measure of Jewish *culture.*

Whatever his misgivings, the proceedings of the first World Zionist Congress were remarkably harmonious. Herzl wielded the gavel throughout, fusing a somber presence with his calculated theatrics. He was elected president by acclamation, and his speeches were met by delirious applause. A brief lapse in decorum occurred only when he withdrew to rest, leaving the delegates on their own. Otherwise, they responded seriously to their responsibility to shift Zionism from Herzl's private undertaking to a Jewish-wide political organization.

Herzl's keynote address is regarded as the Zionist movement's formal beginning. In it he spoke not only of the congress's laying the cornerstone for the Jewish state. He also declared—with exaggeration—that Zionism embraced all Jews, liberal and conservative, modern and traditional, with no conflict between them. He also promised that, in a "civilized, law-abiding and humane manner" the congress would speak for all the segments of the Jewish people.

Herzl's first agenda item for the congress was to establish an institutional framework for Zionism. In his diary, he had written that he was tired of being a one-man show, blaming the "boys, beggars, and prigs" who surrounded him for Zionism's weakness. But much of the fault was surely his own. Herzl disliked delegating authority, or even soliciting advice. While noting his deepening fatigue, he was loath to slow his pace. Dutifully, the congress placed the Zionist organization on a sound institutional foundation, traces of which exist even today.

The structure was named the World Zionist Organization. It was to answer to an annual World Zionist Congress, to which delegates would be elected by members who paid a modest fee, called a "shekel." Between sessions, the congress's instructions would be executed by a Greater Actions Committee, whose members were to be chosen from every part of Europe. It would, in turn, be guided by an Inner Actions Committee seated in Vienna, through which Herzl was to retain his own preeminence.

A more difficult decision was reached on Zionism's level of candor about its aims. At Kattowitz, thirteen years before, Pinsker had chosen not to talk of "statehood," recognizing that it would complicate relations with Rothschild. In his visit to Constantinople, Herzl also learned that any reference to Jewish statehood infuriated the Turks. Some delegates called it dishonest to disguise the Zionist goal, but Herzl insisted it was pointless to complicate the Zionist mission, which all Jews understood anyway, by dwelling on a single word.

In the end, Herzl won unanimous support for declaring that Zionism's goal was "a home in Palestine" for the Jewish people and during the ensuing half-century, the movement rarely used the word "statehood." Zionism was almost always ambiguous about its aim in its public pronouncements. Its restraint, though deceitful, averted many disputes.

The congress also struggled to find a way to impart to the state, once created, the legitimacy that Herzl believed it needed. "It is stupid," he argued, "to build a house without getting title to the building plot. Eventually the owner of the plot will appear and either raze the building or drive us out of the habitation we have erected." The statement explains his fixation on acquiring a charter from the sultan. The delegates themselves, no doubt influenced by the emphasis on law in Jewish tradition, and obedient to their leader, accepted Herzl's argument.

When an early draft called for the "law of nations" to secure the Jews' place in Palestine, it was pointed out that the Turks would read the words as an overture to the Great Powers to push them out. European imperialism, dating back to the "capitulations," was too embedded in the Turkish experience to permit any leeway. Finally, at Herzl's behest, the expression selected was "secured by public law," a term without a fixed juridical definition, and without a noxious place in the Ottomans' historical memory.

The congress's closing resolution, approved unanimously, became the

"Basel Program." Its key assertion read: "Zionism aims to create a home for the Jewish people in Palestine secured by public law." The phrase "in Palestine" allowed for a state in less than *all* of Palestine. It also seemed to preclude the consideration of other sites, which would tie Herzl's hands if he was forced to acknowledge that Palestine was not available. Whatever its flaws, however, the Basel Program remained Zionism's guiding principle in its quest to establish Jewish statehood.

In predicting in his diary that success in this quest would come "perhaps in five years," it is obvious Herzl still looked forward to making a deal with the sultan. But the deal never happened. He covered his prediction by adding "and certainly in fifty," which were the words that proved prophetic. But, given the outcome of the Basel Congress, Herzl possessed no doubt that he had built something permanent. As he headed home to Vienna, he was exultant.

The exultation quickly ebbed, however, in bureaucratic discord. The organizational structure voted by the congress was formally created but did not relieve Herzl's personal burdens. Some of his followers claimed he never intended to dilute his powers. Herzl answered that he was unable to find associates equal to the tasks he asked them to perform. Whatever his intent, the movement continued to be a one-man show.

Herzl, no longer reliant on unwilling financiers, put his energy into founding a Zionist bank to provide the funds needed for a deal with the sultan. When the financiers declined even to help him organize it, he once more turned his wrath on the Rothschilds, threatening them in his diary with "guerrilla warfare." He then mounted a campaign among his widening circle of supporters, which produced much enthusiasm but little money.

After Basel, Zionism's coffers were nearly bare. Herzl's own fortune, long the movement's chief source of funds, continued to recede, and his personal tensions with his newspaper placed even his salary in jeopardy. "Moses had an easier time of it," he told his diary. He could not conceal even to himself, moreover, that his stamina was declining, and he recorded ominously, "I am as tired as an old man, . . . my heart is out of order."

But taking on diplomatic challenges invariably rejuvenated him, and on learning that Germany's Kaiser Wilhelm was planning a visit to the Holy Land, he saw an opportunity. Herzl was as bewitched as ever by Germany, and knew it now had better relations with the sultan than did any other power. He fantasized that the kaiser would take up the Zionist cause and persuade the sultan to reopen the stalled negotiations over a charter.

Relying on a web of contacts, with the Grand Duke of Baden at the center, Herzl finally attracted the kaiser's notice. In a letter to the grand duke, the kaiser stated a readiness to receive Herzl in Palestine as the head of a Zionist delegation. More stunning, he also expressed an interest in placing the Jews of Palestine under Germany's protection—despite, he said, the reluctance of nine-tenths of his subjects to embrace Jewish concerns.

Herzl was thrilled by the response. "The protectorate! Many will shake their heads over it," he wrote in his diary. "But I believe the only right course is to accept it gratefully. . . . To live under the protection of this strong, great, moral, splendidly governed, tightly organized Germany can only have the most salutary effect on the Jewish national character."

As Herzl understood the kaiser's thinking on a protectorate, Palestine's sovereignty would remain in Ottoman hands, while the Jews would exercise local rule under German supervision. "At one stroke," he wrote, "we would obtain a completely ordered internal and external legal status." As an afterthought, he added: "Strange ways of destiny. Through Zionism it will again become possible for Jews to love this Germany, to which our hearts have been attached despite everything."

A few days later, Herzl gave a rousing speech in London before some ten thousand Jews, most of them recent Eastern refugees, in which he laid aside his customary caution to predict an imminent wave of migration to Palestine. Not only did he denounce "protest rabbis and protest bankers," but he moved deeper into social democracy to say, "Our movement belongs to the poor, for whom it is preparing a happier future." He reached his climax with, "Today I declare, I believe the time is not far off when the Jewish people will set itself in motion. . . . I ask you to accept my word." At the time, his audience hailed the words as messianic, though Herzl later found himself embarrassed by such anticipation.

Yet, as he left for his meeting with the kaiser in Palestine, Herzl was stricken with uncharacteristic despondency. "Taking leave from my loved ones," he wrote, "was quite hard this time. I could very well stay in my beautiful house, with my lovely children, whose rosiest childhood is passing without my enjoying it; who are growing up without my observing the delightful details of their development. And I am undertaking such a long journey, one that may not be without danger. I have even been warned that an attempt on my life might be made in Palestine. . . . But it is my duty to go."

Herzl's anxiety vanished, however, when he was received by the kaiser in Constantinople, while both were en route to Palestine. In his diary, he again records his anxiety over whether his gloves and morning coat were the correct dress. But on seeing the kaiser, he fawned. "He looked at me grandly with his great sea-blue eyes," Herzl wrote. "He has truly imperial eyes. I have never seen such eyes. A remarkable, bold, inquisitive soul shows in them." The kaiser tried to conceal his well-known handicap, a withered arm, but Herzl barely noticed, being more interested in the kaiser's "fine, frank, genial and yet bold eyes, which fairly bewitched me."

The Constantinople meeting, an hour long, was rambling, as if the kaiser had no agenda. Herzl was pleased to note that the word "Zionism" tripped familiarly off the imperial tongue, but he was annoyed by the kaiser's equating Jews with usurers. Still, he was pleased that he both lamented anti-Semitism in Russia and the Dreyfus affair. Most important, Herzl wrote, the kaiser endorsed his strategy of exchanging debt relief to the sultan in return for a Palestine charter.

But the kaiser did not mention the protectorate. Herzl acknowledged in his diary that when he raised the subject himself, "the kaiser nodded quickly and contentedly," but revealed nothing. He gently pointed out that a beachhead in Palestine would serve German commercial interests by providing access to a land route across Asia. Finally, the kaiser ended their exchange saying, "Just tell me in a word what I am to ask of the sultan," to which Herzl replied, "A chartered company—under German protection." "Good!" said the kaiser. "A chartered company."

The exchange, much as Herzl was loath to concede it, was conspicuously devoid of commitments. Finally, Herzl reported, "He grandly gave me his hand, which is strong enough for two, squeezed mine good and hard, and went out through the center door." On leaving, the kaiser directed his staff to take Herzl's address in Palestine, where he promised the two would meet again.

The next morning, Herzl boarded a ship for Alexandria with the four-man official delegation that accompanied him. On landing, they transferred to a smaller boat and reached Palestine a day ahead of the imperial party. In stifling heat, they proceeded to visit a Jewish school and two farming villages that depended on Rothschild's largesse. In his diary, Herzl made no secret of his annoyance at finding Rothschild's hand in the Promised Land.

The following day, by chance, Herzl encountered the imperial party on the Jerusalem road, with the kaiser himself on horseback. The kaiser trotted over, and the two chatted amiably. After they parted, Herzl and his companions boarded a train, arriving in Jerusalem after sundown. Herzl was weak with exhaustion, but it was the Sabbath, when Jews are expected not to ride, and with the others he made his way to their hotel on foot.

Herzl was not happy in Jerusalem. The rabbis of the old *yishuv* protested his presence as the embodiment of godless Zionism, and the city itself appalled him. "The musty deposits of two thousand years of inhumanity, intolerance and unseemliness," he wrote, "lie in the foul-smelling alleys. . . ." On visiting the Wailing Wall, he wrote, "a deeper emotion refuses to come, because that place is pervaded by hideous, wretched, speculative beggary." And he concluded, "If we ever get Jerusalem and I am still able to do anything actively, I would begin by cleaning it up. . . . I would build around the holy places a comfortable new city with proper sanitation."

In Jerusalem Herzl now had to await the kaiser's summons. He was nervous not only that the kaiser might forget their promised meeting but, if he overstayed his visa, that the Turkish police would come after him. To pass the time, he checked his companions' "clothes, linen, neckties, gloves, shoes, and hats." He sent the kaiser a packet of photos of Jewish colonies as a reminder of his presence. When he heard rumors that the kaiser planned to spend a few days in Jericho, then return to Berlin, he was disconsolate, but the rumors proved groundless. Finally, an aide to the kaiser called, and Herzl was vexed at having to submit his planned remarks in advance, then was further irritated when the aide insisted he delete some of the passages.

The audience took place after lunch on November 2 in the kaiser's tent in the imperial encampment. The kaiser, Herzl recounted, was dressed in a grey colonial uniform, including riding crop and helmet. Herzl was in a formal suit and wore the decoration the sultan had given him two years before. He introduced his four companions, whom the kaiser greeted cordially. Herzl then read his script, to which the kaiser stated that a German protectorate "still requires study." The two discussed the costs of water to irrigate Palestine's arid soil. "Well, money is what you (Jews) have plenty of, more money than any of us," the kaiser quipped, slapping his boot with his riding crop. Choosing to take no offense, Herzl presented some ideas about cleaning up Jerusalem. At that point, the kaiser, as if bored, ended the talks. As for the protectorate, Herzl later noted to his companions, "He didn't say yes or no."

Still worried about the Turkish police, Herzl promptly booked passage for his party on a freighter sitting in the port in Jaffa. The quarters were so small and stuffy that they spent the night on mattresses on the deck. Deprived for weeks of newspapers, Herzl was unsure what the world knew of his talks. In Alexandria he learned that the Germans had made public the encounter in Constantinople but not the meeting in Jerusalem. In Naples, when the ship next docked, he read a newspaper account based on an imperial press release.

"Kaiser Wilhelm," it said, "has received a Jewish deputation, which presented him with an album of pictures of the Jewish colonies established in Palestine. Replying to an address by the leader of the deputation, Kaiser Wilhelm said that all those endeavors were assured of his benevolent interest that aimed for the improvement of agriculture in Palestine, thus furthering the welfare of the Turkish empire, with complete respect for the sovereignty of the sultan."

Herzl had no trouble deciphering the clumsy diplomatic code. In personally ignoring him, and without reference to a protectorate at all, the message was eloquent in its omissions. It meant that the Germans had given up on Zionism. The final sentence assured the sultan that no change in Palestine's status would take place. Herzl's mission to the kaiser was dead.

In his diary, Herzl noted that he alone in his party did not despair. "I remain undaunted," he wrote, "and that is why I deserve to be the leader. In darker moments than this I have not lost courage. . . ." Then, salvaging what he could, he added, "The fact that the kaiser did not assume the protectorate in Jerusalem is an advantage for the future of our cause."

For a few months Herzl blew on the coals, hoping to rekindle a flame, but the kaiser declined to see him again. In a letter to the German foreign minister, he restated his case that Germany should seize the opportunity to acquire a beachhead on the land route to Asia. He wondered whether the kaiser's shock at the poverty of Jerusalem's pious Jews played a role in the outcome. The real reason, however, surely lay in the kaiser's unwillingness to provoke the sultan, his new military ally, whose attachment to Ottoman sovereignty over Palestine would not budge. Reluctantly, Herzl concluded that "The condition of our cause is now desperate. I cannot deceive myself any longer."

In May 1901, Herzl again visited Constantinople, and the next year visited twice more, convincing himself each time of a resumption of interest on the sultan's part. He was finally granted an audience with the sultan, whom he described as "weak, and cowardly but thoroughly good-natured." Convincing himself that he was on the threshold of a deal, he went back to the Jewish financiers, to find they did not share his optimism. In fact, the Turks may have been using Herzl as a decoy to extract better terms from a team of French lenders who had no Palestine interests at all. Whatever the case, Herzl's last visits to Constantinople represented further defeat for the strategy that had been at the core of his Zionism.

The repeated setbacks unleashed a new wave of self-criticism. On May 2, his birthday, Herzl wrote in his diary, "I am forty-one years old. . . . I must redouble my pace. It is almost six years since I started this movement, which has made me old, tired, and poor."

In another diary entry, he engaged in a sad, almost incoherent recapitulation. "Now I am an aging and famous man," he wrote. "The days of my youth, despite their spells of melancholy, were preferable. . . . In my field I have accomplished next to nothing intellectually, but have merely displayed average political skill, such as is attainable by any horse-dealer, in a matter which is crystal clear to anyone but a blockhead. On the Jewish Question, I am world famous as a propagandist. As a writer, especially as a playwright, I am held to be nothing, less than nothing. People call me only a good journalist. And yet I know that I am or was a writer of great ability. . . ."

In his despair, he returned to an idea he entertained in the earliest days of his Zionist vocation. It was to write a novel that, while glorifying Jewish statehood, would emulate *Uncle Tom's Cabin* in arousing international public opinion. At that time, he had embarked instead on his endless round of diplomacy, but the idea remained in his mind. Herzl's diary records that he started on the novel in mid-1900 and finished it two years later. He called it *Altneuland*, "Old New Land." Clearly, he wanted it judged more for its political content than its literary merit.

Altneuland can be understood as a fictional sequel to *The Jewish State*. Herzl introduced it with the now-famous aphorism: "If you will it, it is no fantasy." The novel looks ahead to the attainment in the 1920s of the utopian vision that *The Jewish State* offered in 1896. Though he departs from the institutional focus of his earlier book, he retains its idealistic spirit. However painful his recent defeats, Herzl was still an unwavering believer.

Fictionally, the Jews' society had been established in Palestine, and it is liberal, tolerant, modern, productive, and humane. The Jews that inhabit it are honorable and secular. It has no peddlers and keeps no standing army. Substantial Jewish migration has taken place, causing anti-Semitism in Europe to ebb. With a weak plot and shallow characters, the novel often falters, but that was not the point. Herzl's message was that the Jews had *willed* it, and so the Jewish state, far from a fantasy, had become a real success.

Within his fictional state, Herzl found a comfortable place not just for Jews but for Arabs. Early Zionist writing is conspicuously wanting in interest in the Arabs; that Herzl gave his attention to them at all was exceptional. In an unusual exchange of letters a few years before, the mayor of Jerusalem had expressed his worry to Herzl about what would happen to the local Arabs if Zionism realized its designs. "What the indigenous population must realize," Herzl answered fancifully, "is that they will gain excellent brothers as the sultan will gain faithful and good subjects who will make this province flourish."

In *Altneuland,* Herzl elaborated on this belief. Amiable Arabs grow rich alongside their Jewish neighbors. The fictional Reshid Bey, a wise Arab, summed up the relationship: "The Jews have brought us wealth and health; why should we harbor evil thoughts about them? They live among us like brothers; why should we not return their kindly feelings?" Herzl never imagined Arabs being attracted, as Jews were, to their own nationalism. The harmony he envisaged in Altneuland was based on the Arabs' gratitude for the benefits brought to them by the Jews.[6]

What *Altneuland* did not examine was Judaism. Herzl, having suppressed the memory of *Jewish* impotence during the Exile, imagined a strong *Hebrew* state. Its foundation was Enlightenment rationalism; at its core was European secularism. As Herzl promised in *The Jewish State,* the government, while respectful of rabbis and the Sabbath, had built a popular consensus on religious freedom. The roots of the state were not in the Torah but in the social values of England, America, France, and, of course, Germany.

Not surprisingly, Herzl's depiction of Altneuland was controversial. It was predictable that pious Jews would reject it, as they rejected Zionism itself. But the depiction also provoked a wave of critics, preponderantly from East Europe, who believed Zionist society had to be infused with a Jewish culture. The leader of those critics, Ahad Ha'am—about whom more appears in the next chapter—published a contemptuous review of the book, dismissing Herzl's state as an imitation of Europe, devoid of Jewish character, designed to please *goyim*.

In fact, the Jewish nationalism that pervaded *Altneuland* was totally bland and un-Jewish. It contained none of the flag-waving that Herzl once extolled. Its nationalism was cerebral, totally lacking in emotion. While he portrayed a dryly rational Jewish state, a major segment of the Zionist movement, including many of his own followers, complained that it was not Jewish at all.

In its impact, *Altneuland* was not *Uncle Tom's Cabin*; it probably had few readers. It surely did not comfort the Turks who, if anything, were drifting further away from a Palestine charter. It was a paradox to Herzl that, even as anti-Semitism swelled in Russia, many of its victims were, for religious reasons, still committed to a territory that was unattainable. Defying the objections within the movement, Herzl determined to look beyond Palestine. In some desperation, and as a last hope, he turned to the English.

The English opportunity arose in 1902, after a Royal Commission was established to study "undesirable immigration"—which meant the influx of Eastern European Jews. Tens of thousands of these Jews had flowed into Britain since the pogroms of the 1880s, provoking an anti-Jewish reaction among trade unions and conservative politicians. Native English Jews had no fondness for these newcomers but, sensing a rising anti-Semitism, they saw the commission as an instrument that would ultimately close the doors to Jewish immigration entirely.

Invited by the commission to testify, Herzl promised Britain's assimilated Jews not to make matters worse. His proposed plan, he told the commission, was to found a Jewish colony on land recently snatched by Britain from the Turks, either on Cyprus or in an arid district in the Egyptian Sinai called El-Arish. Such a colony, while diverting refugees away from Britain, would provide a refuge within striking distance of Palestine, still the ultimate goal. He vowed that Palestine would not be forgotten.

In his testimony to the commission, Herzl kept his pledge to avoid stirring up its members. His most memorable words were, "I am not an Englishman, but if I were, I should not consider industrious, sober, thrifty people 'undesirable immigrants'.... Their only thought is not to starve.... It is a natural force that drives them, like a stream of water which seeks the place of least resistance."

The next morning, Herzl delivered his proposal to Joseph Chamberlain, the colonial secretary, who was known to be sympathetic to Jews. Herzl explained that his interest in Cyprus and El-Arish,—as opposed to, say, Australia—was based on their proximity to Palestine. Ethnic tensions already present between Christians and Muslims, Chamberlain said, made Cyprus unsuitable. As for El-Arish, he pulled out an atlas to find it. "It was like a big junk shop," Herzl joked in his diary, "whose manager isn't quite sure whether some unusual article is in the stock room."

Herzl's knowledge of El-Arish was certainly no greater than Chamberlain's. El-Arish was a patch of the Sinai desert that might get enough water from the Nile, he surmised, to make it habitable. But it was in the jurisdiction of the foreign ministry, Chamberlain explained, which was harder to deal with than the colonial office. Chamberlain arranged for Herzl to meet with the foreign secretary, who in turn directed him to Lord Cromer in Cairo, whose office exercised administrative control over El-Arish. A few days later, a Herzl emissary was on his way to see Cromer.

Herzl kept a sharp eye on the Cairo talks from his headquarters in Vienna. His aim was to obtain a British charter for El-Arish but, unable to give up on a deal with the Turks, he hoped the talks would persuade the sultan to relent. In a crisp message, the sultan made clear that Herzl was fooling himself. The bargaining in Cairo lasted until the spring of 1903, when Cromer announced he would defer to the wishes of Egypt and Turkey, the putative legal sovereigns of El-Arish. The negotiations ended there, since Cromer obviously understood that neither one would endorse Herzl's plan.

The El-Arish scheme was still on the table on Easter Sunday of 1903, when Kishinev, a Russian city of 50,000 inhabitants, was subjected to a horrible pogrom. The local newspaper under the direction of Vyacheslav von Plehve, the czar's interior minister, had for some time been conducting an anti-Jewish crusade, the climax of which was a charge that Jews had murdered a Christian child in a religious ritual. It was a signal for mobs to ravage the ghetto. With the army and police standing idly by, the Jews offered almost no resistance. Fifty died and hundreds were wounded, igniting an international wave of indignation. To Herzl, the Kishinev po-grom reaffirmed that Eastern Jews needed a refuge—anywhere and at once.

Herzl promptly embarked on a mission to Russia to convey his outrage to the czar. But, beyond that, his objective in the Russian capital was unclear. Plehve, probably the most anti-Semitic of the czar's circle, approved Herzl's visit on the condition that he pledge "not to bemoan the irrevocable," which meant foregoing recrimination against Russia over Kishinev. Herzl's own followers joined a wave of Jews in denouncing him for appeasing the Jew-killers. Herzl's answer was that revenge was less important than protecting the surviving Jews from further violence.

Herzl arrived in Russia on August 7, 1903, and met with Plehve a day later. He had prepared a list of requests, among them having the czar use his influence on the sultan on behalf of a Palestine charter. In fact, the czar, an enemy of the Turks, had no such influence. Herzl also asked Plehve, who was famously anti-Zionist, to legalize Russia's fifteen hundred Zionist societies and reverse a ban on spending Jewish funds for emigra-tion to Palestine. Even this was hardly realistic.

Surprisingly, Herzl wrote in his diary that he found Plehve rather like-able. He described him as "tall, a bit obese . . . (with) a sallow face, grey hair, a white moustache and remarkably youthful, energetic brown eyes." When the conversation turned to Zionism, Plehve rose and withdrew from a shelf a "big, handsome volume, with brown binding and gilt lettering, bristling with bookmarks." It turned out to be the interior ministry's files on the Zionist movement. Herzl admitted he was impressed by the orga-nization of Plehve's office.

Plehve insisted to Herzl that he was not anti-Semitic. On the contrary, he said, "I am not blind to the fact that the economic situation of the Jews . . . is bad. I also admit they are required to live in what amounts to a ghetto. . . . [But] the Russian state is bound to desire homogeneity in its population . . . [and] we must demand of all the people in our empire, and therefore also of the Jews, that they take a patriotic view of the Russian state. . . ."

Plehve then added, "Lately it has grown worse, because Jews have been joining revolutionary parties. . . . We used to be sympathetic to your move-ment, as long as it worked toward emigration. But there is less talk now about Palestinian Zionism than there is about culture, organization, and Jewish nationalism. This doesn't suit us."

Herzl was critical himself of revolutionary parties, as he was of economic, cultural, and religious digressions from Zionism's territorial objectives. He found, to his surprise, that he agreed with much of what Plehve said. His own singular focus on Jewish emigration paralleled the goal of Plehve and other Russian anti-Semites, who wanted nothing more than to rid Russia of its Jews.

Though the czar denied Herzl an audience, the subject of emigration came up again when Plehve summoned him for a second meeting. "I had submitted [your requests] to His Majesty the Emperor, the overlord of the country, the head of the government and the autocratic sovereign," Plehve stated. "It was important that the declaration I intended to give you should not come from a temporary official, from a minister who might not be around tomorrow." Plehve insisted the czar's policy still favored Jewish emigration. But his overall message suggested a more immediate interest in urging Herzl to try to curb the international condemnation directed at Russia for the Kishinev violence.

> The czar was extremely hurt that anyone should have dared assert that our government had participated in arranging the excesses or had even passively tolerated them. As head of the state, His Majesty is equally well disposed to all his subjects, and in his well-known great kindness he is particularly grieved at being thought capable of inhumanity. It is easy for foreign governments and public opinion abroad to reproach us for the way we treat our Jews. But if it were a question of letting millions of poor Jews into *their* countries, they would sing a different tune. . . . They leave it to us to cope with the problem.
>
> Now, I certainly don't deny that the situation of the Jews in the Russian Empire is not a happy one. In fact, if I were a Jew, I would probably be an enemy of the state. However, things being what they are, we have no choice but to act the way we have.

Plehve's statement, as Herzl recorded it in his diary, was in part disingenuous, in part self-pitying. But its overall theme had a ring of truth. Plehve unapologetically expressed the intention of the regime, starting with the czar himself, to leave its anti-Semitic practices intact.

Herzl left St. Petersburg feeling defeated, but hours later he was overwhelmed—as he had so often been during his travels among crowds of Eastern Jews—at the fervid welcome he received in Vilna. Home of 65,000 Jews, Vilna was a hub of Zionist activists, as well as socialist, social democratic, and Marxist militants. Supporters had warned Herzl to stay away from the city, contending he faced a threat from Jews who were angered by his visits with Plehve. But, far from finding hostility, Herzl told his diary, he was moved to tears by the ovations of oppressed Jews as he made his way through the teeming streets. Only the czar's police provided a discordant note, he wrote, living up to their reputation by brutally swinging truncheons to suppress the effervescent crowds.

☰

Herzl was still in Russia when Britain's Chamberlain invited him to send a delegation to the colonial office to explore the prospect of a Jewish settlement in East Africa. It was the possibility that Chamberlain, as colonial secretary, had raised with Herzl in conversation some months before. "I have seen a land for you on my travels, and that's Uganda," he had said. "It's hot on the coast but further inland the climate becomes excellent, even for Europeans. . . . And I thought to myself that would be a land for Doctor Herzl. But of course he wants to go only to Palestine or its vicinity." At that time, Herzl had declined Chamberlain's offer.

But after the Kishinev pogrom, Herzl reconsidered. Though the El-Arish proposal had failed, the lesson Herzl took from it was to keep the avenue to Britain open. With only a day's rest after the Vilna visit, he took his accustomed place on the podium at the annual Zionist Congress, again held in Basel. Without prior notice, Herzl sprang the British offer, generally known as the Uganda Scheme, on the assembled delegates.

"The new territory," Herzl stated, "does not have the historic, romantic, religious and Zionist value that even the Sinai Peninsula would have had. . . . The proposal involves an autonomous Jewish settlement in East Africa, with a Jewish administration, Jewish local government headed by a Jewish senior official and, of course, everything under the sovereign supervision of Great Britain. Considering the plight of Jewry and the immediate necessity of finding some way to ameliorate [it], I did not feel justified . . . in taking any steps other than obtaining permission to submit the proposal to the congress.

"It is evident the Jewish people can have no ultimate goal other than Palestine. . . . [But] without our abandoning any of the great principles on which our movement is based, . . . this offer is bound to help improve and alleviate the situation of the Jewish people."

Of the nearly six hundred delegates in attendance, few were ready for such an astonishing offer. To most, Africa was a wilderness populated by savages. Herzl explained that he proposed only to send a research team to report on whether the land was fit for Jewish colonization. But this undertaking, limited though it was, reassured only a small minority. Instead, the proposal ignited a brawl on the congress floor. Herzl's credibility had already been sapped among Eastern delegates by his meetings with the detested Plehve. The same delegates now took the Uganda Scheme as his betrayal of the Basel Program, if not of Zionism itself.

Herzl, by his own admission, did not understand the fierce opposition. Even the Kishinev delegates, whom he assumed would be the first to embrace the proposal, were among those who rejected it. These were the very Jews who most needed a refuge—for whom Uganda was designed not as a homeland but as a temporary sanctuary. As Herzl saw it, they were being driven by a biblical imperative that superseded concern for their personal safety, without their even being practicing Jews. One observer reported overhearing Herzl mumble, "These people have a rope around their necks, and still they refuse."

After an extremely bitter debate, Herzl won a floor vote taken on the Uganda Scheme by 295 to 177. But a hundred delegates had abstained and the majority clearly held reservations. The delegates who actually favored the proposal were almost entirely Westerners, who had no personal stake in Uganda and no experience with pogroms. But they were heavily outnumbered. The margin of victory came from loyal Zionists who, whatever their Uganda position, were unwilling to repudiate Herzl's leadership.

Herzl's largest body of support came from the Religious Zionists, who a year earlier had formed a faction called Mizrachi. Its intellectual lineage dated back to Rabbis Kalischer and Alkalai. Its leader, Rabbi Isaac Jacob Reines, preached that Uganda was not just a refuge in Africa and not a threat to Judaism, but God's signal that the Redemption had begun. The real explanation for Mizrachi's solidarity, however, was its intent to keep Judaism, through Herzl, in the mainstream of the Zionist movement.

But the outcome of the balloting had repercussions that went far beyond Uganda. As soon as the results of the vote were announced, the defeated opposition rose as a body and marched out of the hall. Determined to avert seccession, Herzl chased after them. After he declared the Basel Program intact, the dissidents reluctantly marched back. In his closing talk to the congress, Herzl repeated that though the road to Zionism might require detours, its destination was not in doubt. Solemnly, he pronounced the liturgical vow: "If I forget thee, O Jerusalem, may my right hand lose its cunning." Despite his eloquence, however, much of the opposition announced that it was not bound by the vote approving the Uganda Scheme.

Herzl was now a badly wounded leader, and the rejectionists were not prepared to give up. After the congress adjourned, they reassembled and issued an ultimatum demanding that Herzl not only abandon the Uganda Scheme but restructure the Zionist organization to shift the preponderance of power from West to East. Herzl rejected their ultimatum.

The Uganda dispute dragged on, casting a long shadow over Zionism. In the ensuing months, Britain's ardor for the offer waned in the face of the Zionist dispute, in which it did not want to be mired. Meanwhile, in Russia, anti-Uganda sentiment grew stronger, and Mizrachi lost substantial ground. Uganda clearly was going to remain on the Zionist agenda, fragmenting the movement's unity. Confronted with a decline both in his health and his popularity, Herzl gave serious thought to resigning his presidency.

It is likely, however, that Herzl was incapable of surrender. He wrote to Plehve, asking again that the czar urge a charter upon the sultan. He sent notes to the German and Austrian foreign ministers. He even found energy to travel to Italy to deliver pleas for help to the pope and the Italian king. He proposed to the British that they shift their offer back to El-Arish. Meanwhile, in his free time, he wrote articles for the *Neue Freie Presse* to earn his salary.

The British did not follow up on El-Arish, but at the end of January 1904, they issued a formal invitation to set up a colony in Uganda, and after much agonizing, Herzl conveyed his acceptance. Out of concern for the schism, however, he called a meeting of the Greater Actions Committee, the body empowered to make interim policy decisions. Delegates from ten countries—on both sides of the issue—answered the call, including some who had walked out of the Basel Congress the year before.

"It is my intention to speak only words of peace to you," Herzl said in opening the session. "I know what uneasiness there is among the masses of our good, honest, loyal Zionists all over the world, and particularly in Russia. . . . The British government had offered us a territory for our suffering masses. My personal standpoint is that we have no right to reject such a proposal without asking the people whether they want it or not. I believe it was and is our duty to put this question to the people. . . . I regard this line of action as absolutely proper and perfectly democratic, rather than autocratic or arbitrary."

Though the rejectionists at the meeting fought back, a majority ultimately deferred to Herzl's plea. They not only withdrew their objections to sending a research team to explore Uganda but openly acknowledged that Herzl, faithful to the Basel Program, had not given up his commitment to Palestine as the ultimate Jewish home. The consensus Herzl reached with the opposition was his last triumph as head of the Zionist movement.

Unfortunately, Herzl's diary contains no account of the meeting. Its absence was the product of his failing heart, which left him with physical weakness and severe difficulty in breathing.

Herzl's last diary entry came from a rest home near Vienna. He wrote on May 14, 1904, that "It will probably be a few weeks before I have patched up my heart a bit here, since it is in need of repair." Yet he still dashed off letters to whoever might help the Zionist cause. Two days later, the diary ended with the copy of an acerbic letter Herzl wrote to a New York banker about money in the estate of Baron de Hirsch that might be made available to abate the "misery and filth" of the Jewish masses.

Herzl returned briefly from the rest home to his Vienna apartment, then left for a sanitarium in Edlach, a nearby resort town. Accompanying him was Julie, with whom he now seemed to be on warmer terms. Herzl died in Edlach on July 3, 1904, with his wife and children, his mother, and a few close friends around him. By the eve of his funeral, more than six thousand mourners from all over Europe had arrived to accompany the hearse to the cemetery. Hans, Herzl's son, read the *kaddish* over his father's grave.

Herzl was then forty-four years old. He was buried next to his father in the family plot in Vienna. In 1949, a year after the founding of the state of Israel, his remains were transferred to a hill at the western edge of Jerusalem. The site is known as Mount Herzl.

Were an observer to assess Herzl's life's work at the moment of his death, the conclusion would be that he had failed in his high ambitions on behalf of the Jewish people. He felt that way himself. His efforts to acquire a Palestine charter from the Turks had come to naught. Soon after his death, the proposal to establish a temporary refuge in Africa for beleaguered Jews was rescinded. At the World Zionist Congress of 1905, a majority voted formally to abandon the Uganda plan.

It is true that Herzl had institutionalized Zionism, and left behind an enduring organizational structure. Yet, the movement, at the moment of his death, seemed bereft of leaders, no less than of ideas. With Herzl's death, Zionism itself appeared to many to have run its course.

Yet, in retrospect, what Herzl did must be evaluated by less concrete measures. He took on the challenge of the traditional rabbinic leadership. He defied a historic Jewish self-image of passivity to impart to the Jews a new dynamic sense of themselves. He told Jews that victimhood was not their inevitable fate, and they listened. Whatever his defeats in politics and diplomacy, Herzl aroused Jews from centuries of lethargy to seize control of their future.

It is also fair to say that Herzl understood better than anyone the threat to the Jews that emerged from Europe's disintegrating social order. He recognized that, given the anti-Semitism that lay within Europe's culture, the Jews, if they were not to perish, had to be rescued. He fell short of his goal, and within decades, the oppression, led by his beloved Germany, reached a level that had been unimaginable, even to him. But Herzl's vision of a state where Jews might save themselves lived on. Ultimately, this vision prevailed.

2

Chaim Weizmann
1874–1952

MATCHMAKER

Herzl had no natural heir as leader of the Zionist movement. Though he had fallen short of achieving the goal of a national home, no member of the Zionist community could replace the magic he radiated. In life, he had resisted delegating authority and turned only rarely to advisers for counsel. He groomed no successor. At his death, he passed along the responsibilities and trappings of his leadership to conscientious but lesser men. They kept the organization intact but imparted to it no inspiration.

It was in the turmoil of World War I that Chaim Weizmann emerged from the crowd of claimants to the Zionist throne. By then, the Zionist Congress had repudiated the Uganda Scheme, Herzl's final effort to establish a Jewish refuge. With the Turkish sultan adamant in rejecting a Palestine charter, no other avenue to Zionism's goal presented itself. For a decade after Herzl's death, Zionism seemed paralyzed, without a discernible future. Then, in the disorder of a war-shattered Europe, Weizmann gave the movement a new course and imbued it with new vigor.

Chaim Weizmann would attain eminence not just as a Zionist but as a scientist. Not by chance he titled his memoir *Trial and Error,* a term defined as a method to resolve problems by experimentation and experience rather than by theory or reason. "My personal approach to Zionism," he wrote, "changes every six months. I build a balanced, harmonious theory, and then, when half a year goes by, I have to revise it. . . . How I hate all formulas; how they have entangled and drained us; how useless they are when applied to the Jews!" Weizmann achieved many triumphs in his parallel careers but, given his reliance on trial and error, they were invariably contentious and never easily won.

Weizmann, like Herzl, was an offspring of the Jewish Enlightenment. The Zionism of both derived from secular values. Yet, in the manner of their growing up, the two could hardly have been more different.

Herzl, raised in a Western home, was the spoiled child of bourgeois culture; Weizmann, the fourth of fifteen children, grew up in a household committed to Jewish tradition in Russia's Pale of Settlement. Herzl had little Jewish learning; Weizmann's upbringing was deeply rooted in Judaism. Herzl, to whom Judaism was a mystery, was willing to accept religion into the movement; Weizmann saw Judaism as a barrier to Zionism's objectives. Herzl, a product of German culture, aspired as a youth to be accepted in a Christian world; Weizmann, a son of Yiddish-speaking society, loathed Germany and never doubted, from his earliest days, that he was irrevocably a Jew.

Herzl's Zionism was a response to his own personal crisis of identity; Weizmann's was inseparable from his Jewish sensibility. Such was Herzl's charisma that his preeminence within the movement was never challenged; Weizmann, hounded by rivals, constantly scrambled for recognition and respect. Though Herzl founded modern Zionism, Weizmann in 1917 won the Balfour Declaration, without which Zionism would not have achieved its goal. In 1948, Weizmann became the first president of the newly established Jewish state.

Chaim Weizmann was born in 1874 in a town called Motol, which he described in his memoir as bleak, with unpaved streets and no post office, home to some five hundred families, a third of them Jews. His father, a lumberman—a common Jewish occupation at that time—spent most days away from home, in the forests felling trees, which he then floated downriver to market. Weizmann described his family as "well-to-do" compared to their neighbors. They occupied a large house with fruit trees, chickens, and cows, employed servants, and could afford the tuition to send all fifteen children to good schools.

Growing up, Weizmann wrote, he could feel the presence of the *Haskala,* the Jewish Enlightenment, in his home. Chekhov and Tolstoy stood next to Maimonides and the Talmud on the shelves of his home. Photos of Jerusalem and Baron de Hirsch hung on the walls, and Palestine was the constant subject of dinner-table talk. The pioneers of Hibbat Zion were his heroes. At four, he was enrolled in a *heder,* a religious school where Western ideas were embedded in the curriculum. By adolescence, however, he had chosen science over piety, while at the same time committing himself to the service of the Jews.

Many years later, when an English friend asked what made him "take up" Zionism, Weizmann replied: "I never 'took it up.' We who come from Russia are born and bred in an aspiration toward a new and better Jewish life. It must not be only a comfortable life but a *Jewish* one, a normal Jewish life, just as an Englishman leads a normal English life. . . . In Russia, a most modern and perfect machinery was set up to crush the Jew's body and soul. . . . We claim the right as Jews to be treated as normal human beings, capable of entering the family of nations as equals and be masters of our own destiny."

Having consumed all the schooling that Motol offered, Weizmann was sent to Pinsk, a midsized city nearby, where he enrolled in a Russian high school, a *gymnasium.* Pinsk was a bustling center of Jewish activity, despite the dark clouds cast over the Pale by the pogroms of the 1880s. It was a home of Jewish scholars, shopkeepers, and factory workers. Its writers explored a wide diversity of Jewish questions. Pinsk was a hub from which Hibbat Zion sent young pioneers to Palestine. Weizmann acquired his lifelong attachment to chemistry at school there, and on graduating from the *gymnasium* at eighteen, he faced the choice of competing for a place open to Jews in the Russian university system or continuing his education in a Western country. He chose to go to Germany.

Weizmann enrolled first at the university in Darmstadt, teaching Hebrew and Russian at a nearby Jewish boarding school to defray expenses. Compared to Russia, Germany's freedom exhilarated him, but he was depressed by its Jewish life. Russia's Jews, despite czarist oppression, possessed a valid culture, he wrote, while German Jewry, "obsessed by its social inferiority, . . . exerted itself frantically to efface its own identity, to be accepted as German." Despite a kosher kitchen and required prayers, his school "had no folk background. It lacked warmth and gaiety and color and intimacy." Its director, who described himself as being "of the Mosaic persuasion," insisted anti-Semitism was dying and yearned for full assimilation. In Darmstadt, Weizmann acquired a distaste for Germany that remained with him throughout his life.

After a year in Germany, Weizmann returned home while his father restructured his lumber business to support the education of his brothers and sisters. He then enrolled at the more highly regarded university in Berlin, where he laid the academic foundation for his career in chemistry. He was also introduced into a generation of Jewish students in flight from Russian oppression, who clustered on Western Europe's university campuses. Their common goal was to change the character of Russian-Jewish life. Some were social democrats, others revolutionaries. Weizmann was swept into the magnetic field of the rising movement of Jewish nationalism, just as Theodor Herzl's Zionism was spreading.

"There was not a single university town on the continent," Weizmann recalled years later, "where you could not find a student Zionist society. . . . We used to discuss in our university circle vital questions concerning our people." In these discussions, he wrote, he shed "the vague and sentimental Zionism of my boyhood"—by which he no doubt meant Hibbat Zion's establishment of autonomous pioneer settlements in Palestine—and aligned with Herzl's movement to found a sovereign Jewish state.

Weizmann's generation of students discovered Herzl on the publication of *The Jewish State*. In his memoir Weizmann wrote that, like most Eastern Jews, he was familiar with many of the ideas in the book, since they "had long been the substance of our Zionist tradition." Still, he said, *The Jewish State* was electrifying. "The personality that stood behind the ideas appealed to us," he wrote. "Here was daring, clarity and energy." He and his friends knew instinctively that Herzl was a man of "historic dimension."

Yet Weizmann was burdened by a recognition that Western Jews like Herzl were different from Eastern Jews. He scoffed at Herzl's notion that Zion could be constructed simply by signing a pact with the sultan. Herzl was naive, he said, to believe rich Jews would open their purses or that Jews could rely on pledges from Europe's great powers. Western Jews had much to learn, notably that Zionism "had to be watched, watered, and nursed." Weizmann noted in his diary that Herzl, whatever his grandeur, "was not of the people and did not grasp the dynamic power emanating from the Jews of the East."

As much as Herzl wanted from Zionism, Weizmann wanted more. It was not enough that, out of despair over anti-Semitism, Herzl was proposing a refuge. Herzl's conception of a Jewish state, he said, looked much like modern Germany, a place that he rejected. Herzl had not thought about the state's *character*. Like many of his peers, Weizmann wanted a state reflecting Jewish values, enriched with Jewish culture.

Weizmann was among the young Jews gripped by the ideas of Asher Ginsberg, known by the Hebrew pen name Ahad Ha'am ("one of the people"). A self-taught scholar born in Russia in 1856, Ahad Ha'am was a Zionist dedicated not just to rescuing Jews but to founding a society imbued with the values of a secular Judaism.

Remembered as the father of *cultural* Zionism, Ahad Ha'am distinguished Jewish nationalism in the West from that in the East. The nationalism of the West derived from Jews with a European education, he wrote; nationalism of the East derived from Jews with a *Jewish* education. "One is the product of anti-Semitism, the other of the Jews' link with a millennial culture, and it will remain unaffected even if the troubled Jews all over the world attain comfortable economic positions, are on the best possible terms with their neighbors, and are admitted to the fullest social and political equality."[1]

Ahad Ha'am insisted that Western Jews, whatever their political freedoms, lived in moral degradation. He criticized Hibbat Zion for its unique fixation on land, and Herzl for a Zionism without spiritual content. He described Herzl's novel *Altneuland* as obsequious in imitating European societies. His own vision was to make of Palestine a spiritual hub, where Hebrew would be restored as the Jews' language, and from which Jewish culture would radiate worldwide. Weizmann called Ahad Ha'am's view of Zionism "organic" and argued that Ahad Ha'am's writings corrected a basic weakness in Herzl's vision.

Still, Weizmann recognized Herzl as his leader, and he joined with dozens of students in the spring and summer of 1897 in crisscrossing the Pale to generate enthusiasm for the impending First Zionist Congress in Basel. He was himself elected a delegate from Pinsk but he never got to the meeting. Having discovered a new process in dyestuff chemistry in his university laboratory, he made an illegal journey across Russia to propose it to a Moscow factory owner. The effort failed, though much later he sold the rights elsewhere for a small sum. Weizmann never ceased, however, to lament his absence from the conference at which Zionism was born.

That fall, Weizmann transferred from Berlin to the University of Freiburg in Switzerland, where in time he obtained a doctorate in chemistry and was appointed to the science faculty at the University of Geneva. In Switzerland, he wrote, rival student factions engaged in tumultuous debate, in which anti-czarists of various stripes charged Zionists with inhumanity for having a concern for Jews alone. Weizmann replied that his rivals, especially the Marxists, were assimilationists at heart, and said their complaints rolled off him like rain on a slanted roof. The next summer, at the Second Zionist Congress, he first met Herzl, who knew of his reputation as a young disciple of Ahad Ha'am. The affiliation made Herzl suspicious of him as a troublemaker.

Fluent in Russian, German, and French, as well as Yiddish and Hebrew, Weizmann already lectured on Zionism throughout Europe. His charm, humor, and intelligence captivated his listeners. Though prematurely bald, he was tall and slender, he dressed well, and he made an excellent impression. He also had an engaging face, on which he wore the moustache and goatee favored by the era's intellectuals. But it was not a bland face. Vera Khatzman, a medical student whom he would later marry, described this face as having the burdens of the Jewish world written on it.[2]

By the Second Zionist Congress in 1898, a rift between Herzl and Eastern Jews had already become worrisome. Ahad Ha'am's disciples argued endlessly for "culture," which irritated Herzl, who saw this along with religion as a digression from his priority of acquiring a refuge. "Culture" also enraged Religious Zionists, who opposed admitting Ahad Ha'am's forthright secularism into the movement's tent. Confronted with the impact that Russia's pogroms had on the Jews, Herzl made unity his priority, maintaining that disputes over the *nature* of Zionist society should be deferred until some later, unspecified time.

At the Fifth Zionist Congress in 1901, by which time it was apparent that Herzl's solicitations to the sultan were going nowhere, Weizmann himself ignited a crisis, leading university students in a protest against Herzl's hobnobbing with kaisers and kings. Weizmann's action, Herzl warned, risked his latest negotiations with the sultan, a specious argument. Ahad Ha'am, on the other hand, urged Weizmann to secede from the Zionist Organization altogether. Weizmann refused them both; declaring himself a movement loyalist, he persisted in calling for Herzl to embrace university youth, to bring fresh energy into the leadership ranks.

Weizmann's protest meeting on the eve of the Fifth Congress generated a surprisingly large response among young people. The respondants were not only Cultural Zionists, but Religious Zionists, revolutionary Marxists, and socialist Zionists. The widespread enthusiasm forced Weizmann to concentrate on keeping the protests under control. Only *Zionists*, not rebels, would be admitted to the meeting, he declared, a formula that not only excluded radicals but assured "culture" a preponderant place on the congress floor. There, Weizmann moved to form a standing "Democratic Faction" within the Zionist organization, although democracy occupied only a small part in his program.

Participants in Weizmann's meeting made up about a tenth of the delegates, too many for Herzl to ignore. Reluctantly, he granted recognition to Weizmann's band, establishing the legitimacy of minority Zionist factions. Herzl gave its members time on the floor to express opinions. In the end, the Fifth Congress submitted to the Democratic Faction's pressure to establish a commission, of which Ahad Ha'am and Weizmann would be members, to explore the addition of "culture" to Zionism's agenda.

Among the specific goals on Ahad Ha'am's agenda, which Weizmann adopted, was a Zionist university, which Herzl saw as another digression and endorsed only reluctantly. Weizmann's initial idea was to place the university in Europe, probably England, with the intent of transferring it in time to Palestine. Though nothing came of the project immediately, Weizmann sowed seeds that bloomed decades later in the founding of the Hebrew University in Jerusalem.

Oddly, Herzl made no mention of the Democratic Faction in his diary, though he referred to it amicably in his closing remarks to the congress as "a youthful group, which is faithful, sometimes in a lively way." Without deviating from his own strategy of pursuing a charter, he allowed the Faction to give legitimacy to Cultural Zionism, thus helping to move his Zionism closer to the values that mattered to many Eastern Jews.

Predictably, the Faction angered Religious Zionists, inspiring them to found the rival organization called Mizrachi, which Weizmann promptly labeled the "rabbinical party." Herzl recognized its legitimacy as well, which formally brought the struggle between religion and secularism inside the boundaries of the Zionist movement.

Shortly after the recognition of the two factions, Weizmann sent a puzzling letter to Herzl charging that his pro-Mizrachi sympathies were driving Jewish workers and intellectuals in Russia into radical political groups. Mizrachi is setting a trap, he wrote, to transform Zionism into pietism. Only fusing Jewish culture and tradition with the humane aim of refuge can save the movement, he argued. The Democratic Faction provides Zionism, he wrote, with "modern creativity."

In reply, Herzl acknowledged that Zionism's condition in Russia was "unfortunately very gloomy," but insisted that the Democratic Faction made matters only worse. "I regard you, Dr. Weizmann," he wrote, "as a person who has been temporarily misled, but is nevertheless a useful force who will find his way back and proceed along the right road together with all of us." The exchange took place on the eve of the fierce dispute within the movement over the Uganda Scheme, which left Herzl wounded and Weizmann at an even greater distance to "find his way back."

Weizmann's ambition had by now gone beyond the Democratic Faction, and he was thinking of leadership in the wider Zionist organization. At the Congress of 1903, the Uganda Scheme required him to choose between Herzl and his fellow Easterners, and it was not an easy choice. In the end, upset by Herzl's alliance with Mizrachi, he voted against Uganda and joined in the opposition's famous walkout. But the Eastern leaders, aware of his wavering, denied him the promotion he sought to their inner circle, while Herzl, equally wary, placed him at arm's length. Thwarted in his aspiration to rise in Zionism's ranks, Weizmann, not yet thirty, responded with a resolve to rededicate his life to science.

In the fall of 1903, Weizmann traveled to London, saying little about his plans to his friends. He wrote to Vera, however, "I must regulate my activities so that Zionism does not interfere with chemistry. I shall then be healthier and more creative." Returning to his career in science was an alternative he contemplated whenever his options in Zionism seemed stalled.

From London, Weizmann grumbled to Vera about the "foul weather, fog, din and uproar, and a language that is not easily comprehensible to me." But his complaints did not deter him from seeking an academic post. In March 1904, he received an offer from the University of Manchester to conduct research on dyes, his academic specialty. After writing to Vera of "advantageous opportunities" awaiting both of them, he accepted the offer.

A few weeks after his move to England, Herzl died. Weizmann did not attend the funeral, but he mused in a letter to Vera over the change Herzl's loss would make to his own status. "Verochka, put on mourning. We are all wearing it. . . . All the differences between us have disappeared. And I only have the image of a great creative worker in front of my eyes. I feel a great weight on my heart, the more so as you are not with me, and deep grief. He has left a frightening legacy. . . . I feel that a heavy burden has fallen on my shoulders, and the shoulders are weak and tired."

In the same letter, Weizmann repeated the mantra that in England he would keep his focus on science. Britain was then home to 300,000 Jews, the majority of them recent refugees from Russia. A few years before, they had cheered deliriously at Herzl's speech. Weizmann found them "a wretched sight, herded into a filthy ghetto, perceptibly detached from Judaism, strangers to English culture." Still, they were his people, and he knew he could not isolate himself in a laboratory, distancing himself from them.

Britain, Weizmann soon learned, also had a second community of Jews, descendants of the refugees of Iberian persecution centuries before. Many had prospered in business and been accepted into British society. Some exercised real political influence. Though troubled by the Jews' plight in czarist Russia, they themselves had little to do with the newly arrived immigrants crowded into the London ghettos. Weizmann considered these "native" Jews assimilationists, who were naive about the dangers of anti-Semitism. Mostly, he disapproved of their indifference to Zionism, which most of them regarded as a foreign creed.

In his first weeks in Britain, Weizmann focused on absorbing British culture. He was graciously received at the foreign office, which provided him with useful information, notably about Uganda. Later, in Manchester, he rented an austere flat and worked on putting his laboratory in order. He found the transition difficult, however. From his letters to Vera, it is clear that living among strangers, he felt lonely and depressed.

That summer, Weizmann journeyed to Vienna, where Zionist officials were deliberating on a successor to Herzl. The Uganda issue was still on the table. Weizmann, though he held no office, believed he could be useful in sharing what he had learned in London, and was stunned at being denied admission to any of the Zionist meetings. He promptly packed his bags, expressing to Vera his regret at having made the trip. "My time will still come," he told her, "but later, later, when there will be nothing but fragments."

By the fall of 1904, Weizmann had published two articles in a British scientific journal, which he signed "Charles Weizmann." His command of spoken English had improved, albeit with a heavy accent that he would never lose, and by early 1905 he was delivering regular classroom lectures. He received steady salary increases, was assigned lab assistants and, in letters to old comrades on the Continent, predicted a promotion to professor. He also did off-campus research in dyestuffs for local manufacturers, adding to his income, some of which went to his family in Russia, while the rest he put aside to bring Vera to England.

Among Weizmann's after-hours industrial employers was the head of the local Zionist association, whose dinner invitations brought a touch of luxury to his spare existence. Through these contacts, he received solicitations to speak on Zionism at synagogues and public meetings, initially in Manchester and London, then throughout England. Though he missed the society of the Continent, which he considered intellectually richer, he soon acquired a reputation and some influence in Jewish circles in Britain.

In 1905, the failed revolution in Russia provoked another personal crisis. Weizmann told Vera his life was meaningless while "a sense of death was hovering over" the country of his birth. He worried about his family, and expressed feelings of guilt at observing from afar the killing of Russian Jews. He denounced Jewish financiers for contributing nothing to Zionism while providing loans to the czar's regime. And he also argued irascibly that the assimilated Jews in England were complicit in a new wave of pogroms by desisting from public protests.

Not long afterward, Weizmann met Lord Arthur Balfour, a Scottish aristocrat and politician who had recently been turned out as prime minister and was running in Manchester to retain his parliamentary seat. As head of the government, Balfour had denounced Russia's pogroms as "a disgrace to Christendom" and had played a key role in devising the Uganda Scheme. On the other hand, Balfour proposed to limit the immigration of Russian Jews, declaring to parliament, "It would not be to the advantage of the civilization of this country that there should be an immense body of persons who, however patriotic, able and industrious, however much they threw themselves into the national life, remained a people apart. . . ."

Britain's Jewish elite did not regard Balfour as anti-Semitic, but some of its members questioned whether he was really their friend.

It has never been clear why Balfour invited Weizmann to meet with him in Manchester. As an immigrant intellectual, Weizmann brought nothing to Balfour's political campaign. Balfour, however, was not an ordinary politician. An observant Christian, he had written books on Christianity, in which he referred to Judaism as Christianity's birth mother. Among the aristocratic Jews he knew, Balfour had encountered hostility to Zionism, and he was intrigued by what he had heard of Weizmann's contrary view. Having failed at reelection, Balfour did not see Weizmann again for nearly a decade, and their meeting in 1905 might well have been forgotten. But Weizmann etched it permanently in Zionist lore by treating it as a major stepping-stone to the Balfour Declaration.

Weizmann's account in his memoir says Balfour wanted to understand why Zionists had refused Britain's generous gift of Uganda. Weizmann, still struggling with his English, compared the offer to a hypothetical invitation to Englishmen to accept Paris as their capital; he said it was unthinkable. Asked whether other Jews felt the same, Weizmann replied, "I believe I speak the mind of millions of Jews whom you will never see and who cannot speak for themselves."

According to his biographer, Balfour later said, "From that talk . . . I saw that the Jewish form of patriotism was unique. Their love for their country refused to be satisfied by the Uganda Scheme. Weizmann's absolute refusal even to look at it impressed me." Weizmann claimed that the meeting had turned Balfour into a Zionist.

On the Continent, meanwhile, the Zionist Organization still struggled over Herzl's succession. Weizmann's letters from old colleagues reveal the intrigue that pervaded the organization's politics, and his answers back to them suggest that he missed participating in the intrigues. Competition for offices often had Zionism's East-West schism as a subplot, but a second subplot of nationalist rivalries, particularly between Germans and Russians, was intensified by the Zionist executive's approval of replacing Herzl's Vienna with Berlin as the organization's international headquarters.

Though disqualified from office himself for his self-imposed exile, Weizmann knew the organization had no shortage of competent men clamoring to take charge. Recently naturalized as a British subject, he was elected a provincial vice-president of the English Zionist Federation and was named by the Seventh Zionist Congress to the Greater Actions Committee. But neither office possessed real authority, nor offered the opportunity to rise to the rank that Weizmann believed his contributions had earned him.

Weizmann argued that the Zionist movement was too "Eurocentric," a charge which would later be directed at him as power gravitated from Europe to the *yishuv*. "If the governments give us a charter today," he declared, "it will be a scrap of paper; not so if we work in Palestine. Then it will be written and insolubly cemented in sweat and blood." He called for a synthesis of Zionism's rival wings: Herzl's Zionism based on a deal with the sultan, and the *yishuv*'s Zionism founded on the Hibbat Zion model of establishing settlements throughout Palestine.

At Weizmann's urging, the Eighth Zionist Congress in 1907 voted for the first time to allocate funds for colonization in Palestine. A day after the congress ended, Weizmann left by steamship for his first Palestine visit, leaving behind Vera, now his wife, and their newborn son, Benjamin. Weizmann admitted that the effort he was again putting into Zionism placed strains both on his science and his marriage. In his memoir, he admitted that the chemist within him was forever in conflict with the Zionist, just as his softer, family side was in conflict with his popular image as a globe-trotting, romantic savior of the Jews.

Palestine was "a dolorous country . . . ," Weizman wrote on arriving, "one of the most neglected corners of the miserably neglected Turkish empire." Echoing Herzl's earlier judgments, he described Jerusalem's Jewish quarter as "a miserable ghetto, derelict and without dignity." He was also as critical as Herzl had been of the Rothschilds, arguing that the initiative of the pioneers "had been destroyed by the baron's dictatorial bureaucracy." But while Herzl never changed his view of Edmond de Rothschild, Weizmann did, though only after the family became major supporters of the Zionist cause.

During this visit Weizmann also took notice of the Arabs of Palestine, and the picture he painted of them was not pretty. As cheap labor, he complained, they were a barrier to Jewish economic development. In a later lecture in Manchester, he spoke of "Arabs whose requirements were few and whose mode of living is uncivilized . . . The Jewish colonies cannot be regarded as really Jewish so long as Arabs form so powerful a part of the population."

After the journey to Palestine, Weizmann turned back to the laboratory. He probably had to. His salary fell below what he and Vera spent to keep a fine home, travel often, employ a nanny, and mingle socially above his academic rank. Her income as a public health doctor relieved some of the pressure, and he had numerous patents in his name, though none brought a significant return. In 1913, he was passed over for the promotion to professor that he anticipated and, suspecting anti-Semitism, he considered seeking an academic post elsewhere. It was Vera who put her foot down to keep them in Manchester, Weizmann wrote, but the couple's financial problems persisted.

Weizmann's disappointment over losing the promotion was surely a factor in his metronomic swing back to Zionism, this time by resuming his efforts to found a Jewish university. He made a new argument at the 1913 Zionist Congress: "A university in which the Turkish and Arab populations are accepted would help establish good relations with our neighbors. That indicates its high political significance." Probably offhanded, the remark was an unusual expression of concern for the Jews' relationship with the non-Jewish residents of Palestine. Weizmann rarely repeated it.[3]

Under pressure from Weizmann, the 1913 Congress voted a small sum to a Zionist university, indicating a preference for using its funds to acquire land. Refusing to be discouraged by the congress's cool response, Weizmann took a page from Herzl to solicit the help of Edmond de Rothschild, whose hostility to Zionism had by now receded.

The two met in Paris in January 1914, and Weizmann's description largely echoed what Herzl had written two decades before. Rothschild, Weizmann wrote, was "still something of a dandy . . . both gracious and brutal . . . conscious of his power and arrogant in the possession of it [but] frightened by it." According to Weizmann, Rothschild declared, "Without me, the Zionists could have done nothing, but without the Zionists my work would have been dead." The meeting produced an endorsement by Rothschild and a pledge of funds that would in time make a Zionist university a reality.

Neither man knew, of course, that they were on the cusp of a war that would soon plunge both Europe and the Middle East into flames. With Rothschild's pledge, and the donation by a second philanthropist of a plot of land on Jerusalem's Mount Scopus, the planning for the project began. A few building contracts were actually written before the war broke out, but Weizmann had done his work well. Though delayed for three years, the groundbreaking for the university took place even before the fighting of the world war had ended.

Despite growing instability in the Ottoman East, Western Europe did not seem unusually troubled in 1914. Six years before, the sultan had been overthrown by a cabal of military reformers, called the Young Turks, who promised a European-style political liberalization. The Committee of Union and Progress, its ruling body, even contained a few Turkish Jews. Weizmann, like others, imagined the Young Turks would reverse the Ottoman position on Zionism, and that a deal for Herzl's charter might finally be reached. Instead, the Young Turks' revolution ignited a fierce surge of nationalism, first among the Turks themselves, then among the Empire's European subjects. Insurgencies broke out in the Christian Balkans, culminating in the assassination in Sarajevo of the Austrian archduke, Franz Ferdinand, heir to the Hapsburg throne. The assassination led directly to the war in Europe.

The Young Turks' revolution had also triggered a wave of nationalism in the Ottomans' Arab provinces. Though barely noticed, nationalism had for some time been simmering in Arab student circles. Its main target was the oppression of Arabs by the sultan's regime, which did not vanish under the Young Turks. In Palestine, not only did Weizmann's hope for a charter vanish but Turkish pressure on the *yishuv* intensified. Young Turks and Arab patriots, though each other's enemies, saw eye-to-eye on the dangers to them of Zionism. Then, with the Young Turks' entry into the war on the side of Germany, the possibility that the Ottoman Empire might crumble suddenly seemed real, offering Zionists a ray of optimism.

Weizmann was vacationing in Switzerland with his family when England declared war on Germany on August 4, 1914. Usually quick to adapt, he was surprisingly cautious about proposing a Zionist response. Not only were Zionists scattered across the Continent, but Zionist agencies were also dominated by Jews from both Germany and Russia, which were now at war with each other. Maintaining cordial ties across the battle lines was impossible. The Zionist Organization's most logical course was neutrality, which it formally adopted as policy, but Jews as individuals could not be neutral. Most of them—Weizmann included—took the side of the nation in which they lived. Weizmann thought initially of transferring the conduct of Zionist affairs to America, allowing the headquarters in Berlin to hibernate for the war's duration. But the idea had little support in America—and even less in Berlin.

Weizmann was furious, in fact, when German Zionists decided to keep the Berlin office open, casting suspicion upon Zionism throughout the Allied states. "Even in peacetime we had to fight against the unjustified slander that we are the vanguard of German influence . . . ," he wrote to a friend. "I would protest by all means in my power against any venture which could in any way give our movement a German character." The Zionist Executive set up a branch in Copenhagen, a neutral city, but it could not escape its German shadow. When Weizmann journeyed to Copenhagen, the Executive shunned him, pointing out that he had already violated Zionist neutrality by expressing a preference for a British victory.

By that time, Weizmann had charted a course, which was not neutral at all. He had proclaimed early on that self-interest required Zionism to side with the victor, and since he believed Britain's government was the most sympathetic to the movement, he slipped from his usual critical analysis into wishful thinking. "I am convinced," he wrote, "that the outcome of this catastrophe will be a British and French victory. . . . I cannot and *do not want* to envisage any other outcome." The Jews' dilemma, however, was that the much-loathed czarist regime was an ally of Britain and France. "We as Jews wish and must wish for a victory for the Allies, Russia included," he wrote, "[though] a victorious Russia means a stronger oppressor of the Jews."

At the start of the war, before the Young Turks entered, Britain did its best to keep Turkey out of the fighting. Even afterward, it kept the door open for the Turks' withdrawal from the war. But the plan that took shape in Weizmann's mind required an outright Ottoman defeat. "An imperial synthesis between England and Jewry," he wrote, "would be the greatest thing imaginable." He even drafted a claim, to be delivered at a postwar peace conference, to a Jewish Palestine within the framework of Britain's empire.[4]

Weizmann was not alone, of course, in claiming to act for Zionism independently of the Zionist Organization. In Germany, Zionists exploited the country's ties to the Turks to claim the kaiser's guardianship of the *yishuv,* while denouncing Britain's alliance with the czar. They cited the kaiser's encounters with Herzl in 1898 as proof of Germany's Zionist sympathies. They pointed out that Muslims from the empire were a major component of Britain's armed forces, and that Arabs were more important than Jews to its imperial interests. Like Weizmann, German Zionists believed their own country's triumph would best advance the Zionist cause.[5]

Meanwhile the United States, claiming neutrality, was perceived by both sides as the prize that might determine the war's outcome. Both camps calculated that they might gain an edge by exploiting the influence of America's Jews. A mid-nineteenth-century wave of Jewish immigrants from Germany to America retained a positive memory of their homeland. In contrast, later waves of Russian Jews hated the czar. As the war began, many American Jews believed they could best serve the interests of both their adopted homeland and Europe's Jews by promoting a victory of the Central Powers.

Britain, heavily dependent on America to sustain its war effort, worked hard to overcome this German edge. Weizmann's vision of a Zionist alliance with Britain was emerging gradually, but the British cabinet was far from ready to embrace the Zionist cause. To court world Jewry, Britain sent missions to Russia to urge the czar to soften his anti-Semitic practices, while Germans pressed their ally the sultan to lighten the burdens on the *yishuv*. Neither side had much success. In Britain's case, it was clear that as long as the czar was a member of their camp, the British would face a major obstacle to any rapprochement with Jews everywhere.

Within Britain, the community of assimilated Jews was not insensitive to this dilemma. It felt a duty to support the government in courting the Jews, notwithstanding the czar's practices, but it regarded Weizmann's Zionism as contrary to its own interests. Herbert Samuel, an upper-class Jew welcomed in ruling circles, was an exception. He proposed the cabinet pledge a postwar state to the Jews in Palestine, which would become an imperial outpost. He rooted his argument in Palmerston's nineteenth-century attempt to declare a British protectorate over the Middle East's Jews. Samuel's proposal elicited no official response, but it endeared him to Weizmann, who was later instrumental in his appointment as the first high commissioner in Britain's Palestine Mandate.

Still, Weizmann's influence was feeble compared to that of Britain's assimilated Jews. Their voice was the Conjoint Foreign Committee, known familiarly as the Conjoint, which the Jewish Board of Deputies founded in 1878 to lobby in behalf of Russia's Jews. Its members were shaped by

Emancipation, which in Britain was far more successful than it was any-where on the Continent. The Conjoint scorned "the wider Zionist theory which regards all Jewish communities as constituting one homeless na-tionality. . . . [Zionism] must have the effect . . . of stamping the Jews as strangers in their native lands." Considering Jewish life incompatible with Christian society, said the Conjoint, echoes anti-Semitism.[6]

At the start of the war, the Conjoint was impaled on the Russian stake. If it failed to protest Russia's treatment of the Jews, it would be irrelevant; if it protested too hard, it could be called unpatriotic. The course it chose was to adopt a platform that called on the cabinet to promise the Jews the right of immigration and self-rule in Palestine after the war, along with a free university and recognition of Hebrew as the official language. Such a policy, it declared, would sweep the whole of American Jewry into Brit-ain's arms. The policy looked much like Zionism's Basel Program, but, the Conjoint explained, it was in fact a patriotic adaptation of its historic con-cern for Russian Jewry.[7] When the foreign office replied that it could not issue an obvious rebuke to Russia, the Conjoint came back with a pro-posal for a British pledge that if it held Palestine at the end of the war, it "will not fail to take account of the historic interest that country possesses for the Jewish community." The wording, in rooting the Jewish claim to Palestine in history, went beyond anything Zionism itself had declared. Though the Conjoint's effort languished, the formula did not die, and re-emerged in the deliberations of 1917 over the Balfour Declaration.

Still, Weizmann refused to make common cause with the Conjoint. He repeated an old Zionist axiom, declaring, "The efforts of the emanci-pated Jew to assimilate himself to his surroundings deceive nobody but himself. . . . His position . . . is even more tragic than that of his op-pressed brother in East Europe."[8] The Conjoint must, he declared, "be made to realize that *we* and not *they* are the masters of the situation. We have a program. . . . They stand alone." His words simply widened the breach between Zionism and the strongest segment of Britain's Jewish community.

By early 1915, Britain recognized that victory against the Turks would be harder than it had anticipated. Turkish units had crossed the Sinai to at-tack the Suez Canal, and though they were repulsed, they required Britain to keep a substantial force in Egypt for the defense of the canal. In April,

Britain gambled on taking Turkey out of the war by landing a major force at Gallipoli, with the objective of advancing to Constantinople. Instead, its forces left its Turkish beachhead badly battered, and in the next year Turkish troops attacked Suez twice more.

By then, Britain's Middle East relations with its European allies were in some disarray. Russia gave notice of its plan to annex much of European Turkey as a prize of war, while the French made clear their intent to take over Greater Syria, which included Palestine. These appetites inspired the foreign office to think again about Zionist aims. Palestine was geographically positioned to serve as a buffer on the flank of the Suez Canal, a barrier not just to present Turkish and German forces but, potentially, to the future ambitions of Russia and France.

The Turks' fighting spirit at Gallipoli persuaded Britain that recruiting Arab help could strengthen its battlefield position. In secret negotiations starting in mid-1915, Britain exchanged letters, known as the McMahon–Hussein Correspondence, with Sharif Hussein, the Hashemite ruler of Hejaz, an autonomous province in western Arabia. Sharif Hussein offered to lead an uprising against the Turks in return for his being recognized after Britain's victory as the head of a sovereign Arab nation in the Ottomans' Arab provinces. Britain agreed, but at the same time, it was secretly dealing with France and Russia to produce the Sykes-Picot Agreement, which, contrary to the pledges to the sharif, divided the Ottoman Empire's Arab provinces among the three of them.

The sharif delivered on his commitment in 1916, igniting the Arab Revolt. Under the command of Prince Faisal, the sharif's third son, the Arabs fought honorably against the Turks. In the early stages of the revolt, they harassed Turkish units in Arabia, using guerrilla tactics; in the final stages, they played a key role in the offensive that took Damascus and drove the Turks from the Middle East. In the interval, Faisal captured the Port of Aqaba, which enabled the British army to bypass the Sinai Desert to invade Palestine and occupy Jerusalem.

Meanwhile, in the war in the West, Germany squandered its advantage in the competition for America's favor. Its naval action in the Atlantic, notably its U boats charged with severing Britain's supply lines, alienated the American public. When the liner *Lusitania* was torpedoed in 1915 with the loss of 1,200 lives, President Woodrow Wilson brought America to the edge of war. The threat persuaded Germany to follow a more prudent naval policy, but in January 1917, it shifted course again, announcing "unrestricted submarine warfare." In April, at Wilson's request, the U.S. Congress declared war on Germany.

Germany suffered a second major blow in its quest for America's favor in March 1917, when the czar's regime was overthrown in an uprising of moderate democrats. The provisional government that was set up decided to fight on against Germany, and to appeal to Jews both at home and abroad, it wiped out many of the anti-Semitic provisions in Russia's law codes. But in November, the more radical Bolsheviks, calling for withdrawal from the war, brought down the provisional government. To persuade Russia to stay in the fight, the Allies concluded that the Jews' role was more crucial than ever. In this context, the deliberations in Britain over the Balfour Declaration took on a more serious character.

Weizmann had by then made a major scientific discovery in acetone, a vital component in munitions, and relocated from Manchester to London, the hub of Britain's wartime research, to preside over the transition of his discovery to large-scale production. Years later, David Lloyd George, Britain's wartime prime minister, asserted in a memoir that the Balfour Declaration was Weizmann's reward for his service to Britain's victory; most historians regard the claim as overblown. But Weizmann's scientific renown, if it did not itself give birth to the Balfour Declaration, did enlarge his access to Britain's ruling circles, where he deftly exercised his influence on Zionism's behalf.

Even with his wartime laurels, Weizmann was an unlikely candidate to win British hearts. With his thick Eastern European accent, his self-presentation was that of a Jew of very foreign origin. To be sure, he easily captivated the Jews of East London's immigrant community, who were impressed by his absence of pretense to being an Englishman. But his target audience was now a ruling class of politicians, journalists, academics, and socialites. They were captivated, it turned out, by Weizmann's command of politics, the Bible, and history, and transported by his rational mind. They also resonated to the appeal of his Old World style. Making adroit use of those qualities, Weizmann charmed much of the British elite into embracing the Zionist cause.

Weizmann, it should be emphasized, did not introduce the British to Zionism. The historian Barbara Tuchman, in *Bible and Sword,* presents the case that Protestant reformers who led England's breakaway from the Catholic Church in the Middle Ages substituted the Old Testament for the Papacy as the source of divine authority. Through it, England internalized

God's promise to deliver Palestine to the Jews. The promise, embedded in the British spirit, had inspired Palmerston to propose an English protectorate over Palestine's Jews seventy-five years earlier. In the context of the World War, Britain was ready to renew the promise. Weizmann's triumph was to persuade Britain that its embrace not just of Jews but of Zionism would help the British win the war.

Weizmann, as noted earlier, had met Lord Arthur Balfour in 1906, when he was running in Manchester to retain his parliamentary seat. Earlier, as prime minister, Balfour had denounced Russia's pogroms as "a disgrace to Christendom" and been instrumental in extending to Herzl Britain's offer of the Uganda territory.

In 1916, Balfour returned to the cabinet as foreign secretary, bringing with him his Old Testament conception of the Jews. He took office under David Lloyd George, who, as prime minister, held much the same view. Balfour's biographer, who was also his niece, writes, "I remember in childhood imbibing from him the idea that the Christian religion and civilization owed to Judaism an immeasurable debt, shamefully ill repaid." In Parliament, Balfour stated that Britain's sponsorship of the Jews' return to their homeland is "the ideal which chiefly moves me . . . proving that Christendom is not oblivious to its faith."[9]

Balfour, it should also be noted, held the conventional evangelical view that the Jews, on returning to Palestine, would accept Jesus as their savior. Such a view left ample room in British culture for anti-Semitism, though probably not the vicious variety that pervaded the Continent. After the war, England's sympathetic view of the Jews would be tested against the competing objectives of British imperialism, and it would be found wanting. But while the war raged, religious commitment explains much about why England was so comfortable with Zionism, and why Weizmann was so comfortable with England.

Weizmann, soon to have his own laboratory in London, was reintroduced to Lord Balfour in December 1914, when he was invited to Balfour's home for a chat. The outcome was that both Balfour, then First Lord of the Admiralty, and Lloyd George, then minister of munitions, asked Weizmann to serve as an official adviser. Weizmann met Balfour once more at Lady Astor's dinner table, to which he was often invited, to expound on Zionism. At one of these dinners, Balfour is quoted as saying to Weizmann Zionism is "not a dream. It is a great cause, and I understand it. . . .

You may get your things done much more quickly [than you think] after the war." Weizmann was thrilled by the sentiment.

Both Lloyd George and Balfour, as Old Testament believers, had a vision for Palestine. Lloyd George once told Weizmann that Palestine's place names "were more familiar to me than those on the Western Front."[10] Balfour stated that "the Jews are the most gifted race that mankind has seen since the Greeks. . . . They have been exiled, scattered and oppressed. . . . If we can find them an asylum in their native land . . . [even] the submerged Jews of the ghettoes of Eastern Europe will find a new and powerful identity."

When Lloyd George became prime minister in 1916, with Balfour as his foreign secretary, major decisions on the war's conduct were shifted to a tightly organized war cabinet. Unhappy about the heavy battle losses in France, Lloyd George favored stepping up efforts against the Turks, setting the stage for an "Eastern strategy" that coincided with the cabinet's imperial interest. Weizmann, grasping at the new possibilities, embarked at once on strengthening his ties to Lloyd George and Balfour, who were already so well disposed to him.

By 1917, the war cabinet had reached a consensus that foreshadowed the Balfour Declaration. "Both the prime minister and myself have been influenced by a desire to give the Jews their rightful place in the world," Balfour wrote. "A great nation without a home is not right."[11]

Discussions on Palestine were heating up in March when the foreign office assigned Weizmann a strange mission. Henry Morgenthau, a former U.S. ambassador to Constantinople and a non-Zionist Jew, had embarked on a secret journey to persuade the Turks to withdraw from the war. It was unclear who was behind it, but the task was apparently tied to President Wilson's idealistic vision of a peace without territorial annexations. Morgenthau's mission, if successful, would have required Britain to scrap any plans to extend its empire into the Middle East, snuffing out the Zionist dream as well as the government's pledges to its allies under the Sykes-Picot agreement. Weizmann intercepted Morgenthau in mid-journey in Gibraltar and persuaded him in two days of talks to abandon the undertaking. The achievement made him a hero to the war cabinet, enhancing his influence just as the Balfour negotiations were reaching a critical point.

Britain's Middle East army, meanwhile, was preparing to advance northward from Egypt and Britain's press, at the cabinet's urging, was fanning popular ardor for a Jewish Palestine. With more French than British troops fighting on the Western Front, Lloyd George recognized that France held a strong hand in its plan to include Palestine in its claim to Syria. Over a dinner at the Astors', Lloyd George received from Weizmann a commitment to support the war cabinet in opposing France's Palestine design.

At Balfour's urging the foreign office asked Weizmann to solicit France's endorsement of a Jewish Palestine. Weizmann leaped at the opportunity but, unwilling to leave London during the Balfour negotiations, he assigned the mission to Nahum Sokolow, his right arm on the Zionist Executive. In Paris, Sokolow found the French sympathetic, but apprehensive at being the only Catholic power that backed such a pledge. Sokolow then proceeded to Rome, where he received approval not just from Italy but from the Vatican, which declared that, "The return of the Jews to Palestine is a miraculous event. . . . God has willed it."

On returning to Paris, Sokolow obtained a letter in which France declared it "a deed of justice and of reparation to assist, by the protection of the Allied powers, in the renaissance of the Jewish nationality in that land from which the people of Israel were exiled so many centuries ago." Weizmann was thrilled at what was the first mention by any of the Allies of a Jewish "nationality" in Palestine. On a practical level, it assured Britain's cabinet of French support for designating Palestine a Jewish homeland.[12]

Obstacles, however, remained. Sokolow had not persuaded France or Italy to forego a role in governing Palestine altogether. Russia's provisional regime withheld its endorsement of a Jewish homeland. Germany's Zionists, still faithful to neutrality, objected to Jews' making any arrangement at all with the Allied nations.

President Wilson, having taken his stand against territorial annexation, had grown more influential with the arrival of American forces on the Western Front. But when Balfour floated an offer to have America share in running Palestine, he made no headway. Meanwhile, in response to Wilson, Weizmann argued that a British protectorate was not annexation at all; it was Britain's pledge to hold Palestine in trust for the Jews. Still, talks over the Balfour Declaration languished into mid-1917.

To Weizmann, the chief obstacle to a British declaration came not from abroad but from the Conjoint, whose links to the cabinet were much closer than his own. In calling themselves "native Jews," the Conjoint implied that the Zionists were foreigners, thus of dubious loyalty. What

Weizmann failed to admit was that Zionism would have no need for a refuge at all if Europe's Jews were treated like Britain's Jews. The Conjoint spoke for Jews who regarded Zionism as irrelevant to them, and it had support from cabinet members whose thinking ran along different lines from Balfour's.

By the early summer of 1917, the cabinet—though unhappy at being caught in a dispute between Jews—was closing in on Balfour's target. As the dispute grew more public, it embarrassed even the Jewish Board of Deputies, which sought to quash it by removing the Palestine question from the Conjoint's jurisdiction. It was a victory for Weizmann, and it was followed by an invitation from Balfour to provide a draft statement on a Jewish homeland that he could submit to the cabinet for approval.

Weizmann found himself in a quandary over how far to go, recognizing that overreaching would jeopardize the entire effort. After much discussion, advisers decided not to ask for a Jewish "commonwealth," much less a "state." The best prospect, Weizmann and his circle agreed, lay in a statement of principles, unburdened by detail. The two items deemed crucial were the recognition of Palestine as the Jewish "national home" and the designation of the Zionist Organization as the authority that spoke on behalf of the Jews. Preparing the draft took a month, and three more passed before a statement emerged from the cabinet's deliberations.[13]

Balfour used the interval to build a cabinet consensus. His chief adversary, echoing the Conjoint, was Lord Edwin Montagu, a Jew with a distinguished history in government service. In a memo titled "The Anti-Semitism of the Present Government," Montagu warned the cabinet of being "misled by a foreigner," who insists "the country for which I have worked ever since I left the university—England, the country for which my family have fought"—is not my home, that my national home is Palestine. He called the declaration "an irreparable blow to Jewish Britons . . . [in] endeavoring to set up a people which does not exist."

Weizmann called Montagu "the champion . . . of the dark forces in English Jewry." Montagu carried enough weight, however, to force Balfour to seek an advisory opinion from Washington.

In a letter to Wilson, Balfour solicited America's reaction to an official "declaration of sympathy with the Zionist movement." Not only did Balfour face Wilson's hostility to territorial annexation; it was no less significant that the U.S., though at war with Germany, was not at war with Turkey. Wilson's reply was equivocal, keeping alive the cabinet's indecision. When

Weizmann learned of Wilson's letter, he mobilized influential American Jews to use their energies to turn the president around.[14]

Balfour also alerted the State Department, which was leaning on Jews everywhere to help keep Russia from withdrawing from the war. Balfour insisted, a bit disingenuously, that Germany was working hard "to capture the Zionist movement." The White House staff, meanwhile, was warning Wilson against being used to create an imperial bastion in Palestine. Wilson, in addition, had to take account of Weizmann's American friends, and, with the war's outcome still undecided, he was loath to disregard Britain's objectives. In a second letter, Wilson informed London that he was withdrawing his reservations to Balfour's declaration.

Missing from these deliberations was any input from the Arabs. None were invited to make their case to the cabinet, though Sharif Hussein's forces were now fighting alongside the British army in Palestine. One cabinet member pointed out that Britain could not dismiss five-sixths of the Palestine's population, but he did not press his case. Britain's military command in the Middle East took a sterner view. Its political chief in Cairo—foreshadowing later differences with London—cabled that "it will not help matters if the Arabs . . . are given yet another bone of contention in the shape of Zionism in Palestine as against the interests of the Moslems resident there." But the army's admonition elicited no reaction.

Not surprisingly, Weizmann was pleased at the cabinet's snubbing of the Arabs. Though he clearly foresaw an Arab problem, he considered the Conjoint Jews a greater concern. In the end, reference to "existing non-Jewish communities" crept into the Balfour Declaration. It was an odd expression, the source of which is uncertain. Some believe it was inserted at the request of France and Italy, not to protect Arab Muslims but Arab Christians. The term, however, made no distinction and, once the Balfour Declaration was issued, it was deemed to apply to all of Palestine's Arabs.[15]

Dated November 2, 1917, the Balfour Declaration was made public a week later. Weizmann had hoped to have it published on Rosh Hashanah, the Jewish New Year. He wanted it, he said, to touch the "minds and hearts . . . of Jews all over the world [who] congregate in great masses in the synagogue." But it was not ready in time and, interestingly, the foreign office, commenting on the enthusiasm the Declaration evoked among Jews worldwide, lamented that the delay may have cost the Allies the opportunity to keep Bolshevik Russia from leaving the war. In retrospect, the surmise seems far-fetched.

The Balfour Declaration took the form of a letter addressed not to Weizmann, much less to the World Zionist Organization, which was still dominated by Germans at the headquarters in Berlin. Instead, it was sent to Lord Rothschild, scion of the British branch of the famous family and the honorary president of Britain's Zionist Federation, as well as vice president of the Jewish Board of Deputies. Weizmann, though recently elected president of Britain's Zionist Federation and the major force behind the declaration, was overlooked. No doubt the cabinet felt more comfortable addressing the letter to a "native Jew," who was more acceptable to Britons generally, and certainly to England's Jewish elite, than was a Russian-born, foreign-educated research scientist.

The letter began: "Dear Lord Rothschild, I have much pleasure in conveying to you, on behalf of His Majesty's government, the following declaration of sympathy with Jewish Zionist aspirations which has been submitted to, and approved by, the cabinet." Its self-characterization as a "declaration of sympathy" would later be described by opponents as lacking in legal authority.

The substance of the declaration, in a single convoluted sentence, read: "His Majesty's Government view with favor the establishment in Palestine of a national home for the Jewish people, and will use their best endeavors to facilitate the achievement of this object, it being clearly understood that nothing shall be done which may prejudice the civil and religious rights of existing non-Jewish communities in Palestine, or the rights and political status enjoyed by Jews in any other country."

The declaration thus recognized the interests of three very different communities: the Zionists, the Palestinian Arabs, and the "native" British Jews.

The letter ended: "I should be grateful if you would bring this declaration to the knowledge of the Zionist Federation." It was signed in pen, barely legibly, "Arthur James Balfour."

Balfour's letter was not just a "declaration of sympathy" with the Zionism cause, however; it was an official statement of policy directed at three constituencies whose conflicting concerns were of interest to the cabinet.

The language was cautious. Its imprecision was no doubt deliberate. The text was clearly a compromise, drafted not by a single hand with a clear objective but by an assemblage keeping an eye on diverse political constituencies, the future of the empire, and winning the war. It began as Balfour's brainchild and emerged as a well-meaning, rather strained consensus designed to reconcile the concerns of a wide-ranging audience.

In endorsing a "national home for the Jewish people," the Balfour Declaration was a triumph for Zionism. Not even the Basel Program of 1897, which talked of a Jewish "home," contained the word "national" to describe it. The document was not quite the charter that Herzl had worked so hard to obtain; the British, after all, did not at this point even control Palestine. Only later would the Balfour Declaration acquire international standing through inclusion in a formal treaty of peace. But it vindicated Herzl, as it did Weizmann, by formally recognizing the Jews as a people who possessed a right to inhabit Palestine as their homeland.

To be sure, the text contained elements that left the Zionists uneasy. In his memoir, Weizmann refers to them as an "ambiguity of phrasing," for which he held the Conjoint to blame. But he could not dismiss the significance of the editing done by the cabinet. The initial draft submitted by Weizmann pledged Britain to using its "best endeavors to *secure*" the national home and to consult on "the necessary methods and means with the Zionist Organization." The final text promised Britain's "best endeavors to *facilitate* the achievement" of the national home, and said nothing at all about the role of the Zionist Organization.

Weizmann's original draft, moreover, articulated "the principle that Palestine should be reconstituted as the national home of the Jewish people," using the prefix "re" to assert the Jews' historic right to the territory. The final version made no allusion to a historic right and changed "Palestine" to "*in* Palestine," which left open the option of the land being shared by two peoples.

The final declaration was, actually, closer to Herzl's Basel Program— "Zionism strives to create for the Jewish people a home *in* Palestine"—than to the preliminary draft. Weizmann wrote in his memoir that the cabinet, in omitting the *re*—as in "*re*establish" or "*re*constitute"—also declined to acknowledge a link between present-day Jews and their biblical forebears. The final version clearly reflected a weaker British commitment to a Jewish presence than Weizmann, and Balfour, had envisaged.

Weizmann complained in his memoir that the Balfour Declaration's

guarantees to the Palestinian Arabs and the Conjoint Jews were a gratu-
itous reproach, imputing to the Zionist movement intentions it had never
had. Nonetheless, later events proved the apprehensions justified, at least
in regard to the Arabs. Weizmann is silent on why such safeguards were
not presented to the cabinet in the earlier Zionist draft.

Predictably, the Balfour Declaration contained no reference to a Jewish *state*. Most of its British supporters saw the declaration as an instrument for winning the war by rallying foreign Jews to the Allied cause. Few
Britons intended it as the prelude to statehood. Balfour and Lloyd George
were aware, of course, that a sovereign state was Zionism's aim, despite its
more modest claims. But even after the declaration was issued, the Zionists, to avoid controversy, routinely denied statehood ambitions.

Weizmann was less than candid in lending himself to this denial.
While acknowledging the aim of attaining a Jewish *majority* in Palestine,
he did not admit that the inevitable consequence of a majority was Jewish
sovereignty. He was probably sincere in stating that Zionism would work
to improve the Arabs' economic conditions; Arab prosperity, after all, was,
to the mutual advantage of both communities. But he revealed no concern
about how in the Zionists' society the Arabs might fit.[16]

Whatever his disappointment, however, Weizmann sent Balfour an ef-
fusive note of thanks. "Since Cyrus the Great," he wrote, invoking Persia's
liberator of the Jews in ancient times, "there was never, in all the records . . .
a manifestation inspired by a higher sense of political wisdom, foresighted
statesmanship, and national justice toward the Jewish people." In a note to
Lord Rothschild, he described the declaration as "the Magna Carta of Jewish liberties." Even with its shortcomings, it promised the Jews more control over their destiny than they had enjoyed since the biblical era, which
justified Weizmann's calling it "epoch-making."

Weizmann admitted his true feelings about statehood in a Zionist
meeting after the declaration was published. "We all agree," he said, on
"the final aim, and from now on it is simply a question of tactics as to how
to achieve it. We need an evolutionary tactic. . . . The declaration affords
us the opportunity to become the masters of Palestine. As long as we
do not have people and money, we cannot demand more than that. . . .
There is a British proverb about the camel and the tent: At first the camel
sticks in one leg and eventually it occupies the whole tent. This must be
our policy."

Though in Weizmann's mind there may have been room for Arabs somewhere inside the tent, it was nonetheless to be a *Jewish* tent. While many British—and even a few Jews—were by now becoming more sensitive to the problem of the Arabs' place in a Zionist society, Weizmann shrugged it off. He did not wish to offend the Arabs, or their national feelings, but in his mind the challenge of reaching an accommodation with them took a backseat—far back—to the goal of assuring Jewish rule.

☰

Weizmann's gamble in the early days of the war in placing all of Zionism's chips on a British victory was vindicated a few weeks after the Balfour Declaration, when British forces under General Edmund Allenby captured Jerusalem. The *yishuv,* having suffered severely during the final months under the Turks, was now out of danger. The Zionist Organization was still officially neutral, and Weizmann himself held no high Zionist office. But such was his triumph that no rival could challenge Zionism's ties with Britain, or his own preeminence among the Jews.

Weizmann wasted no time in seeking to assert Zionist authority in Palestine. His first move was to propose to Britain's cabinet that he lead a delegation to Jerusalem, to get started in carrying out a transfer of power. With Balfour's approval, he sat over the next weeks with officials from the foreign office and military intelligence to lay out the delegation's agenda.

Named the Zionist Commission, the delegation was to serve as liaison between Allenby and the *yishuv* to create an administration to govern the country.[17] The commission remained a force, in various incarnations and under different names, until the founding of the Jewish state in 1948. Its initial instructions from the British cabinet specified that establishing friendly relations between Jews and Arabs was a priority. Significantly, Weizmann omitted this item in his own written summary of the commission's responsibilities.

Weizmann himself reached Jerusalem in April 1918, while fighting was still going on, and he perceived at once that the British army was less sympathetic than the British cabinet to Zionist aspirations. British officers, many of them veterans of service in India, were more at ease with Arabs than Jews. An Arab bureaucracy, a vestige of Turkish rule—"just as corrupt and cunning," Weizmann wrote—kept everyday decisions in unfriendly hands. Weizmann's request to Allenby to shift authority to the Jews received no response.

Allenby's chief concern was the Turkish force that was dug in north of the city. "We still hear the thunder of guns," Weizmann wrote to Vera. Focused on keeping order behind the battle lines, Allenby urged Weizmann to convey assurances to the Arabs that Jewish designs would do them no harm. Weizmann was less than enthusiastic about the assignment.

Implementing the Balfour Declaration, Weizmann quickly realized, would be harder than he had foreseen when he was in London. Acquiring land to meet the needs of Jewish immigrants was a high priority, but it was also the Arabs' greatest worry. Even when Arab landowners were willing to sell, Weizmann found Allenby a stickler for international conventions that forbid occupiers to take over conquered territory. Weizmann appealed Allenby's order to London, but the foreign office supported Britain's commander.

To Weizmann's surprise, even the Jewish settlers were wary. "On the one hand," he wrote, "we were hailed as precursors of the Messiah; on the other, we were mistrusted as the vanguard of a set of capitalist exploiters." The *yishuv*'s suspicions were a forewarning of the rivalry that would emerge between Zionism's offices in London and Jerusalem. Weizmann already had trouble with the *yishuv*'s Orthodox Jews who, having been cut off from their sources of funds during the war, lived in grinding poverty. Awaiting the Messiah, they found no reason to embrace this stranger from London, much less to look with favor on a Holy Land run by Zionists.

As for the Arabs, Weizmann tried extending a smattering of goodwill to them. At Allenby's behest, he paid courtesy calls on their notables, in which he talked of the two communities working harmoniously to develop the country. He promised not to intrude on Arab property rights or holy places. At a dinner given by the grand mufti, Weizmann said, "There is land enough in Palestine . . . to sustain a population many times larger than the present one, and all the fears expressed openly and secretly by the Arabs, that they are to be ousted from their present position, are due . . . to a fundamental misconception of our aims and intentions." Jewish immigration, he declared, would benefit both peoples. Deliberately or not, he was misrepresenting the truth, and if he was not aware of it, the Arabs surely were.

But, even if Weizmann believed what he said, he failed to understand the animosities aroused by a half-century of Arab experience with Jewish settlers. Zionism promoted *Jewish* interests, not theirs. When Jews bought land from the local gentry, a few landowners grew rich, while the peasants lost their livelihood and their homes. Allenby praised Weizmann for his efforts at reassuring the Arabs, but the Arabs themselves remained unconvinced that the Jews had any benefits to offer them.

Weizmann simply refused to consider the legitimacy of Arab grievances. As for Arab nationalism, he was unaware that it had grown fiercer as the Turks retreated and as President Wilson's pledges of freedom spread among them. He chose not to understand—as did generations of Zionists, before and after—that the rift between Jews and Arabs had deep *political* roots. Weizmann concluded from his meetings that no prospect existed for a trusting relationship with the local Arabs, which he blamed entirely on them.

In a letter to Balfour from Jerusalem, Weizmann complained that the Arabs he met were "clever and quick-witted . . . but treacherous by nature." In a report to British army intelligence he called them "a demoralized race with whom it was impossible to treat."[18] In his memoir, Weizmann compares talks with Arabs to "chasing a mirage in the desert: full of promise and good to look at but likely to lead you to death by thirst."

✡

In giving up on the Palestinian Arabs, Weizmann shifted to another track, which, after much effort, produced an incongruous and ultimately futile Arab bond. He chose to court Sharif Hussein's son, Prince Faisal, commander of Arab forces in the revolt against the Turks. Inseparable from Faisal was his mentor, the British army officer T. E. Lawrence, widely known for his military exploits as "Lawrence of Arabia."

"I am just setting out on a visit to the son of the King of the Hejaz," Weizmann wrote to Balfour. "I propose to tell him that if he wants to build up a strong and prosperous Arab kingdom, it is we Jews who will be able to help him, and we only. . . . With him I hope to be able to establish a real political entente. But with the Arabs of Palestine—in whom, so far as I can gather, the sharif is little interested—only proper economic relations are necessary, and these will develop in the natural course of things."

Weizmann asserted in this letter to Balfour that Hejaz, the remote segment of Arabia ruled by the sharif, was the real "Arab center of gravity," though he conceded that he was not sure where Hejaz was. He was correct, however, in stating that the sharif had little interest in Palestine's Arabs. Palestinians and Hejazis were largely strangers to one another. Palestinian culture, influenced by Europe and based on agriculture and village life, had little in common with the practices of Hejaz's desert nomads. But Weizmann's claim that "proper economic relations" would ultimately overcome the Palestinians' animosity to their Jewish neighbors proved to be profoundly misguided.

Sharif Hussein, Prince Faisal's father, had once declared his support of a homeland in Palestine for the Jews, but the words did not translate into sympathy for Zionism. The sharif was willing to imagine a Jewish province within the Arab nation that he believed Britain had pledged to him. Only when he got wind of the Sykes–Picot Agreement did he realize that Britain was reneging. Since he, Britain, and the Zionists all opposed French designs in the region, he reasoned that an alliance with the Jews might persuade Britain to deliver on its pledge. With this formulation in mind, Weizmann decided to pay a visit to Prince Faisal and his adviser Lawrence, whose duties had shifted from the military to the political realm.

The rigors of the journey, described by Weizmann, were a measure of the gap between two worlds. Weizmann rode a train from Jerusalem to Suez, where he boarded a "small, grimy, neglected" boat. He was aboard for six days, during which "the heat was unbearable; food, clothes, sheets, everything we touched was covered, permeated with dust." On reaching Aqaba, he set off by car with a British officer and an Arab guide for Faisal's military camp in the Jordanian desert. When the car gave out, he continued on foot and by camel across the inhospitable terrain, "a burning fiery furnace." After a stop at a British air base, he reembarked in a second car, which also broke down. A third finally delivered him to the Arab camp, where Faisal greeted him with cool water and fruit. The voyage had taken ten full days.[19]

Still, Weizmann was dazzled by Faisal, who reassured him of his readiness to cooperate with the Jews in Palestine in thwarting the French. It was the statement Weizmann wanted to hear. Faisal, he wrote to Vera, "is the first real Arab nationalist I have met," which he meant positively. "He is a real leader. He's quite intelligent and a very honest man, handsome as a picture! He is not interested in Palestine but wants . . . the whole of Syria. He talked with great animosity against the French. He expects a great deal from collaboration with the Jews! He is contemptuous of the Palestinian Arabs, whom he doesn't even regard as Arabs."

But when the talk turned specifically to what the Zionists might expect in return, Weizmann ran into an obstacle. Faisal, in the company of Lawrence, said that though he and his father recognized the Jews' claims to

Palestine, any public declaration of support would expose the family to danger from nationalist fanatics. It was public knowledge that Sharif Hussein was not a popular leader, and even during the revolt, few Arabs accepted his authority. Without receiving any pledge from Faisal, Weizmann retraced his steps back to Jerusalem, describing the visit in his memoir as a success, though in fact he had achieved only a conditional offer of tolerance of the Zionist cause.

The high point of Weizmann's visit to Palestine in 1918 was no doubt the laying of the cornerstone of the Hebrew University on the tract in Jerusalem that Zionism had acquired four years earlier. Allenby attended the ceremony, along with Christian and Muslim dignitaries. Ahad Ha'am, Weizmann's mentor, sent a message calling the university the "spiritual foundation of our national home, . . . not a mere imitation of a European university . . . but a university which will become the true embodiment of the Hebrew spirit of old, shaking off the mental and moral servitude to which our people have been so long subjected." A monument to Ahad Ha'am's vision, the university symbolized the triumph of secular Jewish culture in the new society. Getting the university built was Weizmann's achievement.[20]

Allenby's forces resumed their attack on the Turks, in September 1918, determined to force them out of the war. In his memoir, Weizmann maintains he could do nothing constructive in Palestine until the fighting was over and, leaving a team of technicians behind, returned to London. By November, both Turkey and Germany had surrendered, opening a new stage in the campaign to realize Zionism's objective.

A few months later the victorious Allies convened a peace conference in Paris. Weizmann, though still without an official position, was invited by the British to head a Zionist delegation. Faisal, whose final service to the Allies was to lead his army into Damascus at Allenby's side, was his Arab counterpart. The two were enough at ease with each other for Faisal to request a Jewish loan to repair Syria's war damage. In turning him down, Weizmann claimed that such a loan would convey the impression that Faisal was beholden to Zionism. By now the Arabs were squabbling with one another over control of their liberated lands, and Weizmann's assessment on the loan was probably correct.

Weizmann proposed that he and Faisal draw up a common platform to present to the peace conference. Since the Weizmann-Faisal meeting in the desert, the French had intensified their pressure on Britain to evacuate its forces from Syria and turn the country over to them. Faisal countered by demanding that Britain scrap the Sykes–Picot Agreement altogether and grant his family's claim to Syria. Sharif Hussein's right to Syria superseded France's, he insisted, and his case was strengthened by his own election as king of Syria by the makeshift Arab Congress then sitting in Damascus. Weizmann agreed to back Faisal, envisaging Arab support of the Zionist claim to Palestine.

Meeting in London prior to the Paris Conference, the two signed the Weizmann–Faisal Agreement, promising the "closest possible collaboration . . . in the development of the Arab state and [Jewish] Palestine." Weizmann pledged the Zionist Organization's help in establishing an Arab Syria; Faisal pledged to support the Balfour Declaration, including Jewish immigration. He also elicited a vow from Weizmann to protect "Arab peasants and tenant farmers and Muslim custody of the Muslim holy places." It was an accord, Faisal said, "between the two branches of the Semitic family." Weizmann even reversed his earlier refusal and promised Jewish funds to rebuild Faisal's Syria.[21]

The Weizmann–Faisal Agreement gave each side the recognition it sought from the other. But Faisal, at the urging of Lawrence, appended a proviso canceling the entire accord if the peace conference rejected Syria's independence as an Arab state. Faisal's adversaries by now were not just Britain and France however. They were also the Palestinian Arabs, who rejected any concessions by Faisal to Zionism. They were also the radicals sitting in the Damascus congress, who insisted that Palestine was part of Syria and not Faisal's to give to the Jews. With Faisal increasingly isolated from his own people, Weizmann's hopes of a bargain with the Arabs— probably unrealistic from the start—simply evaporated.[22]

By the time the Paris Conference convened, Weizmann's Arab problems were still more tangled. The Arabs of Palestine forcefully demanded that the Balfour Declaration be rescinded. Balfour himself, no longer able to justify his courtship of the Jews as a war measure, witnessed British public opinion move away from Zionism. He also watched hostility toward Zionism grow within Allenby's command. Balfour himself urged Weizmann to proceed cautiously, while unofficial Zionist delegations to the peace conference from America and the *yishuv* squeezed him from the other side, demanding immediate Jewish control of all Palestine.

Meanwhile, as the peace conference approached, Weizmann's hold on the Zionist movement waned. It was not that Zionists failed to appreciate his achievements. They elected him to the Zionist Executive, then to the presidency of the World Zionist Congress, offices to which he had long aspired. But the Zionist Organization had made changes in its distribution of power—splitting the Executive to give greater influence to Jerusalem—in recognition of the importance the Balfour Declaration gave to the *yishuv*. In dismay, Weizmann watched the power of the London office drain away, the inevitable consequence of his own success as the architect of the Balfour structure.[23]

Weizmann drafted a set of demands for the Zionists to present at the Paris talks, taking pains as usual to avoid pressing Britain for more than he thought it would grant. His Zionist rivals, in contrast, urged him to intensify pressure on Britain. The American delegates found his list of demands "too meager . . . as a safeguard against imperialistic domination," while the *yishuv* insisted on powers that Britain intended to keep for its colonial administrators. Together, the Americans and the *yishuv* insisted that "the *whole* of Palestine" be readied for Zionist statehood. In the face of this growing pressure, Weizmann threatened to resign as the official delegation's head.

To avoid a schism, a committee was named to start over in drafting a Zionist position. Weizmann found the provisions it came up with even more disturbing, calling for a Jewish governor of Palestine and a guaranteed Jewish dominance of legislative and executive bodies. Balfour, after consulting with Lloyd George, wrote to Weizmann, "I know how the pressure of constituents urges a political leader . . . to say what is popular. [But] the time to talk of Jewish political predominance in Palestine or of a Jewish state or commonwealth is not yet." Weizmann then took it on himself to prepare a more modest program that, over objections, was adopted by the delegates as a working paper, which Britain's diplomatic team accepted.[24]

Weizmann's chief objective for the the peace treaty was to transform the Balfour Declaration from an expression of intent to a legal obligation. To achieve it, he shuttled tirelessly between London and Paris, and even to Palestine. He met with countless political figures, including President Wilson. On February 27, 1919, he testified on Zionism's behalf before the Council of Ten, the body of high Allied officials to whom the Peace Conference had assigned the task of drafting the treaty.

In his testimony, Weizmann said nothing about a Jewish state but offered the well-remembered vow that the Jewish *nation* in Palestine would be "as Jewish as the French nation is French and the British nation British." Otherwise, his presentation was overblown. He claimed to represent 96 percent of the world's Jews, a clear exaggeration, and asserted that Palestine could absorb five million Jews *without harm to the Arabs*. Zionism, he said, was ready to send 70,000 to 80,000 Jews to Palestine annually, to live "under a Mandatory Power, an administration not necessarily Jewish." Pleased with himself, Weizmann described his presentation to Vera as "marvelous, the most triumphant of my life."

But, meanwhile, the cabinet in London was receiving ominous warnings from Palestine of rising Arab discontent. Officials accompanied their warnings with advice to retreat from the promises of the Balfour Declaration. Balfour's own answer to them was that his declaration was fixed policy, to which the Arabs, as well as the British people, would be wise to adjust.

Yet Balfour understood the problem—as Weizmann did not—of reconciling Britain's policy on Zionism with the pledges made to the Arabs. He also recognized the need to accommodate the declaration to the self-determination that Wilson promised. Of the conflicting claims before him, Zionism was the closest to Balfour's heart. It inspired him to articulate a theory that Zionist preeminence was "rooted in age-long tradition, in present needs, in future hopes, of far profounder import than the desires and prejudices of 700,000 Arabs." Britain, he said, must wait for Jewish migration to catch up in numbers with the Arab population before administering the test of self-determination. But, in the meantime, the British government had no choice, he said, but to do "the next best thing" by offering to the Arabs concessions that the Zionists understandably disliked.[25]

Resolving the Arab-Jewish problem—in fact, dealing with the Middle East as a whole—took much more time at the Paris conference than the negotiators had anticipated. A treaty covering continental Europe, where the victors generally saw eye-to-eye, proved relatively easy. The Middle East, in contrast, ignited not just local animosities but rival imperial ambitions. In the context of less familiarity with the geography, and of societies bearing little similarity to their own, the peace negotiators encountered many more obstacles than they had initially foreseen.

That the Americans lost interest in peace-making made matters worse. Having never declared war on Turkey, the U.S. felt detached from the former Ottoman territories and declined the responsibilities that Britain hoped it would assume. Then Turkish forces under Mustafa Kemal—soon to be known as Atatürk—rose up against the Allied occupation of Turkey and what remained of the sultan's vestigial rule, winning battles that created more disarray. Balfour himself surrendered his post as foreign secretary to Lord Curzon, a man who, in Weizmann's words, "takes the very short view of our question." Under Curzon, Britain began to reconsider the objectives of the Balfour Declaration, further delaying decisions.

After a few months of recess, the Middle East negotiators reassembled in San Remo in Italy. There they finished their work, giving Zionism a major victory, inflicting on the Arabs a severe defeat. Over Arab objections, Britain agreed to withdraw its forces from Syria, which was awarded to France. In return, France waived all claims to Palestine, opening the way for Britain to assume the Palestine Mandate. The final text of the treaty incorporated the terms of the Balfour Declaration and extended the Palestine Mandate across the Jordan River as far as the Iraqi border. The negotiators awarded Britain a mandate over Iraq, as well. In August 1920, the Middle East peace treaty—bearing a strong resemblance to Sykes-Picot—was signed in Sèvres, France.

The Treaty of Sèvres gave the Zionists just about everything Weizmann had asked: a British Mandate and a legal affirmation of the Balfour Declaration. The Palestine Mandate, moreover, was unique. While the Arabs of Syria and Iraq were promised ultimate independence, the Arabs of Palestine received nothing comparable. There was to be no Arab state, such as was envisaged in the McMahon Hussein Correspondence of 1915. In the eyes of Faisal and the Arabs, the British had betrayed the Hashemite family and the Arab people.

Lord Curzon summed up the duties of Britain and France under the Mandatory system: "Each country has left the other with a free hand to proceed with those mandates."[26] France promptly drove Faisal, already weakened, from the Syrian throne, and Britain, in a partial payoff to Sharif Hussein, made Faisal the king of Iraq. Acknowledging the lack of clarity of the Balfour Declaration, Britain also agreed to deposit with the League of Nations a supplemental document setting forth the Mandate's obligations. The task was not easy. Arab resistance to the Balfour Declaration was unyielding. As for the Jews in Palestine, they had by now become deeply suspicious of Britain's long-term designs.

Violence between Arabs and Jews disrupted the Mandate as soon as the Treaty of Sèvres was announced. Arabs attacked Jewish settlements in the north, and the British chose not to respond, leaving the defense to the settlers. In a battle over the village of Tel-Hai, five Jews and five Arabs were killed, among them Joseph Trumpeldor—about whom more is written in the next chapter. A decorated veteran of the Russo-Japanese War, Trumpeldor had fought heroically for the British at Gallipoli. At Tel-Hai, he became a Zionist legend.

A few weeks after Tel-Hai, on a Muslim feast day called Nebi Musa, thousands of Arabs jammed the narrow streets of Jerusalem's Old City shouting, "Independence, independence." The mobs, whether preplanned or not, then attacked Jews, mostly the pious Jews of the old *yishuv*, with whom they had hitherto lived in peace. Besides widespread beating and looting, five Jews and three Arabs were killed. Subsequent riots that began in the port town of Jaffa spread across Palestine, raising the number of fatalities to roughly one hundred. Both sides exalted their victims as martyrs to a sacred cause, imparting legitimacy to further violence.

The response of the Mandatory authorities—"frightened," said Weizmann, "and therefore crawling to the Arabs"—was again to implore the two sides to find a modus vivendi. Trying to be constructive, Weizmann repeated his earlier offers to help build the Arab economy, but he refused to discuss political concessions. Arab leaders, convinced the Jews had no right to be in Palestine at all, rejected any talk of compromise, which they considered a retreat from their rightful claims. Britain's unwillingness to choose sides, since neither had an interest in negotiating, only encouraged the adversaries to engage in further violence.

Britain's refusal to impose restraints on the Arabs, Weizmann complained, contrasted sharply with its conduct in Iraq and Egypt, where they ruled with an iron hand. Arab aggression, he argued, was no different from Russian pogroms. He did not deny that Jews were a puzzle to British officials. "Used to handling natives," he said, they found Jews "bristling with social, political, cultural problems," the product of their history. But the Arabs, he contended, will stop only when they realize their attacks will incur severe penalties. He blamed London for failing to provide its forces in Palestine with clear guidance on suppressing disorders.

Taking the initiative, Weizmann fired off a list of grievances to Lloyd George. In reply, he says in his memoir, Britain agreed to replace the army with a civil administration under his old friend Herbert Samuel as high commissioner. Perceiving the start of a new era, he sent instructions to the Zionist Commission in Jerusalem to have the *yishuv* "observe the strictest self-control and to await in patient confidence the inauguration of the new regime." When he arrived in June, Samuel promptly announced changes that seemed to vindicate Weizmann's confidence.

But Samuel was not long at his post when Weizmann began to perceive weakness. The high commissioner was not the pro-Zionist he knew in London; Samuel saw his mission as keeping the Mandate under control. Samuel himself declared at a royal celebration that "The British government, the trustee under the Mandate for the happiness of the people of Palestine"—meaning the Arabs—"would never impose upon them a policy which they had reason to think was contrary to their religious, political and economic interests." Zionists wondered whether Samuel had been sent to Palestine as a Trojan horse.

Echoing this suspicion, Weizmann grumbled to Samuel, "Everything in Palestinian life is now revolving around one central problem—how to satisfy and to pacify the Arabs. Zionism is being gradually, systematically and relentlessly reduced. . . . We have ceased to exist as a political factor." Weizmann's friendship with Samuel was clearly unraveling, and so were Zionism's bonds with Britain.

In the months of quiet after the Nebi Musa disorders, Samuel ceded no ground to the Jews. He urged them, in fact, "not to put the Zionist flag too high, as too much flag-waving arouses resentment. . . . A great many Arabs are afraid of what they think the Zionists would do, and many influential people in England had sympathy with them." Meanwhile, both the Arab and Jewish camps were arming. Weizmann observed with exasperation that the situation was growing increasingly perilous.

Weizmann's squabbles with Samuel went beyond their everyday administrative differences, extending to the Balfour Declaration itself. In the declaration the British vowed to "use their best endeavors to facilitate the achievement" of a Jewish national home. As Weizmann saw it, Britain's policies did not, by any measure, constitute its "best endeavors."

But what *did* the Balfour Declaration mean? No one seemed sure. Lloyd George had once described it as Britain's pledge to assure the necessary conditions for the Jews to establish their homeland. Weizmann said it was meant to provide no more than an *opportunity* to the Jews to become masters of Palestine. To many observers, the Balfour Declaration was impaled on the semantic conflict between facilitating creation of the Jews' national home and the preservation of the civil and religious rights of the Arabs. Could the conflict be resolved? Did Britain owe more to the Jews than to the Arabs? Weizmann, like most Zionists, saw Samuel's policies as tilting the playing field in the Arabs' favor.

The dispute raged during the negotiations over the language of the document setting out the specifics of the Mandate that Britain had promised the League of Nations. Britain made clear it would not accept the Arabs' demand that the Balfour Declaration be rescinded, but it also acknowledged that it had no right to ignore Arab concerns. Weizmann went directly to Balfour to protest Samuel's policies, but Balfour, now retired, exercised no real power. As for the Arabs, holding the Mandate illegitimate, they boycotted all deliberations, depriving themselves of any influence over the outcome of the argument.

Britain tried to satisfy all the parties in the explanatory text of the Balfour Declaration for the League of Nations. It proved impossible to achieve. While the Arabs desisted from any role, Weizmann busily fended off Zionist societies in America that sent him grand, even ludicrous, proposals to forward to the British. He felt isolated but his tactic was, as usual, to promote only attainable goals.

Samuel tried to persuade Weizmann to officially renounce plans for "a state in which the Jews would enjoy a position of political privilege," but Weizmann refused. At one point, Samuel succeeded in persuading an Arab delegation to have lunch with Zionist leaders in London. According to a British official at the table, Weizmann's words there were conciliatory, but his attitude "was of the nature of a conqueror handing to a beaten foe the terms of peace." Not surprisingly, the Arabs gave no ground.

In the end, Weizmann succeeded in redressing what he considered a major omission of the Balfour Declaration, in having the Jewish Agency, a Zionist political body, serve as adviser to the Mandate. He also obtained a pledge authorizing Jewish immigration, though "under suitable conditions" that the Mandate determined. In his dealings with the British he asked for a committment to a self-governing Jewish commonwealth but got only a promise of "self-governing institutions," which were to apply to Jews and Arabs alike.

In fact, the Samuel administration faithfully went about approving the organization of the "self-governing institutions," of which the Jews took full advantage, and in a few years they built a functional governing structure. The Arabs, in contrast, blocked all attempts to institutionalize their powers. Their persistent boycott not only left them politically impotent but prevented the creation of any forum where Jews and Arabs might meet to achieve some mutual understanding. The Arab boycott closed the door to any possible communal reconciliation.

The British did not give up easily, however. Even as they put the last touches on the explanatory text for the League of Nations, they issued a paper in June 1922, aimed at narrowing the Arab-Jewish abyss. Called the Churchill White Paper—for the newly named colonial secretary who was generally sympathetic to Zionism—it was actually drafted by Samuel, to whom the colonial office deferred as the on-site expert.

The paper assured the Jews that they were "in Palestine of right and not on sufferance," and urged the cabinet to recognize that the Jewish national home rested upon "an ancient historic connection." At the other pole, it assured the Arabs that the Balfour Declaration did not contemplate "the disappearance or subordination of the Arab population, language or culture . . . [It] does not contemplate that Palestine as a whole should be converted into a Jewish National Home but that such a Home should be founded *in* Palestine." Evenhanded as it tried to be, however, the paper did nothing to tamp down animosities.

Weizmann was by now exasperated at the prospect of the Arabs undoing his life's work, but he did not limit the blame to them. "All the shady characters in the world are at work against us," he wrote to his new friend, Albert Einstein, a recent convert to Zionism. "Rich servile Jews, dark fanatic Jewish obscurantists, in combination with the Vatican, with Arab assassins, English imperialist anti-Semitic reactionaries—all the dogs are howling. Never in my life have I felt so alone—and yet so certain and confident." He did not usually indulge himself with such introspection, much less such colorful, hyperbolic outbursts.

When the document that the government had prepared for the League came to the House of Lords for ratification, it provoked a storm. A motion of rejection contended not only that Britain had violated the wishes of the majority of Palestine's inhabitants but—reaching improbably back in time—breached the pledges made to the Arabs during the war. Balfour, a member of the House of Lords, rebutted its arguments, but the rejection prevailed by a vote of 60 to 29. The paper then went to the House of Commons, where the lords were reversed by a large majority. The Council of the League of Nations formally ratified the British document in July 1922, incorporating the terms of the Mandate into international law.

Taken as a whole, however, the document the League approved did little to clarify the issues. Leaving them unresolved meant that its ambiguities would have to be addressed one by one in practice, which foreordained more hostile confrontations. The Arabs scoffed at the document, as did some Zionists who argued it was time for them to move on and start collecting arms for the struggle. Though the conflict was heating up, Weizmann took the position that Zionism had no choice but to accept what Britain had offered, and learn to make the most of it.

"It is true . . . the Mandate is different from the way the Jewish people interpreted the Balfour Declaration in 1917," Weizmann said apologetically to an audience of Zionists in August 1922. "This fact cannot be altered; we can only meet it by an imperishable belief that . . . we go on working and working in Palestine."

Weizmann was forty-eight years old when he made that statement. He had reached the zenith of the Zionist world as president of the World Zionist Organization. He had shepherded the Balfour Declaration from its uneasy wartime birth to its legal endorsement by the League of Nations. Save for Herzl, no man had contributed more than he to the march toward statehood. Weizmann had performed a monumental service to the Jewish people, as he had dreamed of doing since his boyhood.

Then, changing the key of his talk, Weizmann declared, "The Declaration and the Mandate, and our whole life, are nothing but stages on the way to the Redemption."[29]

It was a strange conclusion to reach for this hardheaded secularist, placing his work in such a holy context. But "redemption" for Weizmann was a synonym for "statehood," and he was wise enough to understand that the triumph that Herzl had foreseen still required massive intervention. Weizmann's work was far from finished, and he had many rivals who believed they could do it better. Whether or not he knew it, Weizmann was on the threshold of many new battles to determine the shape of Zionism. What he seemed to be saying was that Redemption, as it had always been for the Jews, was a shimmering vision on a far horizon.

3

Vladimir Jabotinsky
1880–1940

INSURGENT

By the early 1920s, Britain's anti-Zionist practices in Palestine had inflamed debate within the Zionist community. Weizmann, notwithstanding
his growing doubts, remained committed to reliance on Britain to deliver on its promises. But the giants of English politics who had carried
him to his triumphs—Balfour and Lloyd George and their circle—had
passed from the scene. Lesser politicians, more timid by temperament
and more narrowly nationalist and imperialist, replaced them as policy
makers. In the postwar years, Zionism made little headway. Weizmann's
reputation as a result, went into decline, and Zionist talk turned to finding a more aggressive strategy.

In Palestine, an articulate, charismatic Russian Jew named Vladimir
Jabotinsky argued for a Jewish nationalism that embraced arms as a means
to achieve its goals. Jabotinsky admired Britain. He favored democracy and free-market capitalism. He was a tireless advocate of popular
rights and political freedom, and he rejected racial prejudice. Without
being religious, he was respectful of Judaism, and he even recognized the
legitimacy of Arab nationalism as Zionism's rival. But though he revered

Herzl, he also believed Herzl's indifference to arms had left a void in the Zionist vision.

Jewish tradition, even the Bible itself, promoted the use of arms, Jabotinsky asserted. "Sword-fighting belonged to our forefathers," he proclaimed. "The Torah and the sword were both handed down to us from Heaven.[1]" It was not that Jabotinsky broke new ground in calling for the use of force in Palestine; arms were already deeply embedded in both Jewish and Arab practices. But he argued strongly that the Jews would neither merit nor obtain a state of their own without fighting fiercely for it.

"The force of historical reality teaches us a very simple lesson," Jabotinsky wrote. "If we should all be educated people and learn to plough the land and to build houses and be able to speak Hebrew and know our whole national literature . . . and not know how to shoot, then there is no hope. . . . Every Jew and every Gentile who even for a minute thinks of Jewish national problems fully understands that of all the necessities of national rebirth, shooting is the most important of them."[2]

Britain abandoned whatever sympathy it once had for Zionism soon after the World War, Jabotinsky maintained, and the Arabs never had any at all. Weizmann and the mainstream Zionists, he insisted, were deluding themselves about the potential for a diplomatic route to statehood. Though he himself hated war, he said, he was realistic. He shocked much of the *yishuv* by arguing that a Zionist education had to include a "spiritual militarism," by which he meant a readiness to embrace and use weapons.

In an article called "The Ethics of the Iron Wall," Jabotinsky laid out his strategy for overcoming Arab resistance. Arabs might be willing to reach agreement with the Jews, he wrote, but surely not of their own free will. Published in 1923, the article became a classic of Zionist literature.

"Our peace-mongers," the article said, "are trying to persuade us that the Arabs are either fools, whom we can deceive by masking our real aims, or that they are corrupt and can be bribed to abandon to us their claim to priority in Palestine, in return for cultural and economic advantages. . . . I repudiate this conception of the Palestinian Arabs. . . . We may water down and sweeten our aims with honeyed words to make them palatable, but they know what we want, just as we know what they do not want."

Jabotinsky ruled out efforts to persuade the Arabs to consent voluntarily to Jewish statehood. Talk, he argued, only delayed the desired outcome. Weizmann's policy of negotiations, he wrote, was just empty rhetoric, but it was also dishonest. Jabotinsky proposed the creation of a Jewish military force that would establish an "Iron Wall" as an invulnerable barrier to the Arabs' national aspirations.

"As long as in the hearts of the Arabs there remains even one spark of hope to be rid of us," he wrote, "they will not sell this hope for honey-colored words or far-reaching promises. They are not a mob but a living people. Such a people agrees to concessions concerning great issues only when all hope is lost. . . . Only then will radical Arabs whose slogan is 'never' lose their influence. Only then will moderate Arabs approach us to propose mutual concessions on practical issues. . . . When that happens, I believe we will be ready to grant them satisfactory guarantees so that both peoples can live together in peace."

In the context of his belligerent historical image, it is easy to dismiss Jabotinsky's claim to yearn for Arab-Jewish peace. But he had his own definition of peace. He granted Arabs the validity of their nationalism, even when most Zionists chose to deny it. He also warned of its perseverance. But his vision of peace was founded on Jewish military domination. He offered Zionism an ideology to keep the Arabs in a condition of military, and thus political, submission. At the same time, he ignored the threat of perpetual combat and the long-term jeopardy in which endless conflict would itself place a Jewish state.

Vladimir Jabotinsky was born in the Black Sea city of Odessa in 1880, the third child of middle-class, nonobservant Jewish parents. Known to his friends as Ze'ev, he was bright and, in adolescence, became a serious student of literature. Though familiar with Judaic observance, he wrote, he had "no inner contact" with Judaism. Like Herzl, he aspired early to be a writer on secular themes.

Nor was Jabotinsky raised with a commitment to Jewish nationalism. Unlike Chaim Weizmann, he did not belong to a family that reflexively embraced Zionism. As a boy, he thought of himself as Russian. In time he mastered many languages and won fame as a writer and orator in several of them. But Russian was always the language and the culture in which he was most comfortable.

Jabotinsky was happy growing up in Odessa, Russia's most cosmopolitan city. Odessa had a reputation as a home of sailors and fishermen, and as a den of smugglers and swindlers. Newcomers and passersby always seemed to outnumber natives. Jewish life was not centered in ghettos but scattered throughout the city's diverse quarters. Jabotinsky found in Odessa an atmosphere of social acceptance, where his Jewish identity was unchallenged. He described the city as a "peaceful fraternity of nationalities," in which he acquired liberal convictions that were generally unfamiliar to Eastern Jews.

Jabotinsky's early novel, *The Five: A Novel of Jewish Life in Turn-of-the-Century Odessa,* provides a sense of his adolescence. In it, he explores a crowd of intellectual, self-indulgent, warmhearted friends, intrigued by Friedrich Nietzsche, the German philosopher who was then the rage. "Nietzsche had only arrived in Russia," he wrote. "Reports about him, with ensuing debates, had already occurred in our literary circle. I had his books, though I can't guarantee that all the pages had been slit."

Jabotinsky was captivated by Nietzsche's tough individualism, his joyful materialism, his disdain for religious asceticism. Germans in the Nazi era found in Nietzsche a defense of storm-trooper culture. But what became the scaffolding of Jabotinsky's life was Nietzsche's idea of a personal Judaism that resembled early Hellenism in extolling valor, physicality, virility, and a readiness to make war.

At eighteen, Jabotinsky joined the migration of young Jews excluded from the Russian university system to Western Europe to pursue their studies. But he followed his own star. He disliked Berne, where he first settled, for its Germanic flavor, and so moved on to Rome, where few foreign Jews matriculated. He remained there for three years as a kind of scholarly dilettante. He loved Italy's permissive spirit. He flirted with women and with socialism, though he was already repelled by Marxist rigidity. He mastered Italian, read widely, and attended whatever lectures attracted him. He studied some law, which would later prove useful to his Zionist work, but he had no academic plan and earned no degree.

Jabotinsky's idol during his Italian years was Giuseppe Garibaldi, the fiery warrior whose battlefield exploits were crucial to Italy's unification. Garibaldi, he wrote, found "no greater happiness in the world than the nation and the homeland."[3] Garibaldi "demanded unity of rich and poor in the name of love of the homeland, that they forget all conflict and put aside internal quarrels, until the nationalist ideal is realized."[4] Jabotinsky thought of himself very early as a nationalist on the Garibaldi model.

Years later, during Italy's fascist era, Jabotinsky made a curious claim. "I did not get my Zionism from the works of Ahad Ha'am, not even from Herzl . . . ," he wrote. "I learned how to be a Zionist from the Gentiles. The best part of my youth I spent in Rome . . . when Italy was a free and pleasant country, liberal, peace-loving, carefree without the slightest trace of chauvinism . . . harming nobody, persecuting no one. This is how every nation should live, and us Jews, too." This memory, though of dubious accuracy, helps explain Jabotinsky's lifelong deference to Italy, which he called his "spiritual homeland."[5]

Jabotinsky also launched his literary career in Rome, writing witty, nonpolitical pieces reminiscent of Herzl's *feuilletons* for Odessa papers. Published under the pen name Altalena—which would acquire fame in a more violent context during Israel's War of Independence—the articles were warmly received, so that, when he returned home in 1902, his literary reputation preceded him. But the Odessa that he found then was different from the one he had left. Darkened by the prospect of an anti-czarist revolution, Russian society trembled in fear of bloodshed. Barely unpacked, Jabotinsky was arrested on charges of insulting the czar and imprisoned for seven weeks. The experience transformed him from the easygoing youth he had been in Rome into a militant political activist.

At the urging of friends of the revolution, Jabotinsky decided to join the self-defense force that Odessa Jews were organizing in anticipation of pogroms. He wrote letters, distributed leaflets, and raised funds. Though the city escaped serious violence, in April 1903, fifty Jews were killed and hundreds injured in the Kishinev pogrom, and a wave of Jewish self-defense forces formed across the country. Kishinev coincided with Jabotinsky's first serious commitment as a Jew and, soon thereafter, as a Zionist.

The Zionist leaders in Odessa rewarded Jabotinsky for his service by naming him a delegate to the Sixth Zionist Congress, held in Basel in 1903. This was the tumultuous congress to which Herzl presented his controversial Uganda Scheme. Jabotinsky admitted that as a novice, he was thoroughly uncomfortable with the Zionist veterans. He defended Herzl for his much criticized meeting with the czarist minister von Plehve, charging that the congress had confused tactics and ethics. But he followed the other Russians in voting against the Uganda proposal, then joined them in walking out in protest when they lost the vote.

Jabotinsky first met Chaim Weizmann, then a young rebel, in Basel at the congress. He also had a brush with Herzl, who sternly informed him from the podium, he wrote self-mockingly, that the allotted time for the speech he was delivering had expired. But decades later, Jabotinsky wrote, "I remember no person who made such an impression on me, not anyone before Herzl nor anyone after him. Here I felt that I stood before a man chosen by fate, before a prophet and a leader—that even to err and blunder in following him was justified."[6]

The stenographic record of the 1903 congress briefly mentioned Jabotinsky's assertion that Zionism had to become a *force* if it was to succeed, though he did not specify *military* force. He also proclaimed that tactics necessarily trumped ethics in the Zionist struggle, an expression he used often in subsequent years. He further dismissed the value of religion, culture, and pioneering in the existing Zionist program.

In 1907, Jabotinsky married an Odessa girl named Anna Galperin, whom he had known since childhood. Their only child, Eri, was born three years later and grew up a strong disciple of his father. The marriage was regarded as solid, and the two remained dedicated throughout their lives. But his wife did not share Jabotinsky's single-minded ardor for Zionism, much less for travel, and they spent much of their married years living in separate places.

Jabotinsky's work in Odessa came to an abrupt end in the wake of another police incident, and though it was minor, he had no desire to risk a second term in jail, so he fled to St. Petersburg. He took a job there with a Zionist weekly called *Rasswyet* ("Dawn"), where he attracted attention as a solid though undisciplined thinker. Extremely prolific, he also wrote for non-Jewish periodicals, from which his reputation spread, though he was routinely categorized not as a Russian but as a *Jewish* writer.

By now, Jabotinsky was taking extended leaves to deliver speeches across Russia to promote Zionism. He described himself as "a traveling salesman" of Zionism and "a permanent inhabitant of railroads." As anti-czarist fervor in the country rose, his talks aimed increasingly at promoting migration to Palestine. He also attacked the Socialist Bund, Zionism's principal rival, for deluding Jews into believing that Russia's Jewish problem could be solved within its borders by changing the economic system.

In spite of his success as a speaker, Jabotinsky was not physically imposing, like Weizmann. Short and stocky, he had a moon-shaped face. He was clean-shaven, wore thick glasses, and often dressed flamboyantly in bohemian fashion. His voice, however, was powerful and he drew huge audiences wherever he went. Then, in 1907, claiming physical and intellectual fatigue, he took a year's sabbatical, enrolling at the university in Vienna to study national movements. He no longer produced *feuilletons* and wrote not just on the subject of Zionism but on such topics as disarmament, women's rights, and democracy. Though still in his twenties, Jews already spoke of him as Herzl's natural heir, which he did nothing to discourage.

In 1908, when the Young Turks overthrew the sultan, Jabotinsky cut short his studies in Vienna to take a newspaper assignment in Constantinople. He wrote that the Young Turks showed as little sympathy for Zionism as the sultan had shown to Herzl. In a side trip to Palestine, he wrote less about the *yishuv* than about the armed watchmen who safeguarded the Jewish settlements. The Zionist Executive, impressed by his facile style and by the breadth of his knowledge, invited him to open a bureau in Turkey. He agreed, and in 1909 he founded a string of journals in several languages aimed at spreading Zionist sympathies, particularly among Turkish Jews.

Jabotinsky was considered successful, at least marginally, in mitigating the Young Turks' hostility to Zionism. He may also have had some impact, through speeches and personal courtship, in overcoming the wariness toward Zionism of the influential Turkish Jewish community. But he disliked Turkey. "The East? It is entirely foreign to me. . . . Mine is a Western mentality," he wrote.[7] He also complained that he did not get from the Zionist Executive the funds he needed to do his work properly.

Then an internal crisis arose to distract him from his duties. A member of the Executive, transgressing Zionist rules, published a book declaring that the movement's intent was to establish a sovereign Jewish state in Palestine. When Jabotinsky asked the Executive to disavow the book, which he feared would upset the Young Turks, he was turned down, and after persisting, he resigned in protest. It was the first of his many fallings-out with the Zionist establishment. Ironically, the assertion of sovereignty that he sought to suppress was precisely the position he openly promoted a few years later, after the British replaced the Turks as Palestine's rulers.

Leaving Constantinople, Jabotinsky returned to Russia less tolerant of Zionism's inner circle but more ardent in his Zionism. To the dismay of Russia's Yiddish-speaking Jews, he started a campaign to make Hebrew the *lingua franca* of Zionism. He even founded a publishing house to translate world classics into Hebrew. While backing Weizmann's effort to found a university, he insisted its services should be provided immediately to Russia's Jewish students. Over this issue he and Weizmann exchanged the first of the many bitter words that would characterize their relations over the ensuing years.

By the summer of 1914, Jabotinsky was largely alienated from the

Zionist establishment and cut off from any likelihood of a leadership role. "I don't know what I would have done," he later wrote, "if a world catastrophe had not come. Maybe I would have gone to Palestine, maybe to Rome, maybe I would have founded a party." In August of 1914, when Europe exploded into war, Weizmann set out on his path through London's salons that produced the Balfour Declaration. Jabotinsky's path was very different.

☰

Jabotinsky's initial impulse when the war broke out was journalistic, and by early September he was reporting for a newspaper on the battles in France. But the Western Front was not *his* war. Like most Jews, he was tantalized by the prospect of the czar's defeat and overthrow, which was regarded as being a major step forward for Jews. But when Turkey signed up on Germany's side, he found a cause that engaged him even more.

Jabotinsky concluded quickly that the Turks would be defeated, thereby opening to Zionism an opportunity for mass colonization of Palestine. Sent by his paper to North Africa, he wrote articles on the reaction of the former Ottoman provinces to the sultan's declaration of Holy War. His dispatches seemed to confirm the premise that even among Muslims, Turkish support was shallow. The final stop on his tour was Alexandria, where several thousand Jews whom the Turks had expelled from Palestine had taken refuge. In Egypt, the British army was mobilizing for an offensive, which inspired Jabotinsky with an idea.

After the war, Jabotinsky wrote of his idea in *The Story of the Jewish Legion*. "The right thing for the Jews," he stated, "would be to form their own regiment to participate in the conquest of Palestine." Alexandria had hundreds of potential recruits among the exiles from Palestine, fed and housed by Britain and given pocket money by Egypt's Jewish community. Many young men were eager to fight, he wrote, among them a Russian named Joseph Trumpeldor, who agreed to join him in organizing a military force.[8]

Trumpeldor, born in Russia the same year as Jabotinsky, had been drafted for army service in the Russo-Japanese War in 1904 and was sent with his unit to Siberia. Decorated for heroism in battle, he lost his left arm and was taken prisoner by the Japanese. On his release, he was awarded a reserve commission, making him the only Jewish officer in the Russian army. Trumpeldor acquired a university degree in law, then departed for Palestine, where he became an agricultural worker in Tel-Hai.

Jabotinsky wrote admiringly that Trumpeldor was "served better by one arm than most of us are served by two. He washed and shaved and dressed, he ate, he polished his boots, drove his horse and shot—all with his single arm." The two men convened a meeting of refugee leaders, who endorsed the idea of a Jewish regiment. An assembly of young men seconded it with a resolution: "To form a Jewish Legion and propose to England to make use of it in Palestine." A contingent of volunteers elected Trumpeldor their commander and embarked on military training.

Jabotinsky and Trumpeldor presented their proposal—"We forced poor Trumpeldor to put on his four St. George crosses"—at a meeting with Britain's commanding general in Egypt. The reaction was disappointing. The general said he lacked authority to accept foreigners into the army and, besides, he knew of no plans by Britain to undertake a campaign in Palestine. His best offer to the Jews was to form a detachment of mule transport to be deployed on some other battlefield on the Turkish front.

Jabotinsky considered the offer insulting, but Trumpeldor saw potential in it. Mules carrying supplies and ammunition in battle were not demeaning, Trumpeldor insisted, and any sector in which Jews fought Turks was a milestone on the road to Palestine. Jabotinsky later admitted that Trumpeldor was right.

The Zion Mule Corps of six hundred men joined Britain's attack on Gallipoli in 1915 and put Zionism on the military map. A British officer was its first commander, Trumpeldor its second. The British credited the unit, which suffered heavy casualties, with "a more difficult type of bravery than the men in the front line, who had the excitement of combat to keep them going." After Britain's defeat at Gallipoli, and over Trumpeldor's protests, the Zion Mule Corps returned to Egypt and was disbanded. But, Jabotinsky wrote, it opened doors in London for his campaign to establish a fighting Jewish legion.[9]

Jabotinsky's campaign for the Jewish Legion proved long and arduous. Not only did Britain have no plan for a Palestine offensive at the start of the war, but it saw no justification for relying further on the Jews. Turning to the governments of France and Italy, Jabotinsky was met with the same indifference. In Russia, the government, though more positive, refused to soften its anti-Jewish policies, and in Odessa, Jews called him a traitor for soliciting the czar. The Zionist movement, stubbornly neutral in the war, refused him any help at all. When he proposed recruiting the Legion independently of the movement, the Zionist Executive in Berlin denounced him publicly.

Even more discouraging was the response of the thousands of Jewish refugees from czarist rule living in England. Its able-bodied men rejected any service that might, even indirectly, serve Russian interests. Entreaties from Jabotinsky and Trumpeldor had no impact. At one meeting, young toughs in the audience attacked Jabotinsky and broke his glasses. More than once Britain's Parliament and its newspapers proposed that Jews living in Britain and refusing to enlist be sent back to Russia. Even these threats changed nothing. But Jabotinsky, though criticized from many sides, refused to give up the effort.

Weizmann, uncharacteristically, emerged in the campaign for the legion as Jabotinsky's closest supporter. Standing shoulder-to-shoulder against Zionist neutrality, the two were convinced that Jews owed themselves an effort to achieve a British victory. Weizmann arranged meetings for Jabotinsky in London and Paris, and even pleaded his case personally to the Rothschilds. "I know of few people," Weizmann wrote of Jabotinsky in his memoir, "who could have stood up to the difficulties and disappointments. His pertinacity, which flowed from his devotion, was simply fabulous." For months, while lobbying in Britain, Jabotinsky even lived with the Weizmanns in their London home.

Lloyd George's accession as prime minister in 1916 broke the barriers, just as he had broken the barriers to the Balfour Declaration. The Legion took official form when 120 Mule Corps veterans, led by Trumpeldor, enlisted as a unit in the British army. Jabotinsky, describing himself as "not as young or as slim as the others," showed his solidarity with them by signing up as a private, mocking in his book his own clumsiness in training, as well as in his assignment to mop up the sergeants' mess.

In mid-1917, the cabinet officially issued an order to the Mule Corps's first commander, an Old Testament Zionist much like Lloyd George and Balfour, to organize a Jewish regiment. Jabotinsky was made the head of recruitment. In his book, he claims credit on the Legion's behalf for "half the Balfour Declaration," a clear exaggeration; the Legion was never mentioned in the records of the Balfour negotiations. In August, the British cabinet formally recognized the Legion but, to mollify the concerns of the Conjoint, declined to make any reference to Jews in its name. The war ministry designated it the "38th Battalion of the Royal Fusiliers," promising that once under fire it would receive a Jewish name and Jewish insignia.

In June 1918, the 38th Battalion, some eight hundred strong, boarded a ship to Palestine, where it was attached to General Allenby's forces.

Trumpeldor was dropped from the rolls because of his missing arm but Jabotinsky was promoted to lieutenant in command of a fifty-man platoon. The 38th was later joined by the 39th Battalion, composed largely of American Jews, and ultimately by a 40th Battalion, made up chiefly of pioneers from the *yishuv*. Meanwhile, Jewish volunteers swarmed in from friendly countries. Jabotinsky's role in founding the Legion made him, at the time, the Western world's most popular Jew.

The Jewish Legion ultimately reached five thousand men, though only a third of them were ready to participate in Allenby's offensive into Syria in the fall of 1918. They fought well, suffered substantial casualties, and were commended in a dispatch saying they "helped in no small measure to win the great victory gained at Damascus." Jabotinsky acknowledged the pride he felt in wearing a British uniform, and his company received its own citation. After the Turks surrendered in October, the Legion was formally renamed the "Judean Regiment," with a menorah as its insignia.[10]

The Legion, it should be noted, was not the only auxiliary fighting alongside Allenby. Jewish sources generally overlook Faisal's Arab army, twice the Legion's size; and Arabs commit the same sin in overlooking the Legion. Faisal's unit, climaxing the long journey from Hejaz begun in 1916, was the first to enter Damascus. But once the Turks fled, both Jewish and Arab officers, though friendly, turned to partisan politics. Faisal gave his attention to forming an Arab government in Syria, Jabotinsky to advancing the Jewish claim to a homeland in Palestine. To promote their respective political goals, both Jews and Arabs nourished the myth that the battle for Syria culminated in their own military triumph.

Jabotinsky's ambition for the Jewish Legion, always more political than military, was to have Jews play a part in Palestine's liberation, then underpin with military force the promises made by the Balfour Declaration. Their goal, Jabotinsky told his men after the armistice, "was more important now than it ever was before." Britain held a contrary view. One of its first postwar moves was to disband the Jewish Legion, a sure sign, Jabotinsky believed, of its intent to renege on its pledge to promote a Jewish Palestine.

The three battalions of the Jewish Legion were still intact at the start of 1919. Not all its men were motivated by Zionism, and with the war won, many chose to go home. Jabotinsky, as the Legion's senior Jewish officer, sought to discourage them, and Weizmann's Zionist Commission supported him. But the British promptly demobilized whoever applied, and within a few months, only two battalions remained. In March 1920, the first skirmish between Jews and Arabs took place in Tel-Hai, where Trumpeldor was killed. By then, only a few hundred members of the Legion were still under arms.

"As long as the Legion was a visible force in Palestine, there occurred not a single clash," Jabotinsky asserted with some exaggeration. The British garrison left in Palestine consisted preponderantly of Indians, mainly Muslims, concerned chiefly about Atatürk's uprising in Islamic Turkey. From this Jabotinsky concluded with obvious dismay, "So long as the Legion existed, all was quiet and peaceful. . . . When there remained of our Legion only four hundred—only then were Trumpeldor and his comrades killed at Tel-Hai."[11]

Jabotinsky's grudge toward the Zionist establishment had diminished by the end of the war. He was no doubt buoyed by the esteem he had won in the fighting, and in Jerusalem, still wearing a British uniform with an officer's insignia, he decided he was ready to serve the Zionist cause again. Weizmann named him to the Zionist Commission, and at first the two worked together harmoniously. When Weizmann returned to London in late 1918, he chose Jabotinsky to replace him as the Commission's liaison to Allenby's civil administration.

In his new position, Jabotinsky was quickly inundating Weizmann with warnings about the British. In November he wrote, "Precedents are being established that will later be used against us." He followed that with, "Arab impudence is growing daily. . . . The British authorities are acting in a manner which clearly tells them that the Balfour Declaration need not be fulfilled."

Another dispatch began by his asking Weizmann to "forgive the bitterness," then declared, "I did not participate in the organization of self-defense [during the Kishinev pogrom] in order that I should now sit quietly and complacently while the Arabs have it drummed into their ears that they can get rid of us if only they give us a hard enough kick." Still another dispatch said Britain's attitude "suggested to the Arabs that a pogrom would be welcomed; such official attitude cannot help but lead to trouble." Weizmann, in London, was more alarmed by what he saw as Jabotinsky's hyperbole than by what the reports revealed about British rule.

In February 1919, Weizmann, as head of the Zionist Executive, reorganized the Zionist Commission in Palestine, with Jabotinsky his obvious target. In reducing the Commission from twelve to six members, he simply squeezed Jabotinsky out. In his memoir, he criticized Jabotinsky for being "devoid of poise and balance . . . and mature judgment."[12] He would have been more honest had he written that Jabotinsky had told him more about Britain than he wanted to know.

Jabotinsky, as commander of what remained of the Jewish Legion, still had responsibility for his men, whom he felt the British were now mistreating. When ninety-nine of his soldiers were court-martialed on charges of being disorderly, he reached deep into his legal training to defend them. All were sentenced to seven years in prison, and though soon released, he protested to Allenby that his loyalty to Britain was "shattering into pieces under the intolerable burden of disappointment, despair, broken pledges and anti-Semitism permeating the whole administrative and military atmosphere." Allenby by now regarded Jabotinsky as rebellious, and in August Britain discharged him from its military service.[13]

Abruptly, Jabotinsky's ties with the two institutions that made up his public identity—the Zionist Commission and the British army—were forcibly severed. He was again a private citizen, deprived of credentials, living in Jerusalem without a job. But painful as his psychic wounds were, his commitment to Zionism was too firmly rooted, and his energy too irrepressible, for him to sit around brooding.

With the Legion a skeleton and the hostility of the Arabs rising, Jabotinsky embarked on forming a network of independent Jewish self-defense units. Since the turn of the twentieth century, such units had helped guard outlying settlements like Tel-Hai. Its recruits were preponderantly Russian Jews, building on the experience they had acquired during the pogroms and in the Legion. Jabotinsky proposed to unify these units into a force to defend the entire yishuv against Arab attacks. He personally took command, and several hundred men signed up for training. His effort grew quickly into the Haganah ("defense"), which emerged as the precursor of the Israeli army.

Neither the British nor the Zionist Commission authorized the formation of self-defense units, but Jabotinsky did not hide their existence. A secret army, he reasoned, would have no leverage in politics. In fact, he urged that the Haganah serve under British officers, who could offer better training and weapons. The proposal was puzzling. Would British officers not weaken the Jews' political leverage? Was he seeking to relive his glory days serving in the Legion under British officers? Britain, having disbanded the Legion for being Zionist, would hardly want to help build up the Haganah to support the Zionist cause.

The Haganah's initial test came in 1920 with the Nebi Musa disorders in Jerusalem. In response to rumors of impending attacks, Jabotinsky had sought to position his units at strategic sites inside the Old City, to safeguard the old *yishuv*. The British refused to allow it, as did members of the rabbinate, who would admit no Zionists into the Orthodox quarters. Without a choice, Jabotinsky had to station his men outside the walls, but when the rioting began, the British locked the gates, leaving only Arab police inside. Jabotinsky denounced Britain for the Jews' civilian casualties.

Jabotinsky's accusations inflamed British animosity. When the rioting ended, British forces arrested nineteen soldiers in a Haganah billet and, a day later, arrested Jabotinsky himself and placed him in solitary confinement. The *yishuv* was stunned, and four hundred Haganah members signed a plea to the military court to arrest them, too. The Chief Ashkenazi Rabbi, Abraham Isaac Kook, a popular figure—and the subject of chapter 5—circulated a petition of solidarity with Jabotinsky and his men, which thousands signed. Ignoring these collective protests, the court convicted all nineteen soldiers of possessing unauthorized arms and sentenced them to three years at hard labor.

As for the charges against Jabotinsky, the most substantive was that he showed "evil intent" in provoking violence and, contrary to British procedure, he was tried in secret. In his defense, he argued that having lived through pogroms in Russia, he believed that self-defense forces were the only means to protect the Jews of Palestine. British officers testified that Jabotinsky had violated no military orders. The court nonetheless found Jabotinsky guilty and sentenced him to fifteen years in prison.

All of the convicted men were locked up in the famous Crusader castle, now a prison, on the seaside in Acre. When Weizmann did not intercede, claiming a reluctance to jeopardize the talks then under way over the terms of the Mandate, Jabotinsky called him a "moral disgrace." Allenby reduced Jabotinsky's term to a year and the men's to six months, but throughout the world, Jewish organizations and the liberal press, hailing all the prisoners as heroes, deluged Britain with petitions for their release.[14]

A few weeks later Herbert Samuel arrived in Jerusalem as High Commissioner, vowing to bank the fires of conflict. Among his first acts was to issue an amnesty covering the Nebi Musa riots, which included not only

Jabotinsky and his men but also two Arabs convicted of raping Jewish women. Outraged by the pairing, Jabotinsky declared his intention to reject the offer. But leaders of the *yishuv,* joined by his family, begged Jabotinsky to change his mind. He agreed to do so but only when his fellow inmates voted to accept the terms. After ten weeks in Acre, all of the Jewish prisoners were released.

Jabotinsky did not give in on the principle, however. Interviewed by London's *Jewish Chronicle,* he declared that Samuel, in making no distinction between his Jewish fighters and common rapists, desecrated the pursuit of justice. "That the instigators of the pogrom should have been pardoned at the same time proves that the new High Commissioner is willing to place the self-defense corps on the same standing as those who caused the whole trouble." He himself paid to hire lawyers who brought a suit that, to widespread surprise, he won. In March 1921, the army quashed the trial proceedings, erasing all the convictions.[15]

The court victory overcame Jabotinsky's sense of despair. As a free spirit, without organized Zionist support, he had won a major triumph, restoring the Haganah's good name. He had also inflicted an embarrassing defeat on the Mandate and the British army, and both had long memories. It seemed likely that, ultimately, he would have to pay. But if he carried a chip on his shoulder, he chose to conceal it. Jabotinsky was now not just the founder of the Jewish Legion but the savior of Jewish honor, and many wondered how high his surging popularity would take him.

After his release from Acre, and with his wife and child settled in London, Jabotinsky decided to give up his home in Palestine. Having been named a candidate for the Zionist Executive, he assuredly stretched the truth by claiming to the Zionist Congress that he and Weizmann now agreed on nearly everything. As part of his duties, he took a post with Keren Hayesod, a newly created fund to finance Jewish infrastructure in Palestine. Though he disliked the bureaucratic routine, he worked harmoniously with Zionist leaders. Jabotinsky's priority, however, was still to build a Jewish military force; it was an issue over which he and Weizmann would again come into conflict.

"Just as we cannot demand money from England to support Zionism," Jabotinsky wrote, "so we may not demand her blood. If there are casualties . . . the list of killed and wounded must not include the names of

Peter and John but the names of Moses and Isaac. If the standing army must take upon itself the function of scattering the riots by force, this work must be done by those . . . who believe what the League of Nations believes, that Zionism is just, and that driving away its enemies is also just." A standing army does not mean militarism, Jabotinsky declared, but without an army, "Zionism is not feasible."[16]

Throughout the early 1920s, Jabotinsky, as a member of the Zionist Executive, fought aggressively to reconstitute the Jewish Legion, which he still held should be a unit of the British army. The Haganah, he explained, was an assemblage of "Jewish adolescents who know no discipline." His explanations did not persuade the *yishuv*, however, which was already deeply suspicious of British motives. Jabotinsky seemed unable to recognize that the Haganah, composed of the sons and daughters of the *yishuv*, was much closer to the Jews of Palestine than a Legion dependent on Britain would ever be.

In its initial days, the Mandate had proposed to form a *joint* militia, composed of Jews and Arabs, as a way to reconcile the two. But both sides, each fearing the other's dominance, opposed the idea. The unwillingness to work together left responsibility for security in British hands, which London did not like. Finally the Zionist Executive, at Weizmann's urging, dropped the proposal for a Legion entirely, a defeat that further alienated Jabotinsky. Paradoxically, after giving up on a joint militia, the Mandate, acknowledging an unwillingness to handle security alone, began quietly tolerating the Haganah's growth.

In November 1921, Jabotinsky made his first trip to America on a mission to promote the work of Keren Hayesod, the Zionist building fund. He remained for seven months, traveling widely, making speeches, and soliciting money. He was invariably courteous and charming, and kept his distance from local disputes. But, often out of touch, he grew more estranged from the Executive in London, which was happy for the tranquility produced by his absence. On returning, however, he immediately reignited passions, accusing the Executive of jeopardizing the *yishuv* by its soft policy toward Britain.

On the Executive's agenda at Jabotinsky's return was the draft of the White Paper that bore Winston Churchill's name. Among other departures from the Balfour Declaration, it downgraded Britain's responsibility in Palestine to the "development of the existing Jewish community," which it described as "a centre in which the Jewish people may take, on grounds of religion and race, an interest and a pride." The Churchill White Paper made no mention of self-rule, much less Jewish statehood.

Britain's cabinet had submitted the draft to the Zionist Executive with a demand for prompt approval. When Jabotinsky asked whether a serious effort had been made to improve the text, Weizmann answered that he had done all he could. At least, Jabotinsky insisted "our acquiescence should be qualified" by a protest. He chose not to resign from the Executive, he said, only because "I felt it was my moral duty to share with my colleagues even the shame of a defeat, though I had taken no part in the battle." He wrote later that, ever after, he regretted his acceptance of the Churchill White Paper.

Increasingly isolated, Jabotinsky subsequently proposed to counter the White Paper with a set of tough demands, which he knew the British would reject. In the debate over his proposal, he had a talk with Weizmann, which he described as "a good, friendly talk. We both argued intelligently. . . . He believes his way is that of a compromising realist, and mine is the way of a stubborn utopian. I feel that his line is the line of renunciation, while mine is a difficult, stormy way but will lead more quickly to a Jewish state."[17] One by one, however, Jabotinsky's colleagues on the Executive warned him either to fall in line with Weizmann or resign.

In January 1923, the Executive carried out its warning by reaffirming its confidence in Weizmann's strategy of conciliation. The following morning Jabotinsky submitted a letter announcing that he was "no longer bound by the discipline of the Zionist Organization." The Executive's policy, he declared, "threatens to bring the movement to decay and the Jewish work in Palestine to bankruptcy."

The Jabotinsky who resigned from the Executive in 1923 was no longer the popular figure he had been on his release from the Acre prison. Increasingly he built a reputation as an obstinate, self-serving partisan. Even admirers, of whom there were many, asked whether he had made Zionism hostage to his personal gratification. Jabotinsky's foes questioned whether he jeopardized the cohesion of the movement itself.

"When Dr. Weizmann retires—or is forced to retire—he will have a hobby: chemistry," Jabotinsky said after his resignation. "My hobby is literature," and he said he would return to writing. But more ominously he warned, "Being outside the organization, I will employ every means I find feasible to defeat the present Zionist policies. I will listen to no authority, not even the Zionist Congress."

Jabotinsky did indeed temporarily resume his literary career, but it was clear that Zionism had not heard the last of him. Inexorably, his resignation led him into a radical course, which would change not just his life but the course of Zionism itself.[18]

Jabotinsky again opened a publishing house, specializing in translations into Hebrew, but by the fall of 1923 he gave that up. He made another lecture tour of Eastern Europe, insisting that his purpose was only to *inform,* though within a few months he grew restless and decided, he told a friend, "to create some kind of movement out of activists who are scattered throughout the world." His plan, he said, was to campaign, both in Palestine and in Europe, to militarize young Jews for the liberation.

Drawing on Jabotinsky's thinking, right-wing Zionists had already begun organizing in Europe to protest Weizmann's conciliatory strategy. In late 1924, Jabotinsky announced the opening of "an office for the organization of all existing groups and for the creation of new groups" challenging the Zionist leadership. He called the movement "Revisionism," which, he explained, reflected the goal of revising Zionist policies.

In April 1925, Jabotinsky convoked a "Conference of the League of Zionist Revisionists" in a café in Paris. Both young activists and old-line Zionists, mostly Russian émigrés, attended. They elected Jabotinsky their president, but they also emulated the mainstream in avoiding the term "Jewish state" to describe their goal. Instead, they adopted the clumsy pledge to found "a self-governing Commonwealth under the auspices of an established Jewish majority." The conference vowed not to challenge the preeminence of the Zionist Executive, but Revisionism had come far very fast, and it would soon forget the promise.

Though his heart was in Revisionism, Jabotinsky was not yet ready to throw himself fully into rebellion. He remained an admirer of British values and, like Weizmann, believed Britain and Zionism had much in common. "In the Mediterranean, England's corridor to the east . . . ," he wrote in a Revisionist tract, "where there exists a danger of anti-European tendencies, the Jews are building the only mainstay which is morally affiliated with Europe and forever will be part and parcel of Europe."[19] His objective was a sterner Zionist line, he wrote, not a break with Britain.

As his thinking on Revisionism developed, Jabotinsky added another item to its aspirations: Transjordan's inclusion in the Jewish homeland. Transjordan, though regarded as historically separate, had been incorporated into Britain's Palestine Mandate by the Treaty of Sèvres. Though many

Zionists talked of drawing Palestine's border somewhere east of the Jordan River, the issue generated little passion. In fact, in 1921, when Palestine's international borders were being negotiated, Zionism focused on the north, the source of Palestine's water supply and the site of several settlements. In the final agreement, the Zionist delegation received most of what it had asked for in the north. Transjordan was not mentioned at all.

Transjordan reappeared on the agenda soon after, however, when Abdullah, eldest son of Sharif Hussein, led an army in support of his brother Faisal's position in the dispute with France. To appease both Abdullah and the French, while making a payment on its wartime pledge to the Hashemites, Britain created a new state, severing Transjordan administratively from Palestine and placing Abdullah on the throne. Abdullah never entered Syria, and the Jordan River was confirmed as Palestine's eastern boundary. At the time, Jabotinsky was virtually alone in protesting the loss to Zionism.

Over the next few years the issue seemed forgotten, but Jabotinsky raised it again at Revisionism's founding conference in Paris. He repeated it again at the next Zionist Congress, describing Palestine as "an area whose essential geographic characteristic is that the Jordan flows not along its frontier but through the middle of it."[20] The claim of both banks of the river has since been a part of Revisionist ideology, though recognized mainly in the breach.

Meanwhile, Revisionism's institutional ties to the Zionist Congress grew more fragile. Its choices were secession on the one hand or acceptance as a minority faction within the congress on the other. Jabotinsky's clear preference was for independence, and the delegates to the Zionist Congress in Vienna in 1925 waited apprehensively to hear his decision. The highlight of his formal address, however, came when he ran out of his allotted time, and Weizmann, as a conciliatory gesture, invited him to continue. Jabotinsky proceeded to voice his usual complaints about Weizmann's leadership, particularly his indifference to a Jewish Legion, but said nothing about secession. His silence produced a sense of relief among the delegates, but it only delayed the issue of secession for another congress.

Over the next few years, Jabotinsky strengthened his hold over the Revisionist movement, most notably by establishing a tight relationship with Betar, a Zionist youth organiztion with a military orientation and a right-wing ideology. Jabotinsky discovered Betar when he was in Riga, Latvia, to deliver a speech. Its formal name was B'rith Trumpeldor, for

Jabotinsky's beloved mentor in the Jewish Legion; Betar was also Bar Kokhba's last stronghold in his bloody insurrection against the Romans in the second century. Betar was composed largely of students who applauded Jabotinsky's readiness to take up arms. Its members proclaimed their readiness to sacrifice their lives for the Jewish people. Jabotinsky took Betar's vows as an opening to the militant Zionism he was seeking to organize.

Betar's model was the national movement of young Poles who pledged to defend their country's newly regained freedom from Soviet Russia. It emulated the Poles in military organization. In 1931 Jabotinsky, having cultivated Betar for several years, was elected its political leader and military commander.

Jabotinsky and Betar were an ideal match. Jabotinsky felt at ease with its discipline. As leader, he stood at the summit of a pyramid of values, emphasizing not just Jewish nationalism but upright traits of character. He even liked the brown shirts Betaris wore in European fascist style. By the early 1930s, Betar's membership reached an estimated 100,000, concentrated in Poland but spread throughout Europe and Palestine. Jabotinsky, once a committed liberal, moved steadily to the right to accommodate Betar, foreshadowing an authoritarian drift not just in Revisionism but in Zionism's long-standing democratic culture.[21]

In October 1928, Jabotinsky decided to move from London back to Jerusalem, where he would be more directly involved with Betar and the Revisionist mission. Strapped as usual for money, he was promised an administrative post with a private company, as well as work as a writer for Revisionist journals. His reason for relocating, he told a friend, was based not on sentiment but on the Jews' need for rigorous leadership. "I feel sure," he said, "that within a few months after I settle in, there will be at least some knot of muscle within the *yishuv.*"

In Palestine, the Mandatory government remembered Jabotinsky as a troublemaker, and refused to grant him a visa without his pledging to desist from political activity. The condition outraged Zionists, who saw it as a British effort to control the politics of the *yishuv.* Jabotinsky appealed the condition to London, where a few holdovers from Balfour's day came to his support. A standard visa was issued, and within a few days of landing, Jabotinsky led a parade of Betar units through the streets of Tel Aviv.

Palestine, on his arrival, was poised for another round of Arab-Jewish violence. Russian Jews, enduring as much anti-Semitism under the Bolsheviks as they had under the czar, were finding new ways to avoid British barriers to immigration. Some arrived with tourist visas and disappeared into the population. Others crossed over permeable borders from Syria and Lebanon. More Arabs than Jews, in fact, entered Palestine in the 1920s, but the imbalance of wealth belied Zionism's promise of prosperity for all, adding to the society's combustibility.

Tensions reached a climax in August 1929, when a Betari demonstration disrupted the status quo over the rules for prayer at Jerusalem's Wailing Wall. An Arab counterdemonstration triggered riots across the country. Both sides rejected British efforts at mediation. The Haganah tried to contain the disorders, but in many places it had no available forces. In Hebron, a massacre took sixty Jewish lives and, overall, several hundred Jews and Arabs were killed. Britain's response was to convoke a commission of inquiry to assess blame.

Weizmann and Jabotinsky agreed that the body of inquiry—the Shaw Commission—offered an opportunity to make a public statement on the Balfour Declaration's fading promises. Naturally, their approach differed, Weizmann urging conciliation, Jabotinsky confrontation. Still in charge, Weizmann was so sure Jabotinsky's wrath would play poorly that he deleted his name from the Shaw Commission's witness list.

But Weizmann could not stop Jabotinsky from having his say in print. After the commission concluded that Betar was the "immediate cause" of the rioting, Jabotinsky wrote that Betar was not involved at all, adding coyly that he wished it had been. Betar's role, he wrote, was "a necessary, a useful and a fine thing, and if I believed for a moment that Betar was the 'immediate cause,' I should heartily congratulate the promoters." When the commission called his words "intemperate," Jabotinsky replied, "Someone had to get up and say, 'Thus far and no farther.'"

Jabotinsky also contended that Weizmann's conciliatory policies played into the Shaw Commission's intent to exonerate the Mandate for a decade of misrule. Most of the *yishuv* agreed with him, and many local Jews encouraged him to petition the commission for the opportunity to make the Revisionist case in person. To widespread surprise, the commission gave its consent, but said he would have to travel to London to testify, since the proceedings in Palestine were about to conclude.

Jabotinsky's London testimony was never made public, but in a published article he conveyed its essence. The Mandate, he said, gave the Arabs "the impression that Britain regretted its Zionist undertaking, and would be grateful to them if they would provide an excuse to reconsider the matter." He added that Britain "teems with officials who openly hate both the Mandate and the Jews." The anger that Jabotinsky conveyed in his statement was precisely what Weizmann had feared.[22]

The Shaw Commission's report, published in March 1930, confirmed Jabotinsky's prediction. In a virtual whitewash, it chastised the Arabs for rioting, but found them innocent of premeditation. It exonerated the Mandate, focusing responsibility on excessive Jewish immigration and land acquisition, which it said jeopardized the future of the Arabs. Jabotinsky's retort to the report was that "the Zionist political positions have been so undermined that even Moses would have been unable to repair them."

A few weeks later, Britain's cabinet adopted the commission's report and dispatched an agent to examine the disabilities the Arabs faced. The agent concluded that many Arabs, driven off their land, were denied all means of livelihood. The cabinet then issued still another White Paper, named for Lord Passfield, now the colonial secretary, reaffirming the existing ceiling on Jewish entry to Palestine and imposing further limits on Jewish land acquisition.

A wave of protests from Jewish quarters exploded, led by Weizmann himself, who was backed by the British press and the League of Nations. Lloyd George and Balfour also stepped in, declaring the White Paper not just a disavowal of Britain's pledge to the Jews but a betrayal of Britain's honor.

The protests persuaded Ramsay MacDonald, the prime minister, that he had trampled not just on Zionist but on British sensitivities. After consulting with Weizmann, he drafted a letter that largely cancelled the terms of the Passfield Paper. "The obligation to facilitate Jewish immigration and make possible dense settlement of Jews on the land is still a positive obligation of the Mandate," he declared. The letter made clear that Britain had no middle ground in Palestine. It may have bandaged MacDonald's political wounds, but it did not restore the confidence of either Arabs or Jews in British rule.[23]

The Passfield Paper also inflicted wounds on Weizmann and Jabotinsky. Both seemed unhinged at the Zionist Congress in Basel in July 1931. Weizmann, acknowledging that his British policy was going nowhere, resigned as head of the Jewish Agency, one of his several posts, but much of the Zionist community still considered him to be in Britain's embrace. Jabotinsky, however, did not profit from Weizmann's discomfort, since most Zionists questioned whether his relentless criticism of the Mandate served the movement at all.

At the congress, Stephen Wise, a prominent American rabbi, famously taunted Weizmann, "You have sat too long at British feasts," and a few delegates proposed Weizmann's censure for subservience to Britain. Jabotinsky demanded that Britain immediately establish a Jewish state on both banks of the Jordan River, and when his proposal did not even receive the dignity of a vote, he jumped on a chair shouting, "This is not a Zionist Congress anymore." Jabotinsky then ripped up his delegate's card, threw the scraps into the air, and stalked out of the hall.

Weizmann, too, lost his composure. Inexplicably, he stated to a journalist that "I have no sympathy or understanding for the demand for a Jewish majority [in Palestine]. A majority does not necessarily guarantee security . . . or the development of Jewish culture and civilization. The world will construe it in only one sense, that we want to acquire a majority in order to drive out the Arabs." Why he said these words—which did not even represent his position—was a mystery. But his refusal to disavow them assured his fall.

The congress proceeded to censure Weizmann, by a margin of 123 to 106, forcing him to resign, but a greater shock followed when he told an interviewer, "I hope Jabotinsky will be my successor. Because, at any rate, he is an open opponent and I prefer him to some of the others who declare themselves to be my friends, but are ready to stab me in the back."

According to Joseph Schechtman, Jabotinsky's close friend and biographer, Weizmann subsequently revised the interview, crossing out his advice on the succession, but its content nonetheless spread through the hall. Weizmann was said to have repeated it to Jabotinsky personally, who replied enigmatically, "Thanks for the compliment. I regret I am unable to reciprocate."

As for the succession to Weizmann as president of the Zionist Congress, Jabotinsky had an opportunity but no strategy. With Weizmann discredited, he was convinced he was the logical successor. But, instead of seeking out allies, he insisted, to little purpose, that Revisionists be awarded half the seats on the Zionist Executive, a proposal his opponents easily defeated. The congress then proceeded to elect Nahum Sokolow, Weizmann's faithful minion, who had provided vital services in crafting the Balfour Declaration and had served long and ably on the Zionist Executive.

Both Jabotinsky and Weizmann felt betrayed by the events at the 1931 congress. Though they were self-made the congress lost confidence in both of them. It both repudiated Weizmann's intimacy with Britain and Jabotinsky's aggressive alternative. Amid the confusion, Jabotinsky came as close as he ever would to seizing control of the Zionist movement. But he failed, and Revisionism would now have to wait nearly half a century for another opportunity, under another leader.

In Jerusalem, Samuel's successor as High Commissioner no doubt followed what transpired at the Zionist Congress. Though he had failed a year earlier to deny Jabotinsky an entry visa, he had not given up. During the 1929 riots provoked by Betar, Jabotinsky was abroad and could not be charged with criminal intent. But a newspaper had published an address he delivered in Tel Aviv before leaving the country. It was no different from his many other speeches, but the Mandate was lying in wait. In London, Jabotinsky was notified that the High Commissioner had refused to allow his return to Palestine.

Jabotinsky did not accept the decision easily. In a letter to the colonial office, he called the denial "an immoral act of cynicism and ingratitude." Friends in London cited his military service to Britain; in parliament, his defenders charged the Mandate with impropriety. The High Commissioner hinted at a reversal on the same condition as before, that Jabotinsky agree to abstain from politics. Jews everywhere called the condition blackmail, and Jabotinsky rejected it. But he did not get the entry visa, and having given up his British nationality years before, he was henceforth reduced to traveling with documents issued by the League of Nations to stateless persons.

Despite the departure of both Weizmann and Jabotinsky from the leadership circle, the Zionist Organization made no changes in policy. Sokolow's election was an endorsement of the status quo. The Zionist Executive, grateful for MacDonald's quasi-apology for the Passfield White Paper, chose not to undermine its relations with Britain further. Weizmann decided again to use his time to rebuild his career in science, while Jabotinsky renewed his campaign to persuade his followers in Revisionism to secede from the Zionist Organization.

Unable to reverse the High Commissioner's dictum, Jabotinsky never saw Palestine again.

After his unhappy experience at the Zionist Congress of 1931, Jabotinsky embarked on resolving Revisionism's dilemma. In September, he convened a conference in Calais, France, where the Revisionists proposed to remain in the congress without being bound by its decisions. The Zionist Executive rejected the offer.

Jabotinsky was under heavy pressure now from an extreme faction within Revisionism called the "Maximalists," closer to fascism than Betar. Led by an intellectual named Abba Ahimeir, the Maximalists rejected democracy itself. Its models were the Bolshevik Lenin and the radical Jewish insurgent Bar Kokhba of the second century A.D. Jabotinsky recognized the Maximalists' potential to create organizational chaos but he admired their audacity, and he was not disposed to take them on in a fight.

By the mid-1930s, it was clear the Maximalists were undermining Jabotinsky's popular support. "You have proclaimed the slogan 'Back to Herzl,'" a young militant said to him. "We beg you to proclaim 'Back to Jabotinsky.'" When the Maximalists urged him to assume dictatorial powers, Jabotinsky declared, "I believe in the ideological patrimony of Garibaldi and Lincoln. Better not to live at all than to live under such a system." But Jabotinsky's thinking was evolving, and he was not as immune as he claimed to antidemocratic demands.

In rejecting the Calais offer, the Zionist Executive announced that if Revisionism wanted to stay in the Organization, it had to abide by all official decisions. Jabotinsky took the announcement as an ultimatum. He was willing to discuss the matter, he said, but would resign if he did not get the outcome he wanted. As a final gesture, he said he would convene still another Revisionist meeting.

The meeting took place in Kattowitz, the small town, now in Poland, where Hibbat Zion had held its historic conference in 1884. If the first Kattowitz conference left major issues unresolved, the second was even less decisive. The delegates talked day and night about Jabotinsky's secession proposal, but when their meeting adjourned they had resolved on no course at all.

From Kattowitz, Jabotinsky traveled to Łódź in Poland, where, on March 23, 1933, he crossed the Zionist Rubicon. "I, the president of the World Union of Zionist Revisionists, declare that from today I am assuming the direction of the Union and all matters of the world movement.

The activities of the existing central institutions of the world movement are thereby being suspended. . . ." In claiming full personal authority, Jabotinsky did exactly what the Maximalists wanted and he had vowed he would never do. Having long taken pride in being a liberal democrat, he conducted a fascist-style coup d'etat.

In an article a few days later, Jabotinsky ostensibly reversed his action. Kattowitz, he wrote, had caused "despair and hopelessness," and the delegates, in an effort to reconcile their differences, had turned to him. "All Revisionists—or almost all, with a few exceptions—want to go to the Eighteenth Zionist Congress . . . not with a view to seceding. . . . I decided to accept their mandate, irrespective of my personal feelings . . . The Revisionist Party will have the opportunity to 'go' or to 'stay,' through a Revisionist World Conference or a plebiscite."

Even Schechtman, his admiring biographer, had difficulty making sense of Jabotinsky's action. Schechtman's work is rich in research and generally reliable, and he contributes much to any study of Jabotinsky. In leading a Revisionist delegation to the next Zionist Congress, Schechtman writes, Jabotinsky, far from exploiting a coup, wanted simply to eliminate secession as a Revisionist issue. Schechtman's contention strains credulity.

In April 1933, Jabotinsky himself wrote a letter belying Schechtman's interpretation. In tone it sounded much like the deceptions of twentieth-century tyrants. "I look into myself," he said, "but I see no sin, except one: I might have been too soft with my associates, giving them too much leeway. I would be glad to devote myself to literature, to retire to my Paris apartment, but I simply have no right to do so. I see tens of thousands of people who want to follow me, and their number is growing." In opposing him, old colleagues were being "nuisances," he wrote, but he also expressed confidence that they would in time embrace him again.

The plebiscite Jabotinsky promised took place in April 1933, with adult Revisionists everywhere eligible to vote. Rather than focus on the secession, the question put to them—fascist-style—was whether "All the executive functions of the whole Revisionist movement . . . shall be vested in the hands of Vladimir Jabotinsky, President of the Union of Zionist Revisionists." The result was 31,724 votes in favor and 2,066 against. To Jabotinsky, the huge majority confirmed the movement's "sound democracy," validating the Łódź declaration.

Schechtman admitted "a substantial kernel of truth" in the charge that the plebiscite was a fraud, though he rejected comparison with Europe's notorious dictators. Jabotinsky's supporters, he wrote, were moved by respect, not by intimidation, but many Jews were deeply troubled. Schechtman himself writes of crowds jeering at Jabotinsky rallies, often carrying such signs as "Down with Jewish Hitlerism." Ben-Gurion, the socialist leader, provoked a huge row by referring to Jabotinsky as "Vladimir Hitler."

After the plebiscite, Jabotinsky wrote revealingly. "As I grow old, I am beginning to agree with the view that the party must be 'led.' . . . As I near old age, I am beginning to believe in the inevitability of personal leadership." Was the author of these words, who once revered English democracy, suffering from a deep sense of injury over England's repeatedly turning on him? In December 1933, as a gesture of protest, Jabotinsky closed the Revisionist headquarters in London and relocated it to Paris.

By the mid-1930s, David Ben-Gurion—subject of the next chapter—had gone far in creating a foundation of democratic socialism under the Mandate in Jewish Palestine. His supporters extolled his program as building Zionism "immigrant by immigrant, farm by farm." Jabotinsky mocked his efforts as the "cult of the cow." His own priority remained the armed pursuit of statehood, without concern for the character of the state. But now the rivalry between the two men had more immediate implications. With Weizmann apparently out of the running, Jabotinsky and Ben-Gurion were competing for who would rule a forthcoming Jewish state.

Jobs were a major battlefield, on which violence regularly took place. Jabotinsky, hostile to labor unions, argued that Ben-Gurion's Labor Party could not simultaneously promote socialism and statehood. He directed particular animosity at the Histadrut, Labor's organization of workers, which ran exchanges to provide jobs for loyal members. Jabotinsky encouraged Betaris to engage in union-busting and strike-breaking to thwart the exchange. Ben-Gurion branded Jabotinsky the "enemy of the working man."

On May Day, in 1928, Betaris joined with the Mandatory police to break up a workers' demonstration, tearing up socialist flags, and causing a few injuries. Several months later, Betaris attacked a workers' meeting in Tel Aviv, and Ben-Gurion vowed to "root out these hoodlumist outrages." The clashes intensified when Betaris accepted employment by the citrus growers as strike-breakers. Ben-Gurion confronted them with squads of workers that he had organized years before to bar Arabs from taking jobs he thought belonged to Jews.

A year later, Betaris conducted the rowdy protest at the Wailing Wall that led to countrywide bloodshed. The 1929 riots were not just between Arabs and Jews. They inflamed the dispute between Revisionism and Labor, in which Ben-Gurion, in a swipe at Jabotinsky's sympathy for fascist Italy, called Revisionism "a putrid weed drawing sustenance from a befouled source."

In 1933 with talk rising of replacing Sokolow as president of the Zionist organization, Jabotinsky and Ben-Gurion squared off in a campaign to elect delegates to control the Zionist Congress. Both focused their efforts on Poland, the richest source of Zionist votes. Jabotinsky, pressured by the Maximalists, was shrill, declaring Histadrut "a gross cancer" in the body of the *yishuv*. "Our enemies," Ben-Gurion answered, "fight us as Hitler fights the workers. They will use their power to . . . cut us down brutally, with no holds barred."

On June 16, 1933, as the election campaign was drawing to a close, Chaim Arlosoroff, a rising star in the Labor Party's hierarchy, was shot to death while walking with his wife on a Tel Aviv beach. A few days before, Arlosoroff had returned from Germany bearing an accord with the Nazis to allow Jews to emigrate to Palestine, leaving behind property that was to be paid for by German exports. Revisionists raged at him for consorting with Nazis. Most Laborites, Ben-Gurion among them, denounced Revisionism for the murder. Jabotinsky, invoking the medieval charge of Jewish infanticide, called the accusation a "blood libel."

In this bitter atmosphere, a half-million Zionists cast votes for delegates to the forthcoming Zionist Congress. Labor received 44 percent, more than expected. Revisionists were repudiated with just 16 percent. Thrilled by the endorsement, Ben-Gurion announced that Labor's next step would be the "conquest of Zionism."

Within a few days, the British police arrested three suspects, all Revisionists, for Arlosoroff's murder. The most noteworthy was the Maximalist leader Ahimeir, now heading a group called the League of Sicarii, named for Jewish assassins of the Second Temple era. Knowing Ahimeir, the police assumed his involvement. The two others were identified by Arlosoroff's widow. Two Arabs who actually confessed to the killing later recanted their confessions.

Jabotinsky wrote fiery articles comparing the arrests to the Dreyfus case. "Murders of Jews . . . ," he said, "have always been tied to the well-known tensions between Jews and Arabs . . . so it would have been natural to look for the murderers among Arab extremists." Labor took the opposite approach, blaming the killings on Zionist politics, insisting that "moral responsibility . . . falls on the entire Revisionist movement."

By the time the trial opened a year later, the case had ignited a cross-current of abuse among Jews worldwide. The charges against Ahimeir had been dismissed, and one of the two other defendants was acquitted for lack of evidence. The third suspect, Abraham Stavsky—who will re-appear later in different circumstances—was found guilty and condemned to death. Public emotions rose to an even higher pitch. "He belongs to Betar, a youth organization of which I am the head," Jabotinsky wrote of Stavsky, whom he seemed to have known in Poland. "No Betari would lie to me. I pledge my honor that Stavsky is innocent."

A British appeals court reversed Stavsky's conviction a year later. Ja-botinsky remained convinced that Revisionism had been the victim of a Labor conspiracy, while Ben-Gurion was certain the guilty party had gone free. Foreshadowing the later alliance between Revisionism and Religious Zionism, one of Jabotinsky's most outspoken backers was Rav Abraham Isaac Kook, the Chief Ashkenazi Rabbi. The unsolved murder left Zionism under a cloud of mutual recrimination, which has not fully dissipated to this day.

But even as Jabotinsky and Ben-Gurion fanned the flames, both ad-mitted that their mutual hostility had reached a point of inflicting serious harm on Zionism. Whatever their differences, the two parties shared the aim of establishing Jewish statehood. Many Zionists believed the conflict was really about ego and political ambition. Both men admitted that clos-ing the gap would benefit the Zionist cause.

In October and November of 1934, Jabotinsky and Ben-Gurion held a series of secret meetings in London, and to the surprise of both, they got along very well. Ben-Gurion was said even to have made Jabotinsky an omelet for supper. Some of their talking sessions lasted well into the night.

At the end, the two signed a pledge, Jabotinsky in the name of the Re-visionist World Union, Ben-Gurion in the name of the Zionist Executive, to "refrain from all means of party warfare which are outside the limits of political and ideological discussion and are not in conformity . . . with civilized conduct." They further agreed to bar "acts of terror or violence . . .

libel, slander [and] insult to individuals or groups" among their own followers. By the end of the year, they had also signed addendums setting limits on their other differences.

But the accords were not to be valid until ratified by their respective organizations. At the Revisionist World Congress, Jabotinsky coaxed out a fragile majority after much pleading, which included a reminder that "Ben-Gurion . . . wore the uniform of the Jewish Legion in the World War." But Ben-Gurion had less control over his membership and was forced to submit the accord to a referendum of the rank and file. The referendum was defeated by a 60 to 40 percent margin. The animosity that had been built up over the years proved too much for the Labor leadership to overcome.

When the results were in, Ben-Gurion wrote Jabotinsky, "If we must battle each other, remember that among your enemies is a man who esteems you and feels your pain as his own." Jabotinsky sent a similar letter in reply. But there was no undoing the crushing blow to the Zionism movement that the rejection inflicted.

The result was the resumption of conflict. The Zionist Executive rubbed salt in Jabotinsky's wounds by requiring all delegates to the forthcoming congress to waive the right to reject duly approved policy proposals. Some colleagues urged Jabotinsky to defy the requirement, thus daring the Executive to expel them. Jabotinsky chose instead to present his own executive with a motion to have Revisionism secede from the Zionist Organization altogether. Jabotinsky's proposal was adopted unanimously.

Jabotinsky had long awaited this vote. He admitted feeling "as if I were living a new youth." The decision was affirmed in a referendum by Revisionism's 167,000 members. Having seceded from World Zionism, Revisionism then founded an independent body that was named the New Zionist Organization. It elected Jabotinsky its president by acclamation, and ratified a constitution that called for ending the Exile by "repatriating" all Jews to a Jewish state on both sides of the Jordan River. With Hitler consolidating his power in Germany, it was hardly a propitious time for a Zionist schism. But Jabotinsky was now poised to challenge Ben-Gurion for outright control of the Zionist movement.

In 1935, the World Zionist Congress, meeting in Lucerne without the Revisionist faction, voted to restore Weizmann as its president. Ben-Gurion, now the *yishuv's* dominant political figure, raised no objections. Weizmann was still acknowledged as Zionism's most popular figure, known worldwide. His priorities had not changed. He returned to the presidency planning to repair relations with the British, confident that with war against Germany clearly approaching, Britain would recognize the centrality to their interests of the Jews in both Europe and the Middle East.

Jabotinsky, meanwhile, fantasized about replacing Britain with Italy as the Jews' protector. He even petitioned the League of Nations to invite Mussolini to take over the Mandate. He organized a network to expand illegal Jewish entry into Palestine, with Revisionists arranging sea transport in Europe and preparing beaches in Palestine for night landings. By 1938, more than a thousand Jews reached Palestine each month. A large proportion were Betaris, a source of concern to mainstream Zionists, placing them on the alert.

As war approached, Britain grew even more anxious to cool Arab-Jewish animosities in Palestine, but with no greater success than before, Britain had granted at least a smattering of self-rule in Iraq, Egypt, and Transjordan, but the Arabs of Palestine were being asked to share power with the Jews, which they flatly refused. They again dismissed a plan for a joint legislature, but so did the *yishuv*, which feared being permanently outvoted by an Arab majority.

By the mid-1930s, the Arabs were again restless—and ready for a new round of violence. Nazi propaganda helped to incite them. So did a temporary British waiver, in response to rising Nazi persecution of Germany's Jews, of limits on Jewish immigration. Jabotinsky wired the High Commissioner, "Compelled to inform Your Excellency of alarming reports from Palestine voicing acutest apprehension of anti-Jewish outbreaks. . . . Ominous battle cry, 'The government is with us . . .' Such developments inevitably result in bloodshed, especially considering scarcity of imperial troops, inefficient police . . . and absence of legalized Jewish self-defense." Jabotinsky's warning received no response.

In 1936, an Arab Higher Committee was formed under the leadership of the Grand Mufti and called for a general strike in Palestine. Violence began with the killing of several Jews on a bus and was followed by marauding gangs attacking Jewish towns and settlements. Rival Arab factions coalesced, and volunteers arrived from neighboring countries. An organized revolt was clearly under way. The Arab condition for ending the disorders was a total British ban on Jewish immigration and land acquisition.

The *yishuv* mobilized in response to the uprising, with Irgun, the Revisionist militia, drawing the first Arab blood. The Haganah was not far behind, ambushing Arab raiding parties and occupying Arab villages used as guerrilla bases. The British, without modifying their attitude toward the Jews, actually cooperated with the Haganah, but the early fighting was inconclusive and the casualties on both sides kept rising.

Both Jabotinsky and Ben-Gurion agreed in principle on the importance of unifying the Jewish forces under a single command. Though Jabotinsky, being in exile, had no operational power, he was nominally in command of Irgun. Composed preponderantly of Betaris, Irgun called for more aggressive tactics than the Haganah, but the differences between the two went beyond tactics. The Haganah's commanders were Laborites, which made them responsible to Histadrut, thus anathema to Revisionists. When the two sides sat down to talk, Ben-Gurion demanded that the combined forces be an instrument of the *yishuv,* the Jewish community, which meant that Ben-Gurion would be in command. The demand forced the negotiations into an impasse.

Meanwile, the British appointed another commission to assess responsibility for the ongoing Arab revolt. Named for Lord Peel, its chairman, the commission convened in Jerusalem in November to take testimony. The two sides were still negotiating when it was learned that the commission was contemplating a plan to partition Palestine into Jewish and Arab states. However logical, the idea violated a basic Zionist doctrine, but it especially outraged Jabotinsky who, committed to a state on both banks of the Jordan, could not consent to having Revisionists fight and die for what he called "the rump of Palestine."

Weizmann, when presented with the prospect of partition, responded, "Of course, it is cutting the child in two." But Britain, Weizmann admitted, was no longer up to assuring the Jews a home in all of Palestine. Foreseeing an imminent end to the Mandate under any circumstances, he perceived partition as offering to the Jews the chance to become a majority in their own state, whatever its size. If the Peel Commission allowed Zionism to establish a smaller but sovereign state, it would make us "our own masters." With Europe's Jews standing at the edge of annihilation, he reasoned, "we could save a lot of them . . ."[24]

When the Peel Commission invited Jabotinsky to give testimony, it assumed the High Commissioner would honor its request for a visa. Learning of the request, a local Jewish newspaper wrote, "Who of those who saw it can forget the excitement in the streets . . . when an item was published that Jabotinsky might possibly be coming. . . . Electricity seemed to fill the air." The jubilation, however, was short-lived. Jabotinsky pulled the strings that were available to him in London, but in vain. The High Commissioner defied the Peel Commission and reaffirmed the denial of Jabotinsky's entry into Palestine.

In February 1937, Jabotinsky—as he had with the Shaw Commission in 1929—testified before the Peel Commission in London. He conveyed a seething anger, directed at both Britain and his Zionist rivals. Leading the questioning, Lord Peel inquired about disputes within the Zionist movement. Jabotinsky at first disclaimed a willingness to criticize his fellow Jews, but then he changed his stance.

When asked if he objected to the Zionist Organization in "material aspects," Jabotinsky answered curtly, "Yes." Asked on what points they agreed, he waived the opportunity to cite a common dedication to providing a refuge for jeopardized Jewry, and instead answered coldly, "It is for them to decide." Asked to characterize mainstream Zionism, he declared: "They have no plan. They never had any plan of what they meant by colonizing Palestine or carrying out the Zionist program. . . . The first attempt at drawing up such a plan was the Revisionist program." Following up, Peel asked, "You mean you are more definite in your scheme of planning?" Jabotinsky replied, "Not that we are more definite. We are definite. They are not."[25]

Though he spared England itself, Jabotinsky showed no restraint in his criticism toward the High Commissioner on the subject of the visa. "I want the man on the spot," he testified, "to stand before a Royal Commission, before a Judicial Commission, and I want him to answer for his errors. Sometimes a humble man like me has the right to say *J'accuse*. . . . They are guilty of commission, omission, neglect of duty. . . . I believe the persons guilty should be punished, and that is what I humbly demand."

As for the Mandate's future, the central issue faced by the commission, Jabotinsky testified that if Britain was unable to carry out its responsibilities, it should leave Palestine altogether. Yet he could not conceal his ambiguity. Asked to whom he would prefer to entrust its duties, he replied—without specifying Italy—that there were other "civilized peoples as conscientious" as Britain. Then, contemplating the real possibility of Britain's departure, he oddly softened to declare, "I am fully convinced that it will not be necessary. I believe in England just as I believed in England twenty years ago."

Jabotinsky never actually touched on partition, but in the weeks that followed he spoke to sympathetic audiences against what he called the "partition craze." Unreconciled to losing Transjordan, he denounced Weizmann for giving up what he described as four-fifths of the Jews' national home. If "the dark clouds of partition" do not disperse, he declared, "then we shall fight." Vowing to give the order himself, Jabotinsky proclaimed that Betar and Irgun would rebel if Britain sought to impose partition. He himself would fight with them, he announced, even "go to prison and if need be to die together."

The final report of the Peel Commission, issued in July 1937, was a sharp departure from that of any previous body of inquiry, and far more audacious in its advocacy than the British cabinet anticipated. It urged ending the Mandate by dividing Palestine into two states, both sovereign, a Jewish and a much larger Arab state. A third area, which was to include Jerusalem and the port of Haifa, would remain under British control.

In explanation, the report stated, "An irrepressible conflict has arisen between two national communities within the narrow bounds of one small country. About a million Arabs are in strife, open or latent, with some 400,000 Jews. There is no common ground between them. . . . Partition seems to offer at least some chance of ultimate peace. We can see none in any other plan."

Weizmann accepted partition in his own testimony, as did Ben-Gurion. Only Jabotinsky, backed by his Revisionists and a few rebellious Labor Zionists, dissented. At the Zionist Congress in August 1937, Weizmann argued that despite his dissatisfaction over the size, the Peel proposal had set a precedent for Jewish sovereignty, with a state large enough to provide refuge for 100,000 immigrants a year. The Zionist Congress, in a canny compromise, voted to reject partition based on the borders proposed by the commission but offered to negotiate further on all issues. Zionism thus kept the idea of partition alive and on the negotiating table.

The British cabinet initially endorsed the Peel Report, with Foreign Secretary Anthony Eden declaring that "partition is the only solution." In customary fashion, the Arab leadership, save for Transjordan's Emir Abdullah, rejected any compromise at all with the Jews. The Arabs then resumed their revolt. Subsequently, the British cabinet published a policy paper that rejected partition completely. Its final veto was announced on November 9, 1938, the day of the German pogrom known as *Kristallnacht*.[26]

Even as Britain conveyed a willingness to sever its ties to the Jews, Jabotinsky took an unaccustomed step, joining mainstream Zionism in arguing against a final break. But Jabotinsky's voice was no longer what it had been. Visibly aging, he often appeared exhausted. His charisma was fading, his mind was less acute. In the Revisionist office in Paris, he was able to keep dissidence under control, but his long exile had sapped his influence in Palestine, where Revisionists followed their own star. Challenging Jabotinsky, Revisionists in Palestine increasingly perceived Britain as an enemy that they could deal with only with guns and explosives.

The Arab revolt was still raging when the Arab National Congress, a loosely organized popular assembly, announced its formal rejection of partition. Explaining threateningly, it said, "We must make Great Britain understand that it must choose between our friendship and the Jews. Britain must change her policy in Palestine or we will be at liberty to side with other European powers whose policies are inimical to Great Britain." British forces stepped up their attacks on the Arab units fighting in the revolt, but Britain still declined to moderate its hostility toward the Jews.

In Europe in early 1939, after Germany occupied much of Czechoslovakia, Britain made one last effort to resolve the Palestine question. It convened a "round table" at St. James's Palace in London, to which it invited, along with a Jewish delegation, Arabs not just from Palestine but from the neighboring Arab states, signaling its awareness of the spread of Arab antagonism. With war very near, the colonial office was clearly referring to the Arabs, not the Jews, when it declared that Britain "depended on the active support of our allies in the Middle East."

Because the Arab delegates refused to sit with the Jews, or even enter St. James's Palace through the same gate, Britain conducted separate talks with the two sides. Britain's objective, at this point, was to impose new limits, notwithstanding Nazi oppression, on Jewish entry to Palestine. Both sides rejected Britain's proposals, the Jews as a violation of the Balfour pledges, the Arabs as a failure to end immigration completely.

In May 1939, Britain issued the MacDonald White Paper. Conceding that it lacked the means to maintain the Mandate indefinitely, it turned upside down the priorities in the Balfour Declaration. Jewish statehood, it said, was out of the question; henceforth Britain would concentrate on Arab grievances. For the first time, Britain declared openly its intention to apply the Balfour Declaration's pledge to the "non-Jewish communities in Palestine" more seriously than the pledge to the Jews.

The MacDonald White Paper fixed Jewish entry into Palestine over the next five years at 75,000, with illegal immigration to be deducted from the total. After that, immigration was to be permanently closed. Citing "the spirit of the Mandate," Britain further pledged the establishment of self-government in Palestine, stating that, in ten years, Britain would turn the country over to a majority of its inhabitants. Having set strict limits on the Jews' entry, it left no doubt that in 1949, ten years hence, the majority would be Arab.

The White Paper crushed the last hope that Palestine might serve as a refuge for Europe's beleaguered Jews. Weizmann viewed the decision no less as a betrayal than did Jabotinsky and Ben-Gurion. In Palestine, Revisionists initiated a terror campaign against the Mandate, bombing government installations. On August 31, Britain retaliated with the arrest of dozens of Irgun officers. The next day, the Germans invaded Poland, and on September 3, Britain declared war on Germany.

Prime Minister Neville Chamberlain ended any prospect that belligerency might change the reality in Palestine. With Nazi soldiers overrunning Europe, Weizmann offered a military truce between Britain and the Jews in Palestine and, over the protests of Revisionist combatants, Jabotinsky joined him. At this point, it was unlikely Weizmann and Jabotinsky could have enforced a truce, but Chamberlain thanked them for their "expressions of support." He then repeated that the immigration restrictions imposed by the 1939 White Paper would remain in effect.

The coming of war left Palestine's Revisionists in a dilemma. As Jews they recognized the Nazis as the preeminent enemy, but among them were those who were unwilling to give up the fight against Britain. Most of its officers were then in British detention camps, and Revisionism was powerless to fight any war at all. But in mid-1940 Britain released the Revisionist leaders, and it was unclear in which direction they would go.

That summer, the Maximalists broke away from the Irgun completely to form a rogue force known as Lehi, also called the Stern Gang after its leader, Avraham Stern. Its plan was to fight the British, whatever the cost to the war against Germany. Many of the Irgun's soldiers took the breakup poorly. "How was it possible to continue to live," one wrote, "when our commanders, for whom we were willing to kill or be killed, accused one another of being agents of Hitler, or agents of the British police, or lowly and crazed traitors?" Forced to choose between rival wings, some Revisionist soldiers simply abandoned the struggle.

By now Jabotinsky, Revisionism's historic leader and the nominal commander of its armed forces, had become a bystander to events. In early 1940, he left for America, to satisfy his fantasy of re-creating the Jewish Legion. On occasion he sent messages back to his commanders, aimed at narrowing the rift between them, but his efforts came to nothing. Revisionism was leaderless, and by August 1940 Jabotinsky was dead.

Jabotinsky, rejecting the cascading evidence, had insisted until the last moment that war in Europe would not break out. He was almost alone. Was he misreading all the signals or engaged in wishful thinking? Had his analytical powers failed him? What did it mean that he was unable to persuade his followers that the Nazis were the most dangerous threat that Jews had ever faced? In 1914, Jabotinsky's mind had leaped ahead to contemplate the postwar world that the Jews would encounter. In 1940, he was apathetic and unable to find his way.

Before he died, Jabotinsky wrote a book called *The War and the Jew*. Hastily composed, it fell short of his usual standards in style and insight. Still, it was rich in its argument. The foes of Nazism, he declared, must count the Jews as members of their alliance. A Jewish army, he argued, would affirm that "this is the Jews' war, as much as Britain's, France's and Poland's." Yet he also warned that the enemy, to discourage American intervention, was depicting this as a "Jewish war," an admission that the formation of a Jewish army might play into the wrong hands. What Jabotinsky seemed unable to grasp was that the British—lukewarm about the Jewish Legion in World War I—had no intention whatsoever of supporting its re-creation by a man whom they regarded as a persistant troublemaker and who was likely to wind up fighting against them.

Jabotinsky traveled to America in search of a chimera. He hoped to find Jews nostalgic about his Legion, and a pool of young Jewish men ready to wear its uniform. Britain, however, had not given up its vendetta against him. The American consulate in London, no doubt at the urging of Britain's foreign office, delayed issuing him an entry visa, then refused a visa to his wife to travel with him. In Palestine, his son Eri was the last activist to be released from among all the Irgun officers in military detention.

Jabotinsky finally boarded a ship for New York in March 1940, which raised another question. Why did he depart while Revisionism—and particularly the Irgun—was unraveling from within? It could be surmised that Jabotinsky was running away. It seemed as if, to pursue the memory of a Jewish Legion, he was abandoning his command of the Irgun and his responsibility to his movement.

Jabotinsky was well enough received in America, and as usual, he attracted large audiences to his lectures. At all of them he declared that the United States had a duty to forego its neutrality and enter the war, and that Jews had a responsibility to participate in it. But he sparked no mass promises of enlistment in a Jewish Legion. American Jews, while responding warmly to his performances on the speakers' platform, provided little support for his military design.

In fact, Jabotinsky's appeal no longer crossed factional lines in America, as it had in World War I and throughout the 1920s. In the interval too much had happened to undermine his reputation, most notably his role in splitting Zionism by leading Revisionism out of the Zionist camp. His inability to draw support left him in despair. Not only was his effort to mend the schism in the Irgun halfhearted. He even stopped writing articles, explaining to his publisher that "when this mood is upon me, there is nothing doing." Of his failure in America, he wrote to his wife, "Of all the cups of bitterness I have swallowed, this cup is by far the nastiest."

In July, Jabotinsky took a break from his speaking schedule to visit a Betar training camp in upstate New York, where his disciples greeted him enthusiastically. After inspecting the camp facilities, he sang songs, picked flowers, and hiked through the surrounding hills with young Betaris. Being with them improved his mood significantly, even more so when he received word that his wife, with her visa finally in hand, would soon be joining him. On August 3, he made a second trip to the Betar camp. Though he started the day's events in good humor, he was soon exhausted, and after reviewing an honor guard, he adjourned to his quarters to rest. That afternoon his heart gave out and he died. Jabotinsky was not yet sixty years old.

Jabotinsky had conveyed in his will a wish to be buried in Palestine but, until it was possible, his body was to be interred in a Jewish cemetery in Long Island. Thousands made their way to the funeral. An observer reported that because of the many rabbis who sought to honor him, it was politically impossible to select a single one to preside at the graveside. As a result, 150 cantors joined together to chant Jewish hymns, while the rabbis stood by.

Schechtman, his biographer, wrote in summation of Jabotinsky that "All his life long, he was an unhyphenated Zionist: not a Socialist Zionist or a Religious Zionist, but a Zionist *tout court.*" That may have been Jabotinsky's preferred description. But the judgment is untrue. Jabotinsky was a Revisionist Zionist. His huge impact lay in the ideology that he created, which produced a tougher, more rigid, heavily militaristic *and deeply divided* Zionism.

Revisionism thrives today, with an ideology that has grown only harsher since Jabotinsky's time. Jabotinsky inspired a strategy of military confrontation in Palestine that many credit with hastening the formation of the Jewish state. Others, noting a worldwide loss since 1948 of sympathy for Israel, wonder whether the price Revisionism exacted from Zionism was too high.

The diverse crowd of cantors chanting at Jabotinsky's grave summarized the effort of Jews to unite in their struggle for a national home. Jabotinsky did not make the effort easier. Herzl had said that, "If the Jews ever 'returned home' one day, they would discover on the next that they do not belong together," but it was Jabotinsky who, in creating Revisionism and seceding from the Zionist Organization, took a giant step to prove him right. Ben-Gurion contributed to this disunity in denying Jabotinsky's wish to be interred in Israel. It took a prime minister with a warmer heart, twenty-four years after his death, to permit Jabotinsky's burial on Mount Herzl in Jerusalem. There, in a pantheon of men who shaped Zionism, Jabotinsky rests.

4

David Ben-Gurion
1886–1973

STATE BUILDER

On May 14, 1948, the eve of Britain's formal departure from its Palestine Mandate, David Ben-Gurion proclaimed the birth of the sovereign Jewish state of Israel. It was the culmination of the movement for independence that Herzl initiated in 1897, when he declared to the first World Zionist Congress that "we are here to lay the cornerstone of the edifice that is to house the Jewish nation." A few days later, Herzl inscribed in his diary a promise that "perhaps in five years, and certainly in fifty," a Jewish state will exist. In the ensuing half-century, no man did more than Ben-Gurion to transform Herzl's promise into reality.

Even before Jabotinsky's death and Weizmann's decline, Ben-Gurion was the dominant player in Zionist politics. Less naturally charismatic than Jabotinsky, less eloquent than Weizmann, he was a short, stocky figure who wore ill-fitting suits and a flamboyant fringe of white hair on his otherwise barren head. Although all three were of Eastern European background, only Ben-Gurion was born to a poor and struggling family. Dedicated and ambitious Zionists from their youth, each had a different vision of the character of Zionism. But it was Ben-Gurion, the most tireless and stubborn of them, whom the state that emerged would most closely resemble.

Ben-Gurion's own vision of Zionism drew from the Bible, which he treated not as a religious tract but as a work of Jewish history. He was not a traditional Jew. His interest lay in the nationalist message that the Bible contained, which he regarded as the real foundation of Judaism. He was not much interested in the law, the morality, or the religious practices that the Bible taught. He considered the Talmud to be rabbinic sophistry, a device to promote a passive acceptance of the Exile. Throughout his career, Ben-Gurion looked to the Bible as the record of the Jewish people, as his intellectual inspiration, and as the source of his energy.

"The Jewish faith is not only monotheism," Ben-Gurion once said. "Intrinsic to it is the national and territorial motif, which led to the profound spiritual allegiance of the Jews to their ancient land, even while they lived in exile. . . . This motif finds expression in all the books of the Bible. It appears in the first monotheistic revelation, in the first meeting of Abraham, the father of the Jews, with God. It is not important whether the story is a true record of an historic event or not. What is important is that this is what Jews believe. . . . We read in Genesis, 'Now the Lord said unto Abram: get thee out . . . of thy father's house into a land which I will show thee, and I will make of thee a great nation.' This is the first statement of the national and territorial theme."[1]

No less important, Ben-Gurion brought a shrewd practicality to Herzl's grand vision of providing refuge for the Jewish people. It was he who set the course for the governance of Israel by creating institutions that would establish order and prosperity. He also made Israel the most powerful military force in the Middle East. Ben-Gurion's failure was to leave unresolved a conflict with the Arabs that has kept the Jewish state—more in the long term than in the short—in existential jeopardy. Ben-Gurion brought stability to Israel, but he did not assure Israel's future.

David Ben-Gurion was born David Gruen on October 16, 1886, in Płońsk, a small, drab, mostly Jewish town in the Russian Pale. He was the fourth child of Avigdor and Scheindel Gruen. His mother died when he was ten. His father and grandfather called themselves lawyers, though both worked less prestigiously as translators and recorders of legal documents. Ben-Gurion often said he absorbed Zionism from his father, who founded a local society of Hibbat Zion, and his grandfather, who taught him Hebrew and read the Bible to him while he sat on his knee.

Barely ten when Herzl's *The Jewish State* was published, he was surely too young to remember the impact. He later insisted, however, that all Płońsk reacted as if the Messiah had arrived. By adolescence, he said, he was convinced—as was Weizmann—that God had imparted to him a mission to serve the Zionist cause. In his school, shaped by the *Haskala*, he read not only Tolstoy and Dostoyevsky but seminal Zionist thinkers, and with friends he formed a society to promote Zionism called Ezra, named for the scribe who led the ancient Jews back to Palestine from the Babylonian exile. When Herzl urged the Zionist Congress in 1903 to consent to settling Jews temporarily in Uganda, Ben-Gurion said he cried bitterly and vowed to migrate to Palestine as soon as he was able.

Yet, even as his friends from Ezra made the journey, Ben-Gurion delayed. He moved to Warsaw to enroll in an engineering school, claiming it would provide him with skills needed in the Jewish homeland. But he never took the exam, apparently because he was distracted by a young woman named Rachel Nelkin, who was as Zionist as he, and, though never his wife, would be a major presence throughout his life.

He was also active in Zionist politics in Warsaw, and after the Kishinev pogrom, he returned to Płońsk to help organize his friends—much as Jabotinsky did in Odessa—into Jewish self-defense societies. Known by now for fiery speeches and aggressive political action, he took a new satisfaction after Kishinev in learning to use a gun.

As a teen, Ben-Gurion enrolled in Poale Zion—"Workers of Zion"—a Jewish political party that aimed to fuse Herzl's Zionism with Marx's socialism. He did not regard the two goals as equal: socialism was an organizing tool, a distant second in importance to Zionism. As a Poale Zion militant, he became a local hero by leading a workers' strike against capitalists in Płońsk. "Still, my heart was empty," he later said. "I knew that revolution might liberate Russia, but it would not liberate the Jews."[2]

When the Russian revolution of 1905 broke out, Ben-Gurion joined friends in Warsaw in taking up arms against the czar. The blood that was spilled vainly during the fighting, he later said, finally persuaded him to depart for Palestine. Accompanied by Rachel and her mother, he boarded a ship in Odessa in August 1906, shortly before his twentieth birthday. To his father, who paid his passage, he wrote, "A few more hours and I will have left the dark recesses of exile . . . on the way to the land of our rebirth."

On the ship he met his first Arabs, whom he described as "easy to be-friend and almost invariably good-hearted," but otherwise lacking in ap-peal. In September the ship reached Jaffa, where delegates from Poale Zion and some old friends from Płońsk were waiting to greet him.

Ben-Gurion and Rachel set out at once for Petah Tikva, a farm settle-ment several hours away by foot. Founded by Baron de Hirsch, Petah Tikva was now supported by Baron de Rothschild, still Zionism's nemesis. Jews competed with Arabs for pitiful wages in the fields. Ben-Gurion and Ra-chel found work and described their situation in letters home as a Zionist paradise, but in fact the hardships were too much for them both. As a Marxist, Ben-Gurion found Petah Tikva a hub of capitalist abuse, which he could do more to remedy by returning to Zionist politics, his first love.

After barely a month of fieldwork, Ben-Gurion was back in Jaffa, where he participated in establishing a local unit of Poale Zion, a party that was now deeply divided over how to balance workers' rights and the Zionist cause. The party's pro-Marxist wing aspired to build a proletariat of Arabs and Jews within a classless culture; the pro-Zionists called for a purely Jew-ish society, leaving the Arabs to get by on their own. Ben-Gurion was among the pro-Zionists who looked ahead to a Palestine that would be home to separate economies and political systems for Jews and Arabs. It was an objective he never abandoned.

The rift in Poale Zion provided Ben-Gurion with an opening for his political ambitions. In Jaffa he devoted most of his energy to fighting the Marxists, while giving Hebrew lessons to support his daily needs. His success as an organizer led him to imagine bringing his family from Płońsk to Palestine. He even dreamed of becoming a delegate to the next Zionist Congress. Despite his efforts, however, Poale Zion drifted closer to its Marxist pole, which thwarted his aims. So when a few friends were leaving to found a collective colony in the Galilee, he decided to join them.

Instead of sinking roots in the colony, however, Ben-Gurion moved among the Galilee settlements, doing odd jobs. Though he clearly disliked fieldwork, he wrote home glowingly that, "When a Jew walks behind oxen plowing his ancestral soil and sees his fellow Jews nearby doing likewise, is it possible for him not to marvel?" In fact, Ben-Gurion slipped back to Jaffa as often as he could to do party work. In 1908, after Russian officials threatened his father with a large fine if his son did not report for the army, he returned to Płońsk, then served three months in Russian uni-form before deserting and making his way back to Palestine.

Life in the Galilee in these years was characterized by recurring conflict with the local Arabs, though petty thievery was more often the provocation than politics. Ben-Gurion enjoyed serving as an armed settlement guard. He liked the feel of a weapon in his belt. In 1909 a marauder stabbed and robbed him, confirming, he said, "the severity and dangers of the Arab problem." In later years he inflated his Galilee experience to claim that he and his fellow guards—and not his rival Jabotinsky, founder of the Haganah—planted the germ of the Jewish army.

The Young Turks' revolt against the sultan in 1908 got Ben-Gurion out of the fields once and for all. In response to the Young Turks' pledge to treat the empire's diverse peoples as equals, Poale Zion founded a patriotic newspaper called *Ha-Achdut* ("Unity"). At the time, Ben-Gurion—in contrast to most Zionists—believed the destiny of Palestine's Jews was to become Ottoman subjects and participate in building the empire. He even imagined his own election to the Ottoman parliament. Though without training in journalism, he was regarded as politically astute and good with words, and was offered a place on *Ha-Achdut*'s staff. He promptly accepted.

Until then he was still David Gruen, but the offer of a line on the masthead persuaded him to Hebraicize his name. That a "Ben-Gurion" was a hero of the Jews' revolt against Rome influenced his choice. As a journalist, he became an advocate of transferring power to the *yishuv* from Zionism's headquarters in Europe. Though the *yishuv* was then only a tiny fraction of Zionists, and an even smaller fraction of world Jewry, he argued that it should be recognized as Zionism's heart and soul. But Palestine was still a backwater, where life was hard, and as many Jews left as arrived. His plea to shift power to the *yishuv* was premature and went nowhere. After two years as a journalist, Ben-Gurion decided to study law at the university in Istanbul, which he believed would enable him to serve the Zionist cause more productively.

Before enrolling in the university, however, Ben-Gurion returned to Poland, traveling on a false passport to avoid arrest as a deserter. He tried desperately while there to reunite with Rachel, though she was now married to another man and waiting to give birth to a second child; her refusal to go with him produced a sense of grief that it seems he never fully overcame. His second goal was to appeal to his family to help finance his law studies. They agreed in principle, but the family's funds were limited and routinely slow in reaching him, if they reached him at all.

On leaving Poland, Ben-Gurion traveled to Salonika, home of a large community of Sephardic Jews, where he devoted a full year to mastering the Turkish language. Lacking proper academic credentials, he also had to acquire counterfeit documents to obtain admission to the university. Finally, in August 1912, he enrolled in the law school and, for two years, often hungry and sometimes ill, he worked conscientiously at his studies. In July 1914, he boarded a ship in Istanbul to spend his summer recess in Palestine. While he was at sea, war broke out in Europe, putting an end to his academic plans.

In sharp contrast to Weizmann and Jabotinsky, Ben-Gurion was convinced Turkey and its German ally would win the war. Both of them, living under the British flag, had announced their support for the Allies very early. Ben-Gurion's circumstances were different. His home was Palestine, a Turkish province, which he shared with some 85,000 other Jews, two-thirds of them from Russia. Under the rules of war, Russian Jews were enemy aliens. It is possible Ben-Gurion identified sincerely with the Turks; a well-known student photo shows him proudly wearing a Turkish-style moustache and fez. But, more important, the Jews of the *yishuv* were dependent on the Turks for their security and their sustenance, and Ben-Gurion believed he had a duty to stand by them.

Ben-Gurion was not anti-British. But, like most Jews, he regarded the czar as an oppressor, and the czar's regime as the historic foe of both Jews and Turks. Ben-Gurion often expressed his gratitude to the Ottomans for sheltering Jews over the centuries. He did not contemplate that their empire would collapse, much less what the consequences would be if it did. Committed to a Turkish-Jewish bond, he helped to found a Yishuv Ottomanization Committee, which urged Jews in Palestine to support Turkey and even to adopt Ottoman nationality.

The Ottoman governor in Palestine did not reciprocate his good feelings, however. Convinced the Jews were conspiring to set up their own state and secede from the empire, he dismissed Ben-Gurion's claims of loyalty. He disbanded a Jewish militia that Ben-Gurion tried to organize as an auxiliary to the Turkish constabulary. He also regarded Poale Zion, with its Marxist leanings, as subversive. In March 1915, the Turkish government ordered the deportation to Egypt of five hundred Russian Jews as a security measure. When Ben-Gurion published a strong protest in *Ha-*

Achdut, the governor shuttered the paper and placed him on the deportation list. Adding to the insult, the governor arranged for Ben-Gurion's expulsion from the law school in Istanbul.

After a brief jailing, Ben-Gurion was shipped to Alexandria, where he made contact with Jabotinsky and Trumpeldor, who were recruiting for the Zion Mule Corps. He did not join them, however, on the grounds that a Jewish army with an anti-Ottoman mission would make trouble for the *yishuv.* The British, on the other hand, interned him for several weeks for his pro-Turkish sympathies. Trapped between belligerents, Ben-Gurion decided to take off for New York, where he would find a sympathetic community of Russian Jews, many of them Zionists. In the spring of 1915, he left for America and remained there for nearly the entire war.

Ben-Gurion achieved little of service to Zionism during his stay in America. He worked with the local Poale Zion to recruit volunteers to go to Palestine, arguing that the *yishuv* needed them to defend against a possible Russian invasion. But few American Jews were persuaded by the argument or responded positively to it.

Finally, in 1917, with the overthrow of the czar and the issuance of the Balfour Declaration, Ben-Gurion decided to enlist in Jabotinsky's Jewish Legion. Before leaving America, however, he courted a well-educated, articulate, sometimes acerbic daughter of a Russian-Jewish family named Paula Munweis, a committed Zionist who was working as a nurse in New York. Though he would be attracted to many women over the course of his life, and would never forget Rachel, in December he married Paula, who would remain his wife until her death fifty years later. She was four months pregnant when Ben-Gurion went off with the Jewish Legion to fight in Palestine against the Turks.

Ben-Gurion's unit was among those still in training in Egypt when Turkey surrendered. With the war over, he was impatient to get back into Zionist politics. Weizmann had by then installed the Zionist Commission in Jerusalem to provide guidance to the British army on implementing the Balfour Declaration. Ben-Gurion at once perceived him as a rival, and envisaged unifying Palestine's diverse socialist factions into a political force that could compete with Weizmann in representing the *yishuv.*

In December 1918, Ben-Gurion slipped out of camp to make an unauthorized visit to Jaffa to reunite with his old political comrades. When he returned, he was arrested and tried for insubordination. Found guilty, he was stripped of his corporal's stripe. Though now known to the British as a mischief maker, he was not deterred. The changes taking place in Palestine under the Balfour Declaration had made a career in Zionist politics look more inviting than ever.

♆

Based on the Balfour Declaration, Ben-Gurion, like Weizmann, perceived that the campaign for Jewish statehood was moving into a critical phase. But, in contrast to Weizmann, he had no intention of allowing the Mandatory government to dominate the process. The Jews, as he saw it, needed to promote their own political interests, with the socialists taking the lead. His point of departure was to unite the existing socialist factions. By 1920 Ben-Gurion had laid the groundwork for Mapai, the Labor Party, which served as the political voice of the *yishuv* for the next half-century.

Ben-Gurion's Mapai was the beginning of continuous Jewish power in the Mandate. He was also establishing an elected assembly to confront the Mandatory authority. Though religious and secular divisions threatened it, he was good at negotiating and drafting compromises to keep a national consensus intact. The assembly served as a building block in the institutional structure that would, a few decades later, become the government of the Jewish state.

In June 1920, Ben-Gurion traveled to London to help lay the groundwork for the first postwar Zionist Congress. There, for the first time, he met Weizmann, who was famous as the head of a global movement. He and Ben Gurion exchanged a few courtesies before Weizmann accused Ben-Gurion of promoting a breach between Britain and the Jews. Ben-Gurion replied sharply that Weizmann's subservience invited Britain to curry Arab favor. In an open debate, Ben-Gurion went a step too far by declaring the *yishuv* more secure under the Turks. Weizmann's debating skills prevailed in the encounter, but the bitter contest between the two men was now under way.

After this setback in London, Ben-Gurion traveled to Vienna for a conference of Poale Zion. The party, he had concluded, was leading the *yishuv* to absorption into the Communist orbit, which he could not tolerate. Unable to suppress its Marxists, he chose instead to break the party up. The split left Ben-Gurion in control of a social-democratic political force that would support him in his ongoing program of institution building in the *yishuv*.

On his return to Palestine, Ben-Gurion was presented the huge task of integrating thousands of Jews who had arrived since the war ended, pressing the economy to its limits. While he was away, his political comrades had founded the General Confederation of Jewish Labor, called Histadrut, of which he was elected secretary-general. Ben-Gurion now had the power to shape Histadrut at the side of Mapai into what became a comprehensive framework of political and economic action in Jewish Palestine.

Ben-Gurion envisaged Histadrut as the embryo of a Jewish social-democratic state. Zionism's ideological ties to classic socialism were shallow; Histadrut improvised its own socialism, shaping a popularly governed association of workers and employers, while investing funds independently of the British Mandate to found businesses and provide jobs. Histadrut grew to become the backbone of a thriving Jewish society.

From its tentative beginning, Histadrut expanded into an array of trade unions and labor exchanges existing side by side with a network of banks, factories, farms, and construction companies. It ran schools and workers' kitchens, a newspaper, and cultural institutions. It built houses and a health insurance system. In time, it even took command of the Haganah, the militia that Jabotinsky had founded. Ben-Gurion's constant challenge was to come up with funds equal to its ambitions but Histadrut, unique to Palestine, spread its influence to every corner of the *yishuv*.[3]

Ben-Gurion's reputation rose with Histadrut's. He won respect for being clear-sighted and shrewd. Meticulous in observing democratic procedures, he was also creative in crafting organizational structures. He had little time for attending social or cultural events. He was indifferent to personal wealth, though an addict in the collection of books. His basic love was the exercise of leadership, which was synonymous with power. As the dominant force in both Mapai and Histadrut, he achieved his ambition of becoming the *yishuv*'s preeminent public figure before he reached forty.

"His posture on the speaker's rostrum, hands in pockets, exudes awareness of his power," wrote Haaretz, an independent paper, in 1926. "He always looks as though a great party stands behind him, and quite often he proves to be right. . . . At the sight of his serious face, silence prevails in the auditorium. His strong and moderate voice begins to rise more and more. His words are weighty; he does not use a fiery style or big words. . . . He associates the present with the past: there is history and continuity. He Judaizes his socialism, wrapping it in human morality and international justice."[4]

♆

Having outmaneuvered the Communists in 1920, Ben-Gurion continued to face their efforts to infiltrate and control Histadrut and other political institutions. They saw Ben-Gurion's willingness to mix capitalism and trade unionism as class heresy. Sympathetic to Arab nationalism, the Communists proposed to welcome Arabs into all the *yishuv*'s institutions. But what they described as social justice Ben-Gurion regarded as a threat to Jewish rule in Palestine. When the Mandate banned the Communists, they moved the party underground. Ben-Gurion and the Communists engaged in brutal and sometimes violent competition, but in the end he succeeded in purging their influence from Histadrut's diverse bodies.

The Arab question arose in another context in the mid-1920s, when Palestine's economy sank into a depression. Ben-Gurion called for Weizmann to press the Zionist Executive in London into investing in job creation. The Executive, itself short of funds, offered instead to expand the dole, which Ben-Gurion saw as insensitive to workers' self-esteem. But he also saw a political opportunity in unemployment. His plan was to strengthen Jewish labor by excluding Arabs from the labor exchange, which held a near-monopoly on available jobs.

Ben-Gurion applied his strategy in the citrus groves of Petah Tikva, where he once worked as a field hand. In 1924, he adopted strong-arm tactics. The growers, themselves Jews, had long preferred Arab workers, bypassing the exchange to hire them at minimal wages. Ben-Gurion responded by installing picket lines at the gates to bar Arabs from entering the groves. The Mandate's police dispersed the picketers, but the violence spread, continuing off and on for several years, exacerbating the already existing hostility between Arabs and Jews.

In taking personal charge, Ben-Gurion had hundreds of Jewish workers under his command, most of them Histadrut members willing to do battle at a word from him. The growers relied on British constables, who had uniformed Arabs in their ranks. They arrested dozens of Jewish workers. In the end the growers prevailed, but at the cost of transforming an economic dispute into another Arab-Jewish battleground.

Even in defeat, Ben-Gurion kept up the fight over the labor exchange. Herzl, it may be recalled, imagined in *Altneuland* a noble Arab declaring, "The Jews have brought us wealth and health; why should we harbor evil thoughts about them? They live among us like brothers." In choosing his course, Ben-Gurion dismissed Herzl as a dreamer, depicting himself as a pragmatist fighting for the Jews against the growers. When Weizmann objected to the exclusion of Arabs, Ben-Gurion accused him of being "not conscious enough of the dangers to Zionism."[5]

Ben-Gurion's socialist vision never extended to Arabs. He blamed the Arab propertied class, the *effendis,* for popular Arab discontent, while conveying to Jewish workers a sense that he would take great political risks in their behalf. He did not aspire to narrowing the Arab-Jewish prosperity gap. On the contrary, his practices as a labor leader in the 1920s were designed to perpetuate, even widen, the wedge between Arabs and Jews.

Similarly, though Ben-Gurion's rivalry with Revisionism played out chiefly over politics, it was also conducted in economic arenas. On the jobs issue, the Revisionists were more aggressive than the Arabs. Both Ben-Gurion and Jabotinsky regarded themselves as tough-minded militants, disdainful of Weizmann's drawing-room manners, but they differed on economic no less than on political ideology. Revisionism was a capitalist movement, which made it more respectful of Arab workers. Jabotinsky believed that Ben-Gurion was a closet Marxist, while Ben-Gurion thought that Revisionism was a willing oppressor of the Jewish working class.

Conceivably, Ben-Gurion and Jabotinsky could have narrowed the gap between them, and in their meeting in 1934 they tried. But it was never an even fight. Jabotinsky was by nature a propagandist and an outsider, uninterested in competing with Ben-Gurion in the onerous work of administering institutions. He also suspected that once Ben-Gurion controlled the levers of state power, Revisionism would have to resort to force to remain in political competition. Over time, he turned out to be right.

By the mid-1930s, Ben-Gurion was dominant in all of Zionism's centers of power. As a member of the Executive in London he could keep an eye on Weizmann, who reigned even as his influence diminished. In Jerusalem, as head of the Jewish Agency, he maintained a watch over Revisionists as well as *yishuv* politics. As the head of what had effectively become a parallel Jewish government, he could not be ignored by the Mandate. Ben-Gurion's across-the-board preeminence in public institutions remained the source of his indisputable power until the Jewish state was established in 1948, when he would be chosen by acclamation to be Israel's prime minister.

Ben-Gurion was now at middle age and esteemed beyond his dreams, but his life was not easy. In London, he wore expensive suits and fine gloves, but Britain's ruling elite still preferred dealing with Weizmann. His work schedule, and especially his time abroad, had imposed serious strains on his marriage, and Paula made sure he felt guilty about her loneliness. He had affairs with young women, which were a distraction but not a solution to his problems. Meanwhile, British policy grew harsher, even as Hitler's campaign against Europe's Jews grew more oppressive. Then, in 1936, the Arab uprising opened a new chapter in Palestine.

Just before the Arab revolt, Ben-Gurion explored a new avenue to forestall violence, meeting with a group of Arab notables who he thought could broker an arrangement with the Mufti, head of the Arab armed forces. "We are not settling Palestine to the Arabs' detriment but to help them," was his line. The notables had heard such claims before, particularly from Weizmann, and now refused to take them seriously. Arabs, the notables added, preferred poverty to losing their country. The meeting with the Mufti never took place, but the notables, Ben-Gurion said, led him to grasp "the magnitude of Arab fears." The lesson, however, did not persuade him to consider any real changes to the Zionist course.

When the Arab revolt began in 1936, Ben-Gurion turned to Weizmann to keep communications open with the British cabinet. He remained doubtful, however, about whether Weizmann understood that, at a time when Hitler was growing stronger, immigration superseded all other demands. His apprehension was confirmed when Britain, trying to contain the fighting, pleaded with the Jews to make a helpful gesture, and Weizmann offered, on his own, to suspend immigration for a year. Furious, Ben-Gurion saw the offer not only as an Arab victory but an abandonment of Zionism's obligation to rescue Europe's Jews.

Ben-Gurion lectured Weizmann that the Arab revolt, compared to limitations on immigration, was insignificant to the Jews. From the Arab perspective, he recognized that the revolt was legitimate. "Were I an Arab, politically, nationally minded . . . I would rebel vigorously, bitterly and desperately, [knowing] that immigration will one day turn Palestine and all its Arabs over to Jewish rule." Such candor was unusual for Ben-Gurion but, he made clear, Zionism's purpose was not to allay Arab concerns but to save Jewish lives.

The conflict between the two men erupted again when the British sent the Peel Commission to take testimony in Palestine. Retreating in the face of Ben-Gurion's ire, Weizmann withdrew his offer to suspend immigration, but Ben-Gurion did not forgive him. Weizmann cannot be trusted, Ben-Gurion said. Ben-Gurion himself was convinced Britain's goal was to repeal the Balfour Declaration, and even Weizmann agreed on the need for a united Zionist defense. But, out of mistrust for each other, they squabbled over who the leader in dealing with the Peel Commission would be.

Deferring to Weizmann's higher office, Ben-Gurion agreed to have him deliver the opening statement. He was even pleased with Weizmann's formulation of the commission that, "The world is divided into places where the Jews cannot live and places into which they cannot enter." But his approval did not survive Weizmann's leaked testimony in a closed session. Weizmann said he regarded limits on immigration as a fair price for peace in Palestine, adding that Zionism would be glad to bring a million Jews to Palestine, in twenty-five or thirty years. Ben-Gurion was apoplectic.

In his diary, Ben-Gurion noted that, "It is beyond Chaim's power to stand firm before the forceful and courteous English. His will is not strong enough." He demanded that the Executive require Weizmann to declare in writing that he had misstated Zionism's position and, reluctantly, Weizmann did. In his own testimony, Ben-Gurion stated disingenuously that Arab fear of Jewish immigration was misplaced. His statement, however, had no impact, since the commission had by then embarked on the road to partition.

The Peel Commission's report—examined in the previous chapter—had shifted the debate over Palestine from immigration to partition. Ben-Gurion had long contemplated separating Arabs from Jews as a way of attaining a Jewish state. Even Weizmann argued that, separated from the Arabs and ruling over their own territory, Jews could make their own decisions on immigration. Though they were in agreement on partition, the two split over tactics. Weizmann wanted to accept the Peel proposal outright; Ben-Gurion favored playing hard-to-get to squeeze the British for more territory than the Peel Commission offered.

In response to colleagues who complained that partition gave up too much, Ben-Gurion declared: "No borders are eternal. . . . By the time we complete the settlement of our state . . . we shall break through these frontiers." To his son Amos, now an adolescent, he revealed even more. "All our aspiration is built on the assumption . . . that there is enough room for ourselves and the Arabs. . . . [But] I regard this scheme [partition] as . . . an unequaled lever for the gradual conquest of all of Palestine." Clearly, Ben-Gurion regarded partition as a tactical retreat to achieve a more ambitious objective.[6]

Partition was on the agenda at the Zionist Congress of 1937, when Ben-Gurion, to avoid a break with Britain, devised an ingenious formula. It declared that partition was unacceptable to the Jews, while it instructed the Zionist Executive to bargain with Britain for more favorable terms. Though it fully satisfied no one, the proposal passed overwhelmingly. While the Arabs were rejecting partition entirely, the vote of the Congress kept partition alive in the Zionist camp.

But as it turned out, the Peel Commission had a falling-out with its own government, and as war grew nearer partition steadily lost support. The cabinet sent still another commission to Palestine with instructions to reverse the Peel recommendations. The backup commission urged not just the rejection of partition but the loosening of immigration quotas. In accepting its advice, the cabinet ended any prospect of Palestine's serving as a refuge for the Jews confronting doom in Europe.

On November 8, 1938, the Nazis conducted the infamous pogrom remembered as *Kristallnacht*. Britain's response was to dismiss a Zionist request for asylum in Palestine for ten thousand Jewish children. Weizmann, now as outraged as Ben-Gurion, nonetheless urged diplomacy to get Britain to reverse itself. Ben-Gurion, shadowing the path of Jabotinsky, proposed that the Zionist Organization move to a more militant stage, which he called "combative" Zionism.

As the Haganah's commander, Ben-Gurion churned with ideas, some just fantasy, others later evolving into policy. He proposed expanding immigration by harassing the British navy with Jewish speedboats. He talked of declaring a provisional Jewish state surrounding Haifa, where refugees could be landed and housed. He urged construction of a local arms industry. He argued that Britain, once it observed the Jews' ability on the battlefield, would be compelled to switch their allegiance away from the Arabs.

Ben-Gurion reacted with defiance to the collapse of Britain's last-ditch effort at reconciliation at St. James's Palace. When MacDonald, the colonial secretary, proclaimed at the table that only British bayonets stood between Arabs and the *yishuv*, Ben-Gurion declared, "Take your bayonets away . . . we can do without them. . . . Our immigration and our *yishuv* will stand by the strength of the Jewish people. . . . Permit us to protect ourselves. Don't stand in our way."

The MacDonald White Paper, issued on the eve of the war, justified retreat from the Balfour Declaration with the claim that Britain's vow to provide a homeland to the Jews in Palestine had already been met. The *yishuv,* at Ben-Gurion's instigation, replied the next day with strikes and protests. Summoned by the Mandate for censure, Ben-Gurion declared, "Yesterday's demonstration marked the start of Jewish resistance to the disastrous policy proposed by His Majesty's government. The Jews will not be intimidated into surrender, even if their blood is shed."

At the Zionist Congress of 1939, the last before World War II, Ben-Gurion said of the MacDonald Paper, "We shall not reverse these decrees by appealing to the conscience of humanity, but rather by means of our will and strength." He admitted that an incongruity existed between Britain's being the enemy of Palestine's Jews while British forces stood between the *yishuv* and the Nazi armies. When the war started in September, he coined an epigram to make sense of the dilemma. "We shall wage war against Hitler as though there were no White Paper, and wage war against the White Paper as though there were no Hitler." The epigram remained the *yishuv*'s policy throughout the war years.

Palestine was drawn inexorably into the fighting in 1940, starting with Italians bombing Tel Aviv while their army rolled through Libya en route to Egypt. In May, after France fell, Nazi soldiers landed in Syria, and in Baghdad a coup against the pro-British regime placed Iraq in the Axis camp. In exile, the Mufti of Jerusalem worked relentlessly to inflame Palestine's Arabs, thus exposing the *yishuv* to enemies from both within and without. Keeping with precedent, Britain rejected a plea from Ben-Gurion for the formation of a Jewish army to fight alongside Britain, insisting that it would only provoke the Arabs further.

With little explanation, Ben-Gurion decided at that point to move to London to represent the *yishuv* at the hub of the war effort. It was a mistake, if only because London was Weizmann's realm, and there was little he could do there for the *yishuv* that Weizmann could not do better. With time on his hands, Ben-Gurion took lessons in ancient Greek and read Plato. He experienced the Blitz, filling him with awe at Londoners' courage. He squabbled with Weizmann, who he believed—incorrectly—stood as a barrier to a Jewish army. Together they attended a memorial for Jabotinsky after he died, but their relations did not improve. In September 1940, Ben-Gurion left London for New York. Having spent much of World War I in America escaping Jabotinsky's shadow, he ran the reel again in World War II to escape Weizmann's.

Before leaving Britain, Ben-Gurion wrote a paper on what Zionism's policies toward the Arabs should be after an Allied victory. Though the Arabs' expulsion from Palestine would be morally and politically indefensible, he wrote, it would solve many problems. "It would be rash to assert that *in no circumstances* [my italics] . . . can such a transfer take place," he wrote. Zionism, he concluded, should continue to pledge economic assistance to the Arabs, but transfer should not be ruled out.

When the Nazis invaded Russia in June 1941, and six months later Japan bombed Pearl Harbor, Ben-Gurion's expectations suddenly turned optimistic. He decided to move to Washington, now the center of the action, noting with satisfaction in his diary that "in Weizmann's absence, I am the representative of the Jewish people in America." He was especially excited at a vague promise by an American official of a meeting with President Roosevelt, though it never took place. U.S. involvement in the war, however, imparted to him a new insight: Zionism's future depended no longer on Britain's power but on America's.

Weizmann had no intention of conceding representation of the Jews to Ben-Gurion in America, but his own Atlantic crossing had been delayed by the loss in action of his son Michael, an RAF pilot. Weizmann, too, understood that postwar Britain was unlikely to retain its preeminence in Palestine. On arriving in New York in April 1942, he and Ben-Gurion made a new effort to put aside their animosity. Recognizing that the war made convening a Zionist Congress impossible, they decided to hold in its place a major conference of American Zionists. Its goal would be to enlist the American government, now the senior partner in the wartime alliance, in support of Jewish statehood.

On May 6, 1942, Weizmann opened the conference before six hundred prominent Jewish dignitaries in New York's Biltmore Hotel. Since Ben-Gurion had drafted the declaration of its aims, Weizmann deferred to him to deliver the principal address. In five days of speech making and meetings, the conference produced the "Biltmore Program," which succeeded beyond expectations in ending American Jews' long-standing vacillation over Zionism. Claiming to speak for all of America's Jews, the Biltmore Conference aligned itself with the World Zionist Organization's objective of statehood, which, it said, would right "the age-old wrong to the Jewish people."

Still desisting from the word "statehood," the Biltmore Program called for the fulfillment of the Balfour Declaration through the establishment in Palestine of "a Jewish commonwealth integrated in the structure of a new democratic world." It rejected the legitimacy of the MacDonald White Paper's "denial of sanctuary to Jews fleeing from Nazi persecution." It insisted on the Jews' right to control not just the *yishuv*'s social and economic development but the entry of Jews into Palestine. The Biltmore Program, finally, demanded "recognition of the Jews' right to play their full part in the war effort and in the defense of *their* [my italics] country, through a Jewish military force fighting under its own flag. . . ."

The Biltmore Program did not overlook the Arabs who, it claimed, had benefitted from the Jews' colonization in Palestine. While citing no evidence, it asserted that the Arabs "have shared . . . in the new values created" and "the Jews' pioneering achievements in agriculture and in industry, embodying new patterns of cooperative endeavor." It adopted Ben-Gurion's assertion that "the Jewish people in its own work of national redemption welcomes the economic, agricultural and national development of the Arab people and states." The Biltmore Program's promises to the Arabs were far removed from the separation of Arabs and Jews that Ben-Gurion had openly advocated and even further removed from the *yishuv*'s practices in everyday relations between the two peoples.[7]

But whatever the distance between words and intentions, the Biltmore Conference was a huge achievement, especially for Ben-Gurion. Some Zionists, it is true, found the criticisms of the British, an ally in a war yet to be won, too harsh. Some also believed it was still premature to tip Zionism's hand on sovereignty. There was a feeling that, in not mentioning boundaries, the program constituted an unauthorized validation of partition. But, whatever its failings, the Biltmore Program raised the Zionist flag to a lofty height. Over the ensuing months, it was formally endorsed by Jewish organizations around the world as a declaration that the Jews, when the war was over, would be ready to make Palestine *their* state.

The old rancor between Weizmann and Ben-Gurion, however, resumed even before the final gavel came down. Ben-Gurion believed his success as the architect of the conference had earned him a ranking equal to Weizmann's. But Weizmann, as president of the World Zionist Organization and father of the Balfour Declaration, was the singular object of the delegates' adulation. He was greeted with huge ovations everywhere and embraced as Herzl's heir. Though the two were never less divided on issues, Ben-Gurion hurled angry charges that Weizmann had curried the favor of the crowd. Weizmann's charming rebuttals, as usual, only added to Ben-Gurion's frustration.

The rift grew wider after the conference, when Weizmann was summoned to the White House for the private visit with President Roosevelt that Ben-Gurion had yearned for. Ben-Gurion was convinced Weizmann had personally conspired to have the president snub him. That the meeting was limited to polite banalities brought Ben-Gurion no consolation.

In the months after the Biltmore Conference, the war news grew more encouraging each day. A British counterattack defeated the German forces then concentrated on Egypt's frontier, ending the immediate threat to Palestine. Americans landed on the coast of France's North African colonies, cutting off the Germans' westward retreat, forcing them to abandon Africa entirely. Meanwhile, Russia stopped the Nazis' previously invincible army at Stalingrad, imposing on it a brutal battle of attrition from which Germany never recovered. A favorable end to the war now appeared on the horizon.

Early in the war, the Jewish Agency had turned over to the Mandate 100,000 names of young men and women in Palestine who were prepared to enlist in the British army. A third of them actually served with Britain's forces, fighting against the Nazis in Syria and in the African desert. In addition, the *yishuv* supplied Britain with arms from its factories and food from its farms. During the war's darkest days, the British army even solicited the Haganah's military support. While the Mufti of Jerusalem was actively collaborating with the Nazis, winning Arabs to their cause, the Jews believed they had earned Britain's thanks for their contribution to the Allied victory.

Ben-Gurion made no secret of his expectation that Britain would relent in its hostile attitude, and near the end of the war, Prime Minister Churchill agreed to have the Jews form their own units within the British army, though his consent came too late for any of them to engage in combat. Yet Britain continued to enforce the limits on immigration fixed in the 1939 White Paper, along with the naval blockade that kept escapees from the Nazis from entering Palestine. Many ships were stopped and forced to return to Europe, most dramatically the unseaworthy *Struma,* which sank off Turkey in 1942 with the loss of seven hundred Jewish lives. Passengers of the few ships that managed to land in Palestine were routinely locked up in British internment camps.

A few weeks after Germany's surrender in May 1945, Britain's voters surprisingly cast the Churchill government out of office in favor of the British Labor Party. To Ben-Gurion, the presence in office of like-minded socialists raised hopes for a change in policy, but the hopes quickly faded. Ernest Bevin, a former trade union leader, became foreign secretary and, with turmoil spreading throughout the empire, he focused on deterring Muslim populations from challenging British rule. As for Holocaust survivors, Bevin maintained that they had to be settled in Europe, where the Jewish problem originated. Bevin also reaffirmed Britain's determination to continue enforcing the other anti-Zionist provisions of the 1939 White Paper.

In April 1945, Franklin Roosevelt died, and Harry Truman succeeded to the American presidency. Whatever Roosevelt's feelings about Zionism, he had been constrained by wartime obligations to defer to his British ally; Truman faced no such constraints. He outraged not just Bevin but his own State Department by calling for the issuance of Palestine visas for 100,000 refugees. Truman's initiative—no doubt prompted by the Biltmore Program—was the pivot for Zionism's sharp turn from deference to Britain to reliance on the goodwill of the United States.

In October 1945, Bevin resurrected the frayed relic of the royal commission of inquiry to deal with Palestine. When Washington, at Bevin's urging, agreed to join the commission, it became known as the Anglo-American Committee. The messages sent by Zionist witnesses before the commission were familiar: Weizmann sought to revive the Balfour Declaration; Ben-Gurion issued a subtle threat to use force against the recalcitrant Mandate. The Arabs rejected any compromises whatsoever. Despite intensifying U.S. pleas for the admission of the 100,000 Holocaust survivors, Britain stood by its refusal. With Bevin's obstinacy fueling further violence between Britain and the Jews in Palestine, within two years the Mandate would come to an unhappy end.

Lehi, Revisionism's most extreme faction, had been waging a war of terror against the British since 1942. Its climax was the murder in Cairo in 1944 of Lord Moyne, Britain's highest official in the Middle East. Weizmann reacted to the murder by pledging to have the *yishuv* "cut out this evil from its midst." Ben-Gurion instructed the Haganah to suppress "this underground gang." In a campaign called the Season—as in "hunting season"—the Haganah served as an informant to the British, turning in not only members of Lehi but of the less radical Irgun. Two of Moyne's killers were tried by the British, convicted, and hanged.[8]

The anger of the Jewish public over Moyne's killing led both the Irgun and the Lehi to suspend independent operations and submit to the Haganah's command. For a brief time, the three forces limited their efforts to thwarting Britain's sea blockade. But Bevin's unrelenting stand on the refugee issue lured them into more aggressive practices, and with the Haganah taking the lead, Jews succeeded in paralyzing the Mandate by blowing up roads and bridges across the country. On June 29, 1946, designated "Black Sabbath," British soldiers conducted massive searches for weapons, then interned more than a hundred civilian Jewish leaders. Ben-Gurion, who at the time was abroad, eluded the roundup.

A month later the Irgun, now commanded by Menachem Begin—the subject of chapter 6—committed the Jews' most audacious act of terror, bombing Jerusalem's King David Hotel, Britain's civilian and military headquarters. Nearly one hundred Jews, Arabs, and British, most of them noncombatants died in the bombing. Ben-Gurion declared the act a violation of the Irgun's pledge of military discipline. Describing the Irgun as "the enemy of the Jewish people," Ben-Gurion reignited the temporarily dormant conflict between mainstream Zionism and Revisionism.

Meanwhile, British efforts at Arab-Jewish mediation only drove the two sides further apart. A British-American proposal to establish self-governing cantons in Palestine under Britain's umbrella elicited no interest from either camp. When Britain announced a new round of reconciliation talks, neither side agreed to attend. Truman, seeing no way to disentangle the strands, was about to wash his hands of the Palestine issue when Bevin made a dramatic move. On February 18, 1947, he declared Britain would return the Mandate to the jurisdiction of the United Nations and depart from Palestine.

In April, the U.N. General Assembly voted to establish a Special Committee on Palestine (UNSCOP) to determine the Mandate's future. Out of fairness, it excluded the major powers and the Arab states from membership. Its staff conducted field studies in the Middle East and interviews among Europe's displaced persons. In August 1947, UNSCOP issued its recommendation that Palestine be partitioned into sovereign Arab and

Jewish states, while requiring of each of them only the adoption of a constitution assuring full minority rights. Jerusalem was to be placed under U.N.
trusteeship, not part of either state. The Negev desert was assigned to the
Jews, after Weizmann personally lobbied President Truman.

As often as the narrative has been repeated, the General Assembly's vote
in favor of partition remains a miracle in the mind of most Jews. The resolution passed despite Britain's opposition, and though the United States
and the Soviet Union, the U.N.'s most powerful members, were supporters,
the assembly's smaller states were disproportionately influential. With Weizmann their chief advocate, the Zionists made a compelling case for the U.N.
resolution, based heavily on Jewish suffering at Nazi hands. The Arabs made
the mistake of offering no alternative to the undecided delegations, most
of which felt, after the Holocaust, that the world owed a debt to the Jews.

The final vote, taken on November 29, 1947, was 33 to 13 in support of
partition, well more than the two-thirds required. Most of the negative
votes were cast by Muslim states. The Arab delegations, declaring the
resolution illegal, left the chamber, vowing to challenge the outcome by
force. In the *yishuv*, the street celebrations could barely be contained.
Oddly, Ben-Gurion, asleep in a hotel on the Dead Sea where he was taking
a cure for a chronic backache, was among the last to learn of the news.[9]

Ben-Gurion, however, reacted quickly to the resolution. He had labored
throughout his adult life not just to found but to shape a state. With the
goal of establishing a strong central government, he had been instrumental in organizing trade unions, a political party, a national assembly, and
Histadrut. He had put together a shadow cabinet. When the U.N. voted to
create two states, the Arabs had no blueprint for proceeding. But Ben-
Gurion and the Jews were ready to seize the moment.

Ben-Gurion himself was awarded the posts of prime minister and
minister of defense in the state-in-waiting. Around him, he had assembled
a diverse circle of ministers from which were excluded only partition's opponents: the Ultra-Orthodox, who were still awaiting the Messiah, and the
Communists, who demanded a binational workers' republic. Also excluded were the Revisionists, who insisted on a state that embraced all of
Palestine and the territory beyond the Jordan River. Of the three, Ben-
Gurion considered only the Revisionists a threat, since they commanded
their own armed militias.

Ben-Gurion appealed to the Security Council to enforce partition under the terms of the U.N. Charter, but Britain managed to block any action. On the day after the partition resolution was passed, bands of Arab irregulars attacked Jewish communities in Palestine. Though his military experience was limited, Ben-Gurion led the response. His forces were undermanned and under-armed, and though the Irgun had promised to accept his authority, military unity was now a distant dream. What encouraged Ben-Gurion was that the local Arab forces were even more disorganized than the Jews.

Having to wait for the Haganah to mobilize, Ben-Gurion turned to fighters in the Irgun and the Palmach, an autonomous unit tied to Mapai. Both accepted his orders to hold on, whatever the cost, to all the land allocated to the Jewish state by the U.N. In the early fighting, the Palmach beat off an Arab attack on Safed and the Irgun captured Jaffa. A bigger challenge, however, was the relief of Jerusalem, where the Jewish population was besieged by guerrilla bands embedded in the Arab villages that circled the city.

To relieve Jerusalem, the Jews had to overcome Arab control of the road leading from the city to the sea. Among the Palestinian villages standing in their way was Deir Yassin, which the commanders of the Irgun and Lehi requested authorization to capture. Ben-Gurion gave his consent. Though the attack encountered almost no resistance, the attackers slaughtered some 250 men, women, and children. News of the killing panicked Arabs throughout Palestine, triggering the flight of tens of thousands in search of asylum to the neighboring Arab states.

Ben-Gurion was furious at the bloodbath at Deir Yassin, which he blamed on the Revisionist leadership. His chief concern, it should be noted, was not so much the needless killing of Arabs as the reaction of Washington, which was reconsidering its support of the partition resolution. Deir Yassin also provoked Transjordan's Emir Abdullah to the point of ordering his British-trained army to invade Palestine. Ben-Gurion publicly apologized for the "brutal and barbaric deed" committed by the Revisionists at Deir Yassin, which ended any immediate prospect of unifying the Jewish forces. More seriously, the Deir Yassin operation imparted to the founding of the Jewish state a bloody stain that has never been fully washed away.

Also clear by now was that the incipient Jewish state would get no military help from any Western nation. Washington, fearful the fighting might ignite a major new war, suddenly proposed setting up a U.N. trust-eeship for Palestine. To Ben-Gurion, such a trusteeship meant that state-hood, if it was to happen at all, would have to be deferred indefinitely. The time for Jewish sovereignty was now, he had concluded, and it was apparent that on this question the *yishuv* was overwhelmingly behind him.

According to the U.N. partition resolution, the British Mandate was to terminate on May 15, which fell on the Jewish Sabbath. Ben-Gurion convened a provisional council the day before to ratify a declaration of statehood. It adopted the name "State of Israel," and voted to end all bar-riers to Jewish immigration. But rabbinic members of the council refused to permit the declaration to be made on the Sabbath, and then refused to endorse a state that did not refer to the authority of God. In opposition, the council's secular majority rejected any reference to God at all. The two sides argued through late Friday afternoon, when the rabbis, unwilling to violate the Sabbath, made ready to depart for their synagogues.

Their departure raised the intolerable prospect that, at the last mo-ment, the Zionist vision would be snatched away. Ben-Gurion saved the day by proposing to base the state on a foundation of *Zur Israel*, a biblical synonym for God, which all factions agreed to accept. He called it "a nice compromise of Jewish fellowship." Just before sundown on May 14—the date Israel celebrates as Independence Day—Ben-Gurion read the Dec-laration of Independence of the Jewish state.[10]

The Declaration mirrored the dilemmas of the Jews in the modern era. Like Zionism, its roots were in both the Enlightenment and Judaism. It proclaimed the "natural right of Jews to be the masters of their own fate," the secular vision of self-determination, while confirming the Jews' Right of Return, which resonated with the idea of Messianic redemption. It vowed "complete equality of social and political rights to all inhabitants," while pledging free immigration only for "the Ingathering of the Exiles." It promised the Arabs "full and equal citizenship and due representation," which was not part of Zionist ideology at all. It was a jumble of clashing, generally well-meaning contradictions, all but impossible, in its fullness, for Israel to keep.

Weizmann's signature did not appear in the Declaration of Indepen-dence. He was in Washington, soliciting America's recognition of the new state, and sending Ben-Gurion daily reports of his efforts. Truman granted diplomatic recognition to Israel at once, while Britain glowered silently. Ben-Gurion, after reading out the Declaration, generously wired Weizmann that "no one contributed as much as you" to Israel's founding. In Tel Aviv at Ben-Gurion's initiative, Weizmann was elected the first president of the state. On May 25, Weizmann rode with Truman in an open car down Washington's Pennsylvania Avenue, bedecked with American and Israeli flags. A day later, he sailed for Europe, bypassing England to signal his liberation from a badly frayed allegiance to a county he loved.[11]

With the Union Jack flying over Palestine no longer, the neighboring Arab countries—Egypt, Iraq, Transjordan, Syria, and Lebanon—agreed on a joint assault on the upstart state. Though the Jews had defeated the Palestinian irregulars decisively, the regimes of the sovereign Arab states were confident their armies would reverse the defeat. Measuring Israel against its rivals, most outside observers concurred. The triumph of the Jews in the War of Independence has been much chronicled. But given the impact of the war on the course that Israel has since adopted, a few of the episodes bear some review.

At the time of the Arab invasion in May 1948, the Jewish forces appeared clearly inferior. A month later, after heavy fighting without a decisive outcome, both sides accepted a twenty-eight day U.N. truce. But while the Arabs did little to correct their shortcomings, Ben-Gurion seized the opportunity to overcome Israel's deficiencies. He reorganized the army along standard military lines, adopting the name Israel Defense Forces (IDF), with its high command reporting directly to him as minister of defense. Arriving immigrants of military age were inducted at once and subjected to intensified training. Workshops turned out small arms around the clock. Czechoslovakian factories delivered planes, tanks, and artillery authorized by the U.S.S.R., while America and France also opened their arsenals. After the truce, Israel was much better prepared for the fight.

Once again, Ben-Gurion seemed on the way to integrating the Revisionist forces into a national army with the approval of Begin, their commander. Then, in June, a ship called *Altalena*—a Jabotinsky pen name—approached the Israeli coast from France carrying eight hundred Irgun recruits and enough weapons to arm ten battalions. Of this cargo, Begin proposed to reserve 20 percent for his Revisionist forces, a deal Ben-Gurion considered insubordinate, if not central to a plan to take over the state. When the *Altalena* tied up at a small port north of Tel Aviv, Haganah units were there to stop it from discharging its cargo. A firefight broke out in which two dozen Irgun fighters and several IDF regulars were killed. The *Altalena,* with Begin aboard, then turned around and steamed out to sea.

Ben-Gurion's cabinet declared a civil insurrection and, as the ship entered the port of Tel Aviv, it was fired on by IDF guns. On shore, Irgun soldiers, many recently integrated into IDF units, turned on their comrades, and for several chaotic hours, they actually controlled the city. Late in the day, a shell struck the *Altalena,* setting it afire. Begin was among the last to evacuate, but among those killed was Abraham Stavsky, the Betari who was tried and ultimately acquitted for the murder of Chaim Arlosoroff in 1933. In all, nearly one hundred Israelis died, most of them Revisionist fighters. The *Altalena*'s precious cargo sank to the bottom.

Israelis do not like to remember the *Altalena* affair. It says much about Ben-Gurion that with five hostile armies on Israel's borders, he was willing to fight a civil war to affirm the state's authority. After the fighting, both the Revisionist units on the right and the Palmach on the left accepted incorporation into the IDF. Ben-Gurion thus achieved his goal of a unified army, but at a heavy cost. In time, Israel officially recognized the often controversial service rendered by the Irgun and Lehi to the cause of Jewish statehood. But the *Altalena* episode served to widen the political breach between Jews that dated back to Jabotinsky and lasts to this day.

The War of Independence also exposed once again the huge gap between religious and secular Jews. For a century Orthodox rabbis in Eastern Europe had discouraged emigration of their followers both to America, which they considered wickedly secular, and to Palestine, whose existence they regarded as blasphemous. When the Nazis arrived in the 1940s, the Orthodox thus suffered in disproportionate numbers. After the War of Independence, Zionism offered refuge to Orthodoxy's survivors and many accepted, even while refusing to recognize Israel's Judaic legitimacy. When the Arab countries attacked in 1948, the Orthodox rabbinate, faced with conscription of its young men, argued that Jewish learning and prayer were as vital to the Jews' salvation as was victory in battle. Ben-Gurion, sympathetic to Orthodoxy's historic place in Judaism, granted draft exemptions to about four hundred Orthodox Torah students.

After the war, Ben-Gurion's willingness to grant concessions was a temptation to rabbis to enhance their powers. Over the years they maneuvered not only to preserve the draft exemption, which has since swelled to several hundred thousand. They also extracted government subsidies to support Orthodox religious schools, along with the families whose husbands and sons attend them. Further, rabbis extended their powers over rules for marriage, divorce, and inheritance that apply to all Israelis, regardless of religious observance, and they succeeded in requiring state institutions to observe Jewish dietary laws. Initiated to promote national unity during the struggle for independence, Ben-Gurion's precedent instead created a rift between secular and Orthodox Israelis that has become as wide as the strains between mainstream and Revisionist Zionists.

But if Israelis still debate Ben-Gurion's judgment on religious matters, few question that his leadership was a major factor in Israel's victory on the battlefield. By the end of 1948, the Arab armies had been defeated and—with the exception of the West Bank—driven out of Palestine. Israel occupied 20 percent more land than the U.N. partition resolution had allotted to it. Moreover, as many as seven hundred thousand Palestinians had fled the country, and many more were pushed over the borders by the IDF on Ben-Gurion's orders. The "transfer" left Israel more homogeneously Jewish than Zionism ever dreamed possible, but it also initiated a refugee crisis that even now undermines regional stability.

Ben-Gurion's willingness to let Transjordan retain East Jerusalem, including the Old City, and the West Bank was one puzzling outcome of the war. In secret talks, Ben-Gurion had once offered this territory to King Abdullah in return for his neutrality, but the deal fell through. By the fall of 1948, with the IDF clearly superior in the fighting, he proposed an offensive to capture the West Bank, defended by Abdullah's Arab Legion. Ben-Gurion's commanders, however, were not enthusiastic about such an operation, and the cabinet voted narrowly against it. Ben-Gurion did not challenge the decision.

One explanation for his consent to Transjordan's retaining this territory was the presence of a heavy Arab population there. Ben-Gurion recognized that Israel, with so many Jewish immigrants to absorb, did not have the means to take on the burden of a half-million Arabs as well. No less persuasive, he faced the risk of intervention by Britain, whose offices commanded the Legion and which had a security treaty with King Abdullah. With Britain's Middle East empire crumbling, Transjordan anchored whatever regional influence Britain hoped to retain. The IDF had no desire to test its strength on the battlefield against British forces, and the cabinet concurred. Ben-Gurion, while calling the decision "a cause for mourning," decided to leave the issue of the West Bank to another day.[12]

In January 1949, Israel's War of Independence ended in armistice talks conducted under U.N. auspices on the Mediterranean island of Rhodes. Though the meetings were tense, agreements with Egypt, Lebanon, and Transjordan were signed within a few weeks. A Syrian accord took until July. Only Iraq signed nothing at all. The preamble of all the agreements specified that they were to serve as a step to permanent peace. But neither Jews nor Arabs had peace on their agenda.

The armistice borders, hastily drawn, were blurry and volatile, inviting not peace but further violence. Syrian guns on the Golan Heights overlooked Jewish farms and villages in the Galilee. Egypt ruled over the Gaza Strip, where 250,000 restless Palestinian refugees had settled, as well as Sharm el-Sheikh, whose cannon covered the waterway that led to the port of Eilat and controlled Israel's access to the Red Sea. Transjordan's forces in Jerusalem and the West Bank were within a dozen miles of Tel Aviv. A U.N. Emergency Force assigned to police the truce saw fit to apply real constraints on neither side. Israel was admitted to full U.N. membership, and friendly countries opened embassies, but the war's end conveyed no sense of normality. Instability ruled the armistice lines.

The magnitude of his victory surely intoxicated Ben-Gurion. Under his guidance, Jewish arms, untested for two thousand years, had defeated the forces of the Palestinians and five Arab states. Drawing from the Bible, as he so often did, Ben-Gurion asserted that the military aptitude shown by the Jews dated to Joshua's time. Already known as a master of politics and institution-building, he had proven himself an excellent military strategist as well. Israel's triumph vindicated his persistent challenges to Weizmann's cautious ways. The war had left him in charge of a military force that, notwithstanding the *Altalena* affair, was unquestioning in its loyalty to him and to the state.

When he turned from the battlefield to governing the state full time, Ben-Gurion shocked many old Zionist comrades by redefining Jewish sovereignty. Since Herzl, the World Zionist Organization had claimed to speak for the Jewish people. Ben-Gurion, having made his name championing the supremacy of the *yishuv*, now argued that the historic arrangement was outdated. Israel's independence, Ben-Gurion stated, had completed the Zionist Organization's historic mission. Its help was still needed for many tasks, especially to fund the Ingathering of the Exiles. But Zionism no longer made the rules. Sovereign Israel, he declared, was in full charge of the affairs of the Jewish state.

Ben-Gurion also insisted that Israel would not serve as the global representative of the Jews. The Law of Return, inviting all Jews home to Israel, assured to each one a share in governing the state. Jews who waived the right, he argued, "do not understand that they are living in exile." But Israel, he stated, "speaks only in behalf of its citizens and in no way presumes to speak in the name of Jews who are citizens of any other country."[13]

In effect, Ben-Gurion renounced Zionism's historic claim to a bond between all Jews. Israel's ties to American Jews would henceforth be as distant as, say, Italy's to Italian-Americans. His words contained an echo of Weizmann's image that the state would be as Jewish as England is English. But Jewish in what way? It was not to make rules for Jews, as the Vatican does for Catholics. But did that mean that it was to be as Jewish as Saudi Arabia is Islamic? The Declaration of Independence had guaranteed equality to Arab citizens, suggesting a resemblance to the liberal, Western societies that Ben-Gurion admired. But what of the special privileges he granted to Ultra-Orthodox Judaism? Though surely aware of these inconsistencies, Ben-Gurion did not choose to address them—nor has Israel seriously dealt with them since.

Late in his career, Ben-Gurion took a dramatic detour from the Israeli sovereignty he articulated. In May 1960, Israeli agents in Argentina captured and spirited away the Nazi ex-officer Adolf Eichmann, in hiding since Germany's surrender fifteen years before. Eichmann had been the Nazis' chief administrator in liquidating the Jews. His subsequent trial, held in Jerusalem, was highly publicized and lasted five months.

"For the first time in Jewish history," Ben-Gurion declared, contradicting his earlier claim, "justice is being done by the sovereign Jewish people. . . . Israel is judging a murderer of the Jews. . . . Remember that only the independence of Israel could create the necessary conditions for this historic act." Found guilty, Eichmann was hanged as an act of retribution in the name of all Jews.[14]

World public opinion, while sympathetic to the execution of Eichmann, has been much less supportive of the killing in which Israel has been increasingly involved in the name of Jewish security. The explanation for this declining sympathy is not that the world has acquired a be-lated fondness for Arabs, who long remained unyielding. Nor was it, as some Jews insisted, a resurgence of anti-Semitism, for which little evidence exists. Herzl, it might be recalled, had promised in *The Jewish State* to "keep our professional army within the confines of their barracks." Consistently resorting to force to solve problems with Arab neighbors, Ben-Gurion helped erode the reservoir of goodwill that had carried Israel to statehood.

Since his earliest days in Palestine, Ben-Gurion had acknowledged an indifference to reconciliation with the Arabs. Over the years, he did not change, even after Israel repeatedly defeated the Arabs in wars. "I am pre-pared to get up in the middle of the night," he once told a journalist, "to sign a peace agreement—but I am not in a hurry and I can wait ten years. We are under no pressure whatsoever."[15] The obstacle that stood in his way was the high price of peace, which demanded ceding back to the Arabs some of their lost land and allowing at least some of their refugees to re-turn home. Ben-Gurion would not pay this price, and the Arabs of Pales-tine certainly did not have the power to force it upon him.

As Ben-Gurion envisaged them, peace negotiations would reopen the issue not just of the boundaries fixed in the 1949 cease-fire accords but the status of Jerusalem, which had been named a U.N. jurisdiction under the 1947 partition resolution. The War of Independence had ended with the IDF in control of Jewish West Jerusalem, which Israel proceeded to an-nex formally a year later and make the national capital. King Abdullah, meanwhile, having occupied Arab East Jerusalem and the West Bank, an-nexed them to Transjordan. Neither the U.N. nor Israel showed an inter-est after the war in upsetting these annexations. In 1951, all talk of an Arab state in Palestine was suspended indefinitely when Abdullah was as-sassinated by a Palestinian extremist and replaced by a weaker successor.

In the absence of a commitment to peace, Israel's dealings with the neighboring Arab regimes after the War of Independence were routinely confrontational. In the case of Syria, the chief differences were over water, with Ben-Gurion pressing for greater access to the headwaters of the Jor-dan River. In Egypt, army officers under Colonel Gamal Abdel Nasser overthrew the corrupt monarchy in 1952, and Ben-Gurion briefly imagined moving away from mutual hostility; but Nasser did not suppress Palestin-ian infiltration from the squalid refugee camps of the Gaza Strip, which Egypt controlled. As for Transjordan, refugees living in the West Bank routinely crossed the cease-fire lines to their former homes in Israel. Some sought only to visit lost kin, but others were killers and thieves. On Ben-Gurion's orders, Israel responded to all the provocations with equal harshness, using mines, ambushes, and rifle fire, which nullified any prospect of stability.

☙

In the same period, the rising hostility in the Cold War between the West and the Soviet Union aggravated Middle East tensions. Ben-Gurion initially declared a policy of "non-intervention," recognizing that large numbers of Jews lived on both sides of the Iron Curtain. "The interests of the Jewish people," he declared, "are not identical with any state or with any bloc." In response to the IDF's pressing for a new generation of weapons to replace its outdated arsenal, he began reconsidering. His solicitation of America to become Israel's chief arms supplier inevitably led to a strategic recalculation.

When the Korean War began in 1950, Ben-Gurion instructed his U.N. delegation to shift from "non-intervention" to support for the "free world." But Washington was now competing with Moscow for patronage of the Arabs, and it was not ready to accommodate Israel, even as a member of the "free world." Ben-Gurion's attempt to obtain American arms had to wait.

In July 1953, when a weary Ben-Gurion was on a leave of absence from his government posts, infiltrators crossed the border from Jordan and murdered an Israeli family. In retaliation, a young IDF major named Ariel Sharon seized a Jordanian village named Qibya and killed sixty-nine civilians in house explosions, claiming later not to have known the houses were inhabited. To protect the army, Ben-Gurion interrupted his leave to defend Sharon, declaring Israel's raid the work of irate Jewish settlers. Even after the U.N. investigated and condemned the operation, Ben-Gurion stuck to his story.

Qibya initiated Israel's first serious crisis in dealing with international public opinion. Expressing no remorse, Ben-Gurion proclaimed a right to ignore the condemnation, indispensable as the U.N. had been to Israeli independence. The U.N., he insisted, had become an Arab tool. "We must wean ourselves from the preposterous, totally unfounded and baseless illusion," he declared, "that there is outside the State of Israel a force in the world that would protect the life of our citizens. Our own capacity for self-defense is our only security. . . . Our future does not depend on what Gentiles say but on what Jews do."

In reaffirming the Zionist doctrine that Jews were responsible for their own fate, Ben-Gurion was also admitting that Israel was running short of friends. It was not the last time that Israel would, in effect, blame anti-Semitism for its troubles in the world community. To many Jews, being friendless was a recapitulation of their long history in Exile. As policy, Ben-Gurion disguised Israeli vulnerability as strength. His boast was, in reality, an attempt to conceal its dependance on foreign arms imports, which the major powers were now unwilling to supply.

After Qibya, Ben-Gurion, resuming his furlough, turned over the prime minister's office to his foreign minister, Moshe Sharett, the number two in the Mapai hierarchy. The shift, however, was only partial. Watching Sharett over his shoulder, Ben-Gurion maintained ties to government authority through loyal subordinates serving in key positions. Sharett, a far different man from Ben-Gurion, was a peacemaker. He spoke of reducing hostility with Israel's neighbors and he kept a tighter lid on the strife along Israel's frontiers. He even made peace overtures to Nasser. One result of his more moderate course was that neither Ben-Gurion nor the army trusted him.

Shortly after Sharett took office, a spy ring composed of Egyptian Jews bombed American and British cultural facilities in Cairo in an attempt to discredit Nasser and derail the West's efforts at Arab rapprochement. The ring was under the orders of the IDF, not Sharett, and its members were quickly captured. With Israel denying all responsibility, two members of the ring were promptly hanged for the bombings. Named the Lavon Affair—for Ben-Gurion's provisional replacement as defense minister—the episode ignited an explosion in Israeli public opinion. Not surprisingly, it also ended Sharett's peace overture to Egypt.

A month after the Cairo trial, Ben-Gurion returned to the defense ministry and fiercely criticized Sharett for "raising a generation of cowards." Days later, he ordered Ariel Sharon's army units into the Gaza Strip, where they conducted the bloodiest operation since the 1948 war. Thirty-seven Egyptian soldiers were killed, and once again Ben-Gurion lied in denying Israel's involvement. He could not, however, stop Nasser from striking back by recruiting and training Palestinian *fedayeen*— "self-sacrifice" squads—to undertake more raids from Gaza into Israel. Nasser also appealed to Moscow for arms to confront the Israelis, and

Moscow promptly gave its assent, raising the regional confrontation to a new level.

In Washington, President Eisenhower denounced Israel's Gaza raid for undermining U.S. efforts to organize the Arabs against Communism. The deal Nasser was making with Moscow, he stated, could draw the entire Arab world into the Soviet orbit. Eisenhower made no effort to punish Israel, however. He affirmed American concern for Israel's security by offering it the arms the IDF sought, but attached a condition that Israel cease its provocations. Ben-Gurion declined the condition and the talks broke down.

Meanwhile, in the Knesset election of mid-1955, Mapai lost seats to Herut, the Revisionist party, for which Ben-Gurion blamed Sharett's "weakness" in Egypt. Reoccupying the office of prime minister, he demoted Sharett to his old post at the foreign ministry. Again at full power, Ben-Gurion dispatched Sharett to America to restart the arms negotiations with Eisenhower, but in fact he set a trap by ordering Sharon to conduct a large-scale raid into Syria, knowing that Eisenhower would be furious.

Not surprisingly, Sharett returned empty-handed from Washington, and in a fierce cabinet debate he called Ben-Gurion "Satan himself." Within months Sharett was out of office entirely, removing the last obstacle to Ben-Gurion's newly conceived scheme to destroy Egypt's army before it could rebuild itself with the weapons that were due to arrive from Russia.

But Ben-Gurion now more than ever, needed new arms for the IDF. Paris, convinced Nasser was stirring up trouble in France's Arab colonies in North Africa, was itself looking for an ally, and agreed to sell tanks and aircraft to Israel. The U.S., to punish Egypt for its growing intimacy with Moscow, endorsed the French-Israeli arms deal. The U.S. further raised the ante by canceling a loan it had offered Nasser to build a high dam on the Nile at Aswan. Moscow promptly countered by offering Nasser the necessary funds, for which he showed his gratitude by nationalizing the Suez Canal and expelling the last British troops from Egypt. Prolonging the tit for tat, London then joined a brewing French-Israeli plot to attack Egypt. Together, France, Israel, and Britain prepared a bizarre plan to hit the Suez Canal and put an end to Nasser's rule.

Digressing briefly, it might be noted that Ben-Gurion also obtained help from France at this time in developing a nuclear weapon. French-Israeli nuclear talks had begun earlier, when Israel first faced the prospect that America's Middle East strategy might increase its isolation. The initial talks were for a small reactor, without a weapons capacity, but by the time an agreement was signed, it had a major weapons component. Since that time, Israel has, without public acknowledgement, become a nuclear power, casting a shadow across the region. Though the two sets of talks, over Suez and over the bomb, were ostensibly unrelated, the nuclear issue was surely on Ben-Gurion's mind during the preparations for the impending attack.

Israel launched the attack on October 29, 1956, with a paratroop drop in central Sinai. Its forces quickly reached the canal and within days had routed the Egyptians across the wide front from Sharm el-Sheikh to the Gaza Strip. By prearrangement, Britain and France then demanded that both armies withdraw from the banks of the canal, knowing that Nasser would not abandon Egyptian territory. When Nasser refused, they bombed Egyptian military installations, then landed units at Port Said, the canal's northern entry point.

Exultant, Ben-Gurion marched to the Knesset and declared victory. He had already unveiled a proposal during the planning for a "new" Middle East, in which Israel would advance its border to the Jordan River, internationalize the canal, and remake Lebanon into a friendly Christian-run state. Britain and France, interested only in destroying Nasser, dismissed his scheme. Now, with the IDF sitting beside the canal, Ben-Gurion reframed his ambition into restoring "King Solomon's patrimony," which would assert Israeli sovereignty over the Sinai and the Strait of Tiran. Even the Knesset, euphoric as it was, considered the proposal a fantasy.

But for Ben-Gurion, the fantasy was short-lived. The U.S.S.R. said it would not permit the aggressors to remain in their positions, and it showed signs of moving troops into the region. The U.N. General Assembly, with only the Suez allies' three votes in dissent, supported Moscow. Eisenhower ordered his secretary of state, John Foster Dulles, to warn Israel that its advance "cannot fail to bring catastrophe" to it. With the World War III looming, Ben-Gurion recognized that the U.S., though bound to defend its two NATO allies, had no legal obligation to Israel. Britain and France decided to cut their losses and went home, but Ben-Gurion refused to order his forces to withdraw.[15]

In the negotiations with Washington that followed, Ben-Gurion agreed in principle to evacuate the Sinai but haggled over the terms. Dulles, vowing not to reward aggression, at first offered nothing, and reproached Ben-Gurion for preferring short-term security gains to long-term regional stability. Eisenhower proposed sanctions on Israel, then was stunned by the pressure placed on him by America's organized Jewish lobbies. Finally an accord on evacuation was reached, though on terms that fell well short of the goals proclaimed earlier by the U.S. president and his secretary of state.

Under the accord, a U.N. force was to be stationed in the Sinai as a buffer between Israel and Egypt. Ben-Gurion, uninterested in ruling over 250,000 Arab refugees, agreed to the restoration of Egypt's administration of Gaza on the condition of its demilitarization. Prior to evacuation, the IDF leveled Gaza's *fedayeen* bases, which ended guerrilla raids into Israel. Israel also received recognition, notably from Washington, of its right of navigation through the Strait of Tiran to Eilat. In March 1957, four months after Britain and France, Israel withdrew its last military units from Egyptian territory.

But Nasser, Ben-Gurion's nemesis, remained in power, enjoying enhanced stature among the Arab masses, a reward that derived not from a military triumph in the Sinai but from America's diplomatic pressure on Israel. The Suez attack, in linking Israel to the classic colonial powers, had tarnished the country in the eyes of the Third World. Moreover, Egypt's military was now given the time to absorb the Soviet arms, which was the issue that provoked Ben-Gurion in the first place. A decade later, after the U.N. had failed on the promise to serve as a buffer in the Sinai and assure Israel's right of navigation through the Strait of Tiran, Israel faced a far bigger war. The advantages it won in the Suez campaign had done little to make Israel more secure.

Still, most Israelis interpreted the Suez attack as a reaffirmation of Ben-Gurion's toughness and strategic wisdom. He had become the epitome of the fearless Jew, willing to stand up to friend and foe alike. His conduct in the campaign lifted national morale; it also created a sense of invulnerability. Did it matter that Ben-Gurion's policies only positioned Israel for more wars? Many Israelis now reasoned that, at modest cost, all wars with the Arabs could be won, so why make sacrifices to avoid them? Few saw Ben-Gurion's failure to limit, much less to end, the Arab-Israeli conflict as reason to change the nation's strategic course.

Still, Ben-Gurion was foresighted enough to cultivate the principle that the Jewish state needed a patron. Herzl had looked to Germany, Weizmann to England, Jabotinsky to Italy. As a young man, Ben-Gurion had leaned on Turkey. As Eurocentrics, Zionists had not thought much about

America, except as a temptress luring Jewish migrants away from Palestine. Ben-Gurion now allowed his eyes to cross the Atlantic.

Unlike most other Zionists, Ben-Gurion knew America. He had spent much of the two World Wars there, witnessing its growth into global preeminence. He found his wife there and snatched Zionism's reins from Weizmann in New York. It is true he never grasped why most American Jews preferred Exile to the national home. But he understood that with the Cold War raging, America's political horizon extended to the Middle East, generating a dynamism that was driving the United States and Israel into each other's embrace. Ben-Gurion recognized that Zionists could afford to overlook America no longer.

In March 1957, just after Israel's withdrawal from the Sinai, the U.S. issued the Eisenhower Doctrine, pledging its "assistance against armed aggression from any country controlled by international Communism." Nasser's Egypt, where Soviet influence was penetrating deeper, was Washington's chief target. Ben-Gurion had not anticipated such an outcome in launching the Suez war and, during the wrangling over Israeli withdrawal, any benefit at all seemed unlikely. But in testimony to Congress, Dulles interpreted the Eisenhower Doctrine to mean that "preservation of the State of Israel was a vital part of U.S. policy."

In response to Dulles's statement, Moscow described Israel as an American lapdog. Though it was gravitating westward, Israel had no aggressive designs against anyone, Ben-Gurion answered. Without America's military assurances, however, Russia might have contemplated attacking Israel with impunity. The Middle East, once an arena of local wars, Ben-Gurion remarked, had become a playing field where "the world blocs of the East and the West meet as enemies." The Knesset voted overwhelmingly to accept the benefits of the Eisenhower Doctrine, positioning Israel under the shelter of the American military umbrella.

By a similar process, Nasser felt confident he had Moscow behind him in taking on the challenge of the Eisenhower Doctrine. The Suez war had triggered the anti-colonial reflexes of the Arab world, unleashing an unprecedented wave of militant nationalism. To most Arabs, Nasser somehow appeared invincible. With a freshly outfitted army, Nasser saw the prospect of unifying the Arab world against Israel and America under his personal leadership.

On February 1, 1958, Nasser made his initial move, merging Syria with

Egypt, naming the entity the United Arab Republic. In both countries the vote taken to ratify the change was virtually unanimous. In Lebanon in May, pro-Nasser rioters ignited a civil war, demanding membership in the new Arab state. The region's trembling pro-Western monarchies, Iraq and Jordan, promptly announced a union of their own, but it was aborted in Baghdad by a bloody coup, led by officers proclaiming loyalty to Nasser. In Jordan, King Hussein, having suppressed two coups the year before, now readied himself for a third. The Middle East was engulfed in a Nasserite frenzy.

To avoid elevating the Arab fever, Israel kept a discreetly low profile, while Ben-Gurion looked to America for leadership. But while America dithered, Ben-Gurion chose to take security matters into his own hands by negotiating a "peripheral alliance" with Iran, Turkey, and Ethiopia, pro-Western states on the Arab perimeter.

Finally, Eisenhower dispatched fifteen thousand Marines to Lebanon to support the pro-Western government there. The situation escalated when British planes flew through Israeli airspace without authorization to carry men and equipment to embattled Jordan, and Moscow threatened Israel with retaliation. When the U.S. asked permission for its own overflights, Ben-Gurion replied, "Britain and the United States come to us with demands as if we were allies. We indeed are willing to take risks but we do not have the security guarantees granted by the United States to an ally." Israel requested more generous arms deliveries for the IDF, within the framework of the same protection the U.S. pledged to its NATO allies.

Ben-Gurion had maneuvered deftly, satisfying America's Cold War designs while enhancing Israel's military position. On July 25, 1957, Eisenhower, who had so recently denounced Ben-Gurion, sent him a letter stating, "I am deeply impressed by the breadth of your insight into the grave problems that the free world faces in the Middle East. . . . You can be confident of U.S. interest in the integrity and independence of Israel."

Dulles further explained to Congress the impact of the Eisenhower Doctrine on the administration's Israeli policy. "The President" he stated, "has decided that if Israel would be attacked by the Soviet Union, the United States would come to Israel's assistance. . . . The Soviet Union is well aware of that fact. The United States is committed to Israel's existence and would fight for her should an attack by the Soviet Union compel her to do so." Dulles also notified Ben-Gurion of a favorable decision on support for the "peripheral alliance," to which Ben-Gurion reciprocated by approving American overflights through Israeli airspace.

By the end of his term in 1960, Eisenhower had concluded that he could rely only on Israel in the Middle East to confront Nasser and his Soviet patron. Privately, he even expressed regrets for his harsh tone in addressing Ben-Gurion during the Suez dispute. In the fall of 1958, Eisenhower opened the door to America's arsenal, shipping to Israel a thousand recoilless guns along with electronic and aircraft-detection gear. He also authorized American financing of a large delivery of tanks from Great Britain, involving a sum many times greater than any previous U.S.-Israeli military transaction.

Eisenhower did not, however, articulate any change to the premises of U.S. policy from what they were before Suez. He remained convinced the best means of promoting U.S. interests in the region, while thwarting Soviet designs, was to achieve Arab-Israeli peace. He repeatedly sent missions to explore the prospects. All foundered, however, with Ben-Gurion showing no enthusiasm for the U.S. position and the Arabs rejecting any concessions as long as Israel refused to discuss its demands on territory and refugees.

In March 1960, Ben-Gurion, on a visit to America to receive an honorary university degree, was invited for an informal chat with Eisenhower at the White House. Their discussion lasted two hours, a duration that reflected the newly established rapport between them. Ben-Gurion did most of the talking, emphasizing shared social values, but he also renewed an appeal for antiaircraft missiles. Eisenhower politely declined the request—approved a few years later, in the John F. Kennedy administration—explaining to Ben-Gurion that he preferred to leave major weapon sales to America's allies. In that way, he said, the United States could serve as a credible broker for Middle East peace.

Ben-Gurion's talk with Eisenhower was a measure of how the Cold War had narrowed the gap between the two countries. Secretary of State Christian Herter, the recent successor to Dulles, described Ben-Gurion in an internal memo. "We were impressed," his memo said, "by his breadth of vision, his faith in the destiny of his people and his dedication to the great moral verities shared by free men all over the world. We concluded that with such vision, faith, and dedication Israel can assuredly make significant contributions to a better world." Ben-Gurion's visit was a substantial building block in the edifice of Israeli-American friendship.[16]

In June 1963, Ben-Gurion decided to reopen the Lavon Affair, the case of the Cairo saboteurs that had disrupted the government during his leave of absence a decade before. He insisted on determining who ordered the bombing of the American and British facilities, and who lied in denying it. His determination derived from his self-imposed duty to restore the reputation of the army, under whose direction the operation had taken place. But, accompanying his insistence on getting to the bottom of the fiasco was a widespread public feeling that enough had been said about the Lavon Affair, and that after so many years of squabbling, he was holding irrationally to a trifling cause. Faced with a rebuff from the Knesset and his party, Ben-Gurion, at the age of seventy-three, resigned as prime minister.

Increasingly irascible, Ben-Gurion could no longer control either his old comrades or his young disciples. Mapai, the party he founded, was eroding beneath him. His energy had diminished, and even the public, much as it esteemed him, was aware of his decline. But, accustomed to being heeded, he departed in anger. A year later, he withdrew completely from Mapai, grumbling about its spinelessness, and founded a new party focused on himself alone. He ran for the Knesset in 1965, but his list won too few votes to make an impact. Ben-Gurion, at the end of his career, was reduced to being a parliamentary backbencher.

Then, in 1967, as another Arab war approached, a clamor arose—led, oddly, by Herut's Menachem Begin—to restore Ben-Gurion to his familiar post as minister of defense. Israel had never fought a war without Ben-Gurion in charge. He not only declined Begin's offer but argued against going to war at all. During a week of fighting, the Israeli army won its biggest victory ever. Ben-Gurion, even more uncharacteristically, then argued against the permanent occupation of the West Bank—whose absence from Israel's map he once called "a cause for mourning."

Ben-Gurion was now an isolated figure, whom few took seriously. The rapture that gripped the nation after the Six-Day War ignited a new Zionist militancy which left him behind. Ben-Gurion now played the role of an old curiosity, and his opposition to the military occupation made no impact.

Closing in on three-quarters of a century, Ben-Gurion had, however, finished the work he had set out for himself. He had begun his remarkable career as an immigrant from the Pale, a laborer in Palestine's fields and an armed watchman over the settlements. Demobilized from the Jewish Legion, he proceeded to shape Mapai and Histadrut into national institutions. As head of the Jewish Agency and the Zionist Executive in Palestine, he shifted power from London and made the *yishuv* into Zionism's dominant political center. He personally declared the State of Israel before leading it to victory in the War of Independence. He then presided over a freely elected parliamentary government and persuaded America, the strongest state in the West, to serve as guarantor of Israel's survival.

What Ben-Gurion did not do was establish peaceful relations between Israel and its Arab neighbors. In fact, he did not so much as try. That is not to say that peace was ever for the taking. But Ben-Gurion's focus was not on peace; it was on security, which he based solely on Israel's military domination of the region. Brilliant as was his life of service, it was marred by his failure to build sustainable ties with the peoples among whom the Jews now lived.

Nahum Goldmann, a successor to Herzl and Weizmann as president of the World Zionist Organization, wrote in his memoir of an intimate talk with Ben-Gurion over coffee and sandwiches at his home in the Negev one summer night after his retirement. He recalls Ben-Gurion musing, "Why should the Arabs make peace? If I was an Arab leader, I would never make terms with Israel. That is natural: we have taken their country. Sure, God promised it to us, but what does that matter to them? Our God is not theirs. We come from Israel, it's true, but two thousand years ago, and what is that to them? They only see one thing: we have come here and stolen their land. So it's simple. We have to stay strong and maintain a powerful army. Our whole policy is there. Otherwise the Arabs will wipe us out."

Ben-Gurion went on, Goldmann wrote: "The difference between you and me is that I never shrank from giving orders which I knew would mean the death of hundreds of wonderful young men. You would probably have hesitated. And therefore I can lead a people in wartime. You could not." To which Goldmann, known as a committed peace advocate, replied, "You are right, but maybe I could better prevent a war than you, which is still more important."

Admirers of Ben-Gurion's penchant for battle credit the state's founding to his readiness to face up to conflict. No doubt there is much truth in that position. But the reverse argument, which Goldmann makes, also contains truth. War—after centuries of Jewish passivity—has been absorbed into Israel's culture, into its collective personality, into its DNA. In their talk that night in Sde Boker, Goldmann holds Ben-Gurion to blame for modeling the new Israeli Jew in his own belligerent image. Largely as a result of Ben-Gurion's attitude, Goldmann argues, war has arrived too easily and become too common.

When Goldmann asked Ben-Gurion whether his description of the Arabs, if correct, would permit Israel to survive, he answered, "Ask me whether my son Amos, who will be fifty at the end of this year, has a chance of dying and being buried in a Jewish state, and I would answer: 'fifty-fifty.'" Goldmann then asked, "But how can you sleep with that prospect in mind?" Ben-Gurion hesitated a moment before replying: "Who says I sleep?"[17]

David Ben-Gurion died of a stroke on December 1, 1973, at the age of eighty-seven. He was buried next to Paula, who had died five years earlier, in Sde Boker, the austere desert kibbutz that had been their home in their final decades.

"If you seek his monument, look around you," was the epitaph of an admiring biographer, referring not just to the desert kibbutz but to the entirety of the land. During his lifetime, Ben-Gurion was the central figure in the transition of the Jewish community in Palestine from a scattering of idealistic but impoverished pioneers to a well-organized, accomplished, creative, prosperous, and heavily armed society. He died a few weeks after the Yom Kippur War, which was a near-fatal experience for the state. To some Jews, the Yom Kippur victory demonstrated Israel's invincibility. To others, the near-catastrophe showed that the military strength which was so important to Ben-Gurion would not alone assure the preservation of his monument, the Jewish state in the Land of Israel.

5

Rav Abraham Isaac Kook
1865–1935

Rabbi Zvi Yehuda Kook
1891–1982

REVIVALISTS

In 1904, Rav Abraham Isaac Kook, convinced by the pogrom in Kishinev that a secure life for the Jews was no longer possible in his native Russia, left behind a solid rabbinic career to settle with his wife and children in Palestine. Kook had no allegiance to Zionism, which he regarded as impermissibly secular. He also considered Zionism too similar to the aggressive nationalism that was infecting much of Europe. But he had by then turned away from the rabbinic doctrine that the Jews could return to their land only under the Messiah's leadership. In Palestine, Kook shaped an ideology that over the years transformed Zionist thinking, locking Judaism and nationalism in a tight political embrace.

Rav Kook was already a creative force in Jewish theology when he migrated to Palestine. "Rav" was an honorific title signifying his intellectual eminence. He had three daughters, for whom he had no plans, but he also had a son, named Zvi Yehuda, whom he never doubted would follow him into the rabbinate. Yet father and son were quite different. The Rav was a commanding theologian whose mind covered a full range of Jewish spirituality; Jewish nationalism was only one of his interests. His son, less gifted intellectually, grew up a more practical man. Under his father's tutelage, he came to think of nationalism and religion as synonymous. Zvi Yehuda made his mark on Jewish life by engaging in religious activism, fulfilling his father's vision of infusing Zionism with Jewish belief.

The Zionist doctrine devised by Rav Kook, the father, maintained that the secularism which the pioneers brought with them from Europe was a passing fancy, a temporary digression from the Jews' age-old fidelity to their religion. The pioneers may not have perceived God's presence in their settlement of the land, he said. But far from abandoning Judaism, they were conducting themselves according to God's will.

"If a Jewish secular nationalism were really imaginable," Rav Kook once wrote, "then we would be in danger of falling so low as to be beyond Redemption. But secular nationalists do not know how closely they are linked to the spirit of God. A Jewish nationalist, no matter how secular his intentions, is steeped in the divine spirit. A single Jew can sever his bonds to God but the House of Israel cannot. All of its dearest possessions—its land, language, history, customs—are vessels of the Lord's spirit."

"Only in the Land of Israel," he declared another time, "can the people of Israel engage in Jewish independent creativity, whether in the realm of ideas or daily life and action. . . . Revelations of the Holy can be pure in the Land of Israel; in Exile, they are mixed with dross and impurity."[1]

Rav Kook found the roots of his defiance of Orthodoxy deep in the body of Judaism. In drawing widely in his writing from diverse sources, he filled his work not only with conventional theology but with an elusive mysticism. As he saw it, the dogma that barred Jews from returning home in the Messiah's absence was not alone in being invalid; so was the rabbis' corollary requirement that Jews, in the meantime, must accommodate to Exile. The duty of Zionism was to prepare the homeland, in the Rav's view, not just for beleaguered Jews but for a renaissance of Judaism.

Rav Kook's body of work was huge, complex, and often abstruse. Zvi Yehuda, serving as the editor of his writing both during the Rav's lifetime and after his death, was selective, emphasizing the ideas that sanctified the Jews' return to Palestine. Zvi Yehuda was scarcely concerned with the mystical aspects of his father's output; his interest was in Jewish nationhood. During the decades when Religious Zionism was at a low ebb, Zvi Yehuda performed the duty of fanning the coals to keep the flame alive.

Religious Zionism had slipped into a long slumber after Herzl's time, during which it served as the willing servant of Labor Zionism. It emerged to follow its own star only after Israel's victory in the Six-Day War. By then the Rav was dead, but the Religious Zionism that he left behind contained a far worldlier outlook than it possessed in the era of Zionism's founder. It had a core of political dynamism that would place Judaism, the religion, near the heart of Zionism.

Even after Rav Kook's death, father and son were a closely knit team. Together they imparted to Zionism a powerful component of belief, linked to an appetite for the territory they regarded as holy. In doing so, the team of the two Kooks added to the already heavy burden that lay on Israel's quest for peace in the Middle East.

The idea of a Religious Zionism had, to be sure, long predated the Kooks. The rabbis known as the Precursors challenged Orthodoxy's doctrine of the Messiah early in the nineteenth century. Though unwilling to dismiss the Messiah from their theology, they struggled to find scriptural backing for placing the leadership for the return on living Jews. By taking the initiative themselves, the Precursors argued, the Jews were providing conditions to hasten the Messiah's arrival.

After the Russian pogroms of the 1880s, Rabbi Samuel Mohilever became a central figure among rebellious rabbis by joining Hibbat Zion, the society that promoted migration to Palestine. "God," Mohilever contended, "prefers having his children in their land even if they do not observe the Torah to having them observe the Torah properly while living in Exile." The Orthodox rabbinate was not impressed by Mohilever's argument.

By the first Zionist Congress in 1897, the dispute over religion had touched Herzl himself, who was determined to retain the support of observant Jews. "Let us not discourage them," Herzl instructed his followers, "even if we have no intention of handing them the leadership."[2] Herzl ardently wooed Mohilever, who gave his blessing to the Congress by describing it as itself Messianic. Mohilever's embrace helped to legitimize Zionism among religious Jews, especially those from Eastern Europe.

Rabbi Isaac Jacob Reines, a Mohilever disciple, took the Russian pogroms as evidence that Orthodoxy was leading the Jews astray. Zionism had never actually claimed to stand apart from Judaism, but Reines held that it did. Zionism, seeking a refuge from the anti-Semites, was earthbound, he argued, and "in none of its acts or aspirations is there the slightest allusion to a future Redemption." He called Messianism and Zionism parallel visions, which a Jew could embrace separately or together.

"For some decades," Reines contended later, "Jews have shown symptoms of a disease: perversion of the truth. . . . Many supported Zionism in their hearts but spoke against it. Some opposed Zionism with the claim that heretics dominated it, but this was a deliberate distortion. . . . Whether or not freethinkers take part in the movement, no one can deny that all activity on behalf of the Holy Land is sanctified and moral. . . . It would have been much better had they not defended this perversion."[3]

Reines became a player in Jewish politics at the Zionist Congress of 1900, which he attended at Herzl's invitation. Zionist unity was already fraying. Ahad Ha'am's disciples were seeking to have Zionism embrace secular Jewish "culture," which Reines regarded as an effort to exclude religion from the movement entirely. To Herzl, both "culture" and piety were distractions from saving lives, but he was willing to make concessions to both in the interest of preserving Zionism's fragile cohesion.

At the Zionist Congress of 1901, Herzl accepted some of Ahad Ha'am's "culture" while extending funds to aid Reines in making religion into a political force. Reines convoked a meeting the next year in Vilna and founded Mizrachi, an organization that envisaged Palestine as a kind of Judaic Vatican.[4] The Vilna meeting marked the birth of Religious Zionism as a political movement, and in the ensuing months, Mizrachi, touching a popular nerve, established hundreds of branches throughout Europe and America. Its rising appeal convinced Herzl to accept it as a faction within the expanding Zionist tent.

At the Congress of 1903, Reines's Mizrachi provided Herzl with his margin of victory in the vote to establish Jewish colonization in Uganda. In defying the secular delegates from Eastern Europe, Reines accepted that East Africa was a temporary stop on the way to Palestine. Uganda, he declared, gave priority to "the needs of the people, which we love more than the land." He described it as a step toward Redemption, but few Eastern Jews were persuaded. Even his own followers acknowledged Mizrachi's Uganda vote was Reines's repayment to Herzl of a political debt.

Mizrachi's role in the Uganda dispute was its high point in early Zionist history. Reines remained head of the organization until his death in 1915, but by then Mizrachi was already in sharp decline. Mizrachi stayed faithful over the ensuing years to the Herzl tradition of promoting statehood over all other concerns, including religion. But it also succeeded in preserving a religious presence within the Zionist movement during the long years of Labor's political dominance. Mizrachi's influence was, at most, marginal, and almost no one expected it one day to rise from its ashes. But in the third decade of the Jewish state, at the time of the Six-Day War, that is precisely what it did. Under the inspiration of the two Rabbis Kook, Religious Zionism exploded into a major force in Jewish political life.

Avraham Isaac Kook was born in Russian Latvia in 1865, the first of eight children descended from distinguished rabbis on both his mother's and his father's side. Recognized as a prodigy at a very young age, he combined unwavering piety with a wide-ranging intellect. He attended the yeshiva at Volozhin, where the aroma of the *Haskala* was said to permeate the corridors. In his twenties, he married a rabbi's daughter, lost her soon afterward to illness, then married one of her cousins. Appointed to rabbinic posts in a series of small towns, he showed barely a passing interest in Zionism until the Kishinev pogrom, when, poised to advance in the rabbinic hierarchy, he chose instead to accept the offer of a modest pulpit in Palestine.

Kook was named the rabbi of Jaffa, then Palestine's chief port and hub of its agricultural hinterland. He served not just in the town but in the rural settlements that surrounded it. The pioneers respected him for his wisdom in social and economic matters and for his readiness to stand up for them against Turkish bureaucrats, Arab headmen, and Orthodox rabbis. Though he accepted the settlers' secularism, Kook left no doubt about his own allegiance. Even in Palestine's summer heat, he wore a fur hat, a black coat, and an unkempt beard, the costume of medieval rabbis, along with *teffilin* and *talesim,* symbols of the faith. He labored tirelessly to bring the pioneers to *his* Torah, while they worked to move him closer to *their* Zionism.

In 1909, Kook was drawn into the controversy over *sh'mittah,* the religious law that bars Jews from tilling the soil of the Holy Land during the Sabbatical Year. On the agenda since the first migrations, the issue had never been resolved. Secular Jewish farmers naturally objected to rules that threatened not only their income but massive starvation, and perhaps death. Kook outraged the rabbinic establishment by ruling that *halacha* favored rebuilding the land over the outdated Talmudic requirement to keep the land fallow. In helping to waive enforcement of *sh'mittah,* he carved out a lasting reputation for courage, which the pioneers much appreciated.

In 1913, Mizrachi invited Kook to be a delegate to the World Zionist Congress in Vienna. Kook had never joined Mizrachi, despite much overlap of its aspirations with his own. Kook rejected Reines's doctrine that Zionism and Judaism existed in separate domains, and he criticized Mizrachi for settling for second-class status within the Zionist movement. In later years, his opposition to women's suffrage in *yishuv* elections would lead him to an open split with Mizrachi, but when the Orthodox rabbinate urged him to decline the invitation to the Zionist Congress, he refused, insisting that in attending, he would bring holiness to its proceedings.

In the end, however, he stayed home. Zvi Yehuda was then studying at a *yeshiva* in Germany, and the Rav chose to wait a year, until he could visit his son in conjunction with a rabbinic meeting scheduled for Berlin. In July 1914, Kook and his wife sailed from Palestine, arriving in Berlin just as war was breaking out. Still a Russian national, he and his son were interned by the Germans but released at the urging of local rabbis. Unable to get passage home, he settled in Switzerland, where he spent a year writing and studying, his living expenses covered by wealthy Jewish businessmen. In 1915, he accepted the offer of a paid position with a congregation in London's East End, where refugees from Russia were concentrated. He remained in England with his wife and Zvi Yehuda until the war came to a close.

It is not surprising, in a world consumed by conflict, that while in Europe Kook turned to contemplating the meaning of war. The subject was not a familiar one among Jewish thinkers. During the centuries of Exile, Jews had no influence over the starting and stopping of wars, much less a knowledge of how to wage them. His ruminations on the carnage taking place on the battlefield, though murky, yielded a glimmer of hope, however. The war in Europe, he concluded, was the product not of human evil but of God's design. It would end, he wrote, with the attainment of the Zionist goal of reestablishing Jewish sovereignty over the entire Land of Israel.[5]

"God has opened his arsenal and brought forth the weapons of his anger," Kook wrote, "to demolish the evil of present-day civilization. On the ruins of a terrible war, a world order will be established in truth and the knowledge of God." Kook was consistent in applauding the founding of Jabotinsky's Jewish Legion, the first Jewish army since the biblical era. In fact, he regarded the rebirth of a Jewish civilization in Palestine as evidence that Jews were at the brink of resuming an active role in history, "bringing Israel, along with the entire world, to Redemption."[6]

In exploring the meaning of war, Kook also helped reintroduce a respect for physical activity, long absent from Jewish experience. "Athletics, in which our youth in the Land of Israel engages to strengthen the body in the service of the nation," he wrote, "is not different from the moral strength conveyed by the holy sages to increase God's light in the world."[7] Like secular Zionists, he had come to exalt the idea of the "new" Jew, involved in physical games and bodybuilding, Jews who were unafraid to take charge of their national destiny, even to the point of making war.

Kook was also exuberant during these years about the efforts of Weizmann, his neighbor in London, to promote the cause of Zionism in Palestine. Weizmann, however, did not reciprocate the feeling. He urged his trusted colleague Sokolow to meet with Kook, "to bring him into the work," but after their meeting, Sokolow reported that Kook "has ideas of his own concerning Zionist politics . . . which are undoubtedly well meant but are full of *sancta simplicitas* and impracticable."[8] Kook, Sokolow concluded, was ill disposed by temperament to work harmoniously with a circle of secular Zionists, and so Weizmann and the Rav never got together.

Near the end of the war, however, Kook made a defining gesture on his own. He prepared a manifesto, read in his own synagogue and perhaps in others, in which he joined Weizmann in stridently denouncing the assimilated British Jews who were attempting to thwart the issuance of the Balfour Declaration. His manifesto was also conspicuous in its begrudging any gratitude to Britain for what Balfour's declaration promised.

"We demand full restitution for the land which has been robbed from us," his manifesto read. "The crime which cries unto heaven must be completely corrected. Our precious, holy land, full of wonder and splendor, our pride, our human rights and human dignity . . . must be returned to us fully, without compromise, without hypocrisy—entirely, in all completeness. . . . Is it not our duty . . . to inform all humanity, especially the fighting cultured nations, that the crime of crimes will remain hanging over their heads if they do not cleanse themselves of the robbery and butchery that they have perpetrated against us?"

When the Balfour Declaration was published, Kook declared that he saw in it the footprints not of Britain but of the Messiah. Redemption, he told a crowd in London's Albert Hall, would be bestowed at the same time on

Jews as on all mankind. His words seemed to attribute the Balfour Declaration not to Great Britain, but to God.

"I did not come to thank the English people for the Declaration that it
gave us," he told the audience. "I came to congratulate it with the blessing
of *mazel tov* for being a singular nation. The purpose of the existence of
the whole world is the Torah, and he who attaches himself to the Torah is
joined unto the eternity of God. . . . It is the unique glory of your nation to
lend aid to the people of the Torah. . . . I commend the people of England
on their being counted among the supporters of our people."[9]

In 1919, Kook and his family returned from Europe to Palestine. Not surprisingly, Kook was struck by how different the country was, with the Turks
gone and the British in charge. Kook was named, after much debate in
rabbinic circles over his iconoclasm, the Chief Rabbi of Jerusalem, Palestine's
most eminent rabbinic post.

In one of its first acts, the British Mandate had adopted the Ottoman
practice of leaving a large measure of self-rule to each religious minority,
particularly over such "personal status" issues as marriage, divorce, and
inheritance. For centuries, the *yishuv* had been under the jurisdiction of a
chief rabbi, a Sephardi sitting in Constantinople. But as a consequence of
the postwar migrations, the *yishuv* was now heavily Ashkenazi, a shift to
which the Mandate responded by authorizing the appointment of two
chief rabbis, one Sephardi, the other Ashkenazi. Weizmann's Zionist Commission, assured by the Mandate that both rabbis would be Zionists, accepted
the plan, and Rav Kook was formally named Palestine's first Ashkenazi
Chief Rabbi.

In this capacity, Kook, as he had since arriving in 1904, reached out to
all Jews, Ashkenazi and Sephardi, pious and secular, Religious Zionist and
socialist. He opposed the suffrage of women in the *yishuv* election of
1920, however, for which the secular community reproached him. And five
years later, speaking at the dedication of the Hebrew University, the monument of "cultural" Zionism, he urged that "its professors be pious Jews
whose faith will fuel their . . . exploration," a formulation that cost him
heavily in academic circles. By then, the *yishuv* recognized that Kook was
a man of strong mind and eclectic tastes who gave no berth to partisan
politics in his interpretations of Judaism, though that would change over
the ensuing years.

As for Palestine's Arabs, Kook paid them almost no attention at all. The Mandatory government, whose aim was to abate Arab-Jewish tensions, did not look favorably on his indifference. Kook was routinely invited to the Mandate's receptions and garden parties; but in a memoir, Jerusalem's British governor described him with disdain as "a dignified figure with an ample beaver hat who . . . spoke always at formidable length and with confidence . . . that his words must be accepted as *ex cathedra*."[10] Clearly, the British had little respect for Rav Kook, and he had little use for them.

Neither did the Orthodox rabbinate ever accommodate to Kook. Most rabbis had not forgiven the liberal position he took in the *sh'mittah* dispute in 1909. Almost none accepted his contention that Zionism and Judaism were one. Nearly all were angered by the proposal he made to reconstitute the Sanhedrin, the body that had made Jewish law in biblical times, which they saw as a plot to undermine their present-day powers over *halacha*. Some rabbis banned his books; a few even burned them.

With secular Jews suspicious of his piety, the British convinced of his political unreliability, and the rabbinic establishment furious at what it regarded as his heresies, Kook had a narrow political base on which to exercise his influence. He did not make the office of Chief Rabbi into a popular post and certainly not into a position of power. His place in Zionist history was won by the work of his intellect as interpreted by his son, Zvi Yehuda, rather than by any noteworthy political achievements of his own.

Still, one achievement was his contribution to the creation of what came to be called Modern Orthodoxy. Among Kook's mantras was, "The old shall be new and the new will be holy," which he applied to legitimize both his own rigorous piety and the looser observance preferred by religious members of the new *yishuv*. He had no sympathy whatever for Reform or Conservative Judaism, which he regarded as deviations from the faith. With his encouragement, however, Modern Orthodoxy grew among Jews who observed the Sabbath but declined to wear side curls and fur hats or study the Talmud around the clock.

Modern Orthodoxy, as Kook inspired it, told Jews they could be loyal to Judaism within the framework of a contemporary style of life. They could earn their livelihood in the secular economy, while keeping the Sabbath, the dietary laws, and religious holidays, including fast days. The men, like the women, could wear modern dress. They could distinguish themselves from secular Jews by wearing skullcaps at all times. But, with the Rav as their guide, the Modern Orthodox parted most defiantly from traditional Orthodoxy by embracing Jewish nationalism as a divine commandment, independent of the Messiah. By the end of the Six-Day War, the most zealous members of a resurgent Religious Zionism were the Modern Orthodox.

In 1924, Rav Kook founded a yeshiva in Jerusalem to train rabbis in religious nationalism. The yeshiva, taking his honorific title, was called Mercaz HaRav, "The Rav's Center." Since most of its students were Modern Orthodox, Mercaz HaRav looked quite different from any traditional yeshiva. It was, at the time, the only yeshiva in Palestine that taught Zionism as a central element of Judaism. Its language was Hebrew, the nationalist language, not Yiddish, which most Orthodox still spoke and it placed great emphasis on the country's history and geography. It also promised to reexamine *halacha,* with the aim of making the law an instrument of national revival. Students were invited from across the Jewish world to absorb and spread Kook's vision of Religious Zionism.[11]

From its early days, the young men who attended the Rav's yeshiva renounced the tradition of becoming religious scholars in favor of promoting a nationalism based on Judaism. Its graduates were trained to serve Religious Zionist congregations that were scattered around the country. A few also participated in Revisionist activities. But the yeshiva had little success in attracting secular Jews to the Torah, which was a major tenet of Rav Kook's theology. What Mercaz HaRav did accomplish was to build a body of Modern Orthodox rabbis whose passions lay in nationalist activism, and who readied themselves to serve the *yishuv* whenever they might be called.

Rav Kook worked for a decade as the yeshiva's administrator and chief lecturer, assisted by his son Zvi Yehuda. Recognizing that Zvi Yehuda was of lesser rabbinic stature, he proposed at one point that his son prepare to earn a living in circumcision or in kosher slaughter, inferior rabbinic specialties. But he had no problem with Zvi Yehuda as his editor. Zvi Yehuda, the Rav stated, grasped "the inner feelings of my heart."

Zvi Yehuda Kook spent most of his early career organizing his father's diverse and scattered writings into readable form. Specialists recognize him as a competent editor but argue that he made use of his responsibility to emphasize the Jewish nationalism that was only a fraction of the Rav's body of thought. Ultimately, Zvi Yehuda became the chief advocate of the theology that reshaped Religious Zionism. Many scholars of Judaism, acknowledging the intimacy of the father-son relationship, refer to the doctrines that emerged as "Kookism."[12]

Mercaz HaRav was not a success during the Rav's lifetime, however. It had difficulty finding donors, whether religious or secular. The Rav's writings were, for the most part, too esoteric to win a large intellectual following, and his controversial reputation within rabbinic circles was a barrier to attracting students and faculty. The result was that until Zvi Yehuda succeeded to the leadership after his father's death, the academic prestige of Mercaz HaRav never rose to the level of its ambitions.

During his last years, Rav Kook himself became an activist in the secular nationalist cause. He openly rejected the British policy of promoting tranquility in the Mandate by preserving the religious status quo between Arabs and Jews. He scoffed at Muslim claims to many of Palestine's religious sites. When Betaris at the Wailing Wall provoked the Arabs in demonstrations that led to deadly rioting in 1929, Kook denounced the Mandatory authority for blaming the Jews and failing to protect Jewish rights. Though never openly a Revisionist, Rav Kook grew increasingly sympathetic to Jabotinsky's ideas and gravitated steadily toward Revisionism's support.

When Chaim Arlosoroff was murdered in 1933, Kook at first resisted involvement in the controversy over who had killed him. He called for an end to the vilification between Jews, but when the suspects, all Revisionists, were brought to trial, he signed a letter defending "our imprisoned brothers." Jabotinsky, who had once denounced him for opposing women's suffrage, now praised Kook's patriotism, while Ben-Gurion declared him an enemy of justice and proposed to abolish the chief rabbinate altogether. Though uneasy at being seen as a partisan, the Rav took few steps to modify his image.[13]

Rav Kook died at the age of seventy in 1935, no longer considered the man whose grandest ambition was to bring the Jews together. His love for the Torah had become indistinguishable from a fierce patriotism. He was succeeded as head of the yeshiva by an old friend, then by another. Zvi Yehuda remained at his desk, still editing his father's work, while cultivating his own nationalist fervor.

In 1952, seventeen years after his father's death, Zvi Yehuda, now sixty-one, became head of Mercaz HaRav. Israelis, perceiving no particular significance to the succession, took little note of it. Zvi Yehuda settled comfortably into his new responsibilities, continuing the tasks he had performed for most of his adult life: administering the yeshiva and making his father's writing more accessible. The *yishuv* showed little interest in either his work, or in Rav Kook's, but in retrospect it is clear that changes were simmering beneath the surface of Israeli society. On the eve of the 1967 war, Zvi Yehuda dramatically placed his father's theology on the national political agenda. It would take the country by storm.

Zvi Yehuda Kook was born in 1891 in the Lithuanian town of Zaumel, where his father held a pulpit. As a student, he was not regarded as being of his father's caliber. After the family moved to Palestine, he was enrolled in a prominent Jerusalem yeshiva and finished his rabbinic studies in Germany. He spent most of his working life at Mercaz HaRav among the predominantly Modern Orthodox student body, though he himself, like his father, wore a long beard, side curls, and a black caftan throughout his life. In 1922, on a trip to Poland, he married a woman who died childless in 1944. He never remarried.

Zvi Yehuda had attained none of the scholarly benchmarks by which rabbis are measured when he became head of Mercaz HaRav. But his scholarly deficiencies were of little importance in an institution that emphasized scripture far less than the holiness of the land. Mercaz HaRav's motto was "the Torah of Israel, the nation of Israel, the Land of Israel," and it linked Judaism to the Judaization of Palestine from the river to the sea. It also taught that the victory of the Jewish state in 1948 proved that the age of the Messiah had arrived, even if the Messiah himself had not made an appearance. Israel still swelled with patriotic pride over the outcome of the War of Independence, and Zvi Yehuda's nationalist vision suited the temper of his time.

Under Zvi Yehuda, the theology at Mercaz HaRav became barely distinguishable from Revisionism's political platform. Rav Kook, untroubled by Revisionism's secular roots, in his later years enthusiastically embraced Jabotinsky's territorial vision. Like Jabotinsky, he was willing to resort to arms to attain his territorial goal. Interestingly, both the Rav and Jabotinsky left disciples—respectively, Zvi Yehuda and Menachem Begin—who directed their energy into transforming a more radical version of their mentors' ideas into political reality.

Zvi Yehuda, as the head of Mercaz HaRav, required his students to attend military parades. He welcomed army officers at the yeshiva as religious dignitaries and pronounced war-making a sacred practice. He also designated Israel's Independence Day a religious holiday, and on each anniversary he delivered a rabbinic homily on the holiness of all of Palestine's territory. Hundreds of supporters regularly attended.

In 1967, Zvi Yehuda opened his annual homily by recalling that when the Jews of the *yishuv* poured into the streets twenty years earlier to celebrate the passage of the U.N.'s partition resolution, he sat alone, despondent. The loss of holy soil, he said, had been too painful for him to bear. Suddenly, he broke into loud, stunning sobs. "Where is our Hebron, Shechem, Jericho and Anathoth,"—biblical sites now ruled by Arabs—"torn from the state in 1948, as we lay maimed and bleeding?" Weeks later, after Israel's victory in the Six-Day War, his words passed as prophesy into the lore of Religious Zionism.[14]

On June 7, 1967, hours after the IDF's capture of the Old City of Jerusalem from the Jordanian army, students of Mercaz HaRav carried Zvi Yehuda in exultation past the Israeli tanks and artillery to the Wailing Wall. Even secular Israelis found religious meaning, perhaps Redemption itself, in the victory. A few triumphant soldiers had improvised a religious service, immortalized in a photo of a weeping paratrooper kissing the famous Roman stones. On reaching the wall, Kook proclaimed, "By divine command, we have returned to our home, to our holy city. From this day forth, we shall never depart."[15]

The Israeli government promptly passed legislation asserting Israel's sovereignty over the entirety of Jerusalem, including the Old City. Under the partition resolution of 1947, Jerusalem was to have been an enclave under international rule. Instead, at the end of the 1948 war, Israel annexed the western half, Jordan the eastern. Under the 1967 law, all of Jerusalem was to be Israel's. The cabinet not only ignored protests from the U.N. and the United States but, in redrawing the city boundaries, extended Israel's authority deep into the West Bank, taking control of dozens of Arab villages. No part of the annexation has ever been recognized by the international community.

Later that summer, Kook and his followers pressed the government to permit the reoccupation of Kfar Etzion, an Orthodox settlement near Hebron, which in 1948 had fallen to Jordan after brutal combat in which almost no Jews survived. In the ensuing years, Israelis mourned Kfar Etzion as a symbol of national loss. The cabinet, rejecting a warning that reoccupation breached international law, authorized the return of the children—now adults—who had been evacuated during the earlier fighting.

Moshe Levinger, a fiery rabbi who would soon be Mercaz HaRav's most celebrated alumnus, led the ceremony of return. Carrying a Torah, he sanctified a Jordanian administrative building as a synagogue. If

Jerusalem's reunification was driven by irresistible emotion, Kfar Etzion's was a calculated decision by the cabinet to satisfy the increasingly assertive Religious Zionists.

Levi Eshkol, who had succeeded Ben-Gurion as prime minister in 1963, initially signaled a readiness to exchange Israel's conquests for a treaty of peace. The Arab states, however, followed their well-trodden path, refusing at a summit meeting in Khartoum to bargain at all. The U.S., meanwhile, spearheaded a move at the U.N. to win approval of a land-for-peace formula, designated Security Council Resolution 242, based on Eshkol's overture. But a few weeks later, Eshkol notified President Lyndon Johnson that domestic political pressure forced him to withdraw the land-for-peace offer. Israel clearly was no readier than the Arabs to end the Middle East conflict.

In the years prior to the 1967 war, Israel had thought little about changing its borders. Its victory unexpectedly reopened the issue. Eshkol, as had Ben-Gurion in 1948, recognized the demographic dangers to a Jewish majority that lay in Israel's absorbing the West Bank Arabs. But around him were influential Israelis who were determined to hold on. Military officers emphasized security concerns. Jabotinsky's heirs invoked historic rights. Religious Zionists claimed the land in God's name.[16]

Some Israelis were drawn to what was called the Allon Plan, named for a prominent general who proposed building military outposts in the Jordan Valley. Permissible under international law, the outposts were to serve as a trip wire against any later attacks. Some of these outposts were actually built, and later evolved into civilian settlements. But Arab rejection of any negotiations weakened the influence of any Israelis willing to take the opportunity for a permanent peace. Overall the immediate aftermath of the war, notwithstanding heated debate, produced no official policy on military withdrawal, nor any on military occupation.

Of all the claimants of Arab territory, Religious Zionists were the most zealous. Most of their leaders were graduates of Mercaz HaRav. Unlike the traditional Orthodox, they had fought valiantly in the war and claimed the right to make homes in the land Israel had conquered. Some even talked of building a Third Temple and restoring King David's kingdom. Most of Israeli society was too secular to buy into such a mystical notion, but the prospect of retaining the occupied territory was near universally popular.

"Jews did not pray three times a day over the centuries to return to Tel Aviv or Haifa," declared Rabbi Levinger, the most dynamic of the Kook disciples in pressing for control over the conquered territory. "The Bible says Judea and Samaria"—the widely adopted biblical names for the West Bank—"belonged to the Jewish people. Jews lived there during all the years of Exile. For centuries we prayed to return to Jerusalem and Nablus, not to the modern cities of Tel Aviv and Haifa. The tombs of Abraham, Isaac, and Jacob are in Hebron. It was King David's first capital."[17]

Levinger was not just a rabbi but an instinctive strategist. His plan was to have religious settlers seize control of sites, which would require the government either to evict them forcibly, which was sure to be unpopular, or to submit to their presence. On the eve of Passover, in the spring of 1968, Levinger reserved space for ten families in Hebron's Park Hotel, assuring the Arab owner that after conducting a seder they would leave the premises and go home. But on the morning after the seder, Levinger led his followers to the Machpelah Cave, burial place of the Jewish patriarchs and a site holy to both Arabs and Jews. There he declared that under the laws of God, his followers had the duty to remain in Hebron forever.[18]

"We did not have permission from the government to stay here," Levinger said in a later interview. "But why did we need permission? In the Torah it is written that the Land of Israel belongs only to the Jews. Why do Jews need permission to live in their own country?"

The government, as Levinger anticipated, was paralyzed by his action. It had already provided a precedent in annexing East Jerusalem. Many Israelis, both secular and religious, saw annexation as a resurgence of Zionist idealism. When a few officials stated the need for restraint to keep an avenue open to Arab-Israeli talks, Levinger lamented mockingly that the state had been infected by the "virus of peace."

A day later, Levinger paid a visit to Hebron's Arab mayor and declared that he, Levinger, was now in charge. The cabinet did not rebut him and the army, the lawful authority within the occupied territories, took no action. A few weeks later, the cabinet granted permission to Levinger not only to stay but to found a yeshiva, a branch of Mercaz HaRav, as a symbol of Jewish rule. The cabinet also allowed Levinger's followers in Hebron to carry their own weapons, a tactic deliberately designed to generate fear among the Arab inhabitants.

Moshe Levinger, born in 1935, was the son of a doctor who fled Germany with his family after the Nazis took power. Abrasive in manner, he did not look like a leader. He was spindly and unkempt, with bad teeth, thin and disordered hair, and a scraggly beard. But behind thick glasses were eyes flaming with zealotry. Reveling in his takeover, he made a home for his wife and children in the ruins of an ancient synagogue in the Arab marketplace of Hebron. Levinger understood that the government had no choice but to have the army protect him and his family, and that incidents of violence would actually strengthen Israel's determination to retain the land.

Levinger's success brought him into a collision with Rav Kook's belief that the Jewish *state* was "the foundation of God's throne in the world." Zvi Yehuda had even enlarged his father's position, declaring, "We must learn to distinguish between the precious essence embodied in the fact of Jewish sovereignty . . . and the incidental flaws that have accumulated along the redemptive path. The principal overall thing is the state. It is inherently holy."[19] Zvi Yehuda, however, was to change his position as Levinger and Religious Zionism stepped up the campaign against state authority.

In the years after the Six-Day War, Religious Zionism relentlessly challenged the state over territory and consistently won. An Israeli general noted wryly in a memoir, "At the end of the sixties, the world was already watching the finish of the era of colonialism, and precisely then Israel found itself marching in the opposite direction."[20] Led by Kook's followers, Israel's growing domination of Palestine's Arabs had become an irresistible force at the core of Zionism.

Religious Zionism's territorial demands, it should be noted, must not be confused with the quest for power of the Orthodox rabbinate. Both regarded their objectives as divinely inspired, thus on a higher plane than secular power. But Orthodoxy's goal was to salvage in Palestine the authority it exercised for centuries over the life of the Jews in Exile. Over much popular objection, but with the government's consent, the rabbinate narrowed the personal freedoms exercised by Israel's non-Orthodox majority over such private matters as marriage and divorce. Religious Zionism's divine hunger for territorial dominion, in contrast, contributed to countless border conflicts and Israel's loss of the goodwill of much of the outside world.

Early on Yom Kippur day in 1973, the armies of Egypt and Syria undertook a surprise attack to reverse the results of the Six-Day War. The idea had begun with Anwar Sadat, Egypt's president since Nasser's sudden death in 1970. For more than a year, he had sought to lure Israel into talks aimed at the return of Egypt's lost territory in return for peace. After failing to spark a response from Golda Meir, then the prime minister, he persuaded Syria to join him as an ally. Egypt and Syria decided on a two-front attack on Israel, across the Suez Canal and over the Golan Heights.

Sadat's premise was that conquering Israel was beyond the Arabs' reach. His goal was to break the diplomatic stalemate produced by Israel's 1967 victory, and in the early fighting, the two Arab armies made substantial gains, inflicting on Israel huge losses in men and weapons. Had Israel not received emergency arms deliveries from America, it might well have been defeated. In the end, the outcome on the battlefield was more or less a draw, but Sadat succeeded in his objective of shattering the Arab-Israeli status quo.

The close call, however, left Israel in a surly mood, feeling much less sure of itself. It set the stage for the collapse of Labor, the perennial ruling party, transforming Israeli politics. It provided the dynamism for Religious Zionism to become a political powerhouse and opened the door for Revisionism, a political minority since Jabotinsky's day, to take over the government. It also ratcheted up popular dedication to holding on to the land that had been occupied six years before and, by tightening its alliance with America, assured Israel's long-term military dominance in the region. In the aftermath of the Yom Kippur War, Israel became more defiant toward the Arabs, more rigidly nationalistic, more narrow-minded, and even less interested than before in negotiating an end to the conflict.

When Golda Meir became prime minister on the death of Levi Eshkol in 1969, Israel was still debating how to deal with the spoils of the 1967 war. A member of Labor's Old Guard and a loyal disciple of Ben-Gurion, she had served much of her life in the party ranks. She was at ease with Eshkol's circle of cronies, but while Eshkol had been open-minded though indecisive, she was closed-minded and stubborn. Eshkol had recognized advantages in exchanging territory with the Arabs for peace; Meir considered a return of territory, especially to the Palestinians, a humiliation that Israel could not bear.

At roughly the time that Meir took over, Richard Nixon succeeded Lyndon Johnson as the U.S. president. Nixon and his national security adviser, Henry Kissinger, a German-born Jew whose family had fled from Nazism on the eve of World War II, envisaged Israel as an instrument to serve American interests in the Cold War. Deeply anti-Soviet herself, Meir had no quarrel with Nixon's Cold War objectives and was rewarded by a flow of weapons, aimed at keeping Israel's military forces stronger than the combined armies of its neighbors.

The Meir era opened with a resumption of violence on several borders. Yasser Arafat's Palestine Liberation Organization conducted terror attacks from Lebanon and Jordan, while Nasser initiated a deadly "war of attrition" along the Suez Canal, using his newly acquired Soviet arms. In reply to the shelling of IDF bunkers along the waterline, Israeli aircraft struck deep into Egypt, triggering dogfights against Russian-piloted planes. Four hundred Israelis and thousands of Egyptians were killed, and the conflict seemed ready to spread when the U.S., unwilling to get involved in a new world war, managed to impose a fragile cease-fire over the canal.[21]

Nasser's death of a heart attack came shortly after the fighting stopped, and within months, Sadat had welcomed a U.N. emissary to discuss Arab-Israeli negotiations. When Meir refused to reciprocate the gesture, the U.S. proposed a narrower deal, with Israel withdrawing a few kilometers behind the canal in return for an Egyptian pledge of nonbelligerency. Some Israeli generals argued that the proposal made good strategic sense in moving Israeli forces out of the range of Egyptian guns while enhancing their flexibility of deployment. But Meir again exercised her veto.

By 1973, Kissinger, the principal architect of foreign policy in the troubled Nixon era, was serving as a backdoor intermediary between Israel and Egypt. Kissinger's own objective was to coax Egypt away from subservience to Moscow and into the Western camp, and he tried to persuade Meir that negotiations over the Sinai under Washington's sponsorship would serve both Israel's and Egypt's interests. Egypt, Kissinger warned, might well attack Israel, despite its military inferiority, as the only means of ending the diplomatic paralysis. Meir responded that she would consider talks, but only after Israel's Knesset election, scheduled for late October 1973. Her halfhearted acquiescence failed to persuade Sadat to order a delay on Egypt's advancing mobilization for war.

Even on the eve of the attack, Israel did not take seriously the portable bridges and other equipment that Egypt's army was visibly moving to the edge of the canal. The government broadcast no alerts, called up no reserves. After the attack started, Meir knew at once that Israeli forces were reeling, but she denied to the country that the IDF had been caught unaware. She called the attack "an act of madness," but her falsehoods did not fool the public. The Arabs were better trained than Israel had imagined possible, skillfully using the material that Moscow had delivered.

Days later Meir changed her tune, declaring that "the battle has been renewed over the very existence of the Jewish state," which was also untrue. Meir never acknowledged that the Yom Kippur War need not have happened had she responded to Sadat's repeated proposals for territorial talks.[22]

After a few bloody days of fighting, the Meir cabinet had no choice but to appeal to the U.S. for Israel's rescue, which Nixon faithfully provided. By then, what had begun as a local war had changed into a superpower confrontation, with each side committed to supporting its client to advance their own interests. The ties Ben-Gurion established with Eisenhower in the 1950s took the form of a round-the-clock American airlift. Nixon declared that the U.S. aim was to achieve regional stability, but to Kissinger the war was an opportunity to extend American preeminence in the region to Moscow's Arab satellites.[23]

Within a week after the attack, with the help of the American arms, the momentum of battle had shifted, and the IDF was pushing back both the Egyptian and the Syrian armies. An Israeli division under Ariel Sharon crossed the Suez Canal from the Sinai and advanced into Egypt's heartland, threatening Cairo. Moscow, admitting that its own alliance with Egypt and Syria was no match for the U.S. and Israel, proposed an immediate cease-fire. Israel, whose armies were on the move, wanted to fight on. But Kissinger, having by now demonstrated America's capacity to assure Israel's military superiority, saw no advantage in prolonging the conflict.

The U.N. voted a cease-fire on October 21 while each country still had forces tangled with the enemy on the battlefield. The defense of Cairo had become a lesser problem than the encirclement of Egypt's Third Army by Sharon's advancing column. Moscow proposed deploying a joint U.S.-Russian force to stop the Israelis, but Washington had no intention of allowing Moscow to land troops in the region. When Moscow threatened to send in its own army, Nixon placed American military units on global alert, and for a day, the Superpowers stood at the edge of war. Finally the two agreed on a second cease-fire, and Israel's forces halted their advance.

Though Meir vowed publicly to force Sadat to "swallow his defeat," Kissinger was determined to profit from the debt that Israel had incurred as a U.S. client. Promising relief to Sadat, he pressured Israel to permit a

convoy with food and medicines to cross the battle lines to the beleaguered Egyptian troops. He also convinced the two military commands
to negotiate the route of the convoy, and officers of both armies met
unprecedentedly at the front at a site designated Kilometer 101.

Kissinger, meanwhile, had promised Moscow cosponsorship of a peace
conference at Geneva to be based on the land-for-peace Resolution 242, the
goal of which was an all-encompassing peace treaty. But his real intention
was to take over the negotiations himself, with the aim of promoting Arab-
Israeli reconciliation in small, digestible steps, which the U.S. would
control. By dominating the rhythm of the negotiating process, Kissinger
reasoned, he could further American preeminence in the region and keep
Moscow from gaining any advantage from the outcome.

On December 21, Arab and Israeli diplomatic delegations, each sullen
and ill-disposed to sit down with the other, arrived in Geneva. The meeting convened with hard-line speeches and no offers, even to deal with
separating the hostile armies. Kissinger, in the wings, waited impatiently
to embark on what would soon be known as "shuttle diplomacy."

As the negotiations neared, Israel resumed the election campaign
that had been suspended by the Yom Kippur attacks. Before the post-
ponement, Labor and Herut, the Revisionist party, had offered similar
hard-line platforms. When the campaign resumed, Labor, at Kissinger's
urging, scaled back its aspirations. Polls showed that voters blamed the
Meir cabinet for Israel's losses, but that many feared to make a political
change as the Kissinger talks got under way. The unusually narrow margin
of Labor's electoral victory was taken to mean that Israelis had an appetite neither for more war nor for giving up territory for peace.

In January 1974, Kissinger met with Sadat in Cairo to begin talks on
the separation of the armies tangled at the canal, an objective that Israel
and Egypt shared equally. He then flew off to see Meir. In the ensuing days,
he flew back and forth repeatedly, carrying proposals and counterproposals, until he had the approval of both sides.

Under the agreement, Israel consented to redeploy along a line fifteen
miles behind the canal. Egypt advanced into the Sinai to the edge of a
narrow buffer zone that kept the armies apart. As a guarantee of good
intentions, Egypt also agreed to reopen the Suez Canal, blocked since the
1967 war, and rebuild the cities along its banks. It was roughly the plan
that the U.S. had proposed years before, and Israel had refused to discuss. The U.S. pledged to monitor compliance from the air and provide

financial assistance to both countries. The accord ended the immediate Israeli-Egyptian crisis; in fact, it went beyond the limited aim of disengaging the warring forces. Some even saw in it a glimmer of hope for a wider peace accord.

♆

By chance, I was on assignment in Israel when the disengagement agreement was signed. The news that Israelis received from Kilometer 101 was a relief from the casualty notices and the fears stoked by having its army still perilously enmeshed with the enemy. More stunning were the reports that Israeli and Egyptian soldiers were behaving like friends along the cease-fire line. I filed the following dispatch.

> JERUSALEM—The most popular thing to appear on television screens in the postwar season in Israel were the shots of Egyptian and Israeli soldiers in face-to-face meetings just before the military disengagement on the Suez Canal.
>
> I was sitting with friends in a small restaurant in a Tel Aviv suburb when the film was shown as part of an evening news program. The noisy crowd, preoccupied with its dinner conversation, suddenly turned to a little television set in the corner of the room and watched with rapt attention.
>
> Arabic-speaking Israeli soldiers were serving as intermediaries in the dialogue, which was translated into Hebrew in subtitles on the screen. One of my friends translated it into English for me.
>
> The scene was of a dozen men in uniform, about equally divided between the two armies, standing around informally in the desert. The men laughed and joked, and traded cigarettes and souvenirs. I was reminded of similar scenes from our own Civil War, recounted in the colorful histories of Bruce Catton.
>
> All this was commonplace enough among soldiers, but then the dialogue went a step further, when the Egyptians invited the Israelis to visit them in Cairo, and the Israelis asked the Egyptians to come see them in Tel Aviv. The footage ended with the men exchanging addresses, shaking hands and clapping one another on the back.
>
> The entire sequence took no more than a few minutes (and, for all we know, may have been staged). But the Israelis in the restaurant were stunned by it, and one of the women at my table wiped tears from her

eyes. For days afterwards, Israelis everywhere seemed to talk of almost nothing else.

What touched Israelis so much was that the scene was so far removed from the hatred they had come to expect in Arab-Israeli relations. Here were Arabs and Jews actually being civil to one another, even warm. Though a fleeting incident, was it a meaningless interlude, or did it hold promise for the future?

Indeed, what has emerged from decades of uninterrupted warfare between Arabs and Jews in the Middle East is a kind of resignation among Israelis to undying hatred and perpetual conflict. This, in turn, has led to a pervasive intellectual sterility on the questions of how Arabs and Jews might live together in peace.

What dominates Israeli thought today, in the contemplation of the Middle East's future, are strategic problems. How much of the territories won in 1967 can we afford to give back? Will the international community respond when our existence is threatened?

All of these questions are based on the assumption that the Arabs are not only implacably hostile but will continue to be, forever. They are based on the assumption that Israel must remain a fortress against those who would, at any opportunity, try to destroy it.

They are, moreover, based on the assumption that the Arab world is a monolith—that the rage of a Palestinian guerrilla necessarily is the sentiment of a Beirut merchant, that the extremism in Damascus inevitably must triumph as overall Arab policy.

It is true that, given the current state of relations between Arab and Israeli governments, it would be premature to debate long-term questions of coexistence in the political arena. But neither are these questions being debated—even on a theoretical level—among intellectuals in the universities.

At best, a few old Zionists are still alive to remind contemporary Israelis that the first settlers thought a great deal about living with the Arabs. And a handful of left-wing thinkers occasionally talk of it today. But most Israelis regard the former as anachronisms and the latter as kooks—and if they think of Arabs at all, they think of them as a military, not a human, concern.

But when the scene of the canal flashed on the television screen, large numbers of Israelis were reminded of what they had forgotten:

how life could be with Arabs as friends, and without the constant threat of annihilation.

Was the scene on television an omen of promise? One danger is that Israelis, conditioned for so long to be cynics, may be unable to relax long enough even to explore the possibility.

Indeed, if there was a glimmer of hope that arose from the Yom Kippur War, it did not last long. The Labor Party, indifferent to peace-making even under Ben-Gurion, was now led by a woman who was deeply hostile to any compromises. She would soon be replaced in the government by Revisionists, who would take an even harder line than hers, substantially harder than it was even in Jabotinsky's time. Now allied with Revisionism was Religious Zionism, a still rising force which claimed to know that God has no interest in peace. Even Israel's close ties to America did little to promote a peace settlement. The Yom Kippur War was a turning point, in which Israel seemed to give up on peace.

After the rapprochement at Kilometer 101, Kissinger hammered away at the Israelis to move ahead in the negotiating process, but he ran into a wall of intransigence. Golda Meir had, under the terms of the agreement with Egypt, pulled the IDF back from the canal, but declared Israel's forces would never go farther. The Revisionist opposition would not forgive her, however, for ceding any territory at all, and Kook's Religious Zionists went further, declaring she had defied God's strictures on territory. Kissinger had not foreseen how little impact American influence would have on his peace-making mission, more so among the Israelis than among the Arabs.

Meanwhile, Israel's Agranat Commission, established by popular demand to investigate the Yom Kippur failure, concluded that the blame lay with the IDF's leading generals. All of them promptly resigned. But public opinion, in defiance of the Agranat Commission, was unwilling to absolve the civilian leadership, notably Meir herself and the ex-general, Moshe Dayan, her defense minister and most influential adviser. In April 1974, the Meir cabinet fell. After weeks of political bargaining, Yitzhak Rabin, a former general uninvolved in the Yom Kippur debacle, was selected to succeed her.

Kissinger had, meanwhile, embarked on a shuttle to the Syrians, who had never reconciled to the loss of Palestine, which belonged to Ottoman Syria and, which, they believed Britain had pledged to them in World War I. Syria's Golan Heights, captured by Israel in 1967, was unlike Egypt's Sinai in that it was fertile farmland, and the hinterland of Syrian cities. The IDF had advanced beyond the Golan boundaries in the last stages of the Yom Kippur War, and was now dug in fifteen miles from Damascus. Artillery exchanges between the two armies were still going on.

To Kissinger, the two adversaries in the Syrian shuttle were both ungenerous and petty. Making matters worse, PLO *fedayeen* raided two Israeli border towns during the negotiations, in one of which, Ma'alot, twenty-four Jewish schoolchildren were murdered. The raids, said the PLO, were a warning not to forget Palestinian interests. That the killers came from Lebanon, not Syria, made no difference. The Israelis, perceiving all Arabs as assassins, became even more obdurate than before.

In his memoirs, Kissinger berates Meir for badgering the U.S., which "supplies [Israel's] arms, sustains its economy, shelters its diplomacy." Yet, after the trauma of Ma'alot, he gave in to her demand that the U.S. pledge never to deny aid to Israel in reply to reprisals against terrorism. After a month of grueling shuttling, Kissinger achieved an accord that ceded back some of the Golan to Syria. It did not, however, relieve Syrian-Israeli tensions, which actually intensified after the deal.

Yitzhak Rabin was sworn in on the eve of the signing of the Syrian accord. A native-born Israeli, he was a hero of the War of Independence, served as chief of staff in the Six-Day War, then was appointed ambassador to Washington, where he was serving in the run-up to the Yom Kippur attack. In Washington, he established a bond with Kissinger, which paid dividends in arms in the War of Attrition. Rabin sided with Kissinger in White House power struggles and backed him in the controversial Vietnam War. He even campaigned for Nixon among American Jews in the 1972 election. For all of this, Kissinger owed Rabin a debt of gratitude.

Outside Israel, Rabin is generally remembered as the peacemaker who shook the hand of Yasser Arafat on the White House lawn in 1993. But the handshake came in Rabin's second term as prime minister. In the first, making the transition from soldier to politician, he was humiliated by Kook's Religious Zionists. Rabin acknowledged, moreover, that in 1974 he had no interest himself in peace negotiations. The lesson he took from the Yom Kippur War was the need to widen the margin of Israel's military superiority over the Arabs, which he was willing to achieve within the context of Kissinger's strategy for establishing America's hegemony in the Middle East.

After the successful outcome of the Syrian shuttle, Kissinger proposed to Rabin to open talks with King Hussein of Jordan, long the most amenable of the Arab states to establishing cordial relations. Rabin demurred. To be selected prime minister, he had pledged to the Knesset not to relinquish any occupied land without a new election, which none of his party wanted. Moreover, as a professional soldier he considered Jordan and the Palestinians less menacing to Israel than the larger Arab states. In his view, negotiating over West Bank territory contained domestic political perils without redeeming military advantages. In retrospect, it was a very serious error of judgment.

"When I came into office," Rabin said to me in an interview some years later, "I had to decide on my priorities. I knew we had to start with Egypt. Whatever relationship existed between Israel and the Arab world had to start with Israel and Egypt. The disengagement agreement after the Yom Kippur War was a start, but I considered it only to be a consolidation of the cease-fire. Peace would have to come later."

When Rabin proposed to undertake a new round of Egyptian talks, Kissinger, with misgivings over a lost opportunity, accepted the offer. Nixon had recently resigned his office over the Watergate scandal and Kissinger, under the less experienced Gerald Ford, now possessed unprecedented power over U.S. foreign policy. Rabin understood that Kissinger, in order to keep Moscow out of the Middle East, had been openhanded with Israel during the Yom Kippur War. He calculated that he could now squeeze Kissinger for even more.

Kissinger undertook another round of shuttling in February 1975, and found Rabin as difficult to deal with as Meir had been. After two weeks without progress, he returned to Washington, where he publicly blamed Israel for the deadlock. Ford backed him by imposing limits on arms shipments and economic aid, but in his gamble for better terms, Rabin held fast. After quickly resolving Israel's differences with Sadat, Rabin had to wait for Kissinger to swallow the conditions that vindicated his risky diplomatic strategy. After six months, Kissinger did.

The final accord, usually called Sinai II, provided for Israel's withdrawal of its army from the mountain barriers in the Sinai, along with the wells from which it had pumped Egyptian oil since 1967. The agreement reconfigured the buffer zone between the armies, and Egypt consented to renounce force as a means of settling differences with Israel. It also authorized Israel to carry non-military cargo through the Suez Canal. Though Sadat was thwarted in his dream of getting back the entire Sinai, Rabin's concessions took him halfway there.

But Kissinger's commitments to Rabin had wider repercussions. In secret letters, he pledged the U.S. to provide economic, diplomatic, and military support to Israel in its regional quarrels. In agreeing to back any action Israel might take to promote its security, he tightened U.S.-Israeli relations, concentrating power in the region in Israel's hands. Signed in September 1975, Sinai II effectively served as a blank check to Israel, without an expiration date, payable by the United States.

Kissinger reasoned that in neutralizing Egypt as a military factor in the conflict with Israel, he was excluding Soviet power from the Middle East. Sinai II no doubt dealt Moscow a setback. But it also imposed burdens on the U.S. that, in time, undermined its credibility with the Arabs, weakening America's hand in the Middle East. Kissinger agreed to take Palestine off the diplomatic agenda, though it was the key to Arab-Israeli peace. By assuring Israel of permanent military superiority, he eliminated Israel's security as a bargaining component. Kissinger's concessions to Rabin restored the self-confidence of the IDF that the Yom Kippur War had shattered, but Sinai II also spurred an appetite for Israeli adventurism that the U.S. could not control.[23]

A few years after Sinai II, in an interview in Tel Aviv when Rabin was out of office, I asked him whether the agreement with Kissinger had not given Israel, within the limits of American strategy, a free hand to do as it liked. He replied, "No doubt." To be sure I had understood him correctly, I asked whether Israel now had the military power to do whatever it chose in the Middle East. He replied softly, "Of course."

In Sinai II, Rabin simply outbargained Kissinger. It is questionable whether Kissinger's pledges to Israel served any strategic American interests. It is not even clear that his pledge to provide Israel with virtually automatic military support, depriving it of the need to exercise reasonable caution, even served Israel's long-term well-being.[24]

Though Rabin regarded Sinai II as a strategic triumph for Israel, Zvi Yehuda Kook found nothing in it to applaud. His reservations began with his mistrust of Rabin for being a secular, drily intellectual, unemotional, and totally unspiritual man. Rabin called West Bank rabbis "ayatollahs" and the settler communities "Jewish Hamas," referring to the Islamic extremists who ran Gaza. He regarded the prospect of moving Jews into centers of Arab population in the occupied territories as contrary to Zionism's vision. Kook and his followers condemned Rabin not just for giving away conquered territory but for placing obstacles in the way of Religious Zionism's effort to revive the faith throughout the land.[25]

Religious Zionists had no more use for Kissinger than for Rabin. Kook denounced Kissinger as an apostate for having married a Gentile woman. Levinger led protests at the Knesset, vilifying him with anti-Semitic slogans. Religious Zionists described Sinai II as a new stage in the history of Jewish persecution; some called it a resumption of the Holocaust. But, whatever Kissinger's role, they regarded Rabin as responsible. Their rabbis debated whether any Jew, especially a prime minister, was not subject under *halacha* to the death penalty for giving away holy soil. They were still debating the question on the eve of Rabin's murder two decades later.

Religious Zionism took out its frustration toward the government after the Yom Kippur War by organizing Gush Emunim, "Bloc of the Faithful," to challenge the limits imposed on it. Made up chiefly of young followers of Modern Orthodoxy, Gush Emunim aimed to restore the fervor that previous generations had brought to Zionism. Kook explained that Gush Emunim was the instrument of God's command to the Jews to hold on to every inch of land in Palestine and, to assure that the land remained holy.

The principles Kook expounded for Gush Emunim were more rigorous, and more defiant, than any his father had proclaimed. "All this land is ours," Zvi Yehuda stated, "absolutely, belonging to all of us. It is nontransferrable to others, even in part. It is an inheritance to us from our forefathers. Once and for all, it is clear that there are no 'Arab' territories or 'Arab' lands but only the Land of Israel, to which others have come and upon which they have built without our permission, in our absence."[26]

Gush Emunim's grand plan was to build settlements throughout the occupied territories, concentrating on areas of dense Arab population. "It is sometimes the case," Kook declared in the coded language he and his father commonly used, "that leaving the Torah is its fulfillment, especially on the matter of the commandment to settle Israel, which is equivalent in weight to the entire Torah." Decoded, the declaration meant that settling land was more important for Jews than mastering holy scripture.[27]

The Jews who gave their allegiance to Gush Emunim were largely the offspring of Religious Zionist families. They were native-born Israelis, often with young families. Ashkenazim predominated. Unlike the early pioneers, their focus was not on tilling the soil. The men commuted by car to jobs in the cities, while the women stayed at home with the children. Religious Zionists habitually carried weapons, particularly when traveling between Arab villages. Their model was Rabbi Levinger, who prowled through the marketplace of Hebron cradling a machine gun in his arms.

Rabin found dealing with Gush Emunim the most irritating of his official duties. As a newcomer to party politics, he was naive, and having been appointed rather than elected prime minister, he was very vulnerable. Ambitious rivals, most notably Shimon Peres, the defense minister, sought to undermine him. He faced a public that had largely lost interest in Arab-Jewish coexistence. Gush Emunim rejected Rabin's argument that Sinai II had made Israel more secure. Rabin, as prime minister in the mid-1970s, did not have the country with him.

Gush Emunim's strategy followed Levinger's model of defiance of the state. It raised copious funds, much of it from abroad, to build settlements. It won popular admiration for its daring and found the soft spots in the government's enforcement of the laws. Rabin, outraged by Gush Emunim's practices, called it "a cancer in the body of Israeli democracy." But his party rivals, influenced by its growing power, actually abetted its designs.

Rabin's initial confrontation with Gush Emunim came with its occupation of an abandoned Turkish train station in Sebastia, a village near the Arab city of Nablus. A Gush advance guard, eluding army patrols, arrived without notice, then received reinforcements from dozens of volunteers, who announced they would not leave. They established a yeshiva nearby and adopted the name Elon Moreh, which was the biblical site where God told Abraham, "Unto thy seed I will give this land." Rabin's divided cabinet made no immediate responses to the takeover.

While the Gush Emunim contingent prepared to resist the army, Kook warned Peres, the defense minister, of "a civil war in Judea and Samaria, when everyone rises up against the government." In a visit to Elon Moreh, Kook, announcing he was ready to die to defend the settlement, tore open his tunic and challenged the local army commander to shoot him. The commander took him by the arm and gently led him away, but Kook had succeeded in intimidating the cabinet and the state.

Levinger arrived in Elon Moreh in the next wave, which numbered several hundred settlers demanding official recognition. Herut's chief,

Menachem Begin was in the crowd, as was Ariel Sharon, the hero of the Yom Kippur War, now a leader of the right-wing coalition Likud. Rabin saw no alternative to negotiating with them. In a meeting in the train station, he offered to provide temporary housing for thirty families in a nearby military base in return for the departure of the rest. He was convinced the thirty families would soon grow bored and go home. Kook and Levinger, however, knew them better, and proclaimed Rabin's offer a victory.

Six months later, the thirty families were still living on the army base. Rabin's cabinet announced with bravado that they would be forced to disband on approval of a master plan for the territories, but no master plan was forthcoming. Instead, the cabinet authorized the installation of phone and bus service, and construction of a children's clinic on the base. In April 1977, Rabin's government formally legalized Elon Moreh, a milestone for the settlers' movement and a humiliating defeat for the state.[28]

In the national election of 1977, the Labor Party, which was led first by Rabin and then by Peres, lost its parliamentary majority. Nearly half of its supporters had shifted their votes since the previous election. The chief victor was Begin's Herut Party, now the spearhead of the Likud coalition. After the voting, the religious parties, long Labor's loyal partners, joined Begin to form a government. The most dramatic switch was the National Religious Party, the heir to Mizrachi, which was Herzl's faithful ally and for decades was Ben-Gurion's, too. Its defection heralded the end of Labor's dominance of Israeli politics.

The responsibility for Labor's defeat was less Likud's popularity, however, than Labor's fall from grace. The Yom Kippur War had convinced many Israelis that Labor no longer had the spunk to govern. Rabin had failed to regain the public's confidence after Meir's fall. Outmaneuvered by Gush Emunim, he was also wounded by a petty financial scandal involving his wife, which in quieter times he would probably have weathered. Rabin resigned after the scandal broke, and was replaced as party leader by Peres, who was no more able to reverse what later proved to be an enduring anti-Labor wave.

But there were also underlying reasons for Labor's fall, among them its failure to carry out its vows of equality to Israel's non-Ashkenazi underclasses. Jews who had arrived from the Arab world, once grateful to Labor for opening Israel's doors, had come to see the party as the instrument of a self-serving Ashkenazi elite. Labor had become paternalistic and condescending, they said. When young Moroccans mounted street protests against social inequality under Meir, she dismissed them condescendingly rather than inquire into their grievances. By 1977, the Jews from Arab lands had risen to half the population, and only a fraction of them voted for Labor.

But disputes over Sinai II also shaped the new majority. What was now the Likud Party had marched since Jabotinsky's time under the banner of acquiring and retaining land, and it had been joined by Rabbi Kook's Religious Zionists. Reinforcing them were the security-minded voters, persuaded by the near defeat on Yom Kippur that Labor could be counted on no longer. Together, the triad of Revisionism, militarism, and Religious Zionism raised an insurmountable barrier to an electoral endorsement of Labor. The barrier exists to this day.

As his life neared an end, Rabbi Zvi Yehuda Kook turned his mind—as do many Jews—to deciphering the meaning of the Holocaust, in which six million Jews died. Rav Kook, his father, had passed on to him an optimism about world affairs. The Rav regarded World War I as a piece in a divine design to create a Jewish state, and perhaps to abolish evil itself. The Rav lived to witness the coming of Hitler, but not the firing up of the gas chambers. He left his son Zvi Yehuda on his own to reach a judgment on God's relationship to the Jews who perished at the hands of the Nazis. Predictably, the judgment Zvi Yehuda reached provided support for the cause of Religious Zionism.

Zvi Yehuda rejected the conventional Orthodox tenet that the Holocaust was God's response to the sins of the Jews. Like his father he believed in God's control of the universe, and so he felt compelled to find a more positive explanation. Without a virtuous God, there was no reason for Religious Zionism to exist. Without God in control, Judaism itself would not, as Zvi Yehuda understood it, make much sense.

"The blood of the six million represents a substantial excision from the body of the nation," Zvi Yehuda finally concluded. "Our whole people has undergone heavenly surgery at the hands of the destroyers, may their name be blotted out. . . . God's people had clung so determinedly to the impurity of foreign lands that . . . they had to be cut away, with a great shedding of blood. This cruel excision reveals the rebirth of the nation and the land, the rebirth of the Torah and all that is holy."

Zvi Yehuda was saying in his emotional fashion that the Holocaust was God's way of ridding the Jews of the debased culture of Exile. The Holocaust cleansed Jewish life, he said. In that sense it may even have been Messianic. To Zvi Yehuda, the Holocaust was "a deeply hidden, internal, divine act of purification," without which the Jewish state would have been forever corrupt.

Kook's statement came close to *praising* God for the Holocaust. To many, his linking of the Holocaust to the aspirations of Religious Zionism was shocking. It was not that he absolved the killers; he did not. But the terrain on which Kook took his stand held that the Holocaust, in the final analysis, rendered a major service to the Jews by assuring them of a home that was not just *Jewish* but undefiled by an impure past.[29]

Menachem Begin, Israel's new prime minister, did not share Zvi Yehuda's view that the Holocaust was part of the foundation of the Jewish state. Nonetheless, he recognized Kook's contribution to Judaizing Zionism. After the swearing-in of his cabinet in 1977, Begin hastened to Kook's home to kiss his hand and elicit his blessing. Begin's cabinet, in addition to Revisionists, was heavily weighted with ministers allied to the Religious Zionists and to Kook.

Paradoxically, soon after Begin assumed office, Gush Emunim went into eclipse. The explanation lay not in any failure on Gush Emunim's part. On the contrary, Begin, like Kook, regarded its work as patriotic, even holy. Under Labor, Gush Emunim thrived as an independent opposition to the government; under Likud, its services in opposition were no longer required. Begin's government was now fulfilling the mission on which the Rav had laid the goundwork and passed on to his son and to Religious Zionism, which Gush Emunim had fulfilled. This mission was now in the hands of the Jewish state.

Zvi Yehuda Kook died at the age of ninety, having served for thirty years as the head of Mercaz HaRav. After the Six-Day War, Jews—secular no less than religious—seemed hungry for the lessons he and his father taught. Graduates of Mercaz HaRav established dozens more yeshivas, all dedicated to transmitting the Rav's belief that the army, no less than the Torah, were instruments of Jewish belief.

In 1979, Zvi Yehuda was aggrieved that Begin had negotiated the treaty with Sadat that required Israel to restore the entire Sinai to Egypt, and in 1982, as his life ebbed, the IDF was preparing for conflict at Yamit, a town that Jews had built in the heart of the occupied Sinai. Despite talk of armed resistance by its inhabitants, most of them Religious Zionists,

Kook did not—as he had at Elon Moreh—call for civil war. His followers contended that he was giving up his life because he could bear neither the loss of territory nor the prospect of Jews killing Jews over Yamit. In explanation, Religious Zionists cited an obscure biblical verse—"The righteous are taken away from the evil to come"—as evidence that Yamit's loss had brought Zvi Yehuda's long life to a close.

As his father's apostle, Zvi Yehuda was willing to go to war to avoid giving up territory. Does that mean that the Kook doctrine contained no room for peace? Zvi Yehuda would deny such a conclusion, maintaining that he had never turned his back on *authentic* peace. How did he define *authentic* peace? It was the peace which would come after the Jews were reestablished throughout their holy land, and after their neighbors accepted that all of this land belonged to the Jews. At that time, Zvi Yehuda, echoing his father, declared that God would make the Jews a "light unto the nations," and peace would reign throughout the universe.

Though Rabbi Zvi Yehuda Kook may have been a lesser man than the Rav, he surely made a greater impact. Long known as an editor, and later as an interpreter, of his father's work, he came into his own only after he turned sixty. But in the decades that remained to him, he imparted a new dimension to his father's thought and, through it, to Zionist belief. In action Zvi Yehuda proved by far the shrewder of the father-son team. For good or ill, he was the most influential religious leader of Israel's era of independence. To this day, Zvi Yehuda Kook's influence pervades Israeli society, and the body of his ideas drive Zionism.

6

Menachem Begin
1913–1992

LOYAL DISCIPLE

When the Nazis invaded Poland from the west on September 1, 1939, Menachem Begin was serving in Warsaw as head of the Polish branch of Betar, the Revisionist youth organization. A step ahead of the invaders, he and his new wife Aliza hastily fled, with Palestine as their destination. But Russian troops, invading from the east under the terms of the recent accord between Hitler and Stalin, blocked their flight. The couple, often under a rain of German bombs, found refuge among friends in the heavily Jewish city of Vilna in Lithuania. Then, in June 1940, Soviet troops occupied Lithuania, and in September the Soviet secret police took Begin into custody in a roundup of "unreliable elements."

Since the early 1930s, Betar had benefitted from funds, training, and arms provided by the Polish government, and Begin as its leader had become a personage of some importance. Relations between Betar and the Poles were, to be sure, a bit strange. With Europe's largest minority of Jews, Poland was pervaded by anti-Semitism, though not of the malevolence of neighboring Germany's. Poles thought of Betar chiefly as an instrument to persuade Britain to admit their own unwanted Jews into Palestine. But some Poles also saw Betar as an ally-in-waiting against the threatening Nazis and the hostile Soviets. Since most Poles, in this period, considered the U.S.S.R. the more menacing of the two, it was a comfort to them that Betar was as anti-Communist as they were.

Though Begin had no known record of anti-Soviet activity, the Russian secret police considered him a dissident for his involvement with Betar. Begin's book *White Nights* is a personal chronicle of his imprisonment by the Soviet secret police. It begins with an account—familiar in the writings of Soviet political prisoners—of his round-the-clock questioning. The interrogator, Begin writes, began in a friendly enough fashion by asking how long he had been a Zionist. "Since my childhood," Begin answered, "and from the age of fifteen onward in Betar."

The interrogator then volunteered that Begin had long been engaged in "criminal activities." "Why criminal?" Begin asked. "I think my activities were right and proper." "You are a big political criminal," the interrogator answered, "because all your activities were anti-Soviet." By offering Zionism to working-class youths as an alternative to the Bolshevism, he declared, Begin was "worse than a man who has murdered ten people." The Russian called Zionism an artifice devised by British imperialism to entrap Europe's Jews.

Who, the interrogator asked, had sponsored his membership in Betar? "Nobody," Begin replied. "I went to a Jewish school. They knew me in my town and they accepted me without any difficulty." But why did you choose Betar? "I liked its program," Begin answered. "I had read and observed Ze'ev [Vladimir] Jabotinsky." Only when the interrogator described Jabotinsky as the leader of Jewish fascism and a colonel in British intelligence did he upset Begin's equanimity, striking a chord of deep indignation.

When Begin learned of Jabotinsky's death in New York in August 1940, he was in Vilna. He and Jabotinsky had recently had differences; Jabotinsky had become more cautious about confronting the British in Palestine, Begin more militant. Yet Begin delivered a warm eulogy for Jabotinsky in a local synagogue. Begin also knew by now of the mass murders, chiefly of Jews, being committed by the Nazis occupiers of Poland. Jabotinsky's loss, he wrote, intensified the profound fear of "a people trapped by those seeking to annihilate them."

Jabotinsky was "the greatest Jewish political leader of modern times, after Herzl," Begin told his interrogator. He went on to say, "If I filled whole pages, I could not explain what his death meant to me. A stranger will not understand and, in this special instance, 'stranger' also includes some of my own people. And so all I will say is this: the bearer of hope was gone, never to return; and with him—perhaps never to return—hope itself."

Begin's obvious sorrow seemed only to incite his interrogator further. How well did you know Jabotinsky? he demanded. "I think I knew him well . . . ," Begin replied. "In the years before the war, I met him personally. . . . I came when he summoned me. . . . I reckon that in all, I spoke to him a few dozen times." The two discussed the future of Hebrew youth, politics in Palestine, British policy, Palestine immigration, Begin wrote in his memoir. The interrogator insisted that Jabotinsky consistently lied, which Begin vigorously denied. "Jabotinsky was my teacher," he declared. "He gave me my faith."

Shortly before Jabotinsky died he had issued a warning to Poland's Betaris of imminent catastrophe. He coined an epigram, Begin wrote: "Eliminate the Diaspora before it eliminates you." Begin recalled Jabotinsky's stating, "My hair has turned white. I have aged because my heart bleeds that you, the cream of world Jewry, cannot see the volcano which has started to spew out the fire of extermination. Time is short. . . . Listen to my cry. In the name of God, let each one of you save his soul while he can."[1]

Begin, as a loyal disciple, no doubt felt a duty to obey Jabotinsky's instructions to flee. It seems curious, however, that, as the local chief of Betar and with the Nazis approaching Warsaw, he did not recognize a higher obligation to remain with his comrades—and his people. At the time, Betar was said to have as many as one hundred thousand young men under arms in Poland. Its units, organized along military lines, were spread across the country. Betaris had been taught by the Poles to fight an underground, urban war. Betar was the only organization that realistically stood between the Nazis and the annihilation of Poland's Jews.

Some of Begin's old Warsaw friends have since acknowledged that there was a debate within their circle over whether "a captain should leave his ship while it is still afloat."[2] In his own accounts of the period, Begin says nothing about such a debate or of any personal ambivalence about flight.

It is true that Betar's priority was to fight not the Nazis but the British occupiers of the land the Jews coveted. Yet, since the murderous intentions of the Nazis were no secret, could not Betar have turned to face the more immediate danger? Though it had no hope of defeating the Nazis, Betar might have saved Jewish lives by fighting an urban war to slow their juggernaut. Begin, it must be said, did not lack courage; in Palestine a few years later, he repeatedly risked his life to take on the British army against heavy odds. Could he not have taken such risks against the Nazis in 1940, when the extermination of Polish Jews was already underway? Instead, he traveled thousands of miles overland to do battle against an Allied force that was defiantly standing up to the German army in the Middle East.

Over the ensuing decades, Jews have endlessly mused about why the Nazis' Jewish victims—with a few notable exceptions—died without putting up serious resistance. Does the explanation lie in the Jews' tradition of passivity, dating back to the Middle Ages, in the face of a foreign power? Was it a pervasive sense of hopelessness before the Nazi military machine? Did Jews give organized resistance any thought at all?

A companion has reported that, prior to his arrest in Vilna, Begin considered returning to Warsaw to take up arms, but he finally did nothing. He would later become obsessed by the Holocaust, in which his own family was decimated, leaving him with what appeared to be "survivor's guilt." But there is no record of his challenging the Nazis when he could have done so, and he never explained why he did not.[3]

Begin spent nine months with Aliza in the relative safety of Vilna before his imprisonment by the Soviet police. He was initially locked up in a nearby prison, where he learned through underground channels that his wife and a few friends had escaped to Palestine. After his lengthy interrogation, he was convicted in a mock trial by the Soviet authorities as an "element dangerous to society" and was sentenced to eight years in a "correctional labor camp," known popularly as a gulag.

Begin dedicated many pages of White Nights to his gulag experience. It began with days and nights in a tightly crowded cattle car to reach a distant camp. Once there, his life consisted of bitter cold and hunger, pervasive lice, corrupt guards, backbreaking labor, and little sleep. Many prisoners died, but Begin boasts of never wavering in his resolve to survive. His religious beliefs and his love for Aliza kept him alive, he wrote. His release came as a surprise after only a few months of imprisonment. It was the product not of his personal tenacity, however, but of transformation in the politics of the still-spreading European war.

In June 1941, Hitler launched a massive attack on Germany's ex-ally, the Soviet Union. A month later Moscow signed an accord with the Polish government-in-exile in London that formally annulled the Hitler–Stalin Pact. The accord pledged Moscow to restore the borders it had overrun in the joint Nazi-Soviet invasion in 1939. More than a million Poles, a substantial proportion of them Jews, had taken refuge in the Soviet Union as the lesser evil, and as many as half had been interned in gulags. The accord with the government-in-exile required Moscow to release the imprisoned Poles and establish an army led by Polish officers to fight the Nazis, now the enemy of both.

Begin was on a prison ship that was transferring him from one camp to another when he received notice of his release. "He's not a Pole, he's a Jew," cried envious prisoners who had to wait for their own release. A few days later, Begin was taken back to the initial camp and discharged. With a few rubles in his pocket, he was left to find his way from Russia's far north to wherever he wanted to go.

By that time, the reestablished Polish army had set up training camps in southern Russia under the command of General Władysław Anders, who had himself just been released from a gulag.[4] Begin headed in their direction, on foot or, when he could, by hitching train rides. Along the way he encountered Polish Betaris, some of them, like him, recently liberated. Through them he reunited with his sister, living in a small Russian town. He also learned that Aliza was waiting for him in Jerusalem, and he managed to send her a wire. The most promising way to get together with her, these Betaris told him, was to enlist in Anders's army.

Not surprisingly, serious mistrust quickly developed between Anders's forces and Moscow. Russian generals disliked having Polish units based on their soil, consuming their resources while ignoring their authority. When Moscow proposed that Anders deploy his forces on the German front, the Poles objected, convinced that Stalin could not be trusted to help them get their country back. They also knew that the Russians, after they occupied their half of Poland, had executed much of the Polish officers' corps. It required much debate, but Moscow finally gave approval to Anders to lead his army out of Russia through Iran, to join up with the British forces that were fighting the Nazis in the African desert.

Begin did not find it easy to enlist as a Polish soldier. From Anders himself to the ranks of the recruits, the army was permeated with Poland's historic anti-Semitism. Though most of its early recruits were Jews, Anders gradually closed its doors to Jewish enlistment. Some Jews asked to form their own division. Anders rejected the idea, foreseeing that Jewish soldiers, on reaching the Middle East, would be tempted to desert to the Zionists if not to the British. Somehow Begin, despite an impaired heart and poor eyesight, was accepted as a private, vowing to refrain from politics as long as he was wearing a Polish uniform.

After basic training, Begin headed east with his unit, which made much of the long journey on foot. Anders commanded roughly 40,000 soldiers, plus twice as many Polish civilians who traveled with them. The land journey led them to a port on the Caspian Sea, where they boarded a ship to Iran. It was there that many of the civilians remained for the rest of the war. The soldiers proceeded westward across British-ruled Iraq and Jordan to link up with Britain's military command in Jerusalem.

In *The Revolt*, Begin's second wartime memoir, he dates his arrival in Jerusalem to May 1942, just short of a year after his arrest in Vilna. His unit commander assigned him as a translator and clerk, but he had grander plans. Joyously reunited with Aliza, he moved into her tiny apartment. He also made contact with the local leaders of Betar. As Anders anticipated, some Jews who had arrived with him deserted from their units. Begin, however, announced that he would remain until he received a legal discharge, which took him another year to obtain.

Over the succeeding months, Anders's army, with many Jews still in its ranks, joined Britain on the battlefield of North Africa, then Italy. Ironically, some of the Jews who were once their comrades-in-arms were by then fighting to drive Britain out of Palestine. Begin, after his official discharge, was among them.[5]

Menachem Begin was born in 1913, in the Polish town of Brest-Litovsk. The town's population was then about fifty thousand, two-thirds of them Jews. The Jews had first settled in the city in 1388, and, over the centuries, had sporadically experienced forced conversions, mass expulsions, and pogroms. But they also built synagogues, schools, hospitals, and factories, helping to create a substantial and generally stable Jewish community.

When Begin was born, the youngest of three children, Brest-Litovsk was in the last phase of one of its more hospitable eras. Begin's grandfather was a wealthy timber merchant, his father a civic leader. The family lived comfortably in a large, well-furnished house. No one suspected that the city was on the eve of being consumed by a series of wars that were worse than any Poland had ever experienced.

The first of these wars started with a German invasion when Begin was a year old. The Russian army responded by evacuating all the inhabitants of Brest-Litovsk and torching the city. After the war, the Begin family, much poorer, returned to rebuild. In 1939, the Germans invaded again and, this time, stayed for five years. Fewer than a dozen Jews were alive when they departed. Menachem and his sister Rachel were by then in Palestine, but the rest of the family was murdered. The Holocaust left Begin, like so many European Jews, with deep scars on his memory.

Begin's earliest education, when the family was in flight, was spotty, but once back home, he thrived in a school sponsored by Mizrachi, the Religious Zionist movement. He was an able student; he was also a precocious orator, with a natural gift that would serve him throughout his life. At fourteen, he transferred to a state school, where he was exposed to Polish nationalism and instructed in European manners. After graduation, he enrolled in the University of Warsaw to study law. Though religiously observant, Begin led a secular life. By early adolescence, he had also acquired a devotion to Zionism, and was ready to give all of his energy to it.

Zionism had been a major force in Begin's household since Herzl's time. Its influence on him grew at the Mizrachi school and was complemented by the nationalist values he absorbed in the state school system. A frail child with poor vision, he rarely participated with his classmates in sports. His chief diversion was chess. But by the age of twelve, he was a Jewish nationalist, which led him first into a Marxist-oriented Zionist faction. By his early teens, he had switched to Betar, which corresponded with his rising commitment to Jewish militancy.

When he was sixteen, Begin encountered Jabotinsky at a Betar rally in Brest-Litovsk. Jabotinsky had become involved in Betar a few years earlier aspiring to counter what he saw as mainstream Zionism's timidity. With his father a Jabotinsky admirer, the boy was smitten at once.

Begin's commitment to Betar intensified at the university, where he worked as a volunteer at the local Betar office and spent most of his evenings delivering passionate lectures on Zionism around Warsaw. His fiery support of the accused Revisionists in the Arlosorov murder enhanced his reputation, and when Jabotinsky visited Warsaw on a speaking tour, Begin was proud to be named to his honor guard. In his early twenties, Begin became Betar's spokesman in Poland, then was promoted to its chief of information. He also organized anti-British rallies, which upset the Polish authorities and led to a brief jail term. The jail term only enhanced his prestige.

In 1938, with war looming again, Begin had a falling-out with Jabotinsky, though neither publicly acknowledged it. Jabotinsky, obviously depressed, was suffering from the heart ailment that would soon take his life. Alarmed by the Nazis, he advocated reaching an agreement with Britain that would provide refuge for Jews seeking to escape from Europe. Begin, seemingly indifferent to the Nazis, talked audaciously of replacing the British in Palestine through Betar's resort to arms.

Begin showed audacity in taking on Jabotinsky, his idol, but it was not the first time. He had opposed the Ben-Gurion–Jabotinsky attempt at reconciliation in 1934. His quarrel with Jabotinsky reemerged at the Betar world meeting in Warsaw in 1938, after the Mandate in Palestine hanged a young Betari for the ambush of an Arab bus, a reprisal for the murder of a Jew. Begin urged that the Irgun retaliate forcefully against the Mandate. "We can no longer wait patiently," he told a cheering audience. "We must strive for large-scale military activity to become a decisive factor in determining Palestine's fate."

Seated in the audience, Jabotinsky interjected, "Perhaps the gentleman would be kind enough to explain how he intends to get the soldiers of Betar into Palestine." Begin's answer was evasive. "I am suggesting an idea. The experts will say how it is to be done. . . . We shall be victorious because of our moral right." At the same meeting, Begin proposed a change in Betar's bylaws, which required members to pledge "not to bear arms except in defense." In its place he proposed: "I shall prepare my arm for the defense of my nation—and the conquest of my homeland." Jabotinsky considered the proposal bombastic.

"Permit me to say a few sharp words to you," Jabotinsky declared icily. "Indeed, as your teacher, I must do so. . . . It is hard to suffer the noise of a door slamming. . . . The words that we have heard from Mr. Begin represent just such a noise, a noise like that must be ruthlessly suppressed. Betar is not the place for that kind of chatter. Both the speech and the applause are door-slamming that serves no need and no purpose."

Though Begin never ceased to extol Jabotinsky in public, their clash in Warsaw suggests that had Jabotinsky lived, they might well have gone their separate ways. The Warsaw conference voted overwhelmingly to adopt Begin's proposal to change the Betar pledge. Begin was clearly the conference's dominant voice, though Jabotinsky was reelected—more or less honorifically—to head the worldwide Betar movement. The Betar conference was focused solely on Britain's rule in Palestine. The prospect of confronting the Nazis' impending assault on Poland's Jews was, apparently, never even raised.

Over the months prior to the outbreak of World War II, Begin worked by day as a clerk in a Warsaw law office while carrying out his duties to Betar in the evenings with his usual vigor. At his marriage to Aliza in May 1939, Jabotinsky served as a witness. Bride and groom were dressed at the ceremony in brown Betar uniforms. On September 1, when the Nazis invaded, the Polish army put up little resistance, and Betar put up none at all. The invasion ignited the powder keg that blew away the world of Eastern European Jewry.[6]

Arriving in Palestine as a Polish soldier, Begin played only at the fringes of Revisionist politics. Betar in Palestine quietly named him a commissioner, but when the British got wind of it he decided it would be prudent to back away. Begin served as an army clerk in his initial year in the homeland, making no contribution to the Zionist cause.

In the early 1940s, in fact, Revisionism was in disarray. No one had replaced Jabotinsky as the leader. In Europe the movement had all but disappeared before the Nazi onslaught. In British Palestine it was largely inert. The radical Lehi, impatient for action, had split off from the Irgun, taking with it much of the militia's weaponry. Revisionism needed direction. When Begin received his discharge from the Polish forces in 1943, his reputation as a leader in Poland preceded him. Though he had no battlefield experience, he was known as intelligent, articulate, and full of passion. The Irgun officers took a chance by inviting him to be their commander, and he unhesitatingly accepted the invitation.

At his first meeting with Irgun's field commanders, Begin outlined his vision for military action against the Mandate. The Irgun had at most a few hundred men under arms, while British forces in Palestine numbered about 100,000, so his ambition brimmed with bravado. His words revived the Irgun's sense of purpose, however. Begin's first order of business was to declare war against the Mandate. On February 1, 1944, a "Proclamation of Revolt of the Irgun Zvai Leumi" was pasted on walls across Palestine, vowing freedom for the Jews or death.

Two weeks later, the Irgun bombed a string of British government offices in Jerusalem, Tel Aviv, and Haifa. In March, in an attack on a Haifa police station, six Britons and two Irgun soldiers were killed. It was clear now to both Britain and the *yishuv* that a real rebellion was underway. Operating independently of Palestine's existing Revisionist structure, Begin lived incognito in a safe house with Aliza and their infant son, Benjamin. His headquarters were wherever the family was lodged. When Haganah leaders extended a feeler to him on cooperation, Begin declined to meet with them, insisting "they are still emotionally unprepared for war."

Begin looked on the Haganah with ambivalence, and he had even greater ambivalence about its leader, Ben-Gurion. He accepted them as the legitimate agents of the *yishuv,* acknowledging that he was a newcomer with dubious credentials. He also understood that the Irgun was at best a hit-and-run strike force, while the Haganah was potentially an army whose power would ultimately be needed to win independence. Begin stated repeatedly that once the Haganah joined the fight, he would bow to its authority. The road would be bumpy and bloody, however, before the Irgun and the Haganah would be fighting together.

As the end of the war in Europe approached, Begin sent signs that he was ready to explore a merger of forces. Ben-Gurion, he believed, surely understood that the Irgun's attacks on the Mandate strengthened the *yishuv*'s hand in dealing with the British. But while he envisaged an alliance of equals, Ben-Gurion would discuss only the Irgun's placing itself under the Haganah's command. The failed talks left both sides with a foreboding that Zionism was doomed to a struggle over control not only of the Jewish armed forces but of the Jewish state itself.

Soon after the talks, agents of the breakaway Lehi in Cairo murdered Lord Moyne, Britain's chief official in the Middle East. Begin was infuriated with the killing, as was Ben-Gurion. But when Ben-Gurion ordered a crackdown on Jewish "terrorists," he did not exclude the Irgun. In the campaign called the Season, the Haganah seized and turned over to the British dozens of Irgun fighters, who were interned in camps, bring-

ing the Irgun's military activities to a halt.[7] Though outraged, Begin ordered his men not to retaliate. Ben-Gurion called off the Season only in
early 1945, after Britain refused to loosen immigration quotas, even for
survivors of Nazi death camps.[8]

By then, Britain's unrelenting hard line on immigration had again set
the stage for a rapprochement between Jews. The two militias formed a
"Hebrew Resistance," with the Irgun a full partner. In the fall of 1945, the
joint forces conducted attacks on British communications and transpor-
tation throughout Palestine. Humiliated by its losses, Britain struck back
by arresting nearly three thousand Zionist leaders, only by luck missing
both Ben-Gurion and Begin. The two leaders now agreed that dramatic
action was needed to regain the initiative, and they concurred on the Irgun's proposal to bomb Jerusalem's King David Hotel, the Mandate's administrative hub.

In *The Revolt*, Begin spends many pages justifying the controversial
King David bombing. Based on the Irgun's careful planning, the Haganah
had approved the operation. Since the Irgun attacked only legitimate military targets, Begin insisted, the action was not terrorism, setting it apart
from tactics of Arabs, who killed civilians at random. The flaw in the Irgun's plan lay in its failure to anticipate Britain's ignoring a warning to evacuate the building. Ninety-one workers—Jews, Arabs, and Britons—died in
the bombing, and hundreds were injured when Britain dismissed the Irgun's
notice that the King David was about to be blown up.

Disapproval of the attack, however, was global, and ended the brief era
of harmony between the Jewish forces. Ben-Gurion called the Irgun "the
enemy of the Jewish people," while Begin maintained that the casualties
were fully justified, even though he said he mourned only the *Jewish* deaths.
Britain imposed a curfew on the *yishuv* and conducted a vain house-to-
house search to find the culprits. Britain's commanding general aggravated relations by his anti-Semitic vow to "punish the Jews in a way the
race dislikes . . . , by striking at their pockets and showing our contempt."

Jewish reconciliation unraveled further when Ben-Gurion, perceiving
signs of London's acceptance of a partitioned state, suspended temporarily
all of the Haganah's operations. Begin answered by mocking the cease-fire
and reaffirming his rejection of partition. The Irgun then attacked the British prison in the fortress of Acre, where Jabotinsky was once imprisoned,
freeing hundreds of inmates, both Jewish and Arab. The British responded

by whipping Irgun soldiers, an odious practice that Begin then inflicted on several British captives. In July 1947, Britain sent three Irgun soldiers to the gallows; Begin promptly hanged two British sergeants. In the face of anti-Jewish riots in Britain, both the Mandate and the *yishuv* concluded it was time to end the madness. Begin did not help matters, however, by boasting that his policy of brutal retaliation had restored Palestine's calm.

But, recognizing that they were besieged, British personnel in Palestine began conducting their lives behind barbed wire. In Britain, the army's inability to stop Jewish attacks had seeded a national consensus—central to Begin's strategy—that British rule was not worth the cost. That the Irgun's role was crucial in creating this consensus was scarcely in doubt. Ben-Gurion's Labor movement had built the governing institutions of the *yishuv*, but Begin's Irgun had set the stage for ending British occupation.

The U.N. partition resolution followed directly from Britain's decision in November 1947 to relinquish its Mandate. The U.N. vote, while paring down the Zionist vision of a state from the Jordan River to the Mediterranean Sea, awarded sovereignty to both Jews and Arabs. The Jews responded as if this was a victory, the Arabs as if it was a disaster. The Jews dancing in the streets of Palestine left no doubt that in contrast to the Arabs, the *yishuv* was exhilarated by the U.N.'s action.

But Begin and his followers were exceptions. He called the U.N. resolution illegal and insisted that Revisionism was not bound by it. He castigated Ben-Gurion and his circle as marketplace hagglers who settled for a "ghetto state," describing himself as an uncompromising fighters for what rightfully belonged to the Jews. Begin vowed to struggle on, and swore "mutual liquidation" if the Haganah ever again tried to stop the Irgun in its mission to establish a state that covered the entirety of historic Palestine.

Driven by Jabotinsky's hovering spirit, Begin did not renounce—he never would—the dream of Jewish sovereignty straddling the two sides of the Jordan River. Revisionists include it in their anthems to this day. But in time Begin acknowledged that the dream would never be realized, and he confined his criticism of the U.N. resolution to the territory west of the river. No Jewish electorate, he argued, ratified the U.N. decision; nor did any Jews possess the power to do so. "No majority of this generation," he proclaimed, "has the authority to give up the historic right of the Jewish people to their entire country, which belongs as well to all Jewish generations to come."

Even while publicly advocating compromise of Arab-Jewish differences, Begin conducted himself otherwise. He counted on Arab rejection of anything the U.N. offered, which he saw as providing the Jews an opening to nullify partition by military action. The "silly agreement will not be binding," said an Irgun poster pasted on Jerusalem's walls. As Begin predicted, the warfare that followed the Arab rejection would bring the Jews much closer to the borders that Revisionism claimed.[9]

Whatever their public stance, in fact, Begin and Ben-Gurion were not far apart on border issues. Once Begin laid aside the fantasy of taking over Transjordan, neither one envisaged a frontier to the east of the river. Nor did either feel bound by the U.N.'s checkered partition map. They were equally committed to all of Palestine, though they differed on the timing and the circumstances of its achievement. Begin insisted it happen as part of the founding of the state. Ben-Gurion separated the two issues: the state came first; fixing its final borders could be deferred until the state was strong enough to impose its will.

The War of Independence ended with the two still quarreling, but the fighting had changed the balance of their power. By the time of the armistice talks in Rhodes, Begin had lost most of his influence over events. Ben-Gurion, who had made the decisions in war, also made them in peace negotiations. Begin's early contributions to Britain's defeat were largely overlooked amid the IDF's later battlefield victories. Begin protested vigorously on learning that both the West Bank and East Jerusalem would go to Transjordan, forcing Jews to live within what he called "borders of dismemberment." But he had become all but irrelevant. It would take him decades to return to the center of the political stage.

After the war, Begin had no choice but to transfer his competition with Ben-Gurion to the electoral arena. He organized Herut ("freedom") around a core of Irgun veterans as Revisionism's political party. For popular support, he shrewdly did not turn to the Jews who shared his Eastern European heritage; they had become Labor's constituency. He turned instead to the newcomers streaming into Israel from poor Arab countries, whom Labor had helped to migrate, then imprudently ignored.

Begin and Ben-Gurion were as harsh as ever in fighting against each other for votes. Begin ran his party with the secrecy and discipline that one would expect from an underground leader. The Labor Party continued to label him a fascist, though he was no less faithful to parliamentarism than was Ben-Gurion. In Israel's first election in January 1949, Herut won 14 of 120 Knesset seats; Labor won 46. Begin suffered eight consecutive electoral defeats before the tables turned.

Begin's fiercest political attack of the Ben-Gurion era took place in 1952 over an agreement with Germany to pay reparations. Taking German money, Begin argued, meant that Israel placed a monetary price on the lives of the Holocaust's victims. There is "no German who is not a Nazi, who is not a murderer," he shouted on the Knesset floor. Ben-Gurion, who hated Germans no less than Begin, answered that reparations could promote the economic and social development of the Holocaust's survivors.

On the eve of the Knesset vote on the reparations agreement, Begin personally led a parade of protesters through barbed-wire barriers and clouds of tear gas to fling stones that shattered windows of the Knesset building. Invoking his own family, Begin proclaimed, "We who saw our fathers thrown into the river with five hundred other Jews from glorious Brest-Litovsk and saw the river run red with blood . . . who saw events unequalled in history . . . shall we not sacrifice our souls to prevent an agreement with the murderers of our fathers?"

In fact, Begin, having left Poland in 1941, had seen nothing of the Holocaust himself, nor had he confronted any Germans on the battlefield. Ben-Gurion called his protests "a criminal and treacherous plot . . . the first steps in the destruction of democracy."

Ben-Gurion won the Knesset vote on reparations, and Germany duly paid the money it had pledged. Begin was punished for the violence at the Knesset by a brief suspension from his parliamentary seat, and in time the frenzy subsided. But German reparations joined the lengthy list of Revisionism's grievances in its ongoing power struggle with Labor.

Despite his uninterrupted failures at the polls, Begin never adjusted to heading a splinter faction in Israel's multiparty system. On occasion, members of his own party denounced him as a perpetual loser, but he remained in command. In search of a winning formula, he intensified his cultivation of Sephardim and coaxed religious parties, including Mizrachi, to give him their support. But even as Ben-Gurion grew older and more irritable, and Labor's organization began to fray, there was no discernible political trend in Begin's favor.

Through all the turmoil, Begin remained devoted to the vision of an expanding state reliant on military strength. Despite their unseemly exchanges, he invariably supported Ben-Gurion's aggressive practices toward the Arabs. When Ben-Gurion obtained arms from France in 1956, Begin showered him with praise and later cheerfully endorsed his joining Britain and France in the surprise attack on Suez.

"If our teacher and master, Vladimir Jabotinsky, were alive today," he proclaimed, "he would declare—no matter what our differences past or future—that we congratulate the prime minister for having made this wise decision."

Begin turned away only when Ben-Gurion bowed to U.S. pressure by evacuating Egypt's Sinai in the wake of the Suez victory. Invoking what could be called a Begin doctrine, he stated, "The small state must not be ready to make concessions, for once it offers concessions at a time of pressure, it only invites more pressure upon itself." The doctrine, to which he remained dedicated throughout his political life, became a diplomatic principle from which subsequent Israeli leaders rarely departed.[10]

In June 1967, Labor finally invited Begin in from the political cold when the government, facing another Arab war, decided his presence would be useful as a symbol of national unity. After his first cabinet meeting, Begin visited Jabotinsky's grave, where he declared solemnly that "one of your followers is now serving in the government of Israel." Among his first acts, he urged—in vain—that Ben-Gurion, now a Knesset backbencher, be brought into the cabinet. Once the war started, he pressed for the prompt capture of East Jerusalem and the Old City, lest they be lost in a U.N. cease-fire vote. When the fighting ended, Begin took on the mission of barring withdrawal from any territory that the army had captured.

Levi Eshkol, then prime minister, treated Begin respectfully in cabinet sessions, and so did Golda Meir, Eshkol's successor. Begin clearly liked being on the inside. In 1969, when U.S. Secretary of State William Rogers handed Meir a draft treaty with the Arabs based on exchanging land for peace, she wavered, fearful of American retribution. Begin was adamant, however, standing firmly behind Meir on the side of rejection.

America did not dare penalize Israel, its Cold War ally, Begin insisted, and events proved him right. Even as Washington decried Israel's "expansionism," it offered to deliver new aircraft to maintain Israeli military superiority in the region. In the end, though Meir finally accepted the Rogers Plan in principle, no peace negotiations with the Arabs ever came of it. Six years later, however, the American planes proved crucial to Israel in the Yom Kippur War, though by then Begin had quit the cabinet to return to his more familiar place in the Knesset opposition.

Still, Begin's tenure in the unity government served him well in imparting legitimacy to Revisionism's quest for power. The quest gained further momentum in Begin's recruitment of Ariel Sharon, whose ambition to head the army had been thwarted by his brash personality. Turning his prodigious energies to Revisionist politics, Sharon cajoled right-wing politicians to pledge their support to a new political coalition built around the old Revisionist base. The party took the name Likud.

The 1973 election, held in the gloom of Israel's near-defeat in the Yom Kippur War, marked the beginning of a Begin–Sharon partnership that would transform Israel's political culture.[11] Likud did not win the election, but with Sharon running interference Begin came closer than ever before to unseating his historic rivals.

In early 1974, Yitzhak Rabin, on succeeding Meir, took over the negotiations with Kissinger. Begin, furious over the territory given up by Israel in Kissinger's earlier "shuttle" agreements with Egypt and Syria, insisted on no more withdrawals. In retrospect, it is clear that Israel was changing its political direction, and territory was only one of the reasons. But the immediate cause of Rabin's fall was his permitting American military aircraft to land in Israel on the Sabbath, provoking religious members of his cabinet to resign. The episode forced Rabin to call a new election, to be held in May 1977.

The election transformed Israel. Though the campaign focused on land and security, Begin won it on the votes of the sons and daughters of Sephardim who were more resentful than their parents had been of Labor's patronizing attitude. The Orthodox community, both *Haredim* and Modern, had become more comfortable with Begin's piety than with Labor's secularism, helping to tip the scale. Leaping ahead to more recent elections, it can be noted that the migration near the end of the twentieth century of a million newcomers from the former Soviet Union added still another pillar to Likud's structure of support. Beginning in 1977, the outcome of Israeli elections shifted dramatically rightward.

Likud's 1977 victory ended the political preeminence Labor had enjoyed since the pre-independence era. Labor's share of the vote fell by 15 percent. Most of the shift went not to Likud but to a third party that had campaigned as ideologically centrist. The third-party vote led many Israelis to conclude that Likud's victory was a onetime aberration, a calculation that proved to be a serious error.

The best explanation for Labor's defeat lay in its failure to understand how much the electorate had changed over the years. Labor never adapted to the Jewish migrants from the Arab world, who did not aspire to become the free-spirited tillers of the soil that Zionism historically extolled; these immigrants wanted to keep their old traditions alive. Nor did Labor take into account that the Orthodox community never forgave Labor for its rejection of the Messiah. A few years later, Labor was again shortsighted, failing to grasp that the newly arrived Russians were highly nationalistic and far less interested than earlier Zionists in reaching an accommodation with the Arabs. Anti-Labor voters were for the most part at the social margins. Labor's claim to the fatherhood of the state did not impress them.

Begin himself had not expected to win in 1977, and when the results came in, he was scarcely prepared to govern. Neither he nor the members of his circle knew much about running the state, and he did not make the transition smoothly. Begin was, however, heir to a clear-cut ideology. It had survived the death of Jabotinsky and stood the test of time. Though more radical, Begin was, as Israel's leader, Jabotinsky's faithful disciple.

Even before he was sworn in, Begin made a visit of support to Elon Moreh with Sharon and Rabbi Zvi Yehuda Kook at his side.[12] Sharon advised the soldiers on duty to disobey any orders from the army to remove the Gush Emunim squatters. Rabbi Kook tore open his tunic, baring his chest, and proclaimed his readiness for martyrdom. Begin, from the top of a hill adjacent to Elon Moreh, declared, "In a few weeks or months, there will be many more Elon Morehs."[13]

At a press conference during the visit to Elon Moreh, Begin dismissed any notion that once in office, he would soften his ideology. Asked whether he would annex the West Bank, he replied, "We don't use the word 'annexation.' You annex *foreign* land, not your own country." He also rejected the term "West Bank," which implied a link to Jordan, insisting that "Judea and Samaria" was the region's *real* name, derived from the Bible.[14] The squatter-settlers particularly cheered when Begin declared that Gush Emunim, with his help, would soon found twelve more settlements on the occupied land.

In selecting the cabinet for his new government, Begin's most unexpected choice was Moshe Dayan as foreign minister. Dayan, who served as defense minister in 1973, had been drummed out of the Meir cabinet for his mishandling of the Yom Kippur attack. A lifelong member of the Labor Party, Dayan instituted a "normalization" policy after the Six-Day War, which included "open bridges" to the Arab world for the Palestinians living under occupation. The policy was far removed from Begin's ideology and lasted only briefly. Why Begin chose Dayan at all as foreign minister was much debated and remained something of a puzzle.

Not surprising, however, was the choice of Ariel Sharon as minister of agriculture. Though it drew much less attention, since it was ostensibly a lesser post, Sharon became a far more powerful influence. Sharon shared with Begin a conviction, quite the opposite of Dayan's, that the Palestinians should be given virtually no freedom of their own. Sharon's mission was to hammer Begin's often hazy beliefs into hard policy. Begin further enlarged Sharon's portfolio by making him head of the Ministerial Committee on Settlements, which empowered him to rewrite the policies that shaped Israel's military occupation.

By September 1977, Sharon had produced a blueprint titled "A Vision of Israel at Century's End," which was based on settling two million Jews in the occupied lands. The number stunned even Begin, though it corresponded with Sharon's reputation for taking huge risks for high stakes. As a soldier, Sharon had had many successes and a few spectacular failures; he retired from the army because his colleagues blocked his promotion to chief of staff. But Begin made no effort to set limits on Sharon's expansionary vision for the territories.

Sharon's blueprint reorganized Gush Emunim's freewheeling settlement practices. It specified where settlers in the occupied territories could and could not establish homes. His vision was drawn less from ideology than in military security. His blueprint proposed building settlements, first, along a line parallel to the Jordan River, following the objective of the Allon Plan to defend against attacks from the east; second, in a semicircle east of Jerusalem to keep the Arabs from reasserting any claim on the city; and, third, across the Samarian slopes to facilitate military control of heavy concentrations of the Arab population. He also planned to cluster settlers' homes into virtual fortresses to keep at bay enemies approaching from both inside and outside the borders.

In a much studied interview in the *Jerusalem Post* in the fall of 1977, Sharon denied that his strategy would in any way be a barrier to peace. Arab-Israeli peace, Sharon claimed, was his lifelong aspiration. What he meant by peace, however, was what Jabotinsky and Zvi Yehuda Kook meant: Israel's domination of the region, depriving the Arabs of any opportunity to threaten Jews.

"These plans are not prejudicial to the prospects of peace," Sharon stated in the interview. "On the contrary, the creation of bands of settlements through Judea and Samaria will give us a sense of security for the first time, which in turn will permit us to entertain more daring solutions to the question of the Arab population than we can permit ourselves today." He added that "it all depends on what sort of Israel one envisions—an overcrowded, nervous, irritating, and ecologically sick country, or a country with a sound distribution of its millions of inhabitants over a much larger area which will provide for basic security and a healthy economy and society."

Sharon wasted no time in putting his blueprint to work. The Begin government allotted him ample land to distribute both to the army and the settlers. Much of it was public land, previously held by Jordan's government. Additional large tracts had been secretly bought by rich Jews or past Labor cabinets. Some was private Arab land, but Sharon made little distinction between owners. He also received generous funding from clandestine state and private sources, much of which he used to integrate Arab water, electric power, telephone, and transport networks into Israeli systems serving the settlers and the state.

Begin never gave up his goal of annexing the occupied lands into Israel, but—except for the Golan Heights, to which he "extended Israeli law" in 1981—their status remained equivocal. Under army rule, the local Arabs could assert no rights, even as the practices under which they lived grew more oppressive. Western governments, notably the United States, routinely protested that settlement-building violated international law, but they did nothing to stop it. Starting with Begin, Israeli rule showed it did not need annexation to subject Arab society to whatever policies, however harsh, Israel chose to impose.

Under legislation passed by the Begin government, Sharon organized the occupied territories according to his grand plan. Generously subsidized, the settler population quickly grew. Schools, roads, and communication grids were built. Parks were laid out. Inevitably, the juxtaposition of hostile Arab and Jewish cultures generated conflict, much of it at the initiative of the settlers. But the odds overwhelmingly favored the settlers, who had the staunch support of the army. When settler delegations called on Begin, he invariably commended them for dedicating their lives to advancing the well-being of the Jewish people.

"Hundreds of young families have already signed up for settlement projects," Sharon told the *Jerusalem Post* as his efforts gained momentum. "Most come from Israel," he said, "but many arrive directly from abroad. Their parents are well-to-do. They have good jobs and income." When Labor was in power, the settler population in the West Bank was about 10,000, in addition to the 50,000 Jews who populated East Jerusalem. In our own day, the population has surpassed half a million. "Jews will never come here for the purpose of living a materially more comfortable life," Sharon declared. "They will come if we offer them a challenge and a flag," adding, "It is very gratifying."

Early in the Begin era, I was assigned by an American magazine to write an article about the changes taking place in the West Bank. My work began at Neve Tzuf, a settlement of thirty families a mile or so up a narrow road from the village of Birzeit, the site of a small Arab college. Soldiers had surrounded Neve Tzuf with barbed wire. Unlike the early Zionist pioneers, the settlers had no interest in farming. The men held desk jobs in Jerusalem or Tel Aviv, and drove to work every day through the Arab town. Some stopped en route home to buy groceries, but the encounters were not friendly. Every trip through Birzeit contained the potential of trouble.

My visit took place on a Jewish holiday, when carloads of settlers were to pass through Birzeit on the way to a nearby settlement for a pre-annexation rally. The first car, on reaching the main square, was stopped by a barrier of boulders rolled into place by students. The driver, on getting out to clear the road, was pelted with stones. When a second car arrived, more stones smashed into the windshield. Exercising a power granted to them by the military command, the settlers fired rounds of ammunition into the air. Apparently by ricochet, a student was struck in the chest, and was carried off by his companions onto the college grounds.

Birzeit was already considered a problem by the army. Its students often held demonstrations, though searches of the college uncovered no weapons or even subversive tracts. The shooting victim was among a few dozen students who, at a midmorning break in classes, had made their way to the village square. Soon after the shooting, an army unit arrived, lobbed some tear gas grenades, and imposed a curfew. The demonstrators were rounded up, and about half were held for further questioning. A few later claimed they had been beaten. When the soldiers tried to question the settlers about what happened, they refused to answer, claiming it was their right to fire as they chose. The next day, the military governor shut down the college for an unspecified period.

Later that day, I met in Neve Tzuf with one of the drivers in the incident. Small, bearded, in his thirties, he told me he had given up a career as a cardiologist to serve as the settlement administrator, though he still commuted to Jerusalem a few days a week to teach at the Hebrew University. He was religiously observant, he said, but as a Religious Zionist the focus of his faith was the land, not the synagogue.

"We came here because it's our right to settle in Judea and Samaria," he told me, speaking about the settlers. "We must persuade the Arabs of that right. They can stay here. We will not drive them out if they live with us in peace. But this is not their land. It is Jewish land."

I found Neve Tzuf, despite its setting in the magnificent Samarian Hills, a rather bleak place. At its center was a stone fortress, which the British had built as a police station half a century before. The first settlers had lived in it, and when I was there a handful still did, awaiting the arrival of the small prefab houses that the others already occupied. In the schoolyard nearby, children played on swings and slides. The administrator told me the settlers, even the children, had grown accustomed to the barbed-wire fencing and the constant presence of the uniformed guards that watched over them day and night.

After the administrator, I called on a young mother who, with her husband and two daughters, occupied a prefab a few dozen steps away. The family had migrated from Canada several years before, she told me, lived briefly in Jerusalem, then joined Gush Emunim. They owned an M16 rifle and an Uzi machine gun, which the army had taught them to use. The guns, she said, gave her a feeling of safety. Her husband usually carried the Uzi in the car en route to work. She kept the M16 at home. Security was what she and her friends mostly talked about, whether at settlement meetings or over coffee in her tiny kitchen. If she and her husband did not have the guns, she said, the family would move back to Jerusalem.

The young mother admitted her life in Neve Tzuf was hard, much harder than in Canada, or even Jerusalem. But she rejected the Arabs' contention that the Jews had usurped their land. When I asked whether she would acknowledge some uncertainty about the Jews' right to the land, she answered with a firm "no," adding that Judea and Samaria were indisputably Jewish. For her, living in Neve Tzuf was the assertion of an inherent Jewish right of possession. Joining with other Jews to exercise this right, she said, gave her life a sense of purpose that she had never experienced before.[15]

Menachem Begin did not subscribe, as did some Religious Zionists, to the biblical verse that speaks of Jews ruling from the Nile to the Euphrates. His vision of Israel extended to the far side of the Jordan River, but even that was not a priority. To be sure, retaining Judea and Samaria, where King David once reigned, was a moral imperative he inherited from Jabotinsky. But the Sinai, a buffer against a resurgent Egypt, had no historical or theological implications. Determining its future was simply a security calculation.

Basic to this calculation was Egypt's size and population. Egypt was the Arab country with the largest population and the biggest army. Only with Egypt on the battlefield was it imaginable that the Arab states could defeat Israel. In his early years, Gamal Abdel Nasser had considered a shift of national resources from war to economic development, and he made one or two peace overtures to Ben-Gurion. He turned to the Soviet Union only after Ben-Gurion spurned him. Anwar Sadat, Nasser's successor, traveled to Jerusalem to extend a clear offer that in return for getting back the Sinai, Egypt would sign a formal treaty of peace.

Begin was excited at the prospect of being the first Israeli leader to sign a treaty with an Arab state. Peace with Egypt, he reasoned, would surely make Israel more, not less, secure. The obstacle lay, as it always had, in the price. The Sinai had become more than a defensive barrier. Since 1967 it was the site of Jewish settlements, most notably the thriving town of Yamit. Loyal Revisionists, however, were not permitted to give back Jewish settlements, and Begin was even less prepared for a grander concession that Sadat was likely to demand. It was clear that Sadat considered it his duty to restore the West Bank and Gaza to the Palestinians.

In September 1977, Begin and Sadat began to feel out each other's intentions. Separately, they flew to Romania, whose president conveyed to each his belief in the reliability of the other. Dayan, who pushed hardest within the cabinet for negotiations, met secretly in Morocco with a high-level Egyptian diplomat. Though the two sides failed to overcome procedural obstacles, they stayed committed to pressing ahead. The progress persuaded Sadat to undertake one of the most dramatic demarches in diplomatic history: a visit to Jerusalem to bring his case directly to Begin, the Knesset, and the Israeli public.

After intense, last-minute arrangements Sadat arrived in Israel aboard an Egyptian airliner shortly after sundown on November 19, 1977. He was greeted warmly by a delegation of Israeli luminaries. A band played the Egyptian and Israeli anthems. Though Israelis had learned of the visit only a few days before, the entire country watched the ceremony on television. The characteristic reaction was one of disbelief, as if a single gesture had transformed everything about the Arab-Israeli conflict. The euphoria was bound to lead to disappointment.

On assignment in Jerusalem that day, I stood on the sidewalk near the King David Hotel, where Sadat was to stay. Waiting for his motorcade, the crowd could not contain its excitement. An even more vivid memory for me than the cheers, however, is an incident that occurred the next morning when I went for a walk in the Old City. A dozen Arab teenagers had clustered at the Jaffa Gate, and they were very angry. When I asked whether Sadat's visit did not promise an end of the occupation, they let me know in unfriendly fashion how foolish my question was. They could not imagine that Sadat's purpose was to liberate the Palestinians. "He has come to sell us out," they shouted angrily. "He has come to sell us out." And in the end, they predicted the outcome correctly.

On his first day, Sadat prayed at the Old City's Al-Aqsa Mosque, after which he and Begin, each in his own language, addressed the Knesset. Their words sent the message that, after the initial moment of exhilaration, the familiar and grim status quo ante was already reemerging.

Sadat's theme was that Egypt was prepared to erase the hostility of nearly a century of Middle Eastern history. "We used to reject you . . . ," he said. "We were together in international conferences and our representatives did not exchange greetings. . . . But today I tell you, and declare it to the entire world, that we welcome you to live among us in peace and justice . . . within borders secure against aggression."

But he had come to Jerusalem, Sadat went on, to redress not only Egypt's differences with Israel. Speaking for all Arabs, he called on Israel to withdraw completely from the occupied Arab lands. Pronouncing the Palestinian problem "the core and essence of the conflict," he also pleaded for Palestinian statehood. Sadat promised to sign a binding treaty, but vowed not to settle for a separate Egyptian-Israeli peace.

Begin's reply lacked Sadat's grand reach. Narrowly political, it was the opening brief in a bargaining process. It was more banal, emphasizing the problems rather than the solutions. Begin did not mention the West Bank or East Jerusalem. He expressed appreciation of Sadat's courage in making the journey but warned that it would not change Israel's negotiating posture.

"President Sadat knows, as he knew before, that our position on the permanent borders differs from his. . . . But everything will be negotiable . . . No side shall present prior conditions. . . . If there are differences between us, that is not unusual. . . . We shall conduct the negotiations as equals." It was Begin's way of saying he was prepared for the hard bargaining that lay ahead, though, within the context of Sadat's openness, few imagined how hard it would turn out to be.

Over Christmas 1977, Begin and Sadat met again in the Suez Canal town of Ismailia to initiate formal talks. They got no further than appointing two committees to define the issues. Begin admitted the validity of Sadat's demands for withdrawal from the entire Sinai, but he said he planned to fight to keep the settlements, particularly Yamit, that the Jews had built there. As for the Palestinians, he talked of "autonomy" in the occupied territories, but he seemed to imagine it would look like the *kehillot* in which Jews had lived in Exile, which to him meant self-rule for the people but powerlessness over the land.

At the same time, both Begin and Sadat had to fend off adversaries at home who believed they were abandoning inviolable principles. For months after Ismailia, the talks stagnated, emitting a scent of failure. Begin, unlike Dayan, his foreign minister, seemed ready to let the talks collapse if need be. He even went over Dayan's head to solicit advice from Sharon, the cabinet's chief hard-liner.

In Washington, meanwhile, President Jimmy Carter had become

increasingly involved as a kind of gray eminence over the proceedings. After nearly a year passed without results, Carter had grown impatient. He found Sadat generous and farsighted in their contacts and Begin rigid and petty. But Begin, while sticking to his doctrine that a small state need not submit to a large power, was also aware of Israel's reliance on America for its long-term military needs. Begin understood that Carter could not be ignored.[16]

After the journey to Jerusalem, the demands of both Begin and Sadat grew harder. They looked at each other now not as peace partners but as adversaries, perhaps even enemies. That is when Carter stepped in and summoned them to Camp David, his presidential retreat in the woods north of Washington. When they arrived, both carried with them Maximalist diplomatic conditions, aimed not at compromise but at victory.

Bucolic as the site was, it did not relieve the tension. Carter, to promote a friendly informality, had proposed the three bring along only a few advisers, but informality was neither Begin's style nor Sadat's. Having planned for three days of deliberations, Carter showed remarkable tenacity as the meeting dragged on. More than once, mutual recriminations came close to bringing the conference to an end. On the thirteenth day, the two—begrudgingly and in a state of exhaustion—signed an agreement, but two more months of acrimonious bargaining were needed to finish writing the treaty. Even then, much was left unresolved.

The differences over the Sinai were settled with relative ease. Though resigned to giving up the land, Begin argued that forcing Jews to vacate their homes was a dark reminder of their impotence in Exile. The breakthrough came after Sharon assured Begin by phone from Jerusalem that he had no security concerns. After reaching agreement on giving the Sinai back, the parties turned to the more difficult question of Palestine.

Begin maintained that the West Bank and Gaza should not be on the agenda at all. Without a political tie to Egypt, they were not Sadat's business. Sadat replied that since the Palestinians had not been invited to Camp David, he had the duty to look after their interests. Begin rejected Carter's effort to link Palestinian concessions to the deal reached on the Egypt-Israeli issues. Finally he accepted a side agreement, a "Framework for Peace," which offered the Palestinians an undefined "autonomy," along with a pledge of negotiations, not to exceed five years in duration, to resolve the occupied territories' "final status."

Almost immediately after Camp David, Israel and Egypt were accusing each other of violating the "framework" on Palestine. Begin had consented to halt settlement construction, but it was unclear if his pledge extended to the months needed to finalize the peace treaty, as he insisted, or to the five years anticipated to reach the terms of the "final status" agreement on Palestine, which was Sadat's position. Both may have been sincere since, as Camp David came to a close, all the participants were so consumed by fatigue that it is possible none knew exactly what they were signing. The ill will produced by the dispute over the settlement freeze has endured to this day.

By the time talks on drafting the final treaty began, Begin and Sadat had little use for each other. Their ties did not improve when the two—but not Carter, who probably most deserved it—were awarded the Nobel Peace Prize. In fact, Carter's work was still not over. He had to make a round of Cairo–Jerusalem shuttles, which were laden with more animosity than Camp David itself to nail down the last details.

Hardly had the talks on Palestine started than it became clear that Begin would sacrifice the peace with Egypt altogether rather than give up control of the West Bank. Carter flew to Israel to make a plea to the Knesset, but Begin was unmoved. In the end, Begin, the most tenacious of the bargainers, got most of what he wanted, and Carter was left with his mission incomplete. Sadat became the butt of Arab censure for having sold the Palestinians out. It was exactly what the teenagers I met in the Old City had predicted.

On the White House lawn on March 26, 1979, Begin and Sadat signed the treaty that formally ended hostilities between the two countries. It provided for Israel's evacuation and Egypt's demilitarization of the Sinai. It rolled back the results of the Six-Day War by guaranteeing free passage of Israeli ships through the Suez Canal, as well as the Strait of Tiran and the Gulf of Aqaba. It provided for the normalization of Egyptian–Israeli relations, including the exchange of ambassadors. But Israel's control of the West Bank, the Golan Heights, and the Gaza Strip remained intact.

After the signing, Sadat invited Begin to make a state visit to Egypt. "Would any of you citizens of Israel," Begin declared to the crowd at the airport to see him off, "have imagined two years ago that a person holding the position of prime minister would be going to Cairo, there to be welcomed by the army and the playing of *Hatikva*?" Sadat proved to be a gracious host and the mass of Egyptians lining Cairo's streets cheered as Begin drove by. Begin toured the pyramids and prayed at Cairo's main synagogue, though there were now no more than a handful of Jews living in the city. Once back home, Begin phoned Carter, as if in vindication, to report that the visit had gone wonderfully.

But the talks on Palestine, which resumed two months after the signing, went nowhere. Jordan's King Hussein declined to join, and the PLO, which Palestinians regarded as their representative, was not invited to participate. In October, Dayan, the cabinet's last voice of moderation, resigned in disagreement over the government's increasingly tough occupation practices. After that, Israeli and Egyptian diplomats met intermittently, but Begin never relented on his insistence that the occupied territories belonged to Israel. He also made no concessions on limiting the construction of settlements, describing them as "a vital security need to prevent the murder of our citizens and children."

In the fall of 1980, Carter was defeated for reelection. His successor, Ronald Reagan, showed little interest in the Palestine question. The next year, Sadat was assassinated by Islamic extremists in his army. But by then, "final status" talks had lapsed, leaving no hope that the accords reached at Camp David might lead to an Israeli–Palestinian accord, much less a resolution of the Middle East conflict.

Despite his triumph as a peacemaker, Begin did not enter the contest for reelection in 1981 as the favorite. It was not that he failed to indulge his supporters, either Religious Zionists or the relentlessly demanding *haredim*. He provided huge subsidies to religious schools and synagogues. He expanded the draft deferments of their young and took on new obligations to support their families. He had ultra-Orthodox settlements built for them. To pay for the allocations, he cut back on the secular school system, and when the funds ran out, he printed more money, producing triple-digit inflation.

As the election neared, the polls showed that his personal campaigning had narrowed the gap, but what lifted him to victory was surely a daring military exploit. Begin sent Israel's air force to destroy a nuclear reactor in Iraq, which he claimed was soon to produce devastating weapons. The success of the raid, he claimed, avoided another Holocaust, and he won the election by a narrow margin.

Begin's second term in office was much more an expression of Revisionist ideology than the first. He had tipped his hand during the campaign, engaging in vitriolic attacks that whipped up unruly crowds and encouraged zealots to use violence against opposition candidates. Attacks on Arabs in the territories, which he made no effort to contain, became more numerous. In abandoning political restraint, Begin knowingly stirred up a dangerous social fever.

After the election, Begin reoriented his cabinet rightward. He named to the two principle ministries men who had voted against the Camp David treaty. Yitzhak Shamir, a onetime Lehi commander and a central figure in the 1944 murder of Britain's Lord Moyne in Cairo, was named to head foreign affairs, and Ariel Sharon, giving up the ministry of agriculture, was appointed the defense minister, a post he had long coveted. Sharon quickly became the cabinet's dominant member. With Egypt no longer a major factor in the Arab-Israeli conflict, he began preparing plans for suppressing the Palestinian threat to Israel through an Israeli invasion of Lebanon.

Shortly after his reelection, Begin was hospitalized for a broken bone suffered in a household accident, and on his release, he seemed to sense a need to reaffirm publicly his capacity to govern. Notifying no one—neither the Americans nor his own cabinet—he announced the formal annexation of Syria's Golan Heights. The Reagan administration declared the act illegal and threatened retaliation, to which Begin replied, "What kind of talk is that, 'punishing' Israel? Are we a vassal state? . . . This government is composed of men who fought, risked their lives and suffered. You cannot and will not frighten us." Begin's confrontation with Reagan ended quickly, and the annexation remained in force.

Nor did it require much for Sharon to get Begin's approval to invade Lebanon. Palestinians living in the refugee camps of south Lebanon had been crossing the border to harass Israel since their mass flight during the War of Independence. In the 1960s, Yasser Arafat's PLO reorganized and militarized these camps, aggravating the inherent fragility of Lebanese society, sharply divided between Christians, Sunnis, Shiites, and Druzes. In 1975, a civil war broke out, with a Christian militia, called the Phalange, leading one of the sides. Armed with Soviet weapons, the PLO provided much of the firepower for the other side.

In his first term, Begin had sent Israel's army on an incursion into Lebanon, inflicting a severe but temporary setback to the PLO. Sharon's plans in the second term were more grandiose. A full-scale military operation, he reasoned, would destroy the PLO and bring the Christians to power, making Lebanon an Israeli client. He also believed the PLO's defeat would end not just the cross-border raids but Palestinian resistance in the West Bank and Gaza. A week after Begin annexed the Golan Heights, Sharon presented his plan to the cabinet for approval, and when ministers expressed reservations about its magnitude, he promised to limit the army's advance in Lebanon to twenty-five miles. The cabinet, though still dubious about Sharon's intentions, concurred. So did President Reagan's government in Washington.

Begin found a useful pretext for the invasion in 1982 when a Palestinian gunman, who was not affiliated with the PLO, shot Israel's ambassador in London. On June 3, Begin issued the order. "The bullet that hit the ambassador's head," he declared, "was aimed at the head of the state of Israel."[17] Inaction, he said, would be an invitation to return to Auschwitz. Within a few days, the IDF advanced to the promised twenty-five-mile limit and Sharon, without cabinet approval, ordered pursuit of the PLO's forces north to Beirut.

By early August, Beirut, encircled by the IDF, was being subjected to relentless artillery and air attacks. In view of the heavy civilian losses, Washington called for a cease-fire and, to Begin's dismay, initiated independent talks aimed at getting the PLO forces to withdraw by sea to Tunisia. Sharon, however, was committed to Arafat's annihilation, and in a message to Reagan, Begin compared the PLO to the Nazis huddled in their bunkers in Berlin. Despite Reagan's concerns, Begin made no effort to impose on Sharon any limits to Beirut's destruction.

Begin's cabinet by now had come to recognize, however, that Israel, with the prime minister's consent, was fighting Sharon's personal war. When Reagan described Israel's attacks as a "Holocaust," Begin—convinced the term belonged exclusively to the Jews—protested indignantly. Still, with the PLO forces withdrawing to Tunisia under American cover, the war had not gone as Sharon had promised. Sharon's goal of destroying the PLO was out of reach, and a few weeks later, his aim of creating a Christian Lebanon as an Israeli dependency collapsed with the murder of Bashir Gemayel, the Phalangist chief. Begin was beside himself.

The day after Gemayel's assassination, Phalangist units, vowing vengeance, were on the move. Begin, sensing trouble, warned Sharon to keep them in check, but Sharon ignored the order, insisting the Phalange intended only to eliminate PLO terrorists. Instead, with Israeli logistical support, the Phalange conducted a massacre in the Sabra and Shatila refugee camps, which took hundreds, perhaps thousands, of Palestinian lives, many of them women and children. Begin learned of the massacre not from Sharon but from the BBC, and when it became clear that Israel was being held to account for collaborating, he pronounced the now famous words "*Goyim* kill *goyim,* and they blame the Jews."

Begin failed, however, to divert the responsibility. Israel was denounced worldwide, and, in Israel itself, some 400,000 citizens gathered in a square in Tel Aviv to protest. Begin issued no apology but grudgingly named an investigative body, called the Kahan Commission. In his own testimony to the commission, Begin said the IDF had actually limited the killing in the refugee camps. But in its verdict, the commission held Israel *indirectly* culpable of the massacre and recommended that Sharon either be forced to resign or be dismissed outright. Begin sidestepped the recommendation by transferring him from defense minister to a lesser cabinet post.

The commission also targeted Begin himself, citing both him and Shamir, the foreign minister, for official negligence. Even more painful, Begin, having been seduced by Sharon's promise of a quick and easy war, had to explain to the Israeli public the death of five hundred Israeli soldiers. Always moody, the man who had exulted in public approval in a reelection only a year before fell suddenly into black despair.

Amid the turmoil, Aliza Begin died. Ill for some time, she was more than Begin's only love; she was also his only real friend. Begin was in America when she died, preparing for an important meeting with Reagan. Unwilling to forgive himself for his absence from her bedside, he issued instructions for her burial, then raced home for the funeral. Aliza was interred in Jerusalem among the fallen fighters of the Irgun and Lehi.

But without Aliza, Begin was a different man. His melancholy deepened. He rarely ate and even stopped shaving. He avoided his closest aides. He clearly lost his zest for governing and delivered no more speeches. In October 1983, eleven months after Aliza's death, he resigned as Israel's prime minister, saying, "I cannot go on."

Begin never emerged from the depression that followed Lebanon and the loss of his wife. He left his apartment only to say *kaddish* at her grave. Though he lived for nearly a decade after withdrawing from public life, he could justifiably be counted among the casualties of the Lebanon war. Begin felt that the men he had relied on had betrayed him, and that he had failed Israel. He died on March 9, 1992, and was buried in a simple rite at his wife's side. His pallbearers were all veterans of the Irgun command.

♇

The allegiance of Begin and Ben-Gurion to conflicting versions of Zionism was, in considerable measure, fixed by the era in which each arrived in Palestine. It left them with contrasting views of what the *yishuv* required.

Ben-Gurion migrated as a youth when Zionism was turned inward toward providing a structure for the *yishuv*. He worked in the fields and dressed like a field hand. As part of the wave of Eastern European migration, he embodied a Zionism that could be called indigenous. Begin arrived as an adult, already shaped by Europe. Photos repeatedly show him wearing a suit and tie, his hair well brushed, looking very bourgeois. His Zionism, like Europe's nationalisms of the prewar period, focused on power and on the borders of the state.

It is remarkable that Begin, in contrast to Ben-Gurion, won the allegiance of so many Jews who were so different from him. His Zionist career grew with Betar, an urban European, middle-class movement. Yet he won the deference of many Jews who arrived after World War II from Arab lands. Over time, he achieved the approval of black-hatted *haredim*, then of post-Communist immigrants from Soviet lands. They took their place beside Jabotinsky's Revisionists and Rav Kook's Religious Zionists to provide an electoral majority, an odd assortment which over the decades has held together.

Begin's attraction, however, may not have been the mystery that it seemed. His Revisionism succeeded in great measure because Labor Zionism failed. Ben-Gurion and his camp had become the Israeli establishment, behaving as if they ruled by a natural right inherited from Herzl. Begin was not just the political adversary; he was the non-establishment alternative. He and his supporters were outsiders, never invited to belong to the ruling class. In the 1970s, when Labor faltered over the Yom Kippur War, Israel lost confidence in its establishment. Begin led the Jewish state into an anti-establishment era.

To say that Begin changed Israel's course, however, would be an overstatement. Even before the Six-Day War, when Labor under Ben-Gurion was still in charge, Israel possessed a lust for territory. After Begin was elected, Israel shifted away from Labor's historically cautious leadership to become more militant, less tolerant, more colonialist, more willing to play at the edge of international disapproval. It did not so much change direction as adopt riskier practices, which many believed placed the Jewish state in greater peril.

Begin, as distinguished from Ben-Gurion and his Labor successors, never questioned where he wanted Zionism to go. Jabotinsky had imparted the gospel to him. Begin was guided by an ideology, and he had no ambivalence about it. He did not agonize over whether his decisions were good for Israel or the Jews. He wanted what Jabotinsky had taught him to want, and he moved expeditiously to get it.

Begin was not an innovator. Having internalized Revisionist ideology, he made no noticeable contribution of his own. Without Begin, however, Jabotinsky might well have vanished into the archives of Jewish history, along with many other estimable Zionist thinkers. Just as Marx needed Lenin, Jabotinsky required Begin to assure his survival as an icon. Revisionism needed the presence of a man of action to transform its doctrines into deeds. Begin was that man.

Begin's grave error was Lebanon, though he defended the invasion until his death. Reason should have led him to greater prudence; instead, ideology handcuffed him. By the wildest calculation, the invasion in no way served Israel's interests. What is amazing is that Revisionism as a movement emerged from it intact. Israel forgave Revisionism for the Lebanon fiasco in a way that it did not forgive Labor for the Yom Kippur debacle. It is a measure of Israel's transformation that to this day it mourns over the Yom Kippur War, which ended in military victory, while it overlooks Lebanon, which concluded in a terrible defeat.

Revisionism also survived Begin's surrender of the Sinai, including the Jewish settlements there. The treaty with Egypt eliminated the principal Arab threat, not just to Israel's security but to its hold over the remaining conquests of 1967. In the West Bank, the settler population, a few thousand when Begin took office, rose to more than half a million under his direction. It was Begin who triggered Israel's march into the twenty-first century as a Revisionist power. Though Begin is long dead, his heirs rule the Jewish state according to the ideology that he, as Jabotinsky's disciple, imparted to it.

Six years as prime minister is a brief moment of Jewish history, but it is fair to observe that Begin was the architect of what is now the dominant wing of Zionism. That is not to say that the struggle over Zionism's course has been settled. Mainstream Zionism—Ben-Gurion's practical Zionism—still has some fight left in it. But since Begin, the Jewish state has been ruled by the Revisionist vision. Israel and the Middle East—even the world-wide community of Jews—live today in the shadow of Menachem Begin.

7

Arriving at Netanyahu
1983-2015

THE ULTIMATE REVISIONIST

In the third of a century that has passed since the rule of Menachem Begin, seven prime ministers have served in Israel, and no discernible progress has been made toward achieving peace in the land. Israel's conflict with the Palestinians remains an open wound, the product not just of Arab-Jewish differences but of rivalries between Jews. The source of these rivalries, more than any other, is the military occupation of the West Bank, an occupation that is now nearly fifty years old. It derives from competing visions of Zionism, dating back to the bitter struggles between Vladimir Jabotinsky and David Ben-Gurion. Worldwide, the occupation has virtually no approval.

Theodor Herzl, as readers will recall, once wrote in his diary, "If the Jews ever 'returned home' one day, they would discover on the next that they do not belong together. For centuries they have been rooted in diverse nationalisms; they differ from each other, group by group. The only thing they have in common is the pressure holding them together."

Herzl would have understood the ongoing animosities between, say, Russian and Sephardic Jews or Polish and German Jews. These rivalries are the cultural heritage of the societies of which Israeli Jews were once a part. But Herzl did not anticipate the conflict between Labor Zionism and Revisionism. It has been one hundred and twenty years since he expressed his foreboding, but his question remains the same: Do the Jews belong together? Can their state, the progeny of Zionism, remain cohesive in the presence of such deep political divisions?

As a vision for the Jews, Zionism was simple enough to explain in its early days. It aimed to provide a refuge, and, better still, a homeland for a beleaguered people. Zionism's early conflicts were over the process, not the goal. After World War I, Ben-Gurion emerged as the preeminent Zionist; his camp came to represent mainstream Zionism. Ben-Gurion's program was to build the state from within, step by step. By the 1920s, however, the mainstream was under attack from Jabotinsky's Revisionists, more impatient and ready to use force to achieve Jewish sovereignty. Revisionism brought to Zionism an ideology that glorified military struggle. The ideology laid the foundation for what became, in effect, a different country.

Today Israel is a modern state. Its citizens enjoy a high standard of living. It has a significant industrial and technological base. It is rich in artistic and literary accomplishments. Herzl would be dazzled by it. He might, however, be concerned about the powerful army that Israel uses with little restraint to control four million Arabs, most of them in the territories captured in the 1967 war. The chief conflict among Zionists today focuses on whether Israel will make the concessions needed to reconcile with its neighbors or continue indefinitely to use power to dominate them.

The battleground to determine which ideology defines Zionism is the Israeli electoral system. Israel boasts the only democracy in the Middle East, but its electoral politics differ from most other democracies. Under the system called proportional representation, imported from Europe by the early migrants, Israelis vote not for individuals but for party lists that stand for one ideology or another. Knesset members are seated according to the proportion of the total vote each party list receives.

The list system encourages not just an emphasis on ideology but the formation of splinter parties. Some small parties promote only minor deviations from political norms; others—especially the religious parties—have radical differences. No single party has ever won an absolute Knesset majority, i.e., 61 of 120 seats. Coalitions must therefore be organized to form governments, with religious parties often wielding disproportionate power on behalf of their narrow institutional interests. Israel has preserved the proportional representation long after many other democracies have tried and abandoned it.

Ben-Gurion's Labor Party, the voice of mainstream Zionism, dominated Israeli politics until four years after the Yom Kippur War, when it gave way to Likud, the flag-bearer of Revisionism. Since 1977, all national elections have been fought over the issue of the military occupation of the territories conquered a decade before, even when some candidates preferred to talk about social, economic, and religious concerns.

Menachem Begin, in an odd twist on Revisionism, restored the occupied Sinai to Egypt over bitter opposition from within Likud. Supported by the religious parties, he entertained no possibility, however, of giving up Israeli rule over the occupied West Bank, the Gaza Strip, or the Golan Heights. Driven by Jabotinsky's values, Likud vows today to keep all the land that Israel currently holds in reliable Israeli hands, whatever the cost internationally.

The Revisionist dogma has reverberated far beyond Israel's borders. Labor, though not a clear-cut peace party, has always understood that Israel's security depends on benefits derived from the goodwill of the global community. Herzl, from the start, adopted the position that a Jewish state could not survive in the long run without a powerful patron. Begin, like his successors from Likud, was willing to take risks with that patronage, and in that context the conflict between mainstream and Revisionist Zionism goes on today.

In 1983, when Begin resigned in the wake of the failed war in Lebanon, Yitzhak Shamir, a Polish-born former Lehi militant, was elected prime minister by Likud's central committee. Shamir had acquired a reputation for violent exploits in the pre-independence underground. While the war against the Nazis raged, he organized the assassination of Lord Moyne, Britain's chief official in the Middle East. After twice escaping from British prisons, he joined the band that murdered Count Folke Bernadotte, the U.N. representative in Palestine and a dedicated peacemaker. After independence, Shamir enlisted in the Mossad, the Israeli secret service, in which he served for a decade before entering politics.

Short, stocky, and stingy with words, Shamir was elected to the Knesset in 1973, then reelected in the Likud victory of 1977 that made Begin prime minister. He was serving as Knesset speaker when Moshe Dayan resigned as foreign minister over Begin's retreat from the concessions pledged to the Palestinians at Camp David. Begin turned to Shamir despite his vote against the peace treaty with Egypt. As foreign minister, he was cited by the Kahan Commission for negligence in the massacre at Sabra and Shatila, but no penalty was imposed on him.

In a candid memoir called *Summing Up,* Shamir acknowledged that as prime minister he had little interest in reaching peace with any Arabs. He rejected the land-for-peace formula drawn from U.N. Resolution 242 in favor of the formula he called "peace for peace," which ruled out any territorial concessions. Judea and Samaria, Shamir wrote, "are an integral part of the Land of Israel, neither 'captured' in 1967 nor 'returnable' to anyone." He heartily endorsed the settlers' demands that the army exact a heavy price from Palestinians for any shedding of Jewish blood. The "sacred work" of expanding settlements, he declared, "must not stop. It cannot stop. It is the heart of our existence and life."

After only a year in office, Shamir ran for reelection, and fifteen separate parties won Knesset seats, leaving neither major bloc with enough seats to stitch together a majority. He and Shimon Peres, the Labor Party leader, finally agreed that each of them would serve as prime minister for two years, with Peres serving first. Peres, working with Jordan's King Hussein, devised a plan for a Middle East peace conference, but he was unable to win Knesset approval for it. Shamir, when his turn came up, saw no reason at all to disturb the regional status quo.

The next election, in 1988, produced another deadlock—and a similar power-sharing arrangement. But Peres, frustrated at the Knesset's paralysis, took a gamble. He cancelled the rotation agreement, confident of persuading a ninety-two-year-old rabbi who controlled an Ultra-Orthodox Knesset faction to switch from Likud to the Labor camp, enabling him to embark on peace talks. Instead, the rabbi publicly rejected Peres's plan, reaffirming Orthodoxy's disdain to peace talks as well as its mistrust of the Labor Party's secularism. Peres's miscalculation led to his government's fall and Shamir's return as prime minister.

In Shamir's second term, Palestinians for the first time challenged the Israeli occupation in an uprising known as the *intifada.* When the Soviet Union collapsed in 1990, ending the Cold War, U.S. President George H. W. Bush perceived an opportunity to establish stability to the Middle East. Bush assigned his secretary of state, James Baker III, to convene an international conference at which the Arabs would agree to stop the *inti-*

fada in return for an end of the occupation. Shamir interpreted Baker's plan as forcing Israel's capitulation to Arab violence.

Turmoil in the former Soviet Union had, meanwhile, opened the door to the exodus of tens of thousands of Jews to Israel. The Israeli government received them enthusiastically, as it had recently welcomed fifteen thousand Jews from Ethiopia. To most Jews, the influx was vindication of the Zionist dream, but it also required money to feed, clothe, and house the newcomers. Israel planned to borrow most of this money from banks, but to lower interest payments, it sought a U.S. guarantee for the loans. To Shamir's dismay, Bush insisted that Israel, in return, settle none of the migrants in the occupied territories.

Then, in August of 1990, Saddam Hussein's Iraq invaded Kuwait, an independent kingdom to its south, and Bush mobilized a coalition of Western and Arab states to drive Iraq out. Recognizing that the Arabs would quit the coalition if Israel were a member, Bush issued no invitation to Shamir. In January, the coalition forces attacked the Iraqis. Saddam rained missiles on Israeli cities, gambling that Israel would retaliate; it did not, and the coalition remained intact. Overmatched, Iraq capitulated, but Shamir was humiliated at Israel's being excluded from the fighting.

When the war ended, Bush turned again to the peace conference. Much praised for his management of the wartime coalition, he offered the prospect of a "new order" in the Middle East built on Arab-Israeli peace. The Arab states that had joined in the victory accepted Bush's proposal but called on him to pressure Israel to make a confidence-building gesture by stopping the construction of settlements in the occupied territories. Shamir would not hear of it and, in fact, urged Bush to cancel the conference altogether. Only by granting the loan guarantees was the U.S. able to persuade Shamir to attend. In an atmosphere of tension, the peace conference convened in Madrid in October 1991, but the participants were by now hardly in a peace-making frame of mind.

The tension was palpable throughout the halls of the palace in Madrid where the conference convened. Carrying the press credentials of a U.S. magazine, I had the opportuniy to be an eyewitness. In addition to Israel, its neighbors Syria, Lebanon, and Jordan sent negotiating delegations. At Israel's insistence, the Palestinians were deprived of their own representation and were merged into the Jordanians'. In their opening speeches to the assembly, the heads of each of the delegations exacerbated the tone of confrontation by announcing Maximalist negotiating demands.

All of the opening speeches, I wrote in my article, "abused history, abjured self-examination, wallowed in self-pity, preened in righteousness. There is no doubt that the parties to the Middle East conflict, particularly the Israelis and the Palestinians, have more than ample reason to feel victimized, whether by outsiders or by each other, but they had clearly made up their minds to let no one forget their suffering. Every speaker vowed a commitment to fruitful negotiations, but not one suggested letting bygones be bygones—a posture that is probably a sine qua non of Middle East peace. It was almost as though they had met secretly the night before and agreed to get their feelings of persecution off their chests."[1]

At first glance, the Madrid Conference was a bust, nothing more than a sequence of hostile declarations with no real engagement, not even handshakes. Shamir broke the conference up prematurely on the second day, a Friday, claiming he had to be home for Shabbat, a holiday he had never been known to observe. Yet, Madrid may have recorded some modest advance on the avenue to peace. For the first time, Middle East enemies actually sat together around a table, with Palestinians among them. After the adjournment, Israel held closed-door meetings with Arab representatives; nothing came of them, but a precedent was established and a "peace process" inaugurated. The peace process, though it has little to show for itself, has survived—at least in the breach—to this day.

Shamir returned to Jerusalem satisfied with himself for his work at Madrid. He had defeated the threat of losing territory, denied a podium to the Palestinians, and suppressed all substantive negotiations. But that was not enough for the far right of his own Knesset majority, which denounced him as a closet moderate for having gone to Madrid at all. Two months after the conference, several Knesset factions resigned from his coalition, leaving Likud without a majority. Shamir had no choice but to call a new election, six months before the statutory end of his term.

By a narrow margin, Likud lost to Labor in the election of 1992. Not only did right-wing extremists abandon Shamir; so did the ex-Soviet voters who he had brought into the country. Though Shamir had resolved the problem of the American loan guarantees, specifically designed to help the Russians, he also maintained ties to the small Orthodox parties that the secular Russians saw as their adversaries. In his memoir, Shamir acknowledged his pain at the outcome, and claimed that time would reverse the Russian shift away from the Likud. He was right, but in the meantime Labor had been elected to run the government.

Labor's narrow victory surely did not mean that Israelis had rejected Revisionism. The settlements were growing, which seemed to please most of them, including the recent immigrants. Though the Palestinians were still fighting, the *intifada* produced relatively few Jewish casualties, and was more a nuisance than a threat. Clearly, there was not much interest among Israelis in negotiating with the Palestinians. If Labor's newly elected government wanted to try its hand on a peace-making policy, it would have to overcome the ongoing drift by Israel into the Revisionist camp.

Yitzhak Rabin campaigned for peace talks as Labor's candidate in 1992, and for the second time he became Israel's prime minister. Despite his humiliation by the settlers during his first term and his subsequent loss to Begin, he had regained control of the Labor Party. A practical thinker of the Ben-Gurion school, he had long focused on security, as befitted an old soldier. But, while serving as defense minister in the 1980s, Rabin recognized that his "iron fist" practices against the *intifada* were going nowhere, and that Palestinian terrorism was now more of a danger to Israeli society than the armies of the neighboring states. Peace, Rabin concluded, was the correct objective for promoting Israeli security.

"It is our duty to ourselves and to our children," Rabin said in his innovative inaugural address, "to see the world as it is . . . so that Israel will adapt to changes. No longer are we 'a people that dwells alone' and no longer is it true that 'the whole world's against us.' We must now overcome the sense of isolation that has held us in its thrall. . . . We must join the campaign of peace, reconciliation and international cooperation . . . lest we miss the train and be left alone at the station."[2]

Rabin extended friendly overtures very early to both the Palestinians and the settlers, though he succeeded in winning the confidence of neither. He offered limited self-government to the Palestinians, which they considered inadequate, since it was an unlikely step to statehood. As for the settlers, he promised them greater military security, but they rejected his insistence that they scale down their own lawless conduct. Though Rabin's policies led to some decline in Arab violence, he could not bring himself to craft a comprehensive plan to end the occupation, and so the Israeli-Palestinian conflict continued.

Meanwhile, exploratory peace talks were taking place that, at the start, were unknown even to him. In the fall of 1992, a Norwegian diplomat visited Israel and offered his country as host for meetings with the PLO. Secret talks between semiofficial interlocutors began in London, then shifted to Oslo. By early spring of 1993, the PLO's Arafat and Israeli Foreign Minister Peres had taken charge and reached an agreement in principle to transfer the governing power in the occupied territories from Israel to a Palestinian Authority. Israel also consented to have Arafat establish a PLO office as a beachhead in the Arab city of Jericho. The overall agreement that was reached would be known as the Oslo Accords.

The Oslo Accords provided for Israel's withdrawal from Gaza and Jericho as the opening step of a five-year process toward full peace. The Palestinians were to hold a referendum to confer legitimacy on the agreement. Israel was to recognize the PLO as the representative of the Palestinian people, in return for a PLO pledge to desist from violence and recognize Israel's right to exist. Absent from the agreement was any mention of a Palestinian state, or even of such crucial issues as borders, settlements, refugees, and Jerusalem. Still, meant as a "declaration of principles," the Oslo Accords provided guidelines for ending nearly a century of Arab-Jewish war.

The "declaration of principles" was signed dramatically by Rabin and Arafat in the presence of U.S. President Bill Clinton on the White House lawn on September 13, 1993. The event was immortalized by the famous photo in which an unsmiling Rabin reaches out stiffly to shake the hand of a beaming Arafat. Rabin's subsequent speech was more forthcoming.

"Let me say to you, the Palestinians," Rabin declared, "we are destined to live together on the same soil, in the same land. We the soldiers who have returned from the battle . . . we say to you today in a loud and clear voice, 'Enough of blood and tears. Enough!' . . . . We are today giving peace a chance and saying to you, 'Enough.' We wish to open a new chapter in the sad book of our lives together, a chapter of mutual recognition, of good neighborliness, of mutual respect and understanding."[3]

In both camps, however, were anti-peace militants, most of them spilling over with religious fervor. Baruch Goldstein was an extremist settler living in Kiryat Arba, the Orthodox suburb that had grown out of Rabbi Levinger's takeover of Hebron in 1968. Goldstein, a physician, gunned down twenty-nine Arabs praying in the mosque in the Cave of the Patriarchs before losing his own life. Arab suicide bombers promptly exacted revenge by attacking and killing Jews in several Israeli towns. Still, Rabin and Arafat persevered, and in May, the IDF withdrew from Jericho and Gaza, retaining forces only around Gaza's few Jewish settlements.

While Rabin was negotiating with the PLO over the Oslo Accords, he was also reaching for peace beyond Palestine's borders. He opened talks with Jordan's King Hussein, on whom he had turned his back when Kissinger urged a deal in 1974, and signed a formal peace treaty that ended their on-and-off conflict. He even tried making contact with Syria's Assad, to whom he held out the prospect of a return of the Golan Heights; Assad's lack of interest blocked negotiations not just with Syria but with Lebanon, Syria's client.

Rabin, however, took a second major step with Arafat in September 1995 in signing Oslo II, which provided for division of the West Bank into three segments. They were Area A, giving the PLO control of the major Palestinian cities; Area B, setting up a joint Israeli-Palestinian administration over a thinly populated central region; and Area C, where most of the Jewish settlements were located; reaffirming IDF rule over the land.

Rabin understood that, notwithstanding the progress, much remained to be resolved to reach a permanent peace with the Palestinians. The PLO wanted an independent state based on the 1967 borders, with East Jerusalem as its capital. It also wanted the Jewish settlements removed from the West Bank and the Gaza Strip, and recognition of the right of return of the refugees of the War of Independence. Rabin explained to the Knesset that he planned to retain the settlements adjacent to Israel and in the Jordan Valley, but his first priority was to preserve the momentum of withdrawal until agreed borders separating Israel from a Palestinian state were established.

Rabin envisaged winning reelection in 1996—which was no sure thing—as a prelude to completing the peace process. But the Knesset had approved Oslo II by only a 61–59 margin, and some of those votes came from Arab members, which led Likud to protest the absence of a *Jewish* majority, which it claimed invalidated the outcome. Likud also circulated the story that some votes were bought. Clearly the next stage of negotiations, requiring further cession of territory, would be tense, with evidence suggesting no softening of Likud's resistance.

The zealotry of both Likud and the Religious Zionists reached a fever pitch in the months prior to the signing of Oslo II in September 1995. Settlers and Arabs routinely murdered each other, defending the murders as justified. West Bank rabbis, most of them ideological offspring of the

Rabbis Kook, spread the notion that Rabin was a criminal in relinquishing Jewish land to non-Jews. Under *halacha*, many said, Rabin was subject to the penalty of death. The secular Benjamin Netanyahu, who had emerged as the leader of Likud, did not challenge the rabbis in their accusations that Rabin was a traitor.

Rabin, curiously, seemed not to grasp the ramifications of the rising fever. He understood Arab terrorism well enough, but as a native-born secular Israeli raised on Labor Zionist values, he knew little about the beliefs of Religious Zionists, and even less about Revisionism. Still furious at the humiliation inflicted on him by Gush Emunim in 1975, he considered the settlers' lawlessness to be anti-Zionist and anti-Israel. But he never imagined a danger of their killing other Jews.

On the evening of November 4, 1995, at the conclusion of a peace rally in a central square in Tel Aviv, Rabin was assassinated. His assassin was Yigal Amir, a twenty-five-year-old Modern Orthodox Jew studying at the religious Bar-Ilan University. Amir had contemplated the killing since Oslo I. He was enrolled in a government program that combined Torah study with military training, in which he was taught the use of arms. Amir later told the police that "if not for the *halachic* ruling made against Rabin by a few rabbis," he would not have committed the crime. As Rabin approached his waiting car, Amir stepped out of the darkness and fired two shots into his back. Rabin died a half hour later in a nearby hospital.[4]

After the murder, Religious Zionists did not soften their objections to peace. The rabbis who claimed that Rabin's evacuation of territory was a capital offense under *halacha* accepted no blame for his death. Not long after the assassination, I talked with Rabbi Eliezer Waldman, a Gush Emunim founder who was now head of the Kiryat Arba yeshiva. Though mild in manner, he was known for his involvement in deadly acts of settler violence. He and I talked in his apartment beneath framed photographs of the two rabbis Kook.

"Judea and Samaria—yes, Kiryat Arba itself—are our heartland," Waldman told me. "The Six-Day War brought us back here. The process was initiated by God but it depended on the actions of the Jews. Did we need permission of the Arabs to return? Not at all. Was this an Arab land? Never. We were driven out, and now we're coming back. The very notion of trading land for peace is absurd. Our military supremacy is the only basis for peace. Those Jews who do not believe that we must be in command are endangering the Jewish people."

On the morning after Rabin's death, the cabinet named Shimon Peres the acting prime minister. Peres announced immediately that Israel would continue to fulfill its obligations under the Oslo Accords, and in the ensuing days he oversaw the withdrawal of the army from several West Bank cities. He also initiated another overture to Syria, which failed, and even offered negotiations to Saudi Arabia, Morocco, and Tunisia. In January, Arafat moved his headquarters to a compound in Ramallah, instead of Jericho, then held a referendum ratifying his rule. With the shock of Rabin's death subsiding, Peres, at the peak of his popularity, decided to advance elections to renew his mandate. At that point, chaos took over.

In early January 1996, Israel killed a major contributor to Arab terrorism in Gaza by blowing up a cell phone he was using. Hamas, the Islamic organization that dominated Gaza, vowed revenge, and a suicide bomber killed twenty-three passengers on a Jerusalem bus. Two weeks later, another thirteen Israelis were killed and the day after, thirteen shoppers were killed by a bomb on a Tel Aviv street. An artillery exchange with Islamists on the Lebanese border added to the bloodshed. Peres's decision to seal off the occupied territories ended his good relations with Arafat. Israel's mood shifted from accepting peace, albeit reluctantly, to vowing to punish the Arabs for the murders.

Over the course of a few weeks, Peres's popularity collapsed. He continued in his election campaign to defend the steps that were pledged in the Oslo Accords. Likud, however, proclaimed as its motto "Peace with Security," which translated into a warning that it planned to move the government in an entirely different direction.

By chance, Israel was experimenting in the 1996 election with procedural reform in which voters would choose a prime minister in a head-to-head contest, while voting in the usual multi-party fashion for Knesset seats. Peres lost to Likud's Netanyahu by less than 1 percent in the prime ministerial race. In the Knesset contest, Labor came in first by a hair, but the collateral support of the religious and the Russian parties gave Likud a ruling majority. Under Netanyahu, the Likud government suspended peace-making, which has not seriously resumed to the present day.

Benjamin Netanyahu inherited his Revisionism from his father, Benzion, who was a distinguished scholar of Jewish history as well as a secretary to Vladimir Jabotinsky. He was also a friend of Abba Ahimeir, the well-known "Maximalist" of the pre-independence period. He was with Jabotinsky in New York in 1940 when Jabotinsky died. Benzion's firstborn son, Yonatan, was commander of the unit that rescued the Jewish hostages in a captured airliner at Entebbe in 1976; Yonatan was the only Israeli killed in the operation. Benzion's second son, Benjamin, grew up in the shadow of his brother and in his father's intellectual footsteps.

Born in Tel Aviv in 1949, Benjamin Netanyahu spent much of his youth in America, where his father held a series of academic posts. He was an excellent student in both his Israeli and American schools, and reached maturity speaking English flawlessly. At age eighteen, he returned to Israel to fight in the Six-Day War, then served honorably in the IDF for five more years, retiring with the rank of captain. He later traveled back to America to attend the Massachusetts Institute of Technology, where he received degrees in architecture and business.

In 1978, Netanyahu returned to Israel and, in memory of his brother, set up the Yonatan Institute for the study of security against terrorism. He also dabbled in Revisionist politics, which led to his appointment to a post at the Israeli embassy in Washington. In 1984, he was named Israel's ambassador to the United Nations, a position that provided him with widespread media exposure. In 1988 he was elected to the Knesset on the Likud list and subsequently won an election to succeed Yitzhak Shamir as the Likud Party chairman. The chairmanship put him in line to become the next Likud prime minister.

Elected in 1996, Netanyahu had a legal duty to carry out Israel's obligations under the Oslo Accords, but that was not his plan. He had no intention of contributing to a process that moved Israel toward the establishment of a Palestinian state. It was contrary to everything his father had taught him, and everything he had learned from the works of Jabotinsky and Begin. Netanyahu's Likud coalition commanded just 61 of the 120 Knesset seats. His refusal to abide by the terms of Oslo II ended the fragile truce that had been reached between Israel and the Palestinians.

As prime minister, Netanyahu resumed the construction of settlements in the territories. He also pushed the expansion eastward of Jewish neighborhoods in Jerusalem, which all but severed the West Bank into two parts. He bulldozed Arab homes and denied Arabs living in the occupied territories the right to enter Jerusalem. He shrank the West Bank area designated under Oslo II for Palestinian rule and took over Arab water resources, justifying these practices with the claim that Arafat had violated his pledge to suppress terrorism.

In October 1998, U.S. President Bill Clinton summoned Netanyahu and Arafat to the Wye Plantation in Maryland in an attempt to salvage Oslo. Clinton even brought in Jordan's conciliatory King Hussein to help. A week of talks produced an agreement in which Netanyahu pledged to resume Israel's commitment to evacuate Arab territory, while Arafat promised to impose more stringent controls to suppress violence. But Netanyahu had doubts about his concessions, and Arafat's influence in Palestine was declining. The Wye conference, though ostensibly ending in agreement, contributed little to rescuing the peace process.

The Knesset approved the Wye accord, but neither left nor right was reconciled to it. Labor recognized that it did nothing to improve on the status quo; Likud and its Knesset allies were irritated by Washington's resurrecting Oslo just as it was at the point of fading away. At the same time, Netanyahu also lost some of his popularity in a series of minor family scandals.

Netanyahu was thus unable to hold on to his slim Knesset majority, and soon after the Wye meeting he was forced to call elections. Despite a vigorous campaign, he was defeated by a wide margin in the popular balloting. But again it would be a mistake to conclude that Israel's peace forces had triumphed. Netanyahu was rejected by an electorate that was disappointed by his lethargic leadership and, at the same time, tantalized by a Labor Party ex-general named Ehud Barak who, like Rabin, thought of peace as a pragmatic solution to a worsening security situation. In defeat, Netanyahu resigned from both the Knesset and the Likud and took a lucrative job in business.

Ehud Barak, as prime minister, considered himself Rabin's political heir. Born on a kibbutz in 1942, he enlisted at seventeen in an elite army unit that he would ultimately command himself. After many decorations, he attained the IDF's top post, chief of staff. On his retirement from the army, Rabin named him to the cabinet, though clearly Barak aspired to an even higher office. Ideologically, Barak was committed neither to the left's land-for-peace formula nor to the right's dream of a Greater Israel. He thought of himself as a soldier in politics, whose mission was to make Israel more secure, a mission he called "the realization of the Zionist vision."

"The strategic choice made by Shamir and Netanyahu in the face of life's uncertainties," Barak told an interviewer, "was to do nothing, to bypass problems and play for time. My choice and that of Rabin was to act. It was clear to both of us that the processes of (Islamic) fundamentalism, nuclearization, and demography prove that time is not necessarily on Israel's side. . . . Even if you think you have only a 20 percent chance of achieving peace, you know the alternative is a 100 percent certainty of entering rivers of blood. You have a moral duty, and the duty is to act."

Barak liked to compare peace for Israel to a table, of which two legs— the treaties with Egypt and Jordan—were in place. The two unattached legs were Syria, which posed no immediate threat, and the Palestinians, Israel's most dangerous nemeses. There was also a third unattached leg, however, which had been the focus of Barak's election campaign. It was to clean up the debris of the failed war in Lebanon, where 35,000 Israeli soldiers remained in the Shi'ite south, an area Israel called the "security zone." It was a surprise when Barak, soon after his election, bypassed the Palestinians and the "security zone" and announced that Syria was at the top of his diplomatic agenda.

Syria's President Assad had come around to peace-making, declaring he was ready to exchange *full* peace for Israel's *full* withdrawal from Syrian territory—the "full" being particularly emphatic after the recovery by Sadat, his Arab rival, of the entire Sinai in 1979. A treaty would also imply Syria's acceptance of the Sykes–Picot Agreement, which Arabs regarded as Europe's betrayal of its World War I pledge to create an Arab nation of the Ottoman provinces. The presence of the Jewish state was a daily reminder of this betrayal. Regaining only a fraction of the land lost in 1967 would thus constitute a second Zionist dismemberment. Barak never grasped the symbolism for Syria, nor how seriously Assad took it.

Syrian-Israeli talks began in December 1999, with Barak offering to restore all of the Golan Heights save a few hundred yards along the Sea of Galilee. To Barak, the few hundred yards represented a vital guarantee to Israel's water supply. He considered the offer generous, as did Clinton, and in ordinary circumstances it was. But Assad insisted on a pledge of *total* withdrawal from the Golan, after which he was willing to negotiate such issues as security and diplomatic normalization. Barak called Assad's terms "up-front capitulation to his diktat."

As the talks dragged on, opposition in Israel to giving up the Golan

grew stronger. The Golan settlements had been established by Labor supporters, not Likud, giving the left an incentive to join the right in opposing any change. Street demonstrations made further concessions by
Barak increasingly difficult. Clinton made an attempt to resolve the impasse but got nowhere with either Assad or Barak. Taking a gamble, Clinton lured Assad to Geneva, promising to meet Syria's terms, but when he
only repeated Barak's original offer, Assad took it as bad faith and walked
out. A few hundred yards of lakefront thus killed the deal, with Barak and
Assad blaming each other for the failure.

After Clinton's stumble in Geneva, Barak made good on his vow to
withdraw from south Lebanon. The withdrawal, completed by the spring
of 2000, enhanced Barak's international credibility. Clinton by now aspired to include Middle East peace in his presidential legacy, which translated into a personal investment in Barak, and decided to take a page
from Jimmy Carter's book by convoking a summit of Barak and Arafat at
Camp David. With only a few months left in his term, however, there was
hardly time for such a complex and demanding encounter to succeed.

Barak made matters more difficult prior to Camp David by authorizing more settlement construction, and by refusing to carry out the West
Bank withdrawals pledged under Oslo and Wye. Arafat gave Clinton his
candid opinion that, faced with Barak's attitude, a summit was certain
to fail, which would make relations between Israel and the Palestinians
much worse. Clinton answered that if the summit collapsed, Arafat would
not be held to blame, and he plunged ahead.[5]

The second Camp David conference opened on July 11, 2000, but it
was different from Carter's, which had been preceded by a series of
Begin–Sadat encounters that established a foundation for the talks. Carter was also better prepared for his meeting than Clinton, and he was a more
rigorous manager of the proceedings. Both Barak and Arafat, moreover,
were weaker than Begin and Sadat had been. Barak had already lost the support of much of his own coalition, while Arafat was undermined by a radical wave rising through the Islamic world.

Camp David's stated aim was to reach a "final status" agreement
between Israel and the PLO. It would establish a Palestinian state on the West
Bank and in Gaza, formally ending the conflict, and it would resolve the
complex problems associated with founding a state, including borders,
settlements, security arrangements, rule over Jerusalem, and the rights of

refugees to return to their former homes. Given the distance between the positions of the negotiators, it was a substantially greater challenge than Carter faced in 1978.

Barak's refusal to deal personally with Arafat aggravated the challenge. He preferred to use Clinton to convey his proposals, and with the president and Barak working together, Arafat felt increasingly isolated. Throughout the conference, Barak constantly looked over his shoulder at the rowdy demonstrations on Israeli streets, while Arafat kept an eye on Islamic capitals, which were especially concerned with the fate of Jerusalem. Oddly, no record was kept of the daily proceedings. Israeli proposals were submitted orally, without maps, and often modified or withdrawn in later sessions. Clinton never really took charge. The entire process was run unprofessionally.

On some issues, the two sides appeared to approach agreement. Israel talked of ceding back as much as 90 percent of the West Bank, along with the Gaza Strip, and the Palestinians accepted the principle of Jewish settlements annexed to Israel. The two sides explored Palestinian sovereignty over Arab Jerusalem, and Arafat raised the possibility of limiting refugee repatriation to a few hundred thousand in Arab Palestine, with none at all to Israel. But Barak submitted no proposal in writing, and Arafat had no counterproposals to offer. Though some rapprochement occurred between the parties, the conference ended with no decisions.[6]

Could Camp David have succeeded with different dramatis personae? What if Carter, or someone as strong, had been in charge? What if the clear-minded Rabin, rather than Barak, had been there to speak for Israel? What if the Palestinians had been represented by someone other than an unshaven ex-guerrilla chief wearing a *kaffiyeh*? And what if an agreement had been reached and was then turned down by the Knesset or by an Israeli referendum, or by the influential circle of rivals to Arafat within the Palestinian camp?

Clinton reaped what political benefit he could by skewering Arafat, a violation of his pledge. Barak went a significant step further, declaring that Camp David proved Arafat did not really want to end the conflict at all and that Israel had no real partner for peace. Neither Clinton nor Barak presented evidence for their claims that Arafat was to blame for the failure, but in Israel and America the charges stuck. Oddly, when Camp David was over, Clinton still talked of salvaging an agreement.

Six months after Camp David, with George W. Bush recently elected but not yet inaugurated as president, Clinton made a last-ditch effort by calling the two opposing teams back to Washington. They subsequently met in January 2001 in Taba, a resort town in Egypt's Sinai. This time Clinton had his staff prepare bridging proposals—called the Clinton Parameters—based on the Camp David experience. Both sides accepted them as the basis for facing each other again.

But though both delegations took the discussions seriously, none of the three principals at Camp David—Clinton, Barak, and Arafat— attended the Taba talks. With the help of Clinton's bridging points, the negotiators narrowed the gap on some of the outstanding issues. Some observers believed the two sides might have come together if they were able to explore each other's positions for a few months, but at Taba they had only a few days.

Time was only part of the problem, however. In September 2000, Ariel Sharon, now the head of Likud and a driven foe of peace-making, led a contingent of police in a demonstration on the Temple Mount, proclaiming that it had to be eternally Israel's. Barak made no effort to stop him. The demonstration ignited a second *intifada*, a groundswell of violence which firmly implanted in the public mood a sense that Barak had lost control of the government.

Clinton tried to help Barak restore his authority, urging him to grant concessions to the Palestinians. But Barak was unable to summon the necessary initiative, daring, or imagination. When the Taba talks ended, Clinton had nothing more to offer, leaving Barak without political resources. With no choice but to call new elections, Barak threw himself on the mercy of Israel's voters.

On February 6, 2001, Barak was soundly defeated by Sharon, after a tenure as prime minister of only eighteen months. The Israeli peace camp was devastated, as was the international community, which had relied on the negotiations to transform the Middle East. As prime minister–elect, Sharon wasted no time in announcing that offers submitted by Israel at Camp David and Taba were not binding on his new government. Sharon added that he contemplated no more peace talks with the Palestinians.

By the time Sharon took office, Camp David's shattered hopes had made Israelis more frustrated and Palestinians more desperate. The second *intifada* was raging uncontrollably. A suicide bomber massacred thirty Jews at a Passover Seder in a seaside hotel. The IDF besieged Bethlehem's Church of the Nativity, killing eight militants hiding inside. A sniper struck down ten Israeli soldiers at a West Bank checkpoint. The IDF wrecked Arafat's compound in Ramallah, effectively making him a prisoner of war. In an operation ordered by Sharon, the IDF also reoccupied much of the land Israel had ceded to the Palestinians under the Oslo Accords. Then, in the Knesset election of 2003, Sharon won reelection as prime minister, a rousing affirmation of his management of the Likud government.

President George W. Bush had by now concluded that the U.S. should do something about the mayhem. Recruiting the European Union, Russia, and the U.N., he organized a "Quartet" to go beyond a truce to offer Israel and the Palestinians a "Road Map" to a two-state solution to the conflict. The Palestinians agreed to it but Sharon conditioned Israel's acceptance on much narrower Palestinian borders than the Road Map specified. Sharon also ruled out limits on settlement construction, a division of Jerusalem, and any recognition of the refugees' right of return. Notwithstanding Sharon's conditions, Bush promised the attainment of the Road Map's two-state goal within two years.

Not surprisingly, the Road Map ran into hard going from both sides. The *intifada* continued, exacting major losses. Its intensity slowed in 2004, when Arafat took ill and suddenly died, and factional fighting between the PLO and Hamas temporarily diverted the Arabs from the conflict with Israel. In July, Israel and the Arabs agreed to a truce, which led to the release of several hundred Palestinian prisoners. But the lull did not last. Fierce fighting broke out again when Hamas conducted a string of suicide bombings of Israeli buses, and Israel retaliated with a series of "targeted" killings of Hamas leaders. Travel by the Road Map sputtered to an end, with Sharon and the Palestinians, characteristically, blaming each other.

Yet the second *intifada* clearly had an impact on Sharon. Throughout his long career, he had been dedicated to crushing Palestinian hopes for independence. He had a special loathing for Arafat, which deepened after Israel's humiliation in Lebanon. Now in his seventies, he no longer had the slim torso of a soldier, but as a politician he retained his unconventional daring. With hundreds of *intifada* casualties on both sides, Sharon recognized, as Rabin did before him, that Israeli society could not endure such protracted bloodshed indefinitely. Sharon suddenly showed a readiness to lead Israel on a new course.

Unable to crush the second *intifada,* Sharon decided to reconceptualize his long-term strategy. With no advance notice, he told an Israeli news-paper that he would accept the principle of a Palestinian state. He talked of "painful concessions" that Israel had to make. "We have to look at it realistically . . . ," he said. "In the end there will be a Palestinian state . . . I don't think we should be ruling over another people and running its life. I don't think we have the strength for that." A few weeks later, Sharon de-clared, "The occupation is a terrible thing for Israel and the Palestinians. It can't continue endlessly."

Sharon's dramatic departure from his long-held vision of Israel's future was astonishing. The greatest of Israel's field commanders, he had never shown a disposition to sympathize with the Arabs. As a soldier, he had been merciless in delivering blows. He was famous in his politics as the settlers' champion, and he was idolized for his hard line by the Likud faithful. Many supporters now saw him turning away from everything he had stood for. More than a few Israelis suggested that, in his advancing years, he had lost his mind.[7]

Yet it had often been overlooked that Sharon was more soldier than ideologue. He was raised not in a Revisionist home but in a Socialist kib-butz. Like Rabin, in whose government he had once served, his focus was on solving security problems. Even in championing the settlements in the occupied territories, his focus was on security. It was not astonishing that he perceived Israel's strategic needs, after fifty years of independence, as different from what they were at its birth.

At the same time that Sharon was contemplating change, Saudi Arabia sprung a surprise. At an Arab League summit in Beirut in 2002, the Saudis offered a proposal, which the Arab states approved unanimously, that revolutionized—at least on its face—the Arabs' historic perspective toward Israel. Called the Arab Peace Initiative, the Saudis proposed to exchange Israel's consent to a Palestinian state and withdrawal of its forces from all the occupied territories for peace and normalization with all the Arab gov-ernments. Abandoning the traditional Arab claim of the right of all refugees to return to their homes, the Initiative called for negotiating a "just solu-tion" to the refugee problem.

Shimon Peres, again Israel's foreign minister, was practically alone in responding favorably to the overture. "Israel views positively," Peres said, "every initiative aimed at achieving peace and normalization," which seemed like an acceptance of the invitation to discuss the contents further. Washington was silent, however, and the Sharon cabinet overruled Peres.

Some members called the Initiative a trap to get Israel to make sacrifices while the *intifada* raged. Sharon himself declared, rather spuriously, that he could not accept it because it conflicted with Israel's commitment to U.N. Resolution 242. In fact, most Israelis, unaccustomed to Arab peace offers, were bewildered by what to do. For lack of support from the U.S. or Israel, the Arab Peace Initiative faded away, though it would periodically reappear on the Arab diplomatic agenda.

Sharon, soon afterward, announced his own plan for peace, which he called "disengagement." The term had been used at the end of the Yom Kippur War, when enemy armies—one of which he commanded—sat tangled in the Sinai and on the Golan Heights, each of them fearful that the conflict would again break out. By now, two *intifada*s had exposed the huge cost in lives and resources of the pursuit of Israeli rule from the river to the sea. "The Palestinian state is hardly my life's dream," Sharon stated. In disengagement, he said, "we have a solution for future generations."

The first step of the disengagement policy took place in 2002, when concrete was poured for a wall dividing the West Bank from pre-1967 Israel. The wall meant that Palestinians would no longer be able to cross easily into Israel, and especially into Jerusalem. A year later, the initial segments of the wall became effective, and Sharon promptly claimed that it had reduced terrorist infiltration.

Built of concrete slabs eight to ten feet high, the wall was planned to extend nearly five hundred miles along the demarcation line between Israel and the West Bank. Significantly, it looped eastward around the Jewish settlements clustered on the border, placing about ten percent of the West Bank on the Israeli side. Many took the wall to mean impending annexation. Palestinians protested and the World Court declared it illegal. Israel's judiciary ordered changes in the route, and the U.S. criticized it as a useless half-measure on the road to peace. Sharon's response was that it was not up to outsiders to make these judgments. Refusing further talks with the Palestinians, he declared that Israel would continue to carry out the policy of disengagement unilaterally.

Many of Israel's settlers, though satisfied with the limitations imposed by the wall on the daily life of Palestinians, complained that disengagement was an anti-Revisionist, left-wing idea, and worried about what the next step would be. They remembered it was Sharon who, under Begin, located many settlers within heavy concentrations of Arabs, citing strategic grounds. Now Sharon proposed to reposition these settlers away from the

Arabs to reduce friction. His aim, he asserted, was "to draw the most efficient security lines possible."

Then, in late 2003, Sharon made his most daring decision: All twenty-one settlements in the Gaza Strip were to be dismantled and removed. Ex–prime minister Netanyahu, again a cabinet minister, led a band of Likud dissidents in denouncing the move. Religious Zionist rabbis in the West Bank debated placing the ancient curse on Sharon that had been imposed on Rabin. When Netanyahu resigned from the cabinet, taking the Religious Zionist and Russian factions with him. Sharon replied by persuading opposing Labor members to take the place of the defectors. By a slim majority, the Knesset voted final authorization for the Gaza withdrawal.

As an incentive to the 9,500 settlers to leave Gaza peacefully, Sharon offered monetary payments, but at the same time he ordered 50,000 soldiers to remove them if necessary. Only a few settlers took the money. In July, the Gaza border was closed to nonresidents to avoid repeating the mistake made in 1982 at Yamit, when Religious Zionist militants resisted withdrawal with clubs and stones. In Gaza, some settlers barricaded themselves in homes and synagogues, and had to be dragged out forcibly, but the overall violence was contained. In a few days in August 2005, the army completed the evacuation, ending thirty-eight years of Israeli military presence.

When the evacuation was over, Sharon told the Knesset, "I know full well what this decision means for the thousands of Israelis . . . who built homes there and planted trees and grew flowers and raised boys and girls who have known no other home. I sent them there. I was party in this project. Many of these people were my personal friends. I feel their despair . . . But I am convinced in the depths of my soul and with my entire intellect that this disengagement will strengthen Israel's hold on vital territory, will win the support and appreciation of countries near and far, will reduce enmity . . . , and will advance us on the path of peace with the Palestinians and our other neighbors."

He was excessively optimistic, however. With Arafat dead, power struggles intensified between the Palestinians' two main factions, the secular Fatah and the Islamic Hamas, which Israel and the U.S. had classed as a terrorist organization. In June 2006, the Palestinians held elections for control of their parliament. Hamas won a major victory, seriously undermining the Fatah-controlled Palestinian Authority, while refusing to endorse Fatah's peace-making efforts. Though it has at times held out the prospect of negotiating a long-term truce as permitted under Islamic law, Hamas has never wavered in rejecting Israel's legitimacy.

Sharon was also clumsy executing Israel's Gaza disengagement. He refused to hold talks on transition either with Hamas or the Palestinian Authority. He paid no attention to Palestinian politics or the impact of disengagement on the inhabitants' daily lives. He certainly did not take into account that within Gaza there were Fatah sympathizers who might join him on the road to peace.

Under Sharon's post-disengagement system, Israel retained total control over Gaza's borders, airspace, and territorial waters. It kept its hand on Gaza's commuications, water, and electricity networks. In determining who and what could enter or leave, Israel sealed off Gaza from the outside world. In refusing practically all human rights to Gazans, it promoted a permanent hostility that not only failed to curb the bloodshed of the Arab-Israeli wars, which was Sharon's objective, but insured its continuation.

Disengagement, predictably, also served as an invitation for an Arab struggle for control of Gaza, making a civil war all but inevitable. Hamas, having beaten Fatah in elections, then defeated it in bloody fighting, separating Palestinians into two separate political entities, where they remain. For Israel, Sharon's disengagement simply opened a second front in the endless Israeli-Palestinian conflict.

Still Likud's faithful—now preponderantly followers of Netanyahu— were furious at Sharon for emptying Gaza of settlements. In a vote of Likud's central committee, Netanyahu contrived to unseat Sharon, which provoked Sharon to declare, "Likud needs to decide if it is going to position itself at the center of the national consensus or at the extremist margins. . . . The real Likud is a large, centrist, national, liberal movement, not flinching from hard decisions and painful concessions, leading responsibly, sagaciously, in the true national interest." Sharon then announced that he was resigning from Likud to form his own party, composed of disengagement supporters.

Sharon called the new party Kadima, which in Hebrew means "forward," evoking the cry of a military commander to his troops. To a national television audience he stated, "Likud can no longer lead the country in its national goals" Prominent political figures from both the left and the right joined him, including Shimon Peres, the former prime minister and Labor icon. Among them were leading academics and artists looking to change Israeli politics. So was Ehud Olmert, Sharon's deputy. Poised for national elections, Sharon's party appeared invincible

But less than a month later, Sharon, whose doctors had often cautioned him about his weight, was felled by a stroke. During his hospital stay, the doctors found a heart defect that required prompt surgery, which was set for January 5, 2006. Though instructed to rest in the interval, he returned to work at once. A day before the scheduled operation, he was struck down by a more deadly stroke, and despite herculean medical efforts, he did not recover. Olmert succeeded him on an interim basis. Sharon was then transferred to a state medical facility, where he never regained consciousness. He died in January 2014.

Even without Sharon, Kadima achieved a major electoral victory in March 2006, winning 28 Knesset seats to 18 for Labor and 12 for Likud. Ehud Olmert, the new prime minister, was not a political star. He had served in the Knesset for eight terms, and replaced Netanyahu in the cabinet when he resigned in protest over the disengagement issue. Olmert also served a term as the mayor of Jerusalem. Like Sharon himself, Olmert had moved from the far right of Likud to the center. When he was named prime minister, his poll ratings surpassed 70 percent. Within a few months they had fallen to almost zero.

In July 2006, after three Israeli soldiers were killed and two abducted by Hezbollah on the Lebanese border, Olmert launched a war of retribution. Underlying the war was the emergence of Hezbollah, a Shi'ite faction heavily supported by Shi'ite Iran as Lebanon's strongest political and military force. Both Hezbollah and Iran were hostile to Israel. Hezbollah, moreover, had not forgiven Israel for the long occupation of its home soil in south Lebanon, which Ehud Barak had ended only a few years before.

Israel opened the war with heavy air and artillery barrages on Hezbollah installations. It then attacked roads, bridges, and Beirut's international airport, and imposed a blockade on Lebanon's seaports. Hezbollah replied with rocket attacks on towns in northern Israel, reaching as far south as Haifa. In ground operations, Hezbollah units proved to be unexpectedly well trained and equipped, holding the IDF to a stalemate, with heavy casualties on both sides. After thirty-four days of combat, the war was ended by a U.N. Security Council resolution, which both sides welcomed.

Though popular at first, the war quickly ignited protest demonstrations throughout Israel. Olmert sacked his defense minister and replaced him with Ehud Barak, the ex–prime minister and a military hero, but on the battlefield there was no improvement. In an official postwar review, an Israeli commission of inquiry charged that "a semi-military organization of a few thousand men resisted the strongest army in the Middle East, which enjoyed full air superiority and size and technology advantages." More devastatingly, the commission reported that Olmert and his cabinet had started the war without a clear objective, much less an exit plan. In the wake of the report, one hundred thousand demonstrators rallied on Israel's streets to demand Olmert's resignation.

In November 2007, President George W. Bush, perceiving a diplomatic opening, convened a conference at the U.S. Naval Academy in Annapolis in an effort to revive his now moribund Road Map. The central figures, Olmert and Mahmoud Abbas, Arafat's successor, had met a few times privately in recent months, narrowing their long-standing rifts. Among those invited to the conference were representatives of the principal Arab states, which had reaffirmed their commitment to the Arab Peace Initiative, as well as China, Russia, and America's chief European allies. Together they created a carnival-like atmosphere, which was not conducive to serious diplomacy.

The real problem was that both Olmert and Abbas presided over dysfunctional administrations. Olmert's cabinet, bruised by the Hezbollah war, was near dissolution. Abbas ruled over only a half state, with Hamas having effectively removed Gaza from his jurisdiction. The conference closed without results, though Olmert and Abbas agreed to negotiate further. Though both seemed inclined to reach a deal, however, they faced the vetoes of adversaries within their own blocs. Neither could summon the political strength needed to break the historic logjam.

For Olmert, matters grew only worse. Since the Gaza disengagement, Hamas and its extremist allies had been routinely shooting rockets into Israel's southern towns, inflicting few casualties but creating a rising tension. The only practical purpose the rockets served, in fact, was to remind Israel and the world that a million-and-a-half Gazans could not tolerate living under the deplorable conditions that Israel imposed on them.

Israel initiated the first Gaza war by conducting cross-border raids to suppress the rocket fire. Each raid was followed by a brief cease-fire but no practical change. In late 2008, Hamas seemed ready for a wider truce in return for a lessening of the blockade, but Olmert declined to consider its condition. On December 27, Israel launched Operation Cast Lead with air strikes on installations throughout the Gaza Strip, and on January 3, the IDF invaded. Combat lasted until Israel unilaterally declared a cease-fire on January 18. Casualties were estimated at fourteen hundred Palestinians dead, mostly civilians, and thirteen Israelis soldiers. The day after the IDF withdrew from Gaza, the rocket fire resumed.

By this time, Olmert was a lame duck. Dating back to the 1980s, legal authorities had been investigating allegations against him of financial improprieties. The investigations culminated in May 2008, when he was charged with diverting to his personal use substantial sums of money from a Jewish-American donor to his mayoral campaign in Jerusalem. Though claiming innocence, Olmert resigned as prime minister, effective upon the Knesset's selection of a successor.

When no one else in Kadima was able to assemble a governing coalition, Olmert called a new election. Olmert himself was arrested, tried, convicted, and sentenced to a prison term of eighteen months, which he began, after a series of unsuccessful appeals, in February 2016. The national election took place in February 2009, a few weeks after the Gaza cease-fire, by which time Kadima had lost the following it had acquired under Sharon. The victor in the election was Likud's Netanyahu, who had been waiting to return to the prime minister's office since his defeat in 1999. Netanyahu's second term opened a new era in Israeli history.

Benjamin Netanyahu—known as "Bibi" to almost all Israelis—was different from the other prime ministers of the post-Begin period. Except for Yitzhak Shamir, the attitude of all of them toward the Palestinians contained at least a shade of ambivalence. Each recognized—as even Jabotinsky had—that Palestinian Arabs had a legitimate link to the land, even though they gave priority to the Jews. This ambivalence explains why the "peace process" survived, and why a peace plan of some sort was almost always cooking on the political stove. But in contrast, Netanyahu recognized no Arab claim to the land at all and so had no ambivalence.

Netanyahu, in a memoir titled *A Durable Peace*—really a sequence of diatribes against Arabs—reached back to claim that even after Rome crushed the Bar Kokhba revolt in AD 135, the year conventionally regarded as the start of the Exile, the Jews retained power and independence within

Palestine. He asserts, in fact, that the Exile began only with the Islamic conquest of 636, when Muhammad's legions not only overran Palestine but *Arabized* it by importing colonists to take over the land from the Jews. Using italics, Netanyahu concludes: *"Thus it was not the Jews who usurped the land from the Arabs but the Arabs who usurped the land from the Jews."*

The source of this interpretation, Netanyahu acknowledged, was Benzion Dinur, who belonged to a school of Jewish scholars dedicated to rewriting history to promote the Zionist cause. Netanyahu, not himself a scholar, was probably referred to Dinur's work by his father, a historian of the Dinur school. Though most experts regard Dinur's case as weak, Netanyahu relies on it heavily in his book to justify his anti-Arab positions.

Elsewhere in the book, Netanyahu dismisses the contention that the Palestinian problem is at the core of the Middle East conflict. He calls it "a transparent slogan of Arab propaganda." The Arabs, he wrote, have distorted history since the late nineteenth century to portray themselves as victims. "The Arabs took the place of the Jews as the natives," he contends, "and the Jews took the place of the Arabs as the invaders." Netanyahu states that in asserting a right of nationhood, the Palestinians "invented a new identity, in effect creating a 'West Bankian' people who demanded recognition as an entirely new nation." It might be noted that the Arabs in their own accounts say much the same thing about Zionism and the Jews.

"My view of an equitable and secure arrangement for the status of a Palestinian entity," Netanyahu writes, "is based on a simple principle: The Palestinians should have all the powers to run their own lives and none of the powers to threaten Israel's life. . . . I support the Palestinian ability to control their own destiny but not their ability to extinguish the Jewish future. . . ."

Reasonable as this assertion appears, many observers have overlooked the significance of Netanyahu's conclusion: "When I am asked whether I will support a Palestinian state, I answer in the negative." In fact, depending on the politics of the audience, sometimes he claims to support a Palestinian state, and sometimes he does not.

Netanyahu's "simple principle," in fact, resurrected the concept of the *kehillot,* the self-ruling communities in which Europe's Jews lived in Exile in the centuries prior to Emancipation. Most Jews later called them "ghettos." Begin at Camp David offered Sadat such an arrangement for the Palestinians, naming it "autonomy," and Sadat, after much haggling, accepted it. But Begin ultimately backed away even from his own idea, rejecting any dilution whatever of Israeli power in the occupied territories. Netanyahu, despite his occasional equivocations, is clearly committed to Israel's total control of the West Bank.

U.S. President Barack Obama, shortly after his inauguration in 2009, declared in a speech in Cairo directed at the Muslim world that America recognized how "intolerable" life was for the Palestinians under Israel's occupation. He would not ignore, he said, "the legitimate Palestinian aspiration for dignity, opportunity, and a state of their own." "Israelis," he went on, "must acknowledge that just as Israel's right to exist cannot be denied, neither can Palestine's." Obama proceeded to name George Mitchell, a highly regarded international mediator, as his peace envoy in the Middle East.

Netanyahu delivered his response to Obama a few weeks later at Bar-Ilan, the Israeli university that leans toward Religious Zionism. He used the magic words "Palestinian state," describing it as his objective, and for years his government insisted that Israel's policy, as he laid it out at Bar-Ilan, was to make peace by recognizing Palestinian sovereignty.

But the statehood that he laid out was accompanied by substantial conditions. The key phrase of the speech was itself delivered with these conditions: "If the Palestinians recognize Israel as a Jewish state, we are ready to agree to a peace agreement, a demilitarized Palestinian state side by side with a Jewish state." Netanyahu never said what he meant by a "Jewish state," a Zionist goal since Herzl but a term subject to diverse definitions. Nor did he offer guarantees to assure to Palestinians that they would be safe in a "demilitarized" state adjacent to an Israel that has rarely hesitated to make use of its military superiority against them. Netanyahu's Bar-Ilan offer, at best, left much to be resolved.

In other matters as well, the Bar-Ilan speech was not friendly. He reject any Israeli responsibility for hostile relations with the Palestinians. He made no offer to limit the spread of Jewish settlements. He recognized no Israeli responsibility in the refugee crisis going back to 1948. Netanyahu claimed that criticism of Israel's military occupation confused cause with effect, in that occupation was solely the consequence of the Palestinians' relentless attacks on Jews. Still, many in his governing coalition found the Bar-Ilan statement far too generous, if only for its acknowledgment that a "Palestinian state" was not outside the realm of possibility.

Six months after the Bar-Ilan address, with no progress in the U.S. peace mediation, Netanyahu gave in to pressure from Washington and announced a ten-month "partial" freeze in settlement construction. Though he called it a "painful step," a backlog of building permits in the territories suggested the step was easier than he claimed. Then Netanyahu shifted again during a visit by U.S. Vice President Joseph Biden in March 2010, when Israel announced that it would build sixteen hundred new housing units in Arab East Jerusalem. The White House considered the statement a deliberate affront to Biden. Over the ensuing months, the frustrations of the American peace mediation became intolerable, and in May 2011, Mitchell, the U.S. envoy, resigned with nothing to show for his exertions.

That same year, Fatah and Hamas, influenced by the hopes raised in the Arab world by the "Arab Spring," negotiated a fragile reconciliation in which they indicated a readiness to resume talks with Israel. Though Netanyahu no doubt understood that peace required Gaza's participation, he claimed that any accord in which Hamas participated was simply an anti-Israeli ploy. When the two factions later agreed tentatively on a unity government, Netanyahu claimed to see it not as an opportunity but as the death of negotiations. "It's a blow to Israel," he declared. "It's a blow to peace."

In 2013, Netanyahu was reelected to a third term as prime minister and, though his margin was narrow, he formed a government that leaned more sharply to the right than before. A few months earlier Obama was also reelected, and though discouraged by Netanyahu's obstructive practices, had instructed the new secretary of state, John Kerry, to embark once more on a peace mission. Netanyahu again foiled the effort. He publicly dismissed Kerry's work as "an attempt to compel us . . . to withdraw to the 1967 lines . . . [which] would bring Islamic extremists to the suburbs of Tel Aviv and to the heart of Jerusalem. We will not allow that." The Kerry mission soon collapsed, bringing U.S.-Israeli relations to a precarious new low.

Meanwhile, violence between Israel and Hamas-ruled Gaza intensified. Israel continued to tighten its blockade, while Hamas fired longer-range rockets into Israeli targets. In November 2012, the IDF had invaded Gaza and, in a week of intense fighting, some two hundred Palestinians, both combatants and civilians, were killed. Two years later, with little having improved in the interval, the IDF invaded again, targeting the tunnels dug by Hamas to smuggle in food and daily needs, as well as weapons originating in Iran. This time the fighting lasted for nearly a month, taking more than two thousand Arab lives, including hundreds of children. Israel lost sixty-six soldiers, but even costlier was the opprobrium it suffered for its massive use of force. Egypt's effort to broker a cease-fire based on a loosening of the blockade in exchange for an end to the rocketing had no results. "If Hamas," Netanyahu declared, "thinks its losses on the battle-field will be papered over at the negotiating table, it is mistaken." Yet Israel's forfeiture of international esteem constituted a severe defeat.

After the 2014 Gaza war, Netanyahu started thinking ahead to politics. The previous election had left him with a slim majority, its fragility exacer-bated by disputes with the Orthodox parties over their ceaseless demands. Whatever his claims to the contrary, he had not been a victor in Gaza and, if he was to remain in power, he needed a cause that would arouse the voters. In December, he broke up his coalition and called an election for March 2015. The cause to which he turned was the threat to Israel from nu-clear devastation at the hands of Iran, its long-standing Islamic foe.

Israel's problems with Iran had begun with the Islamic revolution in 1979, which overthrew a shah who was friendly to it. The regime took a nastier turn when Mahmoud Ahmadinejad was elected president in 2005 after a campaign that emitted the odor of anti-Semitism. The Ahmadine-jad government furnished arms to Hezbollah in Israel's 2006 war in Leba-non and to Hamas in the Gaza wars. Israeli planes struck back with attacks against Iranian ships carrying arms to its enemies, and even seized a ship loaded with weapons.

In 2008, Israel initiated a secret war on Iran's nuclear research, assas-sinating scientists, initiating cyber attacks, and exploding bombs at nu-clear sites. Olmert, Netanyahu's predecessor, had tried unsuccessfully to persuade President Bush to bomb Iran's reactors, and Netanyahu again promoted the possibility of bombing with Obama, after Ahmadinejad left office. Both prime ministers were told that the U.S. preferred diplo-macy, but Netanyahu did not renounce the threat of Israel's bombing Iran's reactors on its own.

In 2009, Netanyahu told an American political delegation that Iran was already capable of making one bomb, and would soon be able to make sev-eral more. He called Iran's leaders "a messianic apocalyptic cult" in search of atomic arms. On Israel's Holocaust Commemoration Day, he compared his concerns about Iran to the fears of Jews trapped by the Nazi genocide. Netanyahu charged that Obama had made a "historic mistake . . . rendering the world a much more dangerous place" in negotiating an accord to limit Iran's nuclear development. Meanwhile, Israeli intelligence consistently reported that Netanyahu's claims about Iranian bombs were exaggerated, if not totally false.

As the Israeli election of 2015 approached, Netanyahu was running poorly in opinion polls, and the likelihood of his remaining in office dimmed. Israelis, it was said, had grown tired of him. At that point, he took a calculated gamble. In a deal brokered by his ambassador in Washington, he received an invitation—unknown to the U.S. president—from the Republican leader of the House of Representatives to address a joint session of Congress. Many Israelis and Americans regarded the invitation as a political trick. When Netanyahu gave the speech on March 3, Republicans made up an enthusiastic audience, but Democrats in large numbers boycotted it. Netanyahu had for the first time made Israel a partisan issue in American politics.

Netanyahu's speech was delivered just two weeks before Israelis voted. Though the television audience was large, in both countries, the response was generally muted. "The alternative to this bad deal," Netanyahu declared "is a much better deal." Watchers seemed to agree that the message was already familiar. He was silent, however, on how to structure a better deal or how to achieve it. In the ensuing days, his numbers in the polls actually went down.

The numbers stayed down until the eve of the election, when the polls showed Likud a seat or two behind Labor. At that point, Netanyahu took another gamble, appealing to the Israeli electorate's baser instincts. The Arabs, he declared menacingly, were voting "in droves." Reversing the vow he made at Bar-Ilan, he proclaimed that no Palestinian state would be formed as long as he was prime minister. His gamble paid off, and on election day, Likud won 30 Knesset seats to 24 for Labor. Most of the last-minute switch came from more extreme right-wing voters, which helped Likud but undermined the coalition. The appeal worked, however, assuring Netanyahu of another term as prime minister.

The right as a whole had, in fact, lost several seats in the election, leaving Netanyahu with another razor-thin margin. But under Israeli law, he was extended the first opportunity to form a government. The bargaining, which took place over the next six weeks, was grueling. Right-wing minority parties blamed him for their losses and exacted a heavy price for their support. The Orthodox factions extracted a rollback of restraints enacted on rabbinic powers. The Religious Zionist party, called Jewish Home, squeezed out a promise of more settlements and several major ministries. The Russian party simply walked out of the negotiations, perhaps foreshadowing a long-term political shift, but Netanyahu did not need its votes. His new government was sworn in with 61 seats, to 59 for the opposition. The new government was the most radically right-wing in Israel's history.

Netanyahu took office with the Middle East in as precarious a condition as it had been since the fall of the Ottoman Empire. Since the Arab Spring of 2010, inter-Arab wars raged from the Mediterranean to the Gulf, and extremism in the form of the so-called Islamic State was spreading across the region. With the Middle East in chaos, further Israeli-Palestinian bloodshed would only add to the region's instability, but Netanyahu barely seemed to notice. He tried mollifying the White House by recanting his disavowal of Palestinian statehood, but America's leaders did not believe him. Neither did Israelis.

When he convened his new government in May 2015, Netanyahu instructed the members of his majority not to miss a single Knesset session, even for emergencies, lest the opposition spring a surprise vote that could overthrow him. With the odds against him, predictions were rampant that his tenure would be measured in months, not years. As if to reassure his supporters, he repeated his promise that Israel would control all of the occupied territory for the foreseeable future. He then added ominously, "I'm asked if we will forever live by the sword. The answer is yes."

The election of 2015 revealed that most Israelis were still not ready to contemplate a negotiated peace. During the campaign, even Labor was not prepared to raise the issue, as if it could not challenge the Israeli preference for perpetual combat. Israel had no peace party in the 2015 election, and even if Likud had lost, the winner would not have taken office with a popular mandate to negotiate a treaty to end Israel's wars.

As these words are written, the political order that came into existence in the Middle East with the Treaty of Sèvres in 1920, the offspring of the Sykes–Picot Accord, is in the process of shattering. Arabs are killing each other across the region, and names like Al-Qaeda, Al-Nusra, the Houthis, and ISIL, unknown just a few years ago, now trip easily off our tongues. As Arab nation-states—notably Syria and Iraq—fall apart, no one can say how the pieces will come back together, or how long it will take. But it is reasonable to say that in the interstices between the fragments there is probably room to maneuver on behalf of a new Israeli-Palestinian relationship. Establishing even a small oasis of peace between the Mediterranean and the Jordan will not solve the Middle East crisis, but it would certainly be a start.

Can it happen? Not when Israel continues to measure its security solely on its ability to dominate the region by military force. Zionism, unquestionably, has come a long way since Herzl's time, but it is now mired in Jabotinsky's ideals, not Herzl's. Put another way, it is stuck in the Begin era. Given the turbulence that has engulfed the Middle East since the start of the Arab Spring, even Israel is going to have to rethink how to keep the state afloat. Is Israel ready to seize an opportunity to reach out for peace? The answer is certainly: not yet. But, given the turbulence of our times, is it not fair to ask whether it must be soon?

Acknowledgments

I cannot begin to thank all of the people who contributed over the years to my education in Zionism, beginning with grandparents and parents. There are so many. But I want to recognize Ken Jacobson, who read every word of this manuscript and made me rethink much of it. So did Soryl Rosenberg, who drew from her own wide experience. I thank Joyce Anderson and David Myers for their guidance. Yehuda Mirsky, Derek Penslar, Reuven Firestone and Rashid Khalidi provided me with critical assistance in areas of their expertise. Steve Wasserman and Andy Ross, my agents, not only were central to getting the book published but to overcoming rough moments in the process. And I particularly thank my wife Judy, whose judgment as well as whose everyday presence in my life were indispensible.

Bibliography

Zionism chronicles the evolution of an ideal. It follows this evolution through the efforts of a few extraordinary men, generally in conflict with one another, to shape concepts consistent with their own vision. Their energy created and transformed Zionism from the era of Theodor Herzl, who aimed to provide a refuge for a beleaguered people, to our own tempestuous era, when Zionism is identified with war and military occupation.

Such a book necessarily relies on the scholarship that preceded it. In conducting the research, I am indebted to the authors, both men and women, mostly Jewish, whose body of work is extremely rich in its treatment of both Zionism's principal figures as well as the historical age in which they struggled.

These figures had excellent biographers. Some of them, in addition, published their own memoirs or autobiographical statements. A few even wrote novels that explored their thinking. Each of them left behind much other material in their own words—diaries, letters, public speeches, essays, official papers, personal interviews. I have selected information from this extraordinary collection to understand these men and the cause for which, each in his unique way, they labored.

Much of the historical material is familiar to readers and requires no citations. The personal material is based heavily on the biographies and documents mentioned in the notes below. The source of other material is identified within the text. For the most part, I have provided footnotes for information that is likely to be unfamiliar to most readers.

Among the scholars to whom I am particularly indebted are Howard M. Sachar, author of *A History of Israel* and *The History of the Jews in the Modern World*, and Arthur Hertzberg and Shlomo Avineri, editors respectively of *The Zionist Idea* and *The Making of Modern Zionism*. I am also grateful for the sixteen volumes of the *Encyclopedia Judaica* and the two volumes of the *New Encyclopedia of Zionism and Israel*, which filled gaps in the available knowledge. For material too recent to have made its way into books, I relied on

Google, and especially on Wikipedia, which are new and invaluable tools of scholarly research. The bibliography at the end of his section contains a full listing of works consulted for the book.

The responsibility for both the facts and the interpretations in these pages, however, is totally mine.

BIOGRAPHICAL SOURCES

I. Theodor Herzl

Bein, Alex. *Theodore Herzl: A Biography of the Founder of Modern Zionism*. New York: Atheneum, 1970.

deHaas, Jacob. *Theodore Herzl*, 2 vols. New York: Leonard, 1927.

Elon, Amos. *Herzl*. New York: Holt, Rinehart & Winston, 1975.

Herzl, Theodor. *The Complete Diaries of Theodor Herzl*. Edited by Raphael Patai. 5 Vols. New York: Herzl Press, 1960.

   Altneuland. Haifa, Israel: Haifa Publishing Company, no date cited.

   The Jewish State. Minneola, NY: Dover Publications, 1988.

   Zionist Writings, vol. 1, 1896–1898, vol. 2, 1898–1904. New York: Herzl Press, 1975.

Herzl Year Book: Essays in Zionist History and Thought, Raphael Patai, ed., 8 vols. New York: Herzl Press, 1958–1975.

Lewison, Ludwig. *Theodor Herzl: A Portrait for This Age*. New York: World, 1955.

Stewart, Desmond. *Theodor Herzl: Artist and Politician*. New York: Doubleday, 1974.

2. Chaim Weizmann

Berlin, Isaiah & Kolatt, Israel. *Chaim Weizmann as Leader*. Jerusalem: Hebrew University, 1970.

Reinharz, Yehuda. *Chaim Weizmann*, vol. 1. *The Making of a Zionist Leader*, vol. 2. *The Making of a Statesman*, New York: Oxford, 1985 & 1993.

Rose, Norman. *Chaim Weizmann*. New York: Viking, 1986.

Weisgall, Meyer W. & Carmichael, Joel, eds., *Chaim Weizmann: A Biography by Several Hands*. New York: Atheneum, 1963.

Weizmann, Chaim. *The Letters and Papers of Chaim Weizmann, Series A Letters, 1885–1952*. 23 vols. London: Oxford University Press; New Brunswick, NJ: Transaction Press; Jerusalem: Israel Universities Press, 1968–1980; Series B Papers, New Brunswick, NJ: Transaction, 1984.

   Trial and Error. New York: Harper & Brothers, 1949.

3. Vladimir Jabotinsky

Ben-Hur, Raphaella B. *Every Individual a King: The Social and Political Thought of Ze'ev Vladimir Jabotinsky*. Washington: B'nai B'rith Books, no date cited.

Jabotinsky, Vladimir. *Prelude to Delila*. New York: Ackerman, 1930.

   The Five, A Novel of Jewish Life in Turn-of-the-Century Odessa. Ithaca, NY: Cornell, 2005.

   The Story of the Jewish Legion. New York: Ackerman, 1945.

   The War and the Jew. New York: Dial, 1942.

Katz, Shmuel. *Lone Wolf: A Biography of Vladimir (Ze'ev) Jabotinsky*, 2 vols. New York: Barricade, 1996.

Schechtman, Joseph B. *The Jabotinsky Story*, vol. 1 *Rebel and Statesman*, vol. 2, *Fighter and Prophet*, New York: Yoseloff, 1956 & 1961.

Shavit, Jaakov. *Jabotinsky and the Revisionist Movement*. London: Frank Cass, 1988.

4. David Ben-Gurion

Avi-Hai, Avraham. *Ben-Gurion: State-Builder*. New York: John Wiley, 1984.

Bar-Zohar, Michael. *Ben-Gurion: The Armed Prophet*. Englewood Cliffs, NJ: Prentice-Hall, 1966.

    Ben-Gurion: A Biography. New York: Delacorte, 1977.

Ben-Gurion, David. *Days of David Ben-Gurion*. New York: Grossman, 1967.

    Israel: Years of Challenge. New York: Holt, Rinehart & Winston, 1963.

    The Jews in their Land. New York: Doubleday, 1966.

    Letters to Paula. Pittsburgh, PA: University of Pittsburgh Press, 1968.

    Memoirs, with Thomas R. Bransten. New York: World Publishing Company, 1970.

Ducovny, Amram. *David Ben-Gurion in his Own Words*. New York: Fleet, 1968.

Edelman, Maurice. *Ben-Gurion*. London: Hodder & Stoughton, 1964.

Kurzman, Dan. *Ben-Gurion: Prophet of Fire*. New York: Simon & Schuster, 1983.

Litvinoff, Barnet. *Ben-Gurion of Israel*. New York: Praeger, 1954.

Pearlman, Moshe. *Ben-Gurion Looks Back*. New York: Schocken, 1970.

St. John, Robert. *Ben-Gurion: A Biography*. New York: Doubleday, 1971.

Shapira, Anita. *Ben-Gurion: Father of Modern Israel*. Princeton, 2015.

Teveth, Shabtai. *Ben-Gurion, The Burning Ground 1886–1948*. Boston: Houghton Mifflin, 1987.

    Ben-Gurion and the Palestinian Arabs. London: Oxford, 1985.

5. Rav Abraham Isaac Kook & Rabbi Zvi Yehuda Kook

Agus, Jacob B. *Banner of Jerusalem: The Life, Times and Thought of Abraham Isaac Kuk*. New York: Bloch, 1946.

Ben Shlomo, Yosef. *Poetry of Being, Philosophy of Rabbi Kook*. Tel Aviv: MOD, 1990.

Elkins, Dov Peretz. *Shepherd of Jerusalem: A Biography of Abraham Isaac Kook*. Northvale, NJ: Aronson, 1995.

Ish-Shalom, Benjamin. *Rav Avraham Isaac HaCohen Kook*. Albany, NY: SUNY Press, 1993.

Kaplan, Lawrence J. & Shatz, David. *Rabbi Abraham Isaac Kook and Jewish Spirituality*. New York: NYU Press, 1995.

Kipnis, Yuval. *1973: The Road to War*. Charlottesville, VA: Just World Books, 2013.

Kook, Abraham Isaac. *The Lights of Penitence, The Moral Principles*. New York: Paulist Press, 1978.

Mirsky, Yehuda. *Rav Kook: Mystic in a Time of Revolution*. New Haven, CT: Yale, 2014.

    An Intellectual and Spiritual Biography of Rabbi Avraham Yitzhaq HaCohen Kook from 1865 to 1904, unpublished doctoral dissertation at Harvard University.

6. Menachem Begin

Begin, Menachem. *The Revolt*. New York: Nash Publishing, 1951.

Caspi, Dan, Diskin, Abraham & Gutmann, Emanuel. *The Roots of Begin's Success*. New York: St. Martin's, 1984.

Haber, Eitan. *Menachem Begin*. New York: Delacorte, 1978.

Hurwitz, Harry Z. *Begin: A Portrait*. Washington: B'nai B'rith, 1994.

Perlmutter, Amos. *The Life and Times of Menachem Begin*. New York: Doubleday, 1987.

Rowland, Robert C. *The Rhetoric of Menachem Begin*. Lanham, MD: University Press of America, 1985.

Silver, Eric. *Begin: The Haunted Prophet*. New York: Random House, 1984.

Temko, Ned. *To Win or To Die: A Personal Portrait of Menachem Begin*. New York: Morrow, 1987.

White Nights: The Story of a Prisoner in Russia. New York: Harper & Row, 1957.

7. Arriving at Netanyahu

Caspit, Ben & Kfir, Ilan. *Netanyahu: The Road to Power*. Secaucus, NJ: Birch Lane, 1998.

Dan, Uri. *Ariel Sharon: An Intimate Portrait*. New York: Palgrave Macmillan, 2006.

Enderlin, Charles. *Shattered Dreams: The Failure of the Peace Process in the Middle East, 1995–2002*. New York: Other Press, 2003.

Horovitz, David, ed., with the Jerusalem Report Staff. *Shalom Friend: The Life and Legacy of Yitzhak Rabin*. New York: Newmarket Press, 1996.

Kimmerling, Baruch. *Politicide: Ariel Sharon's War Against the Palestinians*. New York: Verso, 1993.

Landau, David. *Arik: The Life of Ariel Sharon*. New York: Vintage, 2014.

Netanyahu, Benjamin. *A Durable Peace: Israel and its Place Among the Nations*. New York: Warner Books, 2000.

Nir, Hefez & Bloom, Gadi. *Ariel Sharon: A Life*. New York: Random House, 2006.

Rabin, Yitzhak. *The Rabin Memoirs*. New York: Little, Brown, 1979.

Shamir, Yitzhak. *Summing Up*. New York: Little, Brown, 1994.

Sharon, Ariel (with David Chanoff). *Warrior: An Autobiography*. New York: Simon & Schuster, 1989.

Sharon, Gilad. *Sharon: The Life of a Leader*. New York: HarperCollins, 2011.

DOCUMENTARY SOURCES

Avneri, Shlomo. *The Making of Modern Zionism*. New York: Basic Books, 1981.

Dawidowicz, Lucy. *The Golden Tradition: Jewish Life and Thought in Eastern Europe*. Boston: Beacon, 1967.

Herzberg, Arthur. *The Zionist Idea*. New York: Atheneum, 1981.

Hurewitz, J.C. *The Struggle for Palestine*. New York: Norton, 1950.

Jung, Leo, ed. *Guardians of Our Heritage, 1724–1953*. New York: Bloch, 1958.

Kaplan, Eran & Penslar, Derek J. *The Origins of Israel, 1882–1948*. Madison: University of Wisconsin, 2011.

Moore, John Norton. *The Arab-Israeli Conflict*. Princeton, NJ: Princeton University Press, 1977.

ENCYCLOPEDIAS & COLLECTIONS

Almog, Shmuel, Reinharz, Jehuda & Shapira, Anita, eds. *Zionism and Religion*. Hanover, NH: Brandeis University Press, 1998.

Appleby, Scott, ed. *Spokesmen for the Despised: Fundamentalist Leaders of the Middle East*. Chicago: University of Chicago Press, 1997.

Encyclopedia Judaica, 16 vols. Jerusalem: Keter, 1972.

Herzl Year Book, 8 vols. New York: Herzl Press, 1958–1978.

Marty, Martin E. & Appleby, Scott, eds., *Fundamentalism Project*, 4 vols. Chicago: University of Chicago Press, 1991–1994.

Rabinovich, Itamar & Reinharz, Yehuda, eds. *Israel in the Middle East: Documents & Readings on Society, Politics & Foreign Relations 1948-Present*. New York: Oxford, 1984.

Sivan, Emmanuel & Friedman, Menachem. *Religious Radicalism & Politics in the Middle East*. Albany, NY: SUNY Press, 1990.

Wigoder, Geoffrey, ed. *New Encyclopedia of Zionism and Israel*. New York: Herzl Press, 1994.

Wistrich, David & Ohana, David. *The Shaping of Israeli Identity*. London: Frank Cass, 1995.

GENERAL JEWISH HISTORIES

Ben-Sasson, H.H., ed. *A History of the Jewish People.* Cambridge, MA: Harvard University Press, 1972.

Edelheit, Abraham J. *A History of Zionism: A Handbook & Dictionary.* Boulder, CO: Westview, 2000.

Gilbert, Martin. *Exile and Return: The Struggle for a Jewish Homeland.* New York: Lippincott, 1978.

Israel: A History. New York: Morrow, 1998.

Johnson, Paul. *A History of the Jews.* New York: Harper & Row, 1987.

Laqueur, Walter. *A History of Zionism.* New York: Schocken, 1972.

Meyer, Michael. *Ideas of Jewish History.* New York: Behrman, 1974.

Pappe, Ilan. *A History of Modern Palestine.* Cambridge, MA: Cambridge University Press, 2004.

Rubinstein, Amnon. *The Zionist Dream Revisited: From Herzl to Gush Emunim and Back.* New York: Schocken, 1984.

Sachar, Abraham L. *A History of the Jews.* New York: Knopf, 1967.

Sachar, Howard M. *A History of Israel from the Rise of Zionism to Our Time.* New York: Knopf, 1979.

A History of Israel From the Aftermath of the Yom Kippur War. New York: Oxford, 1987.

A History of the Jews in the Modern World. New York: Knopf, 2005.

Safran, Nadav. *From War to War: The Arab-Israeli Confrontation, 1948–1967.* New York: Pegasus, 1969.

Shindler, Colin. *A History of Modern Israel.* Cambridge, MA: Cambridge University Press, 2008.

Sokolow, Nahum. *History of Zionism,* 2 vols. London: Elibron Classics, 1919.

OTHER PUBLISHED SOURCES

Abramov, S. Zalman. *Perpetual Dilemma: Jewish Religion in the Jewish State.* Rutherford, NJ: Fairleigh Dickinson, 1976.

Agus, J.B. *The Evolution of Jewish Thought.* New York: Abelard Schuman, 1959.

Ahad Ha'am. *Nationalism and the Jewish Ethic.* New York: Schocken, 1962.

Alteras, Isaac. *Eisenhower and Israel: U.S.-Israeli Relations 1953–1960.* Gainesville, FL: University Press of Florida, 1993.

Avishai, Bernard. *The Hebrew Republic: How Secular Democracy and Global Enterprise Will Bring Israel Peace at Last.* New York: Harcourt, 2008.

The Tragedy of Zionism: Revolution and Democracy in the Land of Israel. New York: Farrar, Straus and Giroux, 1985.

A New Israel: Democracy in Crisis 1973–88. New York: Ticknor and Fields, 1990.

Avnery, Uri. *My Friend, the Enemy.* Westport, CT: Lawrence Hill, 1986.

1948: A Soldier's Tale. Oxford: Oneworld, 1949.

Israel Without Zionism: A Plan for Peace in the Middle East. New York: Collier, 1968.

Bar-Zohar, Michael. *Facing a Cruel Mirror: Israel's Moment of Truth.* New York: Scribner's, 1990.

Bell, J. Bowyer. *Terror Out of Zion: Irgun Zvai Leumi, LEHI and the Palestine Underground.* New York: St. Martin's, 1977.

Benjamin, Uzi. *Sharon: An Israeli Caesar.* New York: Adama, 1985.

Ben-Yehuda, Nachman. *Political Assassinations by Jews.* Albany: SUNY, 1993.

Berkowitz, Michael. *Zionist Culture: West European Jewry Before the First World War.* Chapel Hill, NC: University of North Carolina Press, 1996.

Berlin, Isaiah. *Personal Impressions*. New York: Penguin, 1949.

Bick, Abraham. *Exponents and Philosophy of Religious Zionism*. Brooklyn, NY: Hashomer Hadadi, 1942.

Buber, Martin. *Israel and Palestine*. New York: Farrar, Straus and Giroux, 1952.

Byrnes, Robert F. *Anti-Semitism in Modern France*. New Brunswick, NJ: Rutgers University Press, 1950.

Carter, Jimmy. *Keeping Faith: Memoirs of a President*. New York: Bantam, 1982.

Chomsky, Noam & Pappe, Ilan. *Gaza in Crisis*. Chicago: Haymarket, 2010.

Cohen, Israel. *The Zionist Movement*. New York: Zionist Organization of America, 1946.

Cohen, Mitchell. *Zion and State: Nation, Class and the Shaping of Modern Israel*. New York: Columbia, 1992.

Corbin, Jane. *The Oslo Channel: The Secret Talks that Led to the Middle East Peace Accord*. New York: Atlantic Monthly Press, 1994.

Dieckhoff, Alain. *The Invention of a Nation: Zionist Thought and the Making of Modern Israel*. New York: Columbia, 2002.

Drucker, Malka. *Eliezer Ben-Yehuda: The Father of Modern Hebrew*. New York: Dutton, 1987.

Dugdale, Blanche E.C. *Arthur James Balfour*, 2 vols. London: Hutchinson, 1936 & New York: Putnam, 1937.

   Baffy: The Diaries of Blanche Dugdale 1936–1947. London: Valentine Mitchell, 1973.

Evron, Yair. *Israel's Nuclear Dilemma*. Ithaca, NY: Cornell University Press, 1994.

Ezrahi, Yaron. *Rubber Bullets: Power and Conscience in Modern Israel*. New York: Farrar, Straus and Giroux, 1997.

Firestone, Reuven. *Holy War in Judaism*. New York: Oxford University Press, 2012.

Fisch, Harold. *The Zionist Revolution: A New Perspective*. New York: St. Martin's, 1978.

Flapan, Simcha. *The Birth of Israel: Myths and Realities*. New York: Pantheon, 1987.

   Zionism and the Palestinians. London: Croom Helm, 1979.

Friedman, Isaiah. *The Question of Palestine: British-Jewish-Arab Relations, 1914–1918*. New York: Schocken, 1973.

Friedman, Robert I. *Zealots for Zion: Inside Israel's West Bank Settlement Movement*. New York: Random House, 1992.

Gilner, Elias. *War & Hope: A History of the Jewish Legion*. New York: Herzl Press, 1969.

Goldberg, David J. *The Promised Land: A History of Zionist Thought*. New York: Penguin, 1986.

Goldfarb, Michael. *Emancipation: How Liberating Europe's Jews from the Ghetto Led to Revolution and Renaissance*. New York: Simon & Schuster, 2009.

Goldmann, Nahum. *The Jewish Paradox: A Personal Memoir*. New York: Grosset & Dunlap, 1978.

   The Autobiography of Nahum Goldmann. New York: Holt, Rinehart & Winston, 1969.

Golomb, Jacob. *Nietzsche & Jewish Culture*. New York: Routledge, 1997.

Gorenberg, Gershom. *The Accidental Empire: Israel and the Birth of the Settlements, 1967–1977*. New York: Holt, 2006.

   The End of Days: Fundamentalism and the Struggle for the Temple Mount. New York: Free Press, 2000.

Gratch, Alon. *The Israeli Mind: How the National Character Shapes Our World*. New York: St. Martin's Press, 2015.

Halpern, Ben. *The Idea of the Jewish State*. Cambridge, MA: Harvard University Press, 1961 & Reinherz, Yehuda. *Zionism and the Creation of a New Society*. Hanover, NH: University Press of New England, 2000.

   Clash of Heroes: Brandeis, Weizmann and American Zionism. New York: Oxford, 1987.

Halsell, Grace. *Forcing God's Hand*. Washington, DC: Crossroads, 1999.

Harkabi, Yehoshafat. *The Bar Kokhba Syndrinem: Risk and Realism in International Politics*. Chappaqua, NY: Rossel Books, 1983.

Heilman, Samuel. *Defenders of the Faith: Inside Ultra-Orthodoxy*. New York: Schocken, 1992.

Heller, Joseph. *The Stern Gang: Ideology, Politics and Terror, 1940–1949*. London: Frank Cass, 1995.

Helmreich, Paul C. *From Paris to Sevres: The Partition of the Ottoman Empire, 1919–1920*. Columbus, OH: Ohio State University Press, 1974.

Hess, Moshe. *Rome and Jerusalem: The Last Nationalist Question*. Lincoln, NE: University of Nebraska Press, 1995.

Isaac, Rael Jean. *Israel Divided: Ideological Politics in the Jewish State*. Baltimore, MD: Johns Hopkins, 1976.

Jansen, Michael. *Dissonance in Zion*. London: Zed, 1987.

Jung, Leo. *Guardians of Our Heritage, 1724–1953*. New York: Bloch, 1958.

Kaplan, Eran. *The Jewish Radical Right: Revisionist Zionism and its Ideological Legacy*. Madison, WI: University of Wisconsin Press, 1950.

Karpin, Michael & Friedman, Ina. *Murder in the Name of God: The Plot to Kill Yitzhak Rabin*. New York: Holt, 1998.

Katz, Jacob. *Out of the Ghetto: The Social Background of Jewish Emancipation, 1770–1870*. Cambridge, MA: Harvard, 1973.

Kipnis, Yigal. *1973: The Road to War*. Charlottesville, VA: Just World Books, 2013.

Kissinger, Henry. *Years of Upheaval*. Boston: Little, Brown, 1982.

Kohler, Max. *Jewish Rights at the Congresses of Vienna*. New York: American Jewish Committee, 1918.

Kornberg, Jacques. *At the Crossroads: Essays on Ahad Ha'am*. Albany, NY: SUNY, 1983.

Landau, David. *Piety and Power: The World of Jewish Fundamentalism*. New York: Hill and Wang, 1993.

Leibowitz, Yeshayahu. *Judaism, Human Values and the Jewish State*. Cambridge, MA: Harvard, 1992.

Levine, Daniel. *The Birth of the Irgun Zvi Leumi: A Jewish Liberation Movement*. Jerusalem: Gefen, 1991.

Lewis, Geoffrey. *Balfour & Weizmann: The Zionist, the Zealot and the Emergence of Israel*. London: Continuum, 2009.

Lewittes, Mendell. *Religious Foundations of the Jewish State*. Northvale, NJ: Aronson, 1994.

Liebman, Charles S. & Don-Yehiya, Eliezer. *Religion and Politics in Israel*. Bloomington, IN: Indiana University Press, 1984.

Litvinoff, Barnet. *Zionism's Imprint on History*. London: Weidenfelt & Nicolson, 1965.

Lloyd George, David. *War Memoirs*, 2 vols. London: Odham, no date cited.
    Family Letters, 1885–1936. London: Oxford, 1973.

Lustick, Ian S. *For the Land and the Lord: Jewish Fundamentalism in Israel*. New York: Council on Foreign Relations, 1988.

Luz, Ehud. *Parallels Meet: Religion and Nationalism in the Early Zionist Movement, 1882–1904*. Philadelphia: Jewish Publication Society, 1988.

Makovsky, Michael. *Churchill's Promised Land: Zionism and Statecraft*. New Haven, CT: Yale, 2007.

Marton, Kati. *A Death in Jerusalem*. New York: Arcade, 1996.

Mayer, Arno J. *Plowshares into Swords: From Zionism to Israel*. New York: Verso, 2008.

Medding, Peter Y. *The Founding of Israeli Democracy, 1948–1967*. New York: Oxford, 1990.

———, ed., *Studies in Contemporary Jewry, vol. 2*. Bloomington, IN: Indiana, 1986; vol. 5, New York: Oxford, 1989.

Medoff, Rafael. *Militant Zionism in America: The Rise and Impact of the Jabotinsky Movement, 1926–1948.* Tuscaloosa, AL: University of Alabama Press, 2002.

Morgenstern, Arie. *Hastening Redemption: Messianism and the Resettlement of the Land of Israel.* New York: Oxford, 2006.

Morris, Benny. *The Birth of the Palestinian Problem, 1947–1949.* Cambridge, MA: Cambridge University Press, 1987.

  1948: The First Arab-Israeli War. New Haven, CT: Yale, 1996.

  Righteous Victims: The Zionist-Arab Conflict, 1881–1999. New York: Knopf, 1999.

Muller, Jerry Z. *Capitalism and the Jews.* Princeton, NJ: Princeton University Press, 2010.

O'Malley, Padraig. *The Two-State Delusion.* New York: Viking, 2015.

Parker, Richard B. *The Politics of Miscalculation in the Middle East.* Bloomington, IN: Indiana, 1993.

Patterson, J.H. *With the Judaeans in the Palestine Campaign.* London: Hutchinson, 1922.

Pearlman, Moshe. *The Army of Israel.* New York: Philosophical Library, 1950.

Penniman, Howard R. *Israel at the Polls: The Knesset Election 1977.* Washington, DC: American Enterprise Institute, 1979.

Peres, Shimon. *From These Men: Seven Founders of the State of Israel.* New York: Wyndham, 1979.

Peri, Yoram. *Between Battles and Ballots: Israeli Military in Politics.* Cambridge, England: Cambridge University Press, 1983.

Perlmutter, Amos. *Israel: The Partitioned State.* New York: Scribner, 1985.

Pinsker, Leo. *Auto-Emancipation.* New York: Scopus, 1944.

Poppel, Stephen M. *Zionism in Germany, 1897–1933.* Philadelphia: Jewish Publication Society, 1977.

Quandt, William B. *Decade of Decisions: American Policy Toward the Arab-Israeli Conflict, 1967–1976.* Berkeley, CA: University of California Press, 1977.

  Peace Process, American Diplomacy and the Arab-Israeli Conflict Since 1967. Berkeley, CA: University of California Press, 1993.

Rabinovich, Itamar. *The War for Lebanon, 1970–1983.* Ithaca, NY: Cornell, 1983.

Rabkin, Yakov M. *A Threat from Within: A Century of Jewish Opposition to Zionism.* Winnipeg, Canada: Fernwood, 2006.

Radosh, Allis & Ronald. *A Safe Haven: Harry S. Truman and the Founding of Israel.* New York: HarperCollins, 2009.

Ragins, Sanford. *Jewish Responses to Anti-Semitism in Germany, 1870–1914.* Cincinnati, OH: Hebrew Union College, 1980.

Ravitsky, Aviezer. *Messianism, Zionism and Jewish Religious Radicalism.* Chicago: University of Chicago Press, 1996.

Rosenthal, Bernice G., ed. *Nietzche in Russsia.* Princeton, NJ: Princeton University Press, 1986.

Roy, Sara. *Failing Peace: Gaza and the Palestinian-Israeli Conflict.* Ann Arbor, MI: Pluto Press, 2007.

Ruppin, Arthur. *Memoirs, Diaries, Letters.* London: Weidenfeld & Nicolson, 1971.

Sachar, Harry. *Zionist Portraits and Other Essays.* London: Blond, 1959.

Sachar, Howard M. *Egypt & Israel.* New York: Marek, 1981.

Safran, Nadav. *Israel: The Embattled Ally.* Cambridge, MA: Harvard University Press, 1978.

Samuel, Herbert. *Memoirs.* London: Cresset, 1945.

Saunders, Harold H. *The Other Walls: The Politics of the Arab-Israeli Peace Process.* Washington, DC: American Enterprise Institute, 1985.

Schaeffer, Robert. *Warpaths: The Politics of Partition.* New York: Hill & Wang, 1990.

Schechtman, Joseph B. & Benari, Yehuda. *History of the Revisionist Movement.* Tel Aviv: Hadar, 1970.

Schneer, Jonathan. *The Balfour Declaration.* New York: Random House, 2010.

Schorske, Carl E. *Fin-de-Siecle Vienna: Politics and Culture.* New York: Vintage, 1981.

Segev, Tom. *1949: The First Israelis.* New York: Free Press, 1986.

    One Palestine Complete: Jews and Arabs Under the British Mandate. New York: Holt, 1999.

    The Seventh Million: Israelis and the Holocaust. New York: Hill & Wang, 1993.

Shafir, Gershon. *Land, Labor and the Origins of the Israeli-Palestiian Conflict, 1882–1914.* Berkeley, CA: University of California Press, 1996.

Shapira, Anita. *Land and Power: The Zionist Resort to Force, 1881–1948.* Palo Alto, Stanford Studies in Jewish History and Culture, 1999.

Shapiro, Yonathan. *The Road to Power: Herut Party in Israel.* Albany, NY: SUNY, 1991.

Shindler, Colin. *The Land Beyond Promise: Israel, Likud and the Zionist Dream.* New York: Tauris, 1995.

Shlaim, Avi. *The Iron Wall: Israel and the Arab World.* New York: Norton, 2000.

    The Politics of Partition: King Abdullah, the Zionists and Palestine. New York: Columbia, 1990.

Simon, Leon. *Ahad Ha'am: A Biography.* New York: Herzl Press, 1960.

——, ed., *Selected Essays of Ahad Ha'am.* New York: Atheneum, 1981.

Spiegel, Steven L. *The Other Arab-Israeli Conflict: Making America's Middle East Policy, from Truman to Reagan.* Chicago: University of Chicago Press, 1985.

Sprinzak, Ehud. *Brother Against Brother: Violence and Extremism in Israeli Politics from Altalena to the Rabin Assassination.* New York: Free Press, 1999.

    The Ascendance of Israel's Radical Right. New York: Oxford, 1991.

Stanislawski, Michael. *Zionism and the Fin de Siecle.* Berkeley, CA: California, 2001.

Stein, Leonard. *The Balfour Declaration.* London: Valentine-Mitchell, 1961.

Sternhell, Zeev. *The Founding Myths of Israel.* Princeton, NJ: Princeton, 1998.

Storrs, Ronald. *Orientations.* London: Nicolson & Watson, 1945.

Swisher, Clayton E. *The Truth About Camp David: The Untold Story About the Collapse of the Middle East Peace Process.* New York: Nation Books, 2004.

Sykes, Christopher. *Two Studies in Virtue.* London: Collins, 1953.

Tirosh, Josef. *Religious Zionism: An Anthology.* Jerusalem: World Zionist Organization, 1975.

Tuchman, Barbara W. *Bible and Sword: England and Palestine from the Bronze Age to Balfour.* New York: Funk & Wagnalls, 1956.

Tyler, Patrick. *A World of Trouble: America in the Middle East.* London: Portobello, 2009.

    Fortress Israel: The Inside Story of the Military Elite Who Run the Country—and Why They Can't Make Peace. New York: Farrar, Straus and Giroux, 2012.

Urofsky, Melvin. *American Zionism from Herzl to the Holocaust.* Lincoln, NE: Nebraska, 1975.

Viorst, Milton. *Sands of Sorrow: Israel's Journey from Independence.* New York: Harper & Row, 1987.

    What Shall I Do With This People? Jews and the Fractious Politics of Judaism. New York: Free Press, 2002.

Vital, David. *The Future of the Jews: A People at the Crossroads?* Cambridge, MA: Harvard, 1990.

    The Making of British Foreign Policy. London: Allen & Unwin, 1968.

    A People Apart: A Political History of the Jews in Europe, 1789–1939. New York: Oxford University Press, 1999.

    The Origins of Zionism. London: Oxford University Press, 1975.

    Zionism: The Formative Years. London: Oxford University Press, 1982.

Wanefsky, Joseph. *Rabbi Isaac Jacob Reines: His Life and Thought.* New York: Philosophical Library, 1970.

Wheatcroft, Geoffrey. *The Controversy of Zion*. Reading, MA: Addison-Wesley, 1996.

Wistrich, Robert. *The Jews of Vienna in the Age of Franz Joseph*. Oxford: Littman Library of Jewish Civilization, 1990.

Wright, Lawrence. *Thirteen Days in September: Carter, Begin and Sadat at Camp David*. New York: Knopf, 2014.

Zertal, Idith. *Israel's Holocaust and the Politics of Nationhood*. New York: Cambridge, 2005.

Zertal, Idith & Eldar, Akiva. *The Lords of the Land: The War Over Israel's Settlements in the Occupied Territories, 1967–2007*. New York: Nation Books, 2007.

Zipperstein, Steven J. *Imagining Russian Jewry*. Seattle: University of Washington Press, 1999.

  Elusive Prophet: Ahad Ha'am and the Origins of Zionism. Berkeley, CA: California, 1993.

Zweig, Stefan. *The World of Yesterday: An Autobiography*. Lincoln, NE: Nebraska, 1964.

Endnotes

1. Theodor Herzl

1. Alex Bein provides a full discussion of Dühring and his impact in *Theodor Herzl, A Biography of the Founder of Modern Zionism*, New York, Atheneum, 1970, pp. 36–40.
2. See Herzl's letter to Heinrich Teweles in *The Herzl Yearbook: Essays in Zionist History and Thought*, Raphael Patai ed., New York, Herzl Press, 1968, v. 1, pp. 302–5.
3. For an illustration of Herzl's mix of contempt and envy for "rich Jews," Ibid., p. 307.
4. For more on Herzl's tempestuous relationship with Gudeman, see Robert S. Wistrich, *The Jews of Vienna in the Age of Franz Joseph*, London, Oxford University Press, 1990.
5. David Vital recounts the story of the First Zionist Congress well and at considerable length in *The Origins of Zionism*, London, Oxford University Press, 1975, pp. 309–75.
6. See Derek J. Penslar's balanced study of Herzl's attitude to the Arabs in the *Journal of Israeli History*, v. 24, no. 1, March 2005, "Herzl and the Palestinian Arabs: Myth and Counter-Myth," pp. 65–77.

2. Chaim Weizmann

1. Arthur Herzberg ed., *The Zionist Idea*, New York, Atheneum, 1981, p. 266.
2. Norman Rose, *Chaim Weizmann*, New York, Viking, 1986, p. 26, p. 55.
3. Jehuda Reinharz, *Chaim Weizmann: The Making of a Zionist Leader (Vol. 1)*, New York, Oxford, 1985, pp. 386–88.
4. Ibid., *The Making of a Statesman (Vol. 2)*, 1993, p. 18.
5. Leonard Stein, *The Balfour Declaration*, London, Valentine-Mitchell, 1961, pp. 206–17. Though published more than a half century ago, this remains the classic work on the subject.
6. Ibid., pp. 445–54.
7. Ibid., p. 220.

8. Isaiah Friedman, *The Question of Palestine: British-Jewish-Arab Relations 1914–1918*, New York, Shocken, 1973, p. 386.
9. op. cit. Stein, p. 164.
10. Blanche Dugdale, *Arthur James Balfour*, New York, Putnam, 1917, v. 1, p. 435.
11. Barbara Tuchman, *Bible and Sword: England and Palestine from the Bronze Age to Balfour*, New York, Funk and Wagnalls, 1956, pp. 311–16.
12. Chaim Weizmann, *Trial and Error: The Autobiography of Chaim Weizmann*, New York, Harper & Brothers, 1949, p. 152.
13. op. cit. Stein, p. 152, pp. 157–58.
14. Ibid., pp. 378–385, 394–421.
15. Ibid., pp. 466–471.
16. Ibid., pp. 503–514.
17. Ibid., pp. 522–3, 627.
18. Ibid., p. 625.
19. op. cit. Reinharz, v. 2, pp. 222–24.
20. Ibid., p. 257.
21. op. cit. Weizmann, pp. 233–34.
22. Ibid., pp. 237–38.
23. op. cit. Reinharz v. 2, p. 273.
24. op. cit. Stein, pp. 641–43.
25. op. cit. Rose, pp. 272, 290.
26. op. cit. Reinharz, v. 2, 290–97.
27. op. cit. Stein, pp, 645–47.
28. Ibid., p. 656.
29. op. cit. Rose, pp. 392–96.

3. Vladimir Jabotinsky

1. Joseph Schechtman, *The Jabotinsky Story: Fighter and Prophet (Vol. 2)*, New York, Yoseloff, 1961, p. 79.
2. Mordechai Sarig ed., *The Political and Social Philosophy of Ze'ev Jabotinsky*, London, Vallentine Mitchell, 1999, p. 36.
3. Raphaella Bilski Ben-Hur, *Every Individual, a King: The Social and Political Thought of Ze'ev Vladimir Jabotinsky*, Washington, B'nai B'rith Books, no date cited, p. 29.
4. Mitchell Cohen, *Zion and State: Nation, Class and the Shaping of Modern Israel*, New York, Columbia University Press, 1992, p. 138.
5. op. cit. Sarig, p. 2.
6. op. cit. Schechtman, p. 87.
7. Ibid., (Vol. 1), p. 160.
8. Vladimir Jabotinsky, *The Story of the Jewish Legion*, New York, Ackerman, 1945, pp. 31–35.
9. Ibid., pp. 36–45.
10. Ibid., pp. 64–143.
11. Ibid., pp. 146–7.
12. op. cit. Weizmann pp. 227–28.
13. op. cit. Schechtman, pp. 280–82.
14. Ibid., pp. 329–38.
15. Ibid., pp. 344–65.
16. op. cit. Bilski Ben-Hur, p. 216.
17. op. cit. Schechtman, pp. 422–24.
18. Ibid., pp. 427–9, 434; (Vol. 2), p. 26.
20. Ibid., Schechtman, p. 112.

21. Yonathan Shapiro, *The Road to Power: Herut Party in Israel*, Albany SUNY, 1991, pp. 30–38.
22. Shmuel Katz, *Lone Wolf: A Biography of Vladimir (Ze'ev) Jabotinsky*, New York, Barricade, 1996, v. 1, pp. 166–67.
23. op. cit. Rose, pp. 280–96.
24. The Peel Commission has been the subject of much study by historians. op. cit. Schechtman; Howard M. Sachar, *A History of Israel: From the Rise of Zionism to Our Time*, New York, Knopf, 1979.

4. David Ben-Gurion

1. Moshe Pearlman, *Ben Gurion Looks Back*, New York, Schocken, 1970, p. 226.
2. op. cit. Cohen, pp. 108–11.
3. Shabtai Teveth, *Ben-Gurion: The Burning Ground, 1886–1948*, London, Oxford, 1985, p. 339.
4. Ibid., p. 311.
5. Eran Kaplan and Derek J. Penslar, *The Origins of Israel, 1882–1948*, Madison (Wis.), University of Wisconsin, 2011, pp. 240–43.
6. Ibid., pp. 312–17.
7. The full text appears in the *New Encyclopedia of Zionism and Israel*, New York, Doubleday, 1977, v. 1, p. 202.
8. op. cit. Sachar, p. 248.
9. Martin Gilbert, *Exile and Return: The Struggle for a Jewish Homeland*, New York, Lippincott, 1978, p. 153.
10. op. cit. Rose, pp. 438–42; Weizmann, pp. 478–82.
11. Avraham Avi-Hai discusses this issue at length in *Ben Gurion: State-Builder*, New York, John Wiley, 1984, pp. 219–48.
12. op. cit. Sachar, p. 558.
13. Avi Shlaim, *The Iron Wall: Israel and the Arab World*, New York, Norton, 2000, pp. 51–53.
14. Isaac Alteras, *Eisenhower and Israel: U.S.-Israeli Relations, 1953–1960*, Gainesville (Fla.), Florida University Press, 1993, pp. 247–48.
15. Ibid., pp. 310–19.
16. Nahum Goldmann, *The Jewish Paradox: A Personal Memoir*, New York, Grosset & Dunlap, 1978, p. 99; *The Autobiography of Nahum Goldmann*, New York, Rinehart & Winston, 1969, p. 272.

5. Rav Abraham Isaac Kook/Rabbi Zvi Yehuda Kook

1. Shlomo Avneri, *The Making of Modern Zionism*, New York, Basic Books, 1981, pp. 190–93.
2. Aviezer Ravitzky, *Messianism, Zionism, and Jewish Religious Radicalism*, Chicago, University of Chicago Press, 1996, p. 93.
3. Lucy Dawidowicz ed., *The Golden Tradition: Jewish Life and Thought in Eastern Europe*, Boston, Beacon Press, 1967, pp. 200–6.
4. op. cit. *Herzl Yearbook: Religion and Herzl, Fact and Fable (Vol. 4)*, Joseph Adler, p. 299.
5. Reuven Firestone, *Holy War in Judaism*, New York, Oxford, 2012, p. 157 note.
6. Ibid., pp. 167–77.
7. Abraham Bick, *Exponents and Philosophy of Religious Zionism, an Anthology*, Brooklyn (N.Y.), Hashomer Hadadi, 1942, pp. 41–42.
8. Yehudah Mirsky, *Rav Kook: Mystic in a Time of Revolution*, New Haven (Ct.), Yale, p. 146.

9. Jacob Agus, *Banner of Jerusalem: The Life, Times and Thought of Abraham Isaac Kuk*, New York, Bloch, 1946, p. 93.
10. Ronald Storrs, *Orientations*, London, Nicholson & Watson, 1945, p. 415.
11. Leo Jung ed., *Guardians Of Our Heritage 1724–1953*, New York, Bloch, 1958, pp. 506–7; op. cit. Mirsky, p. 17.
12. Ibid., Mirsky, p. 143; Idith Zertal and Akiva Eldar, *The Lords of the Land: The War Over Israel's Settlements in the Occupied Territories, 1967–2007*, New York, Nation Books, 2007, p. 193.
13. Ibid., Mirsky, pp. 198–210.
14. Gideon Aran, "The Father, The Son and the Holy Land," R. Scott Appleby ed., *Spokesmen for the Despised: Fundamentalist Leaders of the Middle East*, London, University of Chicago Press, pp. 312–13.
15. Ibid., Samuel Heilman, "Guides of the Faithful," p. 330.
16. Gershom Gorenberg, *The Accidental Empire: Israel and the Birth of the Settlements 1967–1977*, New York, Holt, 2006, p. 130.
17. op. cit. Appleby/Heilman, p. 331.
18. op. cit. Gorenberg, pp. 145–46.
19. op. cit. Ravitzky, p. 136.
20. op. cit. Gorenberg.
21. William Quandt, *Decade of Decision: American Policy Toward the Arab-Israel Conflict 1967–1976*, Berkeley, University of California Press, 1977, pp. 72–103.
22. Yigal Kipnis, *1973: The Road to War*, Charlottesville (Va.), Just World Books, 2013, provides a comprehensive and balanced account of the events leading to the Yom Kippur War.
23. op. cit., Quandt, pp. 274–78.
24. Milton Viorst, *Sands of Sorrow: Israel's Journey from Independence*, New York, Harper & Row, 1987, pp. 174–214, contains an earlier discussion by the author of the Kissinger-Rabin relationship.
25. op. cit. Zertal and Eldar, p. 217.
26. Ibid., p. 63.
27. Ibid., pp. 3–54; op. cit, Mirsky, pp. 227–29.
28. op. cit. Ravitzky, pp. 126–27.

6. Menachem Begin

1. Eitan Haber, *Menachem Begin*, New York, Delacorte, p. 82.
2. Eric Silver, *Begin: The Haunted Prophet*, New York, Random House, 1984, pp. 21–23.
3. Ibid., pp. 22–26.
4. The most useful account of the formation and deployment of the Anders army is Yisrael Gutman's "Jews in General Anders's Army in the Soviet Union," published by The International School for Holocaust Studies of the Shoah Resources Center, 50 pages.
5. op.cit., Haber, pp. 48–52.
6. See earlier account in Chapter 4.
7. op. cit. Haber, p. 206; Ned Temko. *To Win or To Die: A Personal Portrait of Menachem Begin*, New York, Morrow, 1987, pp. 108–9.
8. Ibid., Temko, p. 144.
9. See account in Chapter 5.
10. See account in Chapter 5.
11. op. cit. Mirsky, p. 228.
12. op. cit. Temko, p. 198.
13. op. cit. Viorst, pp. 250–53.

14. Jimmy Carter, *Keeping Faith: Memoirs of a President*, New York, Bantam, 1982. pp. 267–430.
15. op. cit. Silver, p. 226.

7. Arriving at Netanyahu

1. Milton Viorst, "Report from Madrid," *The New Yorker*, December 9, 1991, pp. 57–82.
2. Milton Viorst, *What Shall I Do With This People?: Jews and the Fractious Politics of Judaism*, New York, Free Press, 2002, pp. 234–35.
3. Ibid., p. 236.
4. For a fuller account of Rabin's assassination, see Ibid., pp. 237–250.
5. It is not surprising that narratives differ on the failed summit of Clinton, Barak, and Arafat at Camp David. This book draws largely from Clayton Swisher, *The Truth About Camp David: The Untold Story About the Collapse of the Middle East Peace Process*, New York, Nation Books, 2004.
6. David Landau, *Piety and Power: The World of Jewish Fundamentalism*, New York, Hill and Wang, 1993, p. 443.
7. Ibid., p. 503.
8. Ibid., p. 522.

Index

Zionism (*continued*)
  Balfour Declaration's contribution
    to, 62, 71, 77, 80–101, 103, 112, 113,
    114, 118–19, 123–24, 126, 134–38,
    150, 155, 157–60, 161, 191–92
  founding of, 1, 7–12, 22–58
  Hebrew University's founding and,
    67, 73–74, 92, 109, 192, 239
  institutional framework creation for,
    41–42, 43, 57–58
  language associated with, 31, 65, 77,
    109, 194
  the Precursors to, 7–12, 19, 24,
    29–30, 34, 40, 42, 55, 187
  sovereignty's redefinition and, 169–70
  state location considerations and,
    30–37, 42, 50–57, 61, 68, 69, 70–71,
    80, 107, 145, 188
  WWI's influence on, 61–62, 74–101
Zionist Commission, 88, 114–15, 149,
  192
Zionist Federation of Britain, 85
Zion Mule Corps, 111, 112, 149
Zweig, Stefan, 32